How the Obama Presidency Changed the Political Landscape

How the Obama Presidency Changed the Political Landscape

Larry J. Walker, F. Erik Brooks, and
Ramon B. Goings, Editors

BLOOMSBURY ACADEMIC
NEW YORK • LONDON • OXFORD • NEW DELHI • SYDNEY

BLOOMSBURY ACADEMIC
Bloomsbury Publishing Inc
1385 Broadway, New York, NY 10018, USA
50 Bedford Square, London, WC1B 3DP, UK
29 Earlsfort Terrace, Dublin 2, Ireland

BLOOMSBURY, BLOOMSBURY ACADEMIC and the Diana logo
are trademarks of Bloomsbury Publishing Plc

First published in the United States of America by ABC-CLIO 2017
Paperback edition published by Bloomsbury Academic 2024

Cover design by Silverander Communications
Cover photo: A detail of the world's largest beaded mosaic of President Barack Obama
on display in midtown Manhattan, New York, August 5, 2009. (AP Photo/Mary Altaffer)

Library of Congress Cataloging- in- Publication Data
Names: Walker, Larry J. (Consultant)
Title: How the Obama presidency changed the political landscape / Larry J. Walker,
F. Erik Brooks, and Ramon B. Goings, Editors.
Description: Santa Barbara, California : Praeger, 2017. |
Includes bibliographical references and index.
Identifiers: LCCN 2017006671 (print) | LCCN 2017007379 (ebook) |
ISBN 9781440852060 (ebook) | ISBN 9781440852053 (hard copy : alk. paper)
Subjects: LCSH: Obama, Barack. | Political culture—United States. |
United States—Politics and government—2009- | United States—Social policy.
Classification: LCC E907 (ebook) | LCC E907 .H68 2017 (print) |
DDC 973.932092—dc23
LC record available at https://lccn.loc.gov/2017006671

ISBN: HB: 978-1-4408-5205-3
PB: 979-8-7651-3022-3
ePDF: 978-1-4408-5206-0
eBook: 979-8-2160-9929-1

To find out more about our authors and books visit www.bloomsbury.com
and sign up for our newsletters.

Contents

Preface

On January 20, 2009, on a blustery morning I joined thousands of Americans to witness the first African American in U.S. history ascend to the White House. The inauguration of President Barack Hussein Obama was a seminal moment in United States history. After the Trans-Atlantic Slave Trade, Reconstruction, Jim Crow, and the New Jim Crow, there was a belief that times had changed; this included some pundits suggesting we lived in a postracial society. The euphoric feeling emanating from the crowd during the inauguration represented a "deep sigh" from marginalized groups who welcomed a paradigm shift. During the swearing in, I stood between the Washington Monument and the U.S. Capitol and reflected on the moment. Years later it was my hope that in some way I could provide a platform for researchers to properly frame the Obama presidency. Along with my fellow co-editors, Dr. F. Erik Brooks and Dr. Ramon B. Goings, we believe this book provides a nuanced examination of the president's successes and failures.

In contrast to other projects on the Obama presidency, this book deconstructs an array of issues including voting rights, race, education, shifting demographics, social justice, and community policing, among other vital concerns. Each chapter was purposefully written by scholars committed to providing academics, advocates, students, and historians with a critical analysis supported by important facts. We sought to identify researchers with unique experiences that could accurately critique President Obama's policies and proposals. For this reason, *How the Obama Presidency Changed the Political Landscape* is composed of two sections: One: Race, Party Affiliation, and the New Majority; and Two: Coalition Building, Social Media, and Political Messaging. The project reflects several months of hard work by Dr. Kim Kennedy-White from ABC-CLIO; Drs. Walker, Brooks, and Goings; and the contributors for this important book.

This project would not have come to fruition if not for my experience as a Congressional Fellow with the Congressional Black Caucus Foundation (CBCF) and my serving as the Legislative Director for Congressman Major R. Owens. During my tenure on Capitol Hill, I learned under the tutelage of Congressman Owens and my mentor Jacqueline Ellis. Although they are no longer here, I want to acknowledge the impact their mentorship had on my growth as a scholar and policy analyst. The time and effort they took to explain the philosophy behind making tough votes on important political issues taught me how to overcome barriers. In addition, I want to highlight the role the CBCF educational programs play preparing African American political scientists to address a variety of systematic issues. CBCF alumni continue to uphold the ideas of luminaries including Shirley Chisholm, Charles Rangel, William Clay Sr., and Barbara Jordan. The program's continued success is critical.

As with other projects of this scale, there were obstacles. Unfortunately, a few contributors had to withdraw from the project because of personal or professional occurrences. The unmitigated circumstances forced some scholars to make difficult decisions in spite of their commitment to the project. Although their work is not included in the project, I recognize they agonized over the decision to drop out. However, finding contributors to replace individuals mid-project is difficult. Fortunately, Drs. Brooks and Goings helped to identify authors, edit the manuscript, and provide support throughout the process. Working with them on this project was ideal because of their previous experiences as co-editors of other books. Without their dedication and persistence, the project would have stalled.

Readers of *How the Obama Presidency Changed the Political Landscape* should consider a question: What will be the president's legacy? Some pundits would suggest that he exacerbated racial tensions; others believe he couldn't wipe way more than four hundred years of oppression and strife. In spite of being a talented orator and political strategist, there are structural issues that he could not overcome. It is also important to note that some members of the Black community offered harsh critiques on specific policies. To ensure the project was well balanced, we offered contributors with dissenting views an opportunity to outline their concerns.

Overall, we believe this project provides important insight and questions regarding President Obama's eight years in office. Scholars will continue to lament what President Obama could have done differently on a variety of issues. However, what makes this project different is that the co-editors sought out scholars of various ethnic and racial backgrounds and political views to provide a layered analysis. In totality, *How the Obama*

Presidency Changed the Political Landscape is a unique endeavor because it challenges dominant narratives while providing fresh perspectives.

I would like to thank the co-editors of this project, Dr. F. Erik Brooks and Dr. Ramon B. Goings, and Dr. Kim Kennedy-White from ABC-CLIO. In addition, each contributor's passion and diligence provided the foundation to complete the book. Lastly, a personal thank-you to my family, including my wife, Nicola M. Walker, and son, Jacob N. Walker, for allowing me to dedicate time, including weekends, to complete this project.

Onward and upward.

Dr. Larry J. Walker
Co-Editor, *How the Obama Presidency
Changed the Political Landscape*

PART 1

Race, Party Affiliation, and the New Majority

CHAPTER ONE

The Body Politic: How Underrepresented Groups Can Gain Political Power

Christopher M. Whitt

Introduction

President Barack Obama's election and re-election as the first non-White president of the United States of America, as well as the evolution of identity politics during his presidency, shines light to on the progress needed in the interest of gaining political power for underrepresented groups. Unity, solidarity, and internal organization in communities facing underrepresentation are necessary to best develop a cadre of leaders and groups in the interest of increasing political power. Communities seeking to overcome political marginalization through increasing autonomy and self-determination must renew organizing efforts while maintaining previously brokered political coalitions. It is important encourage the people who fill the ranks of each of these groups undergoing organizing and new coalition building to remain open to the possibilities of adjustments in relationships at the base of previous coalitions and new ones in the works.

This chapter brings an emphasis to the initial steps needed in the process of developing civic culture in the Black community and ultimately creating a blueprint for groups who find themselves currently underrepresented to make meaningful gains in political power. To gain real change in civic culture and to truly redirect energy toward gaining political power for any underrepresented group, it is important to recognize power dynamics on local levels in reference to issues of importance across the nation. It is true that the Black community as well as other communities that are underrepresented have many political cleavages. In doing this work, those cleavages much be recognized and respected. None of the underrepresented groups in the United States are political monoliths. In recognizing cleavages, we must differentiate between irreconcilable differences and issues that can more easily be resolved with organizing and working to inform the people.

The initial steps come before building of new political coalitions with other identity groups or entering into partnerships with national political entities. Internal organizing within identity groups on local and regional levels is essential for the success of any group seeking to later harness the political power that may come with the formation of lasting coalitions with other groups. Obama's presidency has shown naysayers that simply having an individual from an underrepresented group win the highest office doesn't automatically make for major positive change for individuals of that group. Members of any of those underrepresented groups still find themselves living daily in a system with many biases and inequities. Members of underrepresented groups surely can benefit from a "political reboot" as they move into this next era of American politics without a person of color in the White House and with many freshly reaggravated wounds of racism and intolerance.

Political power in a modern context is authority held by a particular group over the distribution and administration of resources. Particularly, individuals who are members of identity groups that have continuously found themselves politically underrepresented and historically marginalized end up being on the outside looking in when it comes to that authority. Efforts to increase political power for marginalized groups have to be rooted in first building collective belief in self and collaboration within the particular identity group. It is imperative for operatives seeking avenues to increase political power for the underrepresented to analyze the ever-evolving dynamics of political power.

Looking within as the First Step to Gain Political Power

The electoral successes of Barack Obama in his run for the presidency showed that coalition building could be a very successful tactic in obtaining particular political gains. Efforts rooted in underrepresented groups seeking political power are different from presidential campaigns, though. The type of political power the underrepresented should seek is fundamentally different from the temporary influence sought by a candidate. Long histories and complicated dynamics are intertwined with the need for increased political power of any group of people defined by identity. The particular contexts of their shared experiences simply don't exist for other groups. This is very different from people simply coalescing to support a candidate or a campaign in any given election cycle. To gain real and lasting political power, those who are politically marginalized or underrepresented need to take control of their own destinies through organizing and leveraging that organization for political power.

The coalition that could be labeled as the "Obama Coalition" was something that was built from the top down. It was not rooted in underrepresented communities, even if the face of the movement and the coalition was a person of color. Underrepresented groups seeking to increase their political power need to have control over what will ultimately come out of any coalitions of which their groups may be part. Instead of being classified and organized by outsiders who hold control of political power, underrepresented groups can work to seize control of their political futures. The ways in which unity can be established within a community can later serve as an example for broader coalition building among groups when later moving beyond the front-end tasks mentioned earlier. Coalition politics in the mold of the Obama Coalition is highly dependent on the decisions, whims, and perceptions of the traditional White power structure.[1]

Power dynamics and overall intentions matter very much in many aspects of politics, particularly when seeking to make shifts in political power. Although either of the major political parties may engage in outreach to the Black community or other underrepresented groups, those groups are never their main focus. By focusing within particular identity groups with the intention of a customized approach to gaining political power, it is possible to turn the practice of micro-targeting, so successful for the Obama campaign, on its ear.[2] The groups take control of their own narratives and hold the leverage to negotiate power for support with the major parties, major campaigns, and other entities traditionally in control of political power in the United States.

Groups politically underrepresented and marginalized prior to the Obama presidency, such as Blacks, remained disadvantaged in political power throughout his presidency and beyond. Before seeking to make connections that build bridges between broader identity groups, coalition building must occur internally for those communities. In the interest of increasing power, the first aim should be to bring together a critical mass of interested and politically active people. Solidarity is certainly needed within any given group before looking outward and seeking to unite with other groups in the interest of broader political coalitions. It must be made clear that members of any particular marginalized group in the American body politic both from a group perspective as well as individually face certain political power dynamics that are not favorable and are based on their identity.

There has to be an internal audit or assessment of the political resources available locally before turning attention to similar tactics for national coordination. Any identity group in the United States that sees itself as at least a somewhat cohesive group in any way will only grow and position itself to demand more power when it has a certain level of self-determination. Malcolm X put it very well when he said, "A race of people is like an individual man; until it uses its own talent, takes pride in its own history, expresses its own culture, affirms its own selfhood, it can never fulfill itself."[3] Any community seeking to overcome political marginalization and underrepresentation needs to figure out the best ways to look inward for solutions. Solutions should not be based on decisions of people from outside the groups.

Each identity group has to be positioned to act proactively, and it also should seek to ultimately position itself to eventually join together with other underrepresented groups in coalitions that may look like the Obama Coalition on the surface. The most important difference between these potential coalitions of the future and what has already been seen with the Obama Coalition is the power dynamic. These groups will have stood up and organized on their own before deciding to unite with one another to maximize political influence and power. This certainly is different from having people in power and seeking power at the topic using optics to make their desire for control over voters of color look like the building of coalitions in those communities.

Organization within underrepresented groups and between underrepresented groups puts them in a much better position to hold onto more control of situations when the major political parties and related campaigns come, seeking various forms of support such as in last-minute efforts to "get out the vote." Almost a century ago, Marcus Garvey saw some similar power dynamics at play and opined on challenges facing Blacks seeking to organize. Garvey said, "Negroes should be more determined today than they have ever been, because the mighty forces of the world are operating against the non-organized groups of people, who are not ambitious enough to protect their own interests."[4]

Blacks and any other group seeking to overcome underrepresentation must first position themselves to have control over their group's role in political coalitions. Just like organizing within each group is a necessity prior to seeking inclusion in or creation of coalitions, positing is vital. This step-by-step approach in moving up the ranks of political hierarchy is a necessity if those involved want to fight for transformation of the political system and the ways in which power is distributed.

Change should not be the operative word, because it leads to looking backward at what was. Transformation of the system leads to looking forward to what can be. In seeking to push for transformation of political power structures in the United States, it is important for all involved to recognize the forces of the world that may be standing in the way of the desired progress. Seeking ways to broadly assert direct challenges to the American power structure nationally is something that comes a few steps into this "long game" type of process, after the coalitions have been decided upon and created. In *Rules for Radicals*, Saul Alinsky pointed to another transformation that must come: the way in which attention is paid to the methods in which organizers are developed. "The building of many mass power organizations to merge into a national popular power force cannot come without many organizers. Since organizations are created, in large part, by the organizer, we must find out what creates the organizer."[5]

It is clear that access to political power was historically limited for many identity groups on the margins, originally by law and continually by social traditions, practices, and societal norms. Even as laws and policies have evolved in favor of more inclusive ideologies, various identity groups still find themselves on the outside looking in when it comes to political power. In fact, in recent years political conservatives have actually used legislation and policy in attempts to place new limitations on the political power and lives of some already marginalized groups.[6] As has been mentioned, recognizing these attempts to roll back progress is necessary as groups seek to move forward and break down barriers to progress and increased political power.

In consideration of what is needed to seek and gain political power for marginalized groups, the sentiments of A. Philip Randolph, the historic civil rights leader and organizer, still hold true today:

> At the banquet table of life, there are no reserved seats. You get what you can take and keep what you can hold. You can't take anything, you won't get anything. And if you can't hold anything, you won't keep anything. And you can't take anything without organization.[7]

The first steps in organizing for a particular goal are coming together, recognizing the circumstances, and agreeing to work together with as many people as possible on board for a concerted effort. Any group seeking political power needs to know that they are being denied power systemically, and they need to have a plan to work together in holding onto whatever they may gain. Political power is not simply given out by those mainly in control, and certainly the marginalized will not be allowed to be hold onto it simply out of good will.

The Black Lives Matter movement has embraced the reality that political power and even the control of the political narrative will not be freely handed over by those already in power. They see that even though their message should be easily accepted by people who claim to value liberty and justice for all, it won't be accepted without them pushing. Clarence Page made an excellent point on this issue when discussing the Black Lives Matter vs. All Lives Matter debate,

> The group's founders didn't mean to imply that other people's lives don't matter. Their #BlackLivesMatter hashtag aims to protest how black lives didn't seem to matter in a growing list of scandalous police killings. . . . Those of us who truly believe that "all lives matter" need to elect leaders who can put some action behind those words.[8]

Black Lives Matter has decided that they want to unapologetically express themselves and speak truth to power. They are not waiting for approval from the old guard of Black leadership, the Democratic Party, or any other entity which has held control over the tactics and organization of Black resistance in the last few decades that some consider the "post–Civil Rights Era."

New generations of Black leaders are recognizing the need for organizing with the community on their own terms. Moving forward, this renewed sense of self and renewed confidence is very necessary not only for Blacks seeking liberation and political power but also among each of the groups looking to overcome the state of being perpetually underrepresented. Generations ago, Marcus Garvey saw the need for this sense of self-determination when engaging in acts related to gaining political power. He said, "The Negro who lives on the patronage of philanthropists is the most dangerous member of our society, because he is willing to turn back the clock of progress when his benefactors ask him so to do."[9] Without this mindset, groups allow themselves to ultimately live at the mercy of "benefactors." As has been mentioned, it is vital for groups to take control of their political power through organizing and then leverage that collective power.

Realizing the New Landscape of Identity Politics and Organizing Heading into the Post-Obama Era

> I believe that there will ultimately be a clash between the oppressed and those that do the oppressing. I believe that there will be a clash between those who want freedom, justice and equality for everyone and those who want to continue the systems of exploitation.[10]

Those who seek to gain political power for groups that have been denied fair access and fair representation because of discrimination based on their identities need to focus. Their strategies should center on the fact that the underrepresented are people who must live with being actively and systemically oppressed. There are people in power who knowingly or unknowingly engage in the oppression of others. In the broader populace, there are people who benefit from oppression of the underrepresented, some knowingly so, and others who unknowingly benefit from oppression. The curtain must be pulled back.

The Black Lives Matter movement and other modern social justice movements seem to be becoming skilled in pulling back that curtain. Members of these movements are willing to engage in a variety of methods to work toward opening the eyes of both the oppressed and those who unknowingly benefit from the oppression of others. These are the two groups who need as much information as possible to get mobilized in transforming this system that has marginalized so many for so long. Members of underrepresented groups have remained on the fringes over the course of generations, and the inequities that permeate society must be unpacked.

What can be characterized as a racist backlash in American society has been prompted by the election and reelection of Barack Obama is a mere continuation of the traditions of exclusion that have been in place since the founding of the United States. Recent political uprisings against Black people, and so many other groups simply standing up for equal justice and equal access to the American dream, shows that traditions of exclusion are still very pervasive across the nation and particularly salient in American politics. Inegalitarianism is a fundamental piece of American history, American politics, and the American ethos that is overlooked or ignored far too often.[11]

In the face of pervasive inegalitarianism, those who find themselves being marginalized need to listen closely to messages being used to undermine their gaining power. As has been mentioned, organizing is vital to taking steps to gain political power for those who are currently underrepresented. Those who do not want to see the underrepresented make gains

in political power moving by moving closer to fair representation sometimes attack the means by which that power can be gained. It is not politically smart to outwardly attack an underrepresented group's effort to gain
representation, so veiled comments and dog whistle–type messages are
used to create space for plausible deniability. One of the consistent dog
whistle tactics utilized regularly against candidate Obama included critics
referring to his family background. There were attempts to paint organizing in Black communities or other underrepresented communities as
worthless. People in those communities need not be deterred. Organizing
is needed and should continue.

When Obama's history as an organizer has been attacked, it has usually been in attempts to question his pedigree and his experience. That
same mindset seems to be at play in many attacks against Black communities and organizing efforts in those communities. For Obama, multiple
attempts have been made to attach to him ill-informed negative connota-
tions the attackers may have about the predominantly Black South Side of
Chicago. In fact, Obama's beginnings as a community organizer actually
have been avenues of connection for President Obama and his voter base.

> Mr. Obama's three-year stretch as a grass-roots organizer has figured prom-
> inently, if not profoundly, in his own narrative of his life. Campaigning in
> Iowa, Mr. Obama called it "the best education I ever had, better than any-
> thing I got at Harvard Law School," an education that he said was "seared
> into my brain." He devoted about one-third of the 442 pages in his memoir,
> "Dreams From My Father," to chronicling that Chicago organizing period.[12]

Americans interested in engaging in community organizing in the interest of increasing political power in communities of color and other underrepresented communities can look to Obama's roots as inspiration, not as
something of which to be ashamed.

Barack Obama's early career narrative certainly is an example of what
is needed in communities seeking to gain political power. There has to be
a cadre of up-and-coming Black leaders interested in organizing on the
local level if there is ever ultimately to be a move for real increases of Black
political power nationally. Obama has mentioned that he felt drawn to Chicago to do his work. The election of Harold Washington as the city's first
Black mayor certainly was a big part of that draw. Each generation needs
to inspire the next. Even within generations, those needed cadres of leaders should support and inspire one another. Obama was able to use his
time organizing on the South Side of Chicago to figure out his place not
only in American but also, more importantly, in Black America.

Potential Black leaders have to be allowed space to figure out their place and also their lane. Each of them cannot do everything, so each of them needs to be allowed to come to terms with what slice of the big pie of Black political and social needs they will tackle. That can be said for rising leaders in any group seeking to increase political power and step out of underrepresentation. They too can come to the realization of just what they have to offer within the group and, later, as the group seeks to enter into coalitions. It would be reminiscent of what one of Obama's fellow community organizers, Gregory Galluzzo, had to say about his early years of organizing: "All of a sudden Barack finds himself in one of the most complex African-American communities in the United States and he discovers an energizing capacity to connect with the people in these neighborhoods."[13]

As has been mentioned, organizing will be centrally important to underrepresented groups coming together to gain increased levels of political power. It is actually more than centrally important; it is essential. The desires to be heard and to have control over one's own destiny, as well as reactions to vitriolic statements and actions against members of these groups by people in power, or at least in the majority, will continue to serve as motivation to get people to organize. Saul Alinsky predicted this type of situation, where organizing would spring up from the grassroots because of curiosity: a curiosity of what else there could be in life if the previously powerless or underrepresented finally had some power and a greater political voice.

In order to assemble the much-needed cadre of new and upcoming Black leaders interested in a positive transformation of the political power dynamic for Black people, curiosity must be used as a tool. Those with the potential for leadership need to be intrigued with curiosity for the potential of increased political power for their people on local levels, and ultimately nationally, with international influence. Those deeply involved in grassroots activism need to be vetted for leadership. That leadership should show the potential not only to lead in the community but also to navigate political institutions in the interest of gaining power for their people. Saul Alinsky noted this vital need in developing leaders, who organize:

> Curiosity. What makes an organizer organize? He is driven by a compulsive curiosity that knows no limits. Warning clichés such as "curiosity killed a cat" are meaningless to him, for life is for him a search for a pattern, for similarities in seeming differences, for differences in seeming similarities, for order in the chaos about us, for a meaning to the life around him and its relationship to his own life—and the search never ends.[14]

Even though it is not always discussed publicly, leaders need individual motivation and movements for transformation of political structures certainly need multiple leaders. There need to be many groups with many leaders, each having their own curiosities motivating their actions.

Efforts are necessary within underrepresented groups to turn protestors into voters, and activists into political leaders. The emotions driving people to protest should be directed to mobilizing those people and many others in those communities politically by first showing them the value of politics in a modern context, followed by stages of effort within the group before aiming outward. Basically, any transformation of any political system starts at home. The old adage that all politics are local holds very true in this circumstance of seeking increased political power for groups who find their current representation systemically lacking and unacceptable. It all falls under a general idea similar to natural law. People need to recognize that the system has continually been used to deny them natural rights, and work must be done to transform the system, not simply make well-meaning appeals without fundamentally changing that system.

Many realizations must happen among critical masses of people who are oppressed, before much effort is put into reaching outside the group to build coalitions, seek support, or simply seek empathy. Those finding themselves in states of underrepresentation must choose to come together to fight for political and governmental transformations in systems to create opportunities for fair representation. When Former Senator Bob Graham wrote about making government work for individuals and interest groups, in *America: The Owner's Manual*, he pointed out that pushing for transformation in politics and government involved much more than simply understanding political structures: "In order for citizens to realize the benefits of direct civic engagement, it is not enough to understand the structure or the history of American democracy."[15] People seeking to recreate political power dynamics have to be educated on the many obstacles in their way, as well as the many areas beyond their main focus that also require work for overall transformation.

An example of this that is outside the structure or history of American democracy is the twisted way in which blame is cast on matters pertaining to racism, without first investigating the sordid roots and realities of race in America. Astonishingly, some of his most vocal opponents have blamed President Obama and his administration for current-day race problems in the United States. When blaming Obama, detractors overlook the racist backlash (of which they seem to be a major part) he has faced since taking office or the deep roots of racism that permeate every political institution in the United States.

When Obama is blamed for various manifestations of racism and divisions of public opinion along lines of race, those doing the blaming continually choose to overlook the history of racism and exclusion so integral to the fabric of the United States. In 2016, *The New York Times* did a poll showing that "white Americans were nearly three times more likely to say the Obama presidency itself has driven black and white people further apart, while African Americans were nearly three times as likely to say Obama has brought the races closer together."[16] Those seeking to organize the Black community and other politically underrepresented communities need to take this major divergence of opinion into account as they do their work. At the very least, the first step would be ensuring that those needed to create critical masses of those involved in Black communities were all aware of the pervasive nature of misinformation leading to ill-informed people among the White majority and even in significant numbers in communities of color.

Despite a Black man rising to the highest elected office in the United States, racism in society and in the political arena did not vanish. Political marginalization of Blacks and other people of color did not miraculously disappear. In a 2011 New York Times Opinion piece, Touré made an excellent appeal to America to drop the myth of post racial when by saying:

> Dear America, please, I beg you, stop using the bankrupt and meaningless term "post-racial!" There's no such thing as "post-racial." There's no place that fits the description "post-racial America." There's no "post-racial era." It's a term for a concept that does not exist. There's no there there.[17]

Far too many people within underrepresented groups don't have clear understandings of what they are up against in terms of willful ignorance of their lived experiences and structural interactions with the American Body Politic along lines of race. Some have even bought into, even if only incrementally, the concept that the United States has moved into some sort of postracial or post-identity based era. That is simply not true. It is unfortunate that it takes tragedies like the police involved shootings of unarmed Black citizens along with the constant protest against those racial injustices and many others to even slightly to "move the needle" when it comes to convincing some of the unconvinced that issues still persists.

The fact that denials of racism in America are happening alongside resurgences in attention to racial injustices and an accompanying racist backlash in the era of the first Black president is no surprise to historians and civil-rights legal experts who recall the backlashes of half a century ago—even a century and a half ago, when people came together to fight racial injustices in other eras.

> Khalil Gibran Muhammad, director of the Schomburg Center for Research in Black Culture in New York and author of the 2010 book *The Condemnation of Blackness: Race, Crime, and the Making of Modern Urban America*, has spoken about the clear parallels to how Emancipation and Reconstruction after slavery were met with the wall of segregation codified by *Plessy v. Ferguson*, and how the brutally won civil-rights gains of the 1950s, 1960s, and early 1970s were slowly dismantled by the 20 combined years of President Reagan, both President Bushes, and the conservative-leaning Supreme Court they left behind.

> To the degree that Obama represents an apotheosis of what the nation can achieve; his presidency has also revealed a nation unable to sustain an enduring commitment to civil rights. Obama also represents the unfinished business of America as we're seeing attacks on voting rights and the evisceration of equal protection and due process rights in our criminal justice system. If we think of *Plessy v. Ferguson* as the beginning of one era in our long racial saga, *Shelby v. Holder* represents another milestone. And not one we, as a nation, will look back on and be proud of.[18]

Misinformation and misconceptions are leading to the possibility of limitations arising for underrepresented groups like Blacks being able to transform political structures based largely on perceptions. In addition, forces are at work to fundamentally make governmental structures related to politics more entrenched in the ways in which the underrepresented remain underrepresented. People interested in transforming these systems need to put special effort into making sure they and their followers recognize the odds against which they must fight.

Using the example of the Black struggle for political power is very useful for understanding power dynamics and the fight for political voice. Dr. Ronald Walters, one of the founding fathers of the study of modern Black politics, made an excellent point about recognizing the power dynamics of freedom of those with political power linked to their identity versus those with identities that denote a structural lack of political power, when examining the circumstances of Black people in American politics, "Freedom, to those who have power and citizenship, means the enjoyment of the absence of political restraint on the exercise of civil rights—one of the renowned features of American Democracy" (Walters, 2005). Until people who are underrepresented recognize that being underrepresented does not simply denote the members of their group having obstacles placed in the way to giving voice to their political concerns, they will not be a position to push for real structural transformation. People need to know that this circumstance is a threat and denial of their individual freedom, and they are being limited in their citizenship. People need to know that despite their paying all the "costs of citizenship," they are being denied the benefits of first-class, or full, citizenship.

Underrepresented groups in American politics far too often must live with the reality of being without power or full-fledged citizenship. This reality does not exist in the same way for each group, but Black people seem to fit the bill of being representative enough to provide templates for striving for freedom and political power that could be applied to other identity groups. The mere fact that in 2016 questions abound about the rights of full citizenship curtailed or denied to Blacks is very telling about the true amount of progress made in the United States. Issues of great concern still persist for Blacks, the LGBTQ (lesbian, gay, bisexual, transgender, queer) community, Latinos, and other marginalized populations when it comes to their complete enjoyment of the benefits, opportunities, and protections that come along with true first-class citizenship. The list of issues for each group is far too extensive to explore in this space.

In electoral politics, there is a possibility of people either being sucked into the power and "selling out." Or people may have to "sell out" to get anything done. By organizing within their identity groups and having a grassroots base, there is always a constant to which the overall movement for transformation and political power can return. Leaders and ideas can be cultivated in the grassroots and then pressure can later be applied from those same grassroots. Even though, much of the argument of this chapter revolves around building a cadre of new leaders, that is not a perfect solution.

For those who have more recently already risen to power in very elected positions, they already may have set out on paths that lead to some elements of division and may not have direct connection to the people,

> This latest wave of Black politicians is not immune from criticism. Not least among critics' concerns is whether these new Black politicians will advance the substantive and strategic policy goals of the African American community. Yes, some of these women and men can realistically become senators and president, as Barack Obama has so aptly demonstrated, but at what price? Will they have to sell out Black interests to gain the electoral advantage needed to attain high office?[19]

Everyone cannot and does not have to do the same thing. In an effort to increase Black political power or the power of any underrepresented group, there needs to be recognition that there will be multiple avenues to various types of political power. It would be counterproductive to work against Black elected officials and leaders who may have been considered as selling out Black interest to rise to higher offices. A more effective tactic is to continue organizing internally and, as efforts are made to reach out for allies, count Blacks as people who should be included in negotiations. They can then make decisions if they want to, with the people, or not. Those decisions would be public decisions once the community is organized, whereas if Blacks are part of the process from the beginning, the decisions would not be public, and the pressure would not be on them in the same way.

Even with the nation's first Black president in power, political power structures on each level still are mainly controlled by Whites and the traditionally White-dominated leadership/control that exists in the United States. With that in mind, it is very important to recognize and appreciate the role that grassroots organizations maintain in communities of color having influence over both federal and state policies and politics. Even though President Obama's roots in community organizing served as a punch line for those opposing his candidacy, those roots also serve as inspiration and a blueprint for people who want to ultimately make a mark on American politics.

Tensions exist between those interested in doing away with the status quo and those entrenched in the political power hierarchy; the latter group may feel that the only way to push for real transformation requires working within the very system that so many in the former group view as problematic. "Street-based protest and militancy raises some issues," says Rosemary Feurer, a historian specializing in protest movements. Currently the vanguard of the new civil rights and justice movements are those young activists using a myriad of new tactics in the streets. They are in the belly of the beast, and they are very much needed in order for the movement for true transformation to take shape, but they are not all that is needed. There also must be people who take the broad view into account; "then there are groups that come forward that say, 'We'll address these issues, but we'll be brokers. We're going to direct this anger toward a more detailed purpose.' "[20] There certainly need to be "brokers." The key to having people in those sorts of roles be effective in the overall goal of increasing Black political power or the power of any of the underrepresented groups is for the "brokers" to have been vetted for their intentions to be in line with the overall goal. They simply cannot serve the role of "middleman." They have to truly believe that transformation of political power dynamics can happen and that the supremacy of those who have been in power for generations is not permanently entrench at its current levels.

There are still numerous barriers to overcome, but this type of equity should always be considered as an ultimate goal even if it may not come about until future generation. Systemic barriers are the enemy of Black political power, along with the ignorance or refusal to recognize these systemic barriers, not only by those with the power but also by those who are oppressed. As Harriet Tubman said, "I freed a thousand slaves. I could have freed a thousand more if only they knew they were slaves." In order for the oppressed to rise up and gain political power, they have to know that they are oppressed and also have a clear understanding that the version of freedom and liberty that they may have always considered the goal is limited compared to those who have not been historically oppressed in the society.

Navigate Obstacles of Prevailing Misperceptions in Public Opinion

The body politic of the United States of America has roots and a long history in exclusion. In a broader view, the systems in place in the United States go beyond simple exclusion and end up showing elements of White supremacy. Numerous other aspects of society in addition to political systems and practices fall into categories that are hard to extract from or easily separate from the deep roots of White supremacy in the fabric of the United States. Anti-racism scholar and activist Tim Wise does a good job of clarifying White supremacy in our system and how differs from the general definition of racism:

> White supremacy is the operationalized form of racism in the United States and throughout the Western world. Racism is like the generic product name, while white supremacy is the leading brand, with far and away the greatest market share. While other forms of racism could exist at various times and in various places, none have ever been as effective and widespread in their impact as white supremacy, nor is it likely that any such systems might develop in the foreseeable future.[21]

In the American body politic, one of the ways in which White supremacy, inequities, and other forms of inequality of opportunity persist is through the perpetuation of myths and the inability or the refusal to truly recognize the issues faced by those who are underrepresented and marginalized. Equity is making sure people have what they need in order to have fair access to opportunities available. This concept is one that must be considered by those who find themselves politically marginalized yet decide to fight to transform systems of political power in the interest of justice and fairness.

Barriers along lines of race, social class, gender, sexuality, and other elements of identity continue to stand in the way of significant numbers of Americans genuinely staking their claim in American politics and feeling they can truly make a difference via traditional channels. Activism and grassroots organizing has been the avenue to political voice for particular marginalized groups in the United States for so long that they have become institutionalized. In the Black community and others, there is almost an expectation that people who wish to rise in political power have backgrounds in activism, organizing, or resistance. That expectation can be used as a starting point for these first steps of organizing, with bigger goals of transformation of systems in mind.

The theory and belief that all politics is local specifically pertains to communities of color in the age of Obama. Perhaps more than even other groups, Black people in the United States are struggling with major issues that could easily be boiled down to local levels while still being viewed through the lens of national and state-level politics. Modern movements for justice in the Black community have followed past models in that they have roots in activism and protest on local levels, with connections to trends across the nation; that is the model seen in the Black Lives Matter movement.

The most recent Pew Research Poll on racial attitudes in the United States has shown that Black people have a different view of the circumstances they face, as well as the political strategies needed for progress along lines of race. Black respondents and White respondents certainly have different views on the most pertinent issues of race today. The top takeaways about current-day views of race and inequality in America in the recent Pew Poll go a long way in showing that there are partitions and divisions in the American body politic.

Until there is clear recognition of those in marginalized political positions, will those who are fighting for their political power be able to get real traction in those fights? There are clear splits between Blacks and Whites when it comes to how they view the current state of race relations in the United States as well as what progress President Obama has made on the issue. This sets the stage for a broader analysis of what needs to be done as underrepresented groups seek to gain meaningful political power.

About 6 out of 10 Americans say more changes need to be made in order to achieve racial equality. That fact, found in the Pew poll, shows that there is room for some progress to be made in fights for political power through fights for progress in racial equality. Only 53 percent of Whites say more changes are needed, whereas 88 percent of Blacks and 70 percent of Latinos believe this to be true. The takeaway from that breakdown of the statistics shows the fertile ground in the Black community for instigating change. For far too long, the opinions of Whites have been held as very important to movements seeking political power for underrepresented groups. The new paradigm should focus first on getting as many people from the underrepresented group as possible on board to fight for political power.[22]

The Black community could well be the example for other groups, as has been the case for generations; the 88 percent of Black people who see a need for more change are the prime people who could be targeted for organizing. The next step would be including members of other groups who seek change in the broad movement for change and Black political power. Having non-Blacks on board helps, but it should not be the ultimate goal upon which the broader movements hinge. This seems to be the type of strategy on display with the Black Lives Matter movement as well other current-day movements for social justice in the Black community.

Black people are much more reserved in their opinions when it comes to the possibility of change in the United States. Thirty-eight percent of Whites and only 8 percent of Blacks feel that the country has made the necessary changes to give Black equal rights. When it comes to believing the country will make the changes needed to give Blacks equal rights, 11 percent of Whites and 43 percent of Blacks don't believe this will happen. About 40 percent of both Blacks and Whites think that the country will eventually make the necessary changes, but in the eyes of respondents, there could be different definitions of just how long this will eventually take.[23]

It is clear that views are racially divided on the extremity of problems, the existence of problems, and the optimism of making changes or transformations. These views of Americans of different identities show that those who find themselves underrepresented and marginalized need not waste energy and time continually working to convince the White majority of the merit of their arguments and the validity of their lived experiences. Instead of putting so much social capital into convincing the White majority, energy could be placed in organizing internally and collaborating with those from the White majority, and other groups, who are allies. Organizing and collaborating is the best way to work around inherent obstacles in this system that was originally founded with White supremacy at its core.

Conclusion: Exclusion in the Body Politic and Using the Art of Being Unapologetically Black

The original national vision of freedom and liberty meant that the people of the United States were to be free of their colonial status and therefore free, with the power of governance in their own hands, to pursue their own destiny. As slaves, Blacks were not part of that original vision, but had to seek a place in it, finding that the elements of the vision could not sustain their own freedom and that in fact, their status as slaves was a contradiction to the broader manifest goals of democracy. Sharing broad goals including "life, liberty, and the pursuit of happiness" required the status of citizen, not slave. Thus, full citizenship became a valued goal for Blacks in the United States, a citizenship defined in part as possession of the right to vote, with the vote conceived of an instrument by which citizenship would be meaningful.

—Dr. Ronald Walters[24]

The body politic of the United States of America has roots and a long history in exclusion of Blacks and other groups from consideration as full citizens, as many times those individuals were denied consideration of their full humanity. When the government and society do not recognize certain people as being full citizens, based on their identity, there are problems afoot with the social contract. Unapologetically identifying as Black or being unapologetic about any other element of identity is essential if any group wants to successfully push for the transformation of the society's beliefs and end the perpetuation of practices that foster political, economic, and social marginalization. Continually, marginalized groups have found moments when their activists and politically interested individuals and groups have said, "Enough." In the interest of ultimately succeeding in gaining political power in the post-Obama political era, underrepresented groups have to broadcast there group's "enough moments" to the people who are ready to get involved and fight.

Grassroots efforts have been the choice of groups who have been excluded from the traditional avenues of political expression for so very long. When politically involved people in underrepresented and/or marginalized groups do end up collective saying "enough" on any particular issue or to the political landscape in general, they can begin organizing for changes to their group's civic culture. Historically, the most effective responses and strategies in navigating those "enough moments" come from outside of traditional political arenas and leadership. In order for underrepresented groups to gain and hold onto political power in the years following the Obama presidency, it is imperative that they recognize both their place in the body politic as individuals and as groups, as well as the sub-set of a body politic in which they operate inside their particular identity group.

It is not efficient or effective to pick and choose elements from the strug-gles and grassroots movements of groups when seeking to piece together a plan that can be customized for specific groups facing specific instances of political underrepresentation. The current-day Black body politic relies not only on linked fate but also on shared hope in the face of shared oppression. Linked fate is one view of solidarity that tends to lead people to look backward; shared hope is a view of solidarity that is very forward looking. It has been reinforced in the word and deed of American soci-ety, along with American governmental structure, that Black people and people who are heavily invested as their allies are not fully considered as part of the group of people of the nation, state, and society collectively organized as the broad group of citizens; this is because Black citizenship has been questioned and/or treated as less than first class in so many instances. In light of those realities, Blacks find themselves also being part of a Black body politic.

They end up being people considered collectively as a nation inside a nation. Because that is the case, being unapologetically Black opens the door for Black people to clearly investigate these issues of racism and then raise their grievances. To face the cancer of racism and marginalization, Black people have to be clear about who they are and what they face. This is also true for each group fighting to gain political power. At every point mentioned in organizing on the front end before broad coalitions are estab-lished, being unapologetic is essential to demanding full citizenship. Encouraging pride and self-confidence in the politically active members of any group is vital to politically mobilizing that particular group. The people must have belief and faith that there is something to be proud of in boldly proclaiming their solidarity with the rest of the group before mov-ing on to solidarity with other groups. Not every Black person will be on board with any particular effort to gain political power and justice for Black people as a group. No successful movement takes the time to stall long enough to coddle those in the group who refuse to get on board or to give the vocal majority opposition in power time to come around on their own. There must be active revolution fueled by distrust of government, thirst for freedom, and at least some antigovernment sentiment.

In cultivating a healthy and productive conceptualization of antigovern-ment sentiment, the police violence that is a big part of motivating a move-ment like the #BlackLivesMatter movement can be a unifying force. In seeking to build solidarity in the Black community, it is useful to reach back to the concept of "linked fate" in the Black community. The abuses of Black people and the disrespect of Black life by the state have occurred across lines of age, gender, social class, and geographic location. That bitter reality has worked on its own to reconstitute feelings of linked fate that had somewhat faded in recent decades. A similar approach can be taken when working on political and economic improvement efforts for Black communities like the African American Empowerment Network in Omaha, Nebraska, or the QC Empowerment Network in the Quad Cities region of Illinois and Iowa. Economic marginalization, lack of political influence, and disregard by those in local power are all examples of abuses and disrespect for Black people that are as systemic as the injustices of police violence, but are less immediately visual.

Black people and other underrepresented groups need to embrace their collective anger at the injustices that have been perpetuated for generations instead of instantly forgiving. In taking time to delve into the roots of anger and the related inequities, those seeking to organize the perpetually underrepresented will find touchstones that end up motivating moves toward unity, action, and engagement in those groups and communities. It is clear that there needs to be a harnessing and focusing of the anger found in marginalized communities that is many times rooted in poor levels of political power and representation. That anger can be put to work politically when people are helped in recognizing the political roots that are a major portion of the feelings of anger and exclusion. Never should the anger be allowed to simply fester or morph into blind rage or hopelessness. Far too often, Black people are asked or pushed to forgive the unforgivable. President Obama has been known to say variations of the phrase "Don't boo; vote." Black people and other groups seeking to overcome underrepresentation need to live by the mantra, "Don't rush to forgive; organize." Organizing, for each marginalized group seeking political power, is vital for groups to best position themselves to take political power and fundamentally transform the systems. The systems they seek to fundamentally transform are ones that continue hold them in positions of underrepresentation. Ultimately, the goal would be to forge the bonds of solidarity needed to build lasting and powerful coalitions between groups seeking political power.

Notes

1. Clayton, 2010.
2. Kenski et al., 2010, p. 378.
3. Malcolm X, 2016 (1964).
4. Garvey, 2016.

5. Alinsky, 1989, p. 63.
6. Jackson, 2016.
7. Smiley, 2006.
8. Page, 2016.
9. Garvey, 2016.
10. Malcolm X, 2016 (1965).
11. McClain, 2014.
12. Koveleski, 2008, p. A1.
13. Ibid.
14. Alinsky, 1989.
15. Graham and Hand, 2010.
16. Jackson, 2016.
17. Touré, 2011.
18. Jackson, 2016.
19. Gillespie, 2010.
20. Greenblatt, 2016.
21. Wise, 2014.
22. Pew Research Center, 2016.
23. Ibid.
24. Walters, 2005.

Bibliography

Alinsky, Saul David. 1989. *Rules for Radicals: A Practical Primer for Realistic Radicals.* New York: Vintage Books.

Clayton, Dewey M. 2010. *The Presidential Campaign of Barack Obama: A Critical Analysis of a Racially Transcendent Strategy.* New York: Routledge.

Garvey, Marcus. 2014. "Marcus Garvey. African American Quotes." Africatown/Chinatown News Digest, February 27. https://africatownchinatown newsdigest.wordpress.com/2014/02/17/marcus-garvey-african-american-quotes/.

Gillespie, Andra. 2010. *Whose Black Politics?: Cases in Post-Racial Black Leadership.* New York: Routledge.

Graham, Bob, and Chris Hand. 2010. *America, the Owner's Manual: Making Government Work for You.* Washington, DC: CQ Press.

Greenblatt, Alan. 2016. "Turning Black Lives Matter Protests into Policy." Governing: The States and Localities, May. http://www.governing.com/topics/politics/gov-Black-lives-matter-protests.html.

Jackson, Derrick. 2016. "Race and Representation in the Twilight of the Obama Era." *The American Prospect*, January 15.

Kenski, Kate, Bruce W. Hardy, and Kathleen Hall Jamieson. 2010. *The Obama Victory.* New York: Oxford University Press.

Koveleski, Serge. 2008. "Obama's Organizing Years, Guiding Others and Finding Himself." *The New York Times*, July 7, A1.

Malcolm X. 2016. "Quotes by Malcolm X." Malcolm X. http://malcolmx.com/quotes/. Accessed May 10.

McClain, Paula Denice. 2014. *American Government in Black and White*, 2nd ed. New York; Oxford: Oxford University Press.

Page, Clarence. 2016. "If 'All Lives Matter,' Show That You Mean It." *The Chicago Tribune*, July 8.

Pew Research Center. 2016. "On Views of Race and Inequality, Blacks and Whites Are Worlds Apart." Social & Demographic Trends, June 27. http://www.pewsocialtrends.org/2016/06/27/on-views-of-race-and-inequality-Blacks-and-whites-are-worlds-apart/.

Smiley, Tavis. 2006. *The Covenant with Black America*, Vol. 1. Chicago: Third World Press.

Touré. 2011. "No Such Place as 'Post Racial' America." *The New York Times*, November 8, 2011.

Walters, Ronald W. 2005. *Freedom Is Not Enough: Black Voters, Black Candidates, and American Presidential Politics*. American Political Challenges. Lanham, MD: Rowman & Littlefield; distributed by National Book Network.

Wise, Tim. 2014. "F.A.Q.S." Tim Wise, updated December. http://www.timwise.org/f-a-q-s/.

CHAPTER TWO

The Right to Vote, 50 Years Later: Do We Still Need the 1965 VRA?[1]

Blanche M. Radford-Curry

Introduction

When considering how far African Americans have come in 50 years of voting since the passage of the 1965 Voting Rights Act (VRA), it is instructive to do so not only within the historical context to include the election of the first black president but also within the context of ongoing socio-political issues. Although President Obama's election has been touted as validation of a postracial society, a significant number of political and legal challenges persist with respect to the franchise that render the idea of a postracial society more "apparent" than real.[2]

Beginning with an overview of the electoral and social injustices that necessitated the Fourteenth and Fifteenth Amendments, the 1965 and 1970 VRAs, this chapter argues for the retention and improvement of the 1965 VRA based on current efforts aimed at African American voter suppression. The strategies deployed include gerrymandering or racially and politically biased redistricting, controversial voter ID requirements, and especially the instrumentality of mass incarceration of African American youth. On the bases of such challenges—amid the illusions of a postracial society and the related discourse and campaign rhetoric—it is argued that ending the 1965 VRA now would be premature because it is still needed to ensure justice, equality, and fairness for all Americans.

The History and Justification for the 1965 VRA

The history of the 1965 VRA can be traced back to Abraham Lincoln, toward the end of the Civil War. On April 11, 1865, in what turned out to be his last speech, Abraham Lincoln laid out his vision for the postwar nation and proposed giving some blacks, especially those who had fought in the war, the right to vote. As historian Eric Foner has rightly observed, it was the first time an American president had endorsed publicly any kind of black suffrage.[3] Shortly after the Civil War and Lincoln's assassination, the Thirteenth, Fourteenth, and Fifteenth Amendments to the Constitution were adopted. In 1869, the Thirteenth effectively abolished slavery or involuntary service (except penalty for crime), and the Fourteenth guaranteed liberty and equal protection under the law for all U.S. citizens. Section I reads:

> All persons born or naturalized in the United States, and subject to the jurisdiction thereof, are citizens of the State, where in they reside. No State shall make or enforce any law which shall abridge the privileges or immunities of citizens of the United States, nor shall any State deprive any person of life, liberty, or property, without due process of law, nor deny to any person, within its jurisdiction the equal protection of the laws.[4]

The original intention and justification as well as the optimism engendered by the Thirteenth and Fourteenth Amendments are best captured in the words of Senator Waitman T. Willey, a Republican from West Virginia, who proclaimed from the Senate floor during the debate over the Fifteenth Amendment:

> This Amendment, when adopted, will settle the question for all time of negro suffrage in the insurgent States, where it has lately been extended under the pressure of congressional legislation, and will preclude the possibility of any future denial of this privilege by any change in the constitutions of those states.[5]

Notwithstanding the backing of these constitutional provisions, the initial optimism of Lincoln and Willey regarding the Fifteenth Amendment could not be sustained beyond Reconstruction. Although ratification of these amendments by states implied that states were constitutionally prohibited from engaging in racial discrimination, Southern states continued to prevent blacks from voting as soon as the policies of Reconstruction ended. Blacks, however, did not give up the struggle for their right to vote and persisted against the best mechanisms of their Southern governors, fighting for their voting rights over the next hundred years. In the course of these years, they used several protest movements led by their progressive leaders, such as Frederick Douglass and W.E.B. Du Bois, and the Civil Rights Movements of the 1950s and 1960s.

Subsequently, President Lyndon B. Johnson signed the 1965 VRA into law on August 6, 1965, one hundred years after Lincoln's initial voting rights amendments. It was a historical and ceremonial moment, witnessed by Rev. Dr. Martin Luther King Jr. and other civil rights leaders. At the end of the debates, the voting rights bill was passed with a vote of 77 to 19 in the U.S. Senate on May 26, 1965. Less than two months later, on July 9, 1965, the U.S. House of Representatives passed the bill, with a vote of 333–85, after a lengthy discussion that went beyond a month.[6] One of the immediate impacts of the 1965 VRA was that on the following day, voter registration officials in Sumter County, Georgia, dropped their opposition to a black registration drive that had been going on for some two weeks. David Garrow also notes that some three hundred new black voters were registered in Sumter County on August 6 that year alone.[7]

Even more remarkable has been the effectiveness of the black vote on presidential elections in favor of democratic presidents including John F. Kennedy, Jimmy Carter, Bill Clinton, and Barack Obama.[8] Not only has the African American vote played an important part in the election of these presidents, but if we consider the work of Garrow (1978) as well as Laney (2003), we learn about much earlier historical instances. In Garrow's discussion of pre-1965 voting rights history, he notes three frequent starting points for the Civil Rights Movement. Many scholars, he notes, begin with *Brown v. Board of Education of Topeka*, May 17, 1954, or Mrs. Rosa Park's Montgomery bus boycott, December 1, 1955. He informs us of the *Smith v. Allwright* Supreme Court ruling of April 1944. Of significant interest here is Garrow's further discussion of *Smith v. Allwright* with respect to African Americans and voting rights. With the favorable ruling of this case, the number of registered African Americans substantially increased. Although their record number of votes were not adequate to seat a given politician, it is important to note this early historical evidence about African American's voting as a possible impact in determining the election of a given candidate.[9] Earlier than 1944, Laney notes that Senator Cole Blease of South

Carolina, in his address to the 1927 Congress, related that the 1895 South Carolina Constitution was "to disfranchise African Americans" and that Calvin Coolidge received 1110 votes from his state in the 1922 election. "I do not know where he got them. I was astonished to know they were cast and shocked to know they were counted."[10] It is no exaggeration to infer that without black votes, not one of these democratic victories could have been secured. Even though Hilary Clinton lost to Donald Trump, it cannot be denied that black votes were critical in making the election so close and enabling Clinton to win the popular vote.[11]

It was necessary to reauthorize the Fourteenth Amendment in 1870 with the Fifteenth Amendment, which allowed only African American men the right to vote. Only with the Nineteenth Amendment in 1920 did the Constitution grant women the right to vote. Nevertheless, African American men under the Fifteenth Amendment and African American women under the Nineteenth Amendment faced obstacles to exercise their right to vote, such as poll taxes, literary tests, registration requirements, and intimidation. One of the most powerful of these obstacles was the use of state constitutions to undermine black voting rights guaranteed by the Fourteenth, Fifteenth, and Nineteenth Amendments. A striking example occurred in Kentucky, whose 1792 constitution allowed the state to permanently deny voting rights to individuals with convictions unless the governor chose to restore their rights. Given Kentucky's history of racism, it goes without saying that blacks were discriminated against in their voting rights restoration. Florida and Iowa also imposed indefinite disenfranchisement on all persons convicted of any felon, even after they had served their sentences and were rehabilitated.[12] In 1890, for example, Mississippi held a constitutional convention to contrive measures to permanently disenfranchise most blacks. Their example emboldened many other Southern states to create similar measures to disfranchise their black citizens.[13] It was only with the passage of the 1965 VRA that we begin to see an increase in African American women and men exercising their right to vote.

Despite its importance for a multiracial, inclusive, and truly representative democracy, the history of the 1965 VRA cannot be complete without reflection on the struggles by African Americans and well-meaning whites to ensure its survival amid formidable and sometimes ferocious opposition, especially from Southern states. No matter how vicious the opposition, African Americans, as well documented within the Civil Rights Era, "had their eyes fixed on the prize" and were not prepared to give up on their right to vote.

When considering how the 1965 VRA came to be, its' birth, the work of Garrow, provides us with an insightful examination of the dynamics of protest that was woven from the struggle for voting rights, to the VRA as a law. He notes that "the story of the Voting Rights Act is inextricably tied to the story of the SCLC [Southern Christian Leadership Conference] protest campaign in Selma. Selma [Alabama] is the nexus at which the voting rights story and the dynamics of protest come together so vividly."[14]

The March 7, 1965, voting rights march from Selma, Alabama, to the state capital in Montgomery was one of the most historical and pivotal voting rights endeavors in the Civil Rights Movement marches of the 1950s and 1960s. This march was led by the Rev. Dr. Martin Luther King Jr., in conjunction with other notable organizations like the Student Nonviolent Coordinating Committee (SNCC), lay people, and clergy from all over the United States. The vicious assaults on the protesters, including severe beatings, water hosing, dog attacks, and police brutalities, were seen around the world on national television. The media effect propelled many other clergy, black and white, out of sympathy, empathy, and compassion generated by humane feelings and the *agape* Christian love or a sense of social justice, to join the march or support the movement.

Ava Dunernay's 2015 documentary film *Selma* chronicles many of the social injustices against African Americans and details obstacles to the franchise. The telling examples include election officials intentionally dismissing African Americans from voting lines under the false pretense that they had come to the wrong polling location or they had come on the wrong polling date. Some were illegally asked to show evidence of paid poll taxes, and others were required to take discredited and unfair literacy tests, or to recite parts of the Constitution. Also brought to life is Garrow's discussion of the dynamics of the VRA protest. Elevating moral interest in African Americans' struggles was the goal of the SCLC voting rights protest. Selma leaders learned lessons from earlier marchers in Albany, Georgia (1961 and 1962) and Birmingham (1963). African Americans' use of violence and weapons proved to be counterproductive in response to the horrific violence by the police and created a lack of sympathy from whites and other non-white supporters of Civil Rights. With the fusion of King's nonviolent method and a clear single goal that "could be easily conveyed both *to* and *by* news media," SCLC achieved memorable national and moral attention of African Americans voting rights with the 1965 Selma protest.[15]

African American protestors had proven to a larger "audience" that their immediate opponents' reaction to their nonviolent voting rights struggle was unacceptable. Garrow explains that although the larger "audience" is not directly involved in the conflict at the outset, it influences "the outcomes of political conflicts."[16] He also references political analyst E. E. Schattschneider, who explains the importance of ongoing vigilance of the *relations* between the protestors and the opponents, as it is the audience who decides the outcome. Additionally, as noted in the *Selma* documentary, the media plays an important part. Garrow references further the sociologist James S. Coleman, who explains that the factors that influence the audience's decision—whether to support the protestors or their opponents—center on each group's ability to have its basic values and dispositions supported by the audience while decreasing the other group's support. Whether the audience decides to support the protestors or their opponents is largely influenced by the news media portrayal of each group's position.[17]

So disappointing was the implementation of the 1965 VRA that, beginning in the 1960s, the federal government was pressured into taking action to address racial discrimination and other blatant injustices at the polls. For a while, all three branches of the federal government seemed to work in harmony on the VRA. For example, while Congress passed legislation to enforce voting rights and remove legal barriers to the ballot box, the Executive branch sued state governments and local officials for depriving African Americans of their voting rights. Ultimately, the judiciary stepped in to remove (or at least reduce) some of the legal obstacles to black suffrage. For example, in 1965, in *Louisiana v. United States*, the Supreme Court struck down Louisiana's so-called "understanding test." This controversial law allowed local voting registrars to decide whether individuals attempting to register had a sufficient understanding of state and federal constitutions to be qualified to vote. Also in 1966, the Supreme Court (*Harper v. Virginia State Board of Elections*) determined that the imposition of a poll tax as a prerequisite to voting in state elections violated the Fourteenth Amendment. Some Southern states continued to implement the poll tax until long after the passage of the Twenty-Fourth Amendment in 1964; thusly, the Supreme Court stepped in again and struck it down in 1966, banning all poll taxes throughout the country as a precondition for registration to vote. Furthermore, in response to state noncompliance, Section 10 of the VRA empowered the attorney general to challenge the use of poll taxes in the states. In spite of all these judiciary and other federal efforts, several credible studies have shown that these and other institutional barriers continued to suppress minority voting.[18] Additional evidence is provided later to show that voter suppression efforts by the states have not abated at the end of the presidential election in 2016.

To counter state noncompliance and their innovative obstacles to black suffrage, the U.S. Congress also adopted additional innovative instruments. For example, states and localities were designated as "VRA covered jurisdiction" if they posed a serious threat to the rights of blacks to vote. Thus, the VRA designated a state or county government as a "covered jurisdiction" if it implemented any discriminatory test or device, or if the voting registration rate or the voter turnout in the presidential election among the voting population in 1964 was lower than 50 percent.[19]

By 1965, the VRA had designated several Southern states as "covered jurisdictions": Alabama, Georgia, Louisiana, Mississippi, South Carolina, and the Commonwealth of Virginia. Additionally, 40 out of the 100 counties in North Carolina were designated as "covered jurisdictions." The aforementioned states resented this designation for several reasons. Once designated as a "covered jurisdiction," the state would need preclearance from the federal government for any change in rules that could affect public elections. Also, on the request of residents, federal officials have the power to review the voter registration process and monitor the elections in covered jurisdictions. The aim of the strategy is to severely limit the ability of Southern governments to discourage minority representation and voting rights. The idea of being monitored has been compared to the monitoring of elections in emerging democracies in the Third World by the United States and other Western nations and their nongovernmental organizations (NGOs), with the implication that the states under provision are being treated like third-world countries. The effectiveness of this measure became apparent by research conducted in 2008. For example, Rosenberg found that African American voter registration rates within VRA-covered states rose from 27.9 percent in pre-VRA to 54.7 percent in post-VRA years.[20] Instead of celebrating the positive outcome of this policy, Southern states rather dreaded the prospect of minority voters affecting policy making in the near future. Consequently, they started to look for new ways to make the black vote less meaningful or impactful. This VRA backlash should therefore be deemed as one of the explanations for the massive pro-Trump vote from the Southern states in the 2016 presidential election.

Why the 1965 VRA Is Still Needed

Opposition to continuing the VRA has been growing steadily in recent years, and especially since the two-term election of President Barack Obama as the first African American president of the United States and a liberal democrat. The anti-VRA voices reached their crescendo when, in 2013, Chief Justice of the Supreme Court John Roberts concluded that the protection for the VRA is no longer necessary because "times have changed" and that African American ballots were no longer blocked by tests and other devices. Moreover, he claimed, the African American level of registration and voting is equivalent to or higher than those of whites.[21] Justice

Roberts further argued that the VRA should not be sustained because it was a violation of a threat to the sovereignty of each state.

Responding to the ruling, President Obama, who had benefitted immensely by the most historic black voter turnout in 2008 and 2012, said he was *"deeply disappointed"* [emphasis added] with the decision. He explained:

> For nearly 50 years, the Voting Rights Act—enacted and repeatedly renewed by wide bipartisan majorities in Congress—has helped secure the right to vote for millions of Americans, "Today's decision invalidating one of its core provisions upsets decades of well-established practices that help make sure voting is fair, especially in places where voting discrimination has been historically prevalent."[22]

To remedy the negative impact of the ruling, President Obama appealed to Congress "to pass legislation to ensure every American has equal access to the polls." Unlike John Roberts, Obama believes there is sufficient evidence for discrimination to the VRA Section 4 for it to be retained as it is.[23]

The premises of Chief Justice Robert's argument were either factually wrong or legally suspect. Fortunately, Justice Ruth Bader Ginsburg would not let him get away with the unacceptable legal premise. She argued:

> [T]he court in upholding the original 1965 Voting Rights Act, "held, in no uncertain terms, that the principle [of equal sovereignty]" applies only to the terms upon which States are admitted to the Union, and not to the remedies for local evils which have subsequently appeared.[24]

In other words, although the Constitution recognizes a state as sovereign, the state cannot violate the civil and human rights of its citizenry and expect the federal government and the Supreme Court to remain silent. That is because every state is committed to the Union and its Constitution, which, if violated by the state, makes it imperative for the federal government to intervene and impose corrective measures.

Besides Justice Ginsberg, a former justice of the U.S. Supreme Court, John Paul Stevens, argues that there has been an extensive history of discrimination against blacks, especially against their voting rights, and that Congress determined after much deliberation that the 1965 VRA was necessary as a remedy to the ongoing voter discrimination. Rather than overturn a decision made by Congress (which is the people's representation), Stevens argued it was better for the Supreme Court to honor that decision by upholding the 1965 VRA.[25] It is also pertinent to add that

Justice Stevens's challenge to Justice Robert's factual premises on voter discrimination against African Americans is well supported by volumes of credible evidence and data provided by the American Civil Liberties Union (ACLU) and the Southern Poverty Law Center at their respective websites.[26]

Mass Incarceration as an Instrument for Black Voter Suppression

The feminist philosopher, ex-Communist and ex–Black Panther, and antiprison activist Angela Davis has been mostly a lone voice crying in the wilderness against the U.S. prison system as a prison–industrial complex built primarily on the profit motive, and not for crime prevention, reform, rehabilitation, or even retributive justice.[27] But recent research by social sciences appears to be confirming her belief based on her personal experience as an inmate for almost two decades. Her radical views on the prison system and her activism on social justice and other controversial issues have earned her the title "The Notorious Philosopher."[28]

The issue, however, is more than a criminal justice issue. It is also a political and a civil rights issue. It is becoming increasingly clear that as a result of a collusion between politicians and private businesses running the prison system, there is now a vicious cycle in which young African Americans arrested for any minor crime (such as the use, sale, or possession of marijuana; a street fight; or even jaywalking) is given a long prison sentence by white prosecutors who advertise themselves to their campaign sponsors, including the CEO or owners of prison-related businesses, as "tough on crime." To sustain the mutually beneficial partnership, such prosecutors have to do "what they have to do" to ensure that as many unstable and vulnerable young men as possible, mostly black (who are easily tempted by drugs and money given their poverty level and dysfunctional homes) are caught in the system. As Adam Gopnik Gospen has observed in *The New Yorker*, with a population of 6 million inmates, if the American prison system were a city, it would be the second-largest city in the United States, behind New York. Of these 2 million inmates, one-third are black Americans. Filling the prison cells to capacity means profits, and overcrowding means less expenditure and more profit.[29]

Besides prosecutors, many city managers and mayors, governors and lawmakers, Congressmen, and even judges advertise themselves as "tough on crime," "three-strikes-and-you're-out," or "no-nonsense candidates" as a way to attract sponsors within the private prison–industrial complex. There are even reports of free or cheap inmate labor exploited by these prison-related for-profit businesses, with the connivance of prison officers or their supervisors.[30]

One does not need to search far to find evidence for the existence of the prison–industrial complex and their modus operandi. Described as the most chilling document in recent American life is the 2005 annual report of the Corrections Corporation of America, the biggest of these firms. In the quote below, the company is obliged to caution its investors and lobbyists about the risk of losing convicted men in the prison system.

> Our growth is generally dependent upon our ability to obtain new contracts to develop and manage new correctional and detention facilities. . . . The demand for our facilities and services could be adversely affected by the relaxation of enforcement efforts, leniency in conviction and sentencing practices or through the decriminalization of certain activities that are currently proscribed by our criminal laws. For instance, any changes with respect to drugs and controlled substances or illegal immigration could affect the number of persons arrested, convicted, and sentenced, thereby potentially reducing demand for correctional facilities to house them.[31]

Prior to reading it oneself, it's hard to imagine such a document actually exists, portraying in the words of the perpetrators themselves how an amoral and inhumane capitalist enterprise feeds on the misery of fellow human beings and does all it can to ensure that no one within its grip escapes legally or otherwise from such misery.

Before this revelation based on her decades of experience and reflection from behind the bar, Angela Davis had disclosed the collusion between law enforcement and politicians, as reflected in her online article "Masked Racism: Reflections on the Prison–industrial Complex," published in 1999.[32] In an earlier article on prisons, she argues that, among other things, imprisonment in the United States has become big business, as it is now the first response to far too many poverty-related social problems facing mostly people of color:

> Imprisonment has become the response of first resort to far too many of the social problems that burden people who are ensconced in poverty. These problems often are veiled by being conveniently grouped together under the category "crime" and by the automatic attribution of criminal behavior to people of color. Homelessness, unemployment, drug addiction, mental illness, and illiteracy are only a few of the problems that disappear from public view when the human beings contending with them are relegated to cages. Prisons thus perform a feat of magic. . . . But prisons do not disappear problems, they disappear human beings. And the practice of disappearing

vast numbers of people from poor, immigrant, and racially marginalized communities has literally become big business.[33]

The point in raising the issues of mass incarceration in this essay is, of course, not to condone criminal behavior, but to point out how incarceration and other legal restrictions unfairly lead to mass disenfranchisement of incarcerated and previously incarcerated African Americans. While they are incarcerated, prisoners, disproportionately black, forfeit the right to vote. Moreover, many years after their incarceration and rehabilitation, most of them are still denied the right to vote based on their status as ex-convicts. Although some states allow ex-cons to register to vote after one year, others make them wait five years, and still other states never allow them to exercise their right to vote. The lack of uniformity in the application of the relevant laws in this case represents a clear violation of the equal protection clause of the Fourteenth Amendment.

Those who try to deny the reality of the prison–industrial system and its impact on voting rights often refer to the notion of a postracial society as the elimination of racial discrimination against blacks. In her book *The New Jim Crow: Mass Incarceration in the Age of Color Blindness*, Michelle Alexander explains that with the support of lawmakers, prisons have increasingly become privately owned. Consequently, prisons have become sources for profit run by private owners. The structure that supports this process, she explains, involves an unjust legal system that allows the incarceration of African Americans at a rate seven times higher than that of whites. This is the result of the unjustifiable differences in the types of charges and length of their incarcerations. According to Alexander, this process represents "a modern day racial caste system."[34] The irony is not that it exists, but that it is embedded within the American democratic system of all places!

In "The Caging of America," Adam Gopnik notes,

> For a great many poor people in America, particularly poor black men, prison is a destination that braids through an ordinary life, much as high school and college do for rich white ones. More than half of all black men without a high-school diploma go to prison at some time in their lives. Mass incarceration on a scale almost unexampled in human history is a fundamental fact of our country today—perhaps the fundamental fact, as slavery was the fundamental fact of 1850.[35]

As noted by Angela Davis, no longer is the prison system a place for dangerous criminals to protect society or even a place for retributive justice. Rather, it has become a for-profit business by private owners, and corporations have been upended with a more perfidious practice of mass punishment built on profit and convenience.[36] American's incarceration rate has tripled since 1980, although violent crime has been declining. Almost 13 million people have contact with American jails in any given year, and 6 million have "correctional supervision." Because of the excessive sentencing policies of the 1980s and 1990s, many are serving time for convictions relating to minor drug offenses, smoking and/or selling marijuana. Additionally, there are new laws like "three strikes" and "truth in sentencing," which unfairly increase a person's incarceration period. Persons are sentenced to 25 years to life for multiple felony convictions and are required to serve most of that time.

Recent research into the prison system has shown that the intent of these laws is to increase the incarceration rate for continued profit. Among these recent exposés is the 2009 Luzerne County, Pennsylvania, scandal about "kids for cash." William Ecenbarger's book of the same title speaks volumes to the corruption of our "justice" system. For more than a decade, two judges were paid over $2.8 million for convicting over 5000 kids in their courtrooms. The children were sent to prison for petty crimes like stealing DVDs from Walmart and trespassing in vacant buildings. Eventually the two justices were caught and sentenced to 17.5 and 28 years in prison, respectively. But the tragedy is that the lives of those young victims were forever ruined.[37]

Issues for Further Discussion

Cynics about the criminal justice system, and especially about the prison–industrial complex, dismiss the possibility of reform while revolutionaries call for a violent response. It is therefore worth noting that, motivated by care ethics and compassion, Virginia Governor Terry McAuliffe and Maryland Governor Larry Hogan invoked legal measures have full voting rights restored, to over hundreds of thousands of its citizens with previous conviction records. Governor McAuliffe's action received immediate backlash from Republican legislatures. Governor Hogan's efforts to end disenfranchisement to those sentenced only to probation were vehemently opposed by the Maryland legislature. The argument presented was that ex-convicts have the right to vote because they have completed their sentences. For states where over half of the felony convictions are for African Americans, this action would go a long way toward undoing the effects of decades of racially skewed suffrage restrictions. States like Maine and Vermont have always refused to limit their citizens' right to vote, even their ex-cons.[38]

What would happen if the 1965 VRA were to be abolished? Certainly, it would be a serious blow to the Obama legacy, which, in spite of the determination of Republican Congress and other leading conservatives to ensure its failure, still is a legacy most blacks and many other people could be proud of. Take, for example, the reversal of the dire economic trend he inherited in 2008, cutting unemployment down from 10 percent to under 4.6 percent nationally, and black unemployment from 14 percent to 7 percent or lower in December 2016. One cannot also forget the abundance of gas at prices below two dollars a gallon in most places for the last two or three years, and the expanded use of alternate sources of energy, including solar, liquid gas, and hydroelectric, which have reduced our dependence on foreign oil. Take also his signature health care program, The Affordable Health Care Act, or Obamacare; hunting and taking down America's number-one enemy, Osama bin Laden; and ending two major wars in Iraq and Afghanistan. Also take his initiatives in ensuring more equitable sentencing across racial lines; minimizing or eradicating predatory lending that targets poor blacks and others; instituting federal laws to limit sexual harassment in schools, colleges, and universities; increasing special grant initiatives for historically black colleges and universities (HBCUs); and expanding the Pell Grant to cover more poor people, not to mention the pride and dignity he has brought to the White House, especially for most blacks.

Obama's critics often ask what has he done specifically for African Americans or other minorities. One of the most important legacies achieved by Obama, which his critics might not appreciate or may need to be reminded of, is the passing of the 2015 Voting Rights Advancement Act (VRAA). In his reaction to the attempt by Chief Justice John Roberts and the majority conservative Supreme Court to undermine the black vote guaranteed by the 1965 VRA in the *Shelby County v. Holder* case, Obama asked Congress to help him pass a law that would ensure that the VRA would remain a permanent provision for African Americans and their future generations. This Act was surprisingly passed with bipartisan backing on June 24, 2015. Among other things, this Act provides for the following:

1. Modernize the preclearance formula to cover states with a pattern of discrimination that puts voters at risk.
2. Ensure that last-minute voting changes won't adversely affect voters.
3. Protect voters from types of voting changes most likely to discriminate against people of color and language minorities.
4. Enhance ability to apply preclearance review when necessary.

5. Expand the effective federal observer program.
6. Improve voting rights protection for Native Americans and Alaskan Natives.[39]

Although no law by itself can guarantee that one's right to vote is never violated, the 2015 VRAA includes a mechanism for ensuring compliance with the act in affected states:

> A federal court shall retain jurisdiction to enforce constitutional voting guarantees, but also certain violations of the Act as well as of any federal prohibition against discrimination on the basis of race, color, or membership in a language minority group, for an appropriate period to prevent commencement of new devices to deny or abridge the right to vote.[40]

Philosophically speaking, critical questions may continue to be asked about the 1965 VRA, such as the following:

- Should we be concerned about the possibility of new legislators and Supreme Court justices nullifying the 1965 VRA in the future?
- Will the Voting Rights Advancement Act end amendments to the 1965 VRA without transformative moral consciousness?
- Is there no better resolution such as rewriting the relevant section of the U.S. Constitution to guarantee that no state could tamper with the 1965 VRA?

Without grappling with such questions and making serious changes, to quote Roger Smith and Desmond King:

> The future of American politics is rather bleak on the voting rights front. As long as the conservative movement sees voting rights suppression as a partisan tool, racial policy alliances will continue to structure American politics and American elections and governance might be paralyzed by voting wars.[41]

Our goal, as articulated by the titles of three notable publications in regards to this issue, should be the right to vote and not *The Fight to Vote*[42] as we move "From Vote Participation to Meaningful Representation,"[43] and toward "The Last Will and Testament"[44] in the words of Michael Waldman, Olivier Richomme, and Mary McLeod Bethune, respectively.

Conclusion

In conclusion, 50 years of the 1965 VRA is certainly worth celebrating; but in so doing, one must not forget that the fight to protect it for future generations is far from over even with the Voting Rights Advancement Act of 2015. As noted in the forgoing history of the 1965 VRA, the right to vote has not been offered freely for the African American, as it has been whites. The right to vote was fought for during the Civil War and was lost and regained repeatedly until the VRA of 1965. The historical review has also shown that, despite its moral and legal justification, African Americans and their allies in the liberal movement and the Democratic Party have fought gallantly to defend it up until now. If the controversial and unprecedented presidential election of 2016 has anything to teach us in this regard, it must be that, in spite of the 2015 Voting Rights Advancement Act signed by Obama, the struggle to defend the 1965 VRA is not over. The 1965 VRA was severely tested in multiple ways, including by closing down voting stations, limiting advance early voting, cancelling Sunday after-church voting, prohibiting voting without a picture ID or driver's license, so-called security provided by gun wielding, pro-Trump supporters, and so on.

The lesson from the prison–industrial complex and the efforts of the Virginia and Maryland governors in defending the VRA for African Americans is not enough. We cannot afford to ignore the history of states like Kentucky, Mississippi, Iowa, and Florida, which were so determined to end the black vote that they either amended their constitutions or passed new bills to disenfranchise the black vote permanently. It is therefore critical that more governors emulate the actions of Virginia and Maryland governors. On his part, President Obama has begun a substantial conversation on ending the disenfranchisement of ex-felons, which would have to be continued by democrats and liberal-leaning civil rights organizations now that he has left office. It is necessary, therefore, that we continue to educate ourselves and the general public on the need for social justice in order to end the adverse effects of the prison–industrial complex system.

Another lesson is that we should embark on a systematic education process that will maximize critical moral consciousness and critical thinking for our youth in their preteen years, so they will understand the danger that is out there looking for them. We must also empower and encourage them to learn to resist temptation so they do not fall victim to the vicious cycle of the prison–industrial complex that will not only deprive them of their freedoms but also take away their right to vote and reduce them to second-class citizens.

The struggle to preserve the 1965 VRA should not be perceived as just for the right to vote for any political candidate, or to preserve the Obama legacy—important as that is for our posterity; it must be perceived above all as the struggle to preserve our common identity, our dignity as black people, and how far we have come socially, politically, and otherwise. For, as Aristotle observed over 2000 years ago, by nature, man or every human being is "a political animal."[45] In effect, if we lose the right to vote, then we lose our humanity just as we lost our humanity through the institution of slavery.

Notes

1. I wish to acknowledge research assistance from graduate students Kelisha Graves and Terri Walker West. Also, I am appreciative for the review of this work by my philosophy colleague, Dr. Joseph Osei, Fayetteville State University.

2. Rodney E. Hero and Carline J. Tolbert, "Race and the 2012 Election: A Post-Racial Society, More Apparent Than Real Mini-Symposium," *Political Research Quarterly* 67(3): 628–31.

3. Eric Foner, *The Fiery Trial: Abraham Lincoln and American Slavery* (New York and London: W.W. Norton & Company, 2010).

4. U.S. Constitution, Fourteenth Amendment, Section I.

5. Cited in Lee Epstein and Thomas Walker, *Constitutional Law for a Changing America: Rights Liberties and Justice* (Washington, DC, 2007), p. 749.

6. Voting Rights Act (n.d.), http://www.History.com/topics/black-history/voting-rights-act, accessed December 16, 2016.

7. David J. Garrow, *Protest at Selma: Martin Luther King, Jr., and the Voting Rights Act of 1965* (New Haven, CT: Yale University Press, 1978), p. xi.

8. Eddie S. Glaude, "The Black Vote: History Demands a Strategy for Change," time.com, September 24, 2016, http://time.com/4504138/black-vote-blank-out/.

9. Garrow, *Protest at Selma*, pp. 6–8.

10. Garrine P. Laney, *The Voting Rights Act of 1965: Historical Background and Current Issues* (Novinka Books New York, 2003), p. 5.

11. Glaude, http://time.com/4504138/black-vote-blank-out/.

12. M.T.C. Shafer, "Race is the Reason Felons Don't Vote," SCALAWAG-Magazine.org, June 14, 2016, http://www.scalawagmagazine.org/articles/race-is-the-reason-felons-dont-have-the-right-to-vote.

13. Laney, *The Voting Rights Act of 1965*, pp. 3–5.

14. Garrow, *Protest at Selma*, p. 1.

15. Ibid., pp. 2–3

16. Ibid., pp. 4–5.

17. Ibid., pp. 212–213.

18. J. E. Filer, L. W. Kenny, and R. B. Morton, "Voting Laws, Educational Policies, and Minority Turnout," *Journal of Law & Economics* 34(1991): 371.

19. Olivier Richomme, "The Voting Rights Act at 50: From Vote Participation to Meaningful Representation," *Transatlantica* 1, 2015.

20. Jennifer S. Rosenberg and Margaret S. Chen, *Expanding Democracy: Voter Registration Around the World* (New York: Brennan Center for Justice, New York

University School of Law, 2009), http://www.brennancenter.org/sites/default/files /legacy/publications/Expanding.Democracy.pdf.

21. Noah Berlatsky, ed., *Shelby County v. Holder John Roberts*, 'The Court Was Right to Strike Down Section 4 of the Voting Rights Act,' *Opposing Viewpoints Series, Vol I. Voting Rights* (Farmington Hills, MI: Greenhaven Press, 2015), p. 20.

22. Stephanie Condon, "Supreme Court Strikes Down Section of Voting Rights Act," cbsnew.com, June 25, 2013, http://www.cbsnews.com/news/supreme-court -strikes-down-section-of-voting-rights-act/.

23. Ibid.

24. *Shelby County v. Holder*, Supreme Court 2013.

25. John Paul Stevens, "The Court Should Not Have Struck Down Section 4 of the Voting Rights Act," in Noah Berlatsky, ed., *Opposing Viewpoints Series* (Farm-ington Hills, MI: Greenhaven Press, 2015).

26. American Civil Liberties Union and the American Civil Liberties Union Foundation, www.aclu.org, accessed November 21, 2016.

27. Angela Davis, *Are Prisons Obsolete?* (New York: Seven Stories Press, 2003).

28. Judith M Green and Blanche Radford-Curry, "Notorious Philosopher: The Transformative Life and Work of Angela Davis," in *Hypatias*, 1500 years of Women Philosophers, ed. Indiana Lopez McAlister (Bloomington, Indiana Uni-versity Press, 1996).

29. Michelle Alexander, *The New Jim Crow: Mass Incarceration in the Age of Col-orblindness* (New York, NY: The New Press, 2010).

30. Ibid.

31. Adam Gopnik, "The Caging of America: Why Do We Lock Up So Many People?" *The New Yorker*, January 30, 2012, http://www.newyorker.com/magazine /2012/01/30/the-caging-of-america.

32. Angela Davis, "Masked Racism: Reflections on the Prison Industrial Com-plex," Colorlines.com, September 10, 1998, http://www.colorlines.com/articles/ masked-racism-reflections-prison-industrial-complex.

33. Ibid.

34. Alexander, *The New Jim Crow*.

35. Gopnik, "The Caging of America."

36. Davis, *Are Prisons Obsolete?*

37. William Ecenbarger, *Kids for Cash: Two Judges, Thousands of Children, and a $2.6 Million* (New York: New York Press, 2013).

38. Ibid., Shafer, pp. 25–26.

39. Voting Rights Advancement Act of 2015, http://vrafortoday.org/current -legislation/.

40. Voting Rights Advancement Act of 2015, SB1659.

41. Desmond King and Rogers M. Smith, *Still a House Divided* (Princeton, NJ: Princeton University Press, 2011); Richomme, "The Voting Rights Act at 50."

42. Michael Waldman, *The Fight to Vote* (New York: Simon and Schuster, 2016).

43. Richomme, "The Voting Rights Act at 50."

44. "History," Bethune Cookman University, http://www.cookman.edu/about_bcu/history/lastwill_testament.html (accessed December 16, 2016).

45. Aristotle, *Politics, Book 1*, section 1253a, edited by Richard McKeon (New York: Random House, 1970).

Bibliography

Alexander, Michelle. *The New Jim Crow: Mass Incarceration in the Age of Colorblindness*. New York: The New Press, 2012.

American Civil Liberties Union and the American Civil Liberties Union Foundation. www.aclu.org (accessed November 21, 2016).

Aristotle. *Politics, Book 1*, section 1253a. Edited by Richard McKeon. New York: Random House, 1970.

Berlatsky, Noah, ed. *Opposing Viewpoints Series*. Farmington Hills, MI: Greenhaven Press, 2015.

Condon, Stephanie. "Supreme Court Strikes Down Section Voting Rights Act." cbsnew.com, June 25, 2013. http://www.cbsnews.com/news/supreme-court-strikes-down-section-ofvoting-rights-act/.

Davis, Angela. *Are Prisons Obsolete?* New York: Seven Stories Press, 2003.

Davis, Angela. "Masked Racism: Reflections on the Prison Industrial Complex." Colorlines.com, September 10, 1998. http://www.colorlines.com/articles/masked-racism-reflections prison-industrial complex.

Ecenbarger, William. *Kids for Cash: Two Judges, Thousands of Children, and a $2.8 Million*. New York: New Press, 2013.

Epstein, Lee and Thomas G. Walker. *Constitutional Law for a Changing America: Rights, Liberties, and Justice*. Washington, DC: CQ Press, 2007.

Filer, J. E., L. W. Kenny, and R. B. Morton. "Voting Laws, Educational Politics and Minority Turnout." *Journal of Law & Economics* 34(1991): 371.

Foner, Eric. *The Fiery Trial: Abraham Lincoln and American Slavery*. New York and London: W.W. Norton & Company, 2010.

Garrow, David. *Protest at Selma: Martin Luther King, Jr., and the Voting Rights Act of 1965*. New Haven, CT: Yale University Press, 1978.

Glaude, Eddie S. "The Black Vote: History Demands a Strategy for Change," Time Magazine, September 24, 2016. http://time.com/4504138/black-vote-blank-out/.

Gopnik, Adam. "The Caging of America: Why Do We Lock Up So Many People?" *The New Yorker*, January 30, 2012.

Green, Judith M., and Blanche Radford-Curry. "Notorious Philosopher: The Transformative Life and Work of Angela Davis." In *Hypatias: 1500 Years of Women Philosophers*, edited by Linda Lopez McAllister. Bloomington, IN: Indiana University Press, 1996.

Hero, Rodney E., and Caroline J. Tolbert. "Race and the 2012 Election: A Post-Racial Society, More Apparent than Real Mini-Symposium." *Political Research Quarterly* 67(2014): 628–31.

"History." www.cookman.edu, http://www.cookman.edu/about_bcu/history /lastwill_testament.html (accessed December 16, 2016).

History.com Staff. "Voting Rights Act." History.com. www.history.com/topics /blackhistory/voting-rights-act (accessed December 22, 2016).

King, Desmond, and Rogers M. Smith. *Still a House Divided*. Princeton NJ: Princeton University Press, 2011.

Laney, Garrine P. *The Voting Rights Act of 1965: Historical Background and Current Issues*. Novinka Books: New York, 2003.

Richomme, Olivier. "The Voting Rights Act at 50: From Vote Participation to Meaningful Representation." *Transatlantica* 1 (2015). https://transatlantica. revues.org/7465.

Rosenberg, Jennifer. "Expanding Democracy: Voter Registration Around the World." New York: Brennan Center for Justice, 2009. https://www.bren nancenter.org/publication/expanding-democracy-voter-registration-around -world.

Shafer, M.T.C. "Race Is the Reason Felons Don't Have the Right to Vote," *SCALA-WAGMagazine.org*, June 14, 2016. http://www.scalawagmagazine.org/arti cles/race-is-the-reason-felons-dont-have-the-right-to-vote.

U.S. Constitution, Amendment XIV, Section I.

Voting Rights Advancement Act of 2015, http://vrafortoday.org/current-legislation/ (accessed December 16, 2016).

Waldman, Michael. *The Fight to Vote*. New York: Simon and Schuster, 2016.

CHAPTER THREE

The Latino Vote: Growth, Influence, and How Obama Changed the Game

Andrew Martinez and Paola Esmieu

The 2012 reelection of President Barack Obama was the first time in history that a presidential candidate won by a margin of votes that was smaller than the number of voters in the Latino voting bloc.[1] In and of itself, the Latino vote did not result in the reelection of Barack Obama. However, the importance of the Latino vote in Obama's reelection demonstrated the exigency for candidates to intentionally and strategically target Latinos and discuss the issues they face in the United States, as part of their political platforms. As the Latino population continues on its trajectory of rapid growth, the Latino electorate is projected to be 40 percent higher in 2016 than in 2008 and will make up a record 11.9 percent of all U.S. eligible voters in 2016.[2] The sheer numbers of the Latino population will give Latinos more political power than ever before due to the number of eligible Latino voters as more Latinos come to age and become naturalized citizens. Since 1988, the number of Latinos voting during presidential elections has increased consistently and has broken records election after election. Despite this unprecedented growth, the percentage of registered Latinos who actually vote has remained largely unchanged, and it is likely that Latinos will continue to be underrepresented among voters compared with their share of eligible voters. As we examine here, Latinos played a critical role in both the 2008 and 2012 federal elections, and demonstrated that when mobilized to participate in the political process, their voting power can sway the direction of a federal election.

In this chapter, we discuss the importance of the Latino vote in federal elections and the impact of Obama's efforts on increasing Latino political engagement during his presidential campaigns. First, we provide a historical overview of voting trends and partisanship within Latino origin groups. Next, we discuss how the Obama presidency reshaped American politics by recognizing the power of the Latino vote on a national platform through his campaigns in 2008 and 2012. We then explore the state of the Latino vote by looking at current demographic trends and explain the effect these trends will have on Latino voter engagement in upcoming federal elections. We also identify key motivators that influence Latino political participation and what conditions have to exist for them to have a significant impact on federal elections. Lastly, we end with a discussion on Latino voter projections and how this population will play a major role in the future of American politics.

Latino Partisanship and Voting Trends

The study of Latino voting patterns—and that of specific Latino origin groups—is a recent emergence. Interest in the growth and evolution of Latino political engagement was spurred primarily by the protests and civil disobedience during three major political developments: the Civil Rights Movement, the 1965 Immigration Act, and the expansion of the Voting Rights Act in 1975.[3] The Civil Rights Movement led to numerous efforts to change practices in politics to address equity among minority groups including Latinos. The Immigration Act of 1965 prompted an increase of immigration from Mexico that drastically changed the demographics of the United States. The Voting Rights Act in 1975 addressed language discrimination and resulted in an expansion of opportunities for Latinos to register, vote, and run for political office. Together, these three political developments radically changed who was eligible to vote and opened doors for increased political engagement of Latinos and other racial/ethnic minorities.

Historically, Latinos had not been major candidates in federal elections and were fairly unknown for engaging in the political process. As such, for most of the 20th century, little attention was devoted to understanding Latino partisanship. Partisanship among the group is complex given the diverse nationalities, races, and histories of the overall Latino population.

In attempting to answer the question "Does a Latino public opinion exist?," Castro, Félix, and Ramírez believe that "intraethnic differences of class, race, gender, immigrant status, and national origin run through the Latino community and make it difficult to speak of a singular political agenda." They argue, "Latino public opinion should not be seen as an artifact of discrete individual-level variables but rather should be understood in light of the larger shared history of displacement and discrimination, of struggle and solidarity that characterizes the Latino community."[4] Subgroup context matters, and the unique histories of the different ethnicities within the Latino umbrella play an important role in the formation of the political views for the group.

To facilitate our discussion on Latino partisanship, we focus on the three origin groups that make up most of the Latino vote: Mexican Americans, Cuban Americans, and Puerto Ricans. Together these three origin groups comprise about 77 percent of the total Latino population.[5] By examining political preferences of these three groups, we gather a broad understanding of voting trends and partisanship of the overall Latino population.

Mexican Americans make up 64 percent of Latinos in the United States and 60 percent of the Latino electorate. Traditionally, Mexican American voters tend to align themselves with the Democratic Party because of the party's progressive platform on immigration, support for social services, and support for bilingual education.[6] However, when examining the group in more detail, certain factors like age, generational status in the United States, geographic location, and whether the individual speaks Spanish play a role in its political affiliation. Mexican Americans—and other Latino origin groups in general—who do not speak Spanish are more likely to support stricter immigration practices. However, younger Mexican Americans identify with the "common struggle" Latinos face in regards to discrimination, and buy into the idea of "pan-ethnicity," making them more likely to support progressive platforms.[7]

Puerto Ricans represent the second largest Latino origin group in the United States and account for 9 percent of the Latino population (15% if you include those that live on the island). Although Puerto Ricans are considered the second largest group of Latinos in the United States, 6 percent of all Puerto Ricans do not have the legal right to vote during presidential elections. Because of the island's status as an unincorporated territory of the United States, Puerto Ricans on the island can only vote in the primaries during federal elections.[8] Based on trends of local elections and the voting patterns of Puerto Ricans both on the island and mainland, we see that Puerto Ricans generally support politicians with liberal and progressive platforms that most often align with the Democratic Party.

Accounting for about 4 percent of all Latinos in the United States, Cuban Americans are the third largest Latino origin group.[9] Although Salvadoran Americans account for a similar percentage of all Latinos, Cuban Americans have a more prominent and complicated political history in the United States. Voting trends and partisanship of Cuban Americans are sometimes unaligned with the overall voting trends and partisanship we see of Latinos as a whole; thus, focusing on this group helps give us a broader scope of what the Latino partisanship spectrum looks like.

Cuban Americans are more likely to affiliate with the Republican Party or as Independent.[10] To escape communism under Fidel Castro, Cubans were granted unique access to U.S. citizenship. During the 1980s, the Reagan campaign courted Cubans to the Republican Party with their anti-Castro rhetoric. Since then, Cubans have consistently supported the Republican Party at higher rates than other Latinos during federal elections. This support is important in states like Florida, where Cubans represent 6.5 percent of the population, and 34.3 percent of the residents in the Miami-Dade voting district. Despite the consistency in Cuban support of the Republican Party, the GOP experienced a decline in support from Cuban Americans during the 2012 presidential election. Although there were conflicting reports on the polls tallying Cuban American support for both candidates Barack Obama and Mitt Romney, Obama won by a small margin. This marks an important shift from prior elections, where the Cuban vote was almost exclusively in support of Republican candidates. Political scholars speculate that the Republican Party is losing the Cuban American vote because of adjustments in foreign policy the Democrats have made in order to be more appealing to Cuban Americans. In addition, many Cuban Americans increasingly reject the extreme fiscal and social conservatism of the Republican Party.[11]

There have been efforts to mobilize the different Latino origin groups to work together. Organizations such as the League of United Latin American Citizens (LULAC) have focused on creating a pan-ethnic agenda for politicians to focus on, while mobilizing Latinos to understand their common struggle as one ethnic group. As an overall ethnic group, Latinos are culturally collectivist, and presidential candidates do best among Latino voters when they "can best tap into shared identity and improve a voter's perception that the candidate is 'on their side.'"[12] In addition, some researchers have found that political engagement and partisanship of Latinos can also be situational and dependent on their mobilization and the racial hostility felt within party politics and political platforms.

Despite the differences in priorities, voting trends, and partisanship among Latino origin groups, the majority of Latinos across all origin groups typically favor candidates who support progressive immigration reform, bilingual education, and social services for underrepresented and disadvantaged groups. Furthermore, when discussing voting trends and partisanship, it is important to mention that the Latino population is young, diverse, and disproportionately poor. Voting patterns across all racial and ethnic groups indicate that younger voters and those who are from lower socioeconomic statuses have a tendency to vote Democratic.[13] It should not escape our notice that, although diverse and complex, Latinos are a group disproportionately made up of young and poor citizens. As a whole, Latinos have demonstrated a strong favor toward Democratic candidates, a trend that we have seen in the past and that is likely to continue into the 2016 and 2020 federal elections.

The Election and Reelection of President Barack Obama

During the late 1950s and early 1960s, Latinos—specifically Mexican Americans—and Latino issues received intentional and targeted attention for the first time in American history. During his presidential campaign, a campaign worker convinced John F. Kennedy that the often-overlooked Mexican American voters had significant numbers to sway the 1960 election. As a result, the "Viva Kennedy" outreach program was created as a means of engaging Mexican American voters. This outreach program was the first organized presidential outreach effort geared toward Latinos during an election and set the tone for a positive relationship between Latinos in the United States and the Democratic party.[14] The "Viva Kennedy" campaign, coupled with the Chicano Movement and United Farm Workers Movement of the 1960s, actively tied issues the Mexican American community was facing with an urgency to become politically engaged in order to make a difference.[15] The concentrated and intentional inclusion of Mexican Americans in the political process started by Kennedy laid the groundwork for President Barack Obama's 2008 presidential campaign, during which he was able to mobilize more Latinos than ever before.

The Obama campaign in 2008 was a great success because of its concentrated efforts at mobilizing young and underrepresented citizens to become politically engaged in innovative ways, using social media. The campaign made targeted outreach efforts to distinct populations by creating online peer groups like "Latinos for Obama." These affinity-based groups campaigned for Obama through outreach and community events to inform others about his presidential platform and to encourage voter registration and participation in the 2008 federal election. In addition, the Obama campaign team ensured that their website was easily translatable;

spent a significant amount of money for Spanish ads and signs, particularly in key battleground states; and ensured that the Democratic National Convention (DNC) had well known Latino politicians present and ready to mobilize Latino voters for the election of Obama.

Tailoring his platform to address salient issues within the Latino community was a major part of Obama's campaign. Former governor of New Mexico Bill Richardson claimed that more Latinos than ever before voted for Obama because "he spoke to them not as an ethnic group but as American voters pursuing the American Dream."[16] By making progressive immigration reform a key issue in his campaign, Obama was endorsed by the Service Employees International Union, the largest immigrant union in the country.[17]

The Obama campaign was able to successfully court the Latino vote in 2008 through the "La Promesa de Obama" plan, which included a comprehensive immigration reform bill that he would carry out during his first year in office. During his first presidency, not only was Obama unable to bring "La Promesa" plan to action, but he was also unable to get less comprehensive plans to pass through the legislative process. Instead of making significant strides with immigration reform, the Obama administration was responsible for increased deportations and increased funding for border patrol. Obama also supported the Secure Communities Program, which allowed officers to racially profile Latinos and run their fingerprints in efforts to deport undocumented immigrants with a criminal background, although less than 40 percent of undocumented immigrants who were deported from this program had criminal records. Obama's unfulfilled promises and support for anti-immigrant policies led to a 77 percent disapproval rating from Latinos who were aware of his legislative failures in immigration reform.[18]

Despite the failures of Obama's first presidency, the 2012 reelection of President Obama was the first time in U.S. history that the support of the Latino electorate was greater than the margin a candidate won by. In the 2012 presidential election, Latinos supported Barack Obama over Mitt Romney by a margin of 71 percent to 27 percent and were vital to the coalition that reelected President Obama.[19] Although often criticized for deporting more immigrants than any other president, Obama's support for the Dream Act, a challenge to Arizona's SB-1070 law, and executive order DACA reconfirmed his commitment to issues important to the Latino community for the 2012 campaign.[20]

Contrary to popular belief, immigration reform is not the sole primary issue Latinos are concerned about during federal elections. Since 2000, the rates of Latino immigrant arrivals to the United States have steadily declined.[21] Increasing birth rates of Latinos have become the new drivers of population growth;[22] thus, Latino children will sharply outnumber Latino seniors for at least the next three decades.[23] There is no question that the primary concern of voting age Latinos is their children and ensuring that sufficient resources are allocated to supporting children and education. Through his first term, Obama was able to make progress in both education and health policy, two public policy issues salient to the Latino community, especially in consideration of the changing demographics of the United States. In 2010, Latinos constituted 30.7 percent of people in the United States who were uninsured compared to 11.7 percent of Whites.[24] Through the Affordable Health Care Act, Obama was able to increase access to affordable health care. In addition to Obama's successes in education and health care reform, Obama also successfully appointed and received Senate approval for 35 Latinos to top-ranking positions in the government, more than any president before him.[25]

Race Saliency and the Obama Presidency

As the nation's first Black president, on his journey to the White House, Obama could not have avoided addressing race relations in the United States. During the Democratic primary in 2008, Obama had to address racism in the United States skillfully, not only to entice people of color in America but also to keep and increase the support of White voters. In his "A More Perfect Union" speech, given during his campaign in Philadelphia in March of 2008, Obama contextualized the problems of racism in America as it relates to the principles of our nation to provide opportunity for everyone to pursue the American dream—a primary draw of Latino immigrants to this country. By centering his campaign on the American Dream and identifying how problems stemming from racism affect all Americans, Obama emphasized that many of the issues in America transcend race, while pointing out that until racism is addressed, conflict will persist and progress will be limited.[26] During his campaign, his ties to Reverend Jeremiah Wright—the pastor of the Trinity United Church of Christ in Chicago, whose sermons compared the United States to KKK and other racist extremist groups—were used to challenge Obama's ideologies and fitness to be president. However, Obama overcame this challenge by emphasizing that despite our different racial identities, "we all want to move in the same direction: toward a better future for our children and our grandchildren."[27] Under that rhetoric, Obama was able to make addressing racism in the United States salient to improving and creating a stronger nation.

Addressing racism proved to be a strength for Obama during his campaign after politicians claimed that his attitudes toward affirmative action, health care, and immigration reform would exacerbate problems in the economy. He discredited their claims by explaining the contributions of immigrants in America. Obama appealed to Latino voters (and other minority voters) by calling out his adversaries' xenophobic ideologies and promising better access to education, jobs, and health care for historically underrepresented minorities and immigrants,[28] which led to their support for his presidency.

Although support from White voters was crucial to Obama's election, the overwhelming support he received from underrepresented minorities established the importance of that voting bloc. Had only White votes been accounted for, John McCain would have won by a landslide, with a 12-point victory.[29] This implies that politicians running for office must acknowledge, understand, and commit to working on issues affecting historically underrepresented minorities—such as Latinos. Obama's commitment to immigration reform, education, and accessible health care mobilized Latinos and other minorities to campaign and vote for him during the primaries and subsequent election.

The media had also played a critical role in elevating race as a focal point during federal elections. During the 2008 federal election season, changes in news coverage on the "Latino vote" increased in almost every state during the campaign.[30] Both presidential candidates spent millions of dollars on Spanish ads to reach the Latino community. Obama's unsuccessful attempt to pass comprehensive immigration reform and his inability to prevent voter identification laws during his first term made racial profiling among Latinos a key issue for Latino engagement in politics during his next run for president. Spanish news outlets, like Univision, raised these issues to challenge Obama's efforts and elevate the consciousness of their viewers to keep politicians accountable to their promises.

During Obama's 2012–2016 term, the deaths of Trayvon Martin, Sandra Bland, Freddie Grey, and many more evoked discourse on police brutality against Black men and women in the United States, which heightened conversations about systemic racism in the nation. Through the #BlackLivesMatter movement, other historically underrepresented minority groups, including Latinos, have become more engaged in politics. As the problem persists toward the end of Obama's term as president, 2016 presidential candidates Hillary Clinton (Democrat) and Donald Trump (Republican) have faced constant criticism on their historical and present-day approaches to addressing racism in this country. Campaign efforts against Donald Trump have focused on his xenophobic rhetoric toward

Mexicans, the Chinese, and Muslims, and his history in his businesses of racist practices toward African Americans. Those who oppose Hillary Clinton often refer to her commentary associating Black men as "super predators." Furthermore, the popularity of Vermont Senator Bernie Sanders among millennial voters was largely attributed to Sander's intentional focus on how racism is one of the most pressing issues facing the United States. These examples demonstrate how salient race has become in the United States during and after the election of Obama. Though important for all racial/ethnic minority groups, candidates attempting to court the votes of Latinos will need to acknowledge that Latino political concerns are directly related to their racial and ethnic identity, as xenophobia disproportionately affects Latinos.

The Latino Vote

As previously mentioned, through most of the 20th century, little attention was paid to Latino partisanship and engagement in the political process. Today, this looks very different. Obama's efforts at mobilizing Latinos effectively started the modern-day shift in American perceptions of the importance of the Latino vote. In addition, as drastic demographic shifts occur and the exponential growth of the Latino population gains more recognition, devoting attention to the Latino vote has become inevitable.

Latinos constitute one of the largest and fastest growing populations in the United States, estimated at 55 million.[31] By the year 2060, the U.S. Census Bureau projects that 28.6 percent of the population will be of Hispanic origin.[32] As with most underrepresented groups, there is disproportionality between the number of Latinos who actually vote in comparison to the Latino population that is eligible to vote. Although eligible Latino voters have grown exponentially, from 8.8 million in 1992 to about 28 million possible voters in 2016, their registration rates have remained at about 58 percent.[33] In addition, more than half (52%) of the national Latino population is either too young to vote or does not currently hold U.S. citizenship. Despite this, the exponential growth of the Latino population will be felt in all presidential elections to come.

Latinos are projected to make up 11.9 percent of the electorate in 2016.[34] Since the presidential election of 1988, we have seen a pattern of record turnout of Latino voters in presidential elections.[35] This pattern can be attributed to the changes occurring within the Latino population and the electorate. Two trends that can be credited as the primary sources of growth for the Latino electorate are the coming of age of Latino millennials and the naturalization of adult Latino immigrants. These trends have resulted in a 40 percent growth of the Latino electorate since the 2008 presidential election.

The Latino population is relatively young; among the nation's estimated 35 million American-born Latinos, the median age is only 19. After the 2012 election, a significant number of American-born Latinos (3.2 million) will have reached the legal voting age, making them eligible to vote in November 2016's presidential election. The coming of age of the Latino youth is important, as they will join the projected 44 percent of Latino eligible voters who identify as millennial—a share greater than any other racial or ethnic group of voters. As notable as this may be, the Latino voter turnout rate may not meet its potential given that Latino millennials are less likely to register to vote compared to other millennial groups (50% Latino millennials registered to vote in 2012 compared to 61% White millennials and 64% Black millennials). Not only are Latino millennials less likely to register, they are also less likely to actually cast a ballot in a presidential election (37.8% Latino millennials voted in 2012 compared to 47.5% White millennials and 55% Black millennials).[36] The lack of millennial participation can result in lower than expected Latino voter turnout rates; however, the growing population and increased naturalization of Latino immigrants will help boost voter turnout rates and continue the record-breaking trend of Latino participation in presidential elections.

U.S. births have overtaken new immigrant arrivals as the main driver of Latino population growth.[37] However, Latino immigrants who are in the United States legally still account for a sizable portion of the Latino population. Since 2012, approximately 1.2 million of these Latino immigrants have naturalized and will contribute to the exponential growth of the Latino electorate for the 2016 presidential election. In both the 2012 and 2008 presidential elections, naturalized immigrant Latinos voted at higher rates compared to American-born Latinos (2012: 53.6% naturalized immigrant Latinos voted; 46.1% American-born Latinos voted. 2008: 54.2% naturalized immigrant Latinos voted; 48.4% American-born Latinos voted).[38] Despite the lower voter turnout expected from Latino millennials, naturalized immigrant Latinos have consistently showed up at the polls and bolstered the growth of the Latino electorate, a trend that is likely to continue.

Some states in particular have seen a large increase in Latino voter turnout. In New Mexico, Latinos have made up the largest percentage of total voters since the mid-1990s, accounting for about 35 percent of the state's voters. In California, Latino voter turnout has increased from 11.7 percent to 23.5 percent between 1996 and 2012. Both Florida and Nevada have experienced increases in Latino voter turnout between the 1996 and 2012 federal elections. In Florida, Latino voter turnout grew from 9.2 percent to

17.3 percent. Latino voter turnout grew from 3.9 percent to 15 percent in Nevada.[39] Despite these remarkable increases in Latino voter turnout, until Latino voter registration rates begin to increase at the rate of the population growth, the Latino voting bloc's power and impact will not reach its full potential.

Conditions Needed to Actualize the Impact of the Latino Vote

Although political leaders have taken more interest in Latinos, and there are more initiatives in place to increase Latino voters, Latino voter registration has arguably remained unchanged since the 1990s. The number of eligible Latino voters who actually vote is not reflective of the total Latino population, which is detrimental to passing legislative policies that advance the interests of Latinos and other racial/ethnic minorities. Increasing engagement of Latino eligible voters in federal elections is essential in order to ensure that issues affecting Latino communities in the United States are at the forefront of candidate platforms. To ensure Latino issues become relevant in an election, certain conditions must exist in order for Latinos to exert strong political influence. These conditions are a large Latino population, rapid growth in Latino voter registration, more partisan cohesiveness, a competitive electoral environment, and extensive campaign outreach and mobilization of Latinos.[40]

A Large Latino Population

We know that the overall Latino population in the United States is substantial and is expected to only get larger. However, about half of the Latino population is concentrated in a few regional areas, limiting the total impact of the population's electorate. Though the bulk of the Latino population is primarily located in gateway regions (Los Angeles, New York, Miami, Chicago, Houston), they are increasingly dispersing into geographic regions not known as traditional Latino settlement areas.[41] The spread of Latino growth is seen not only in sheer population numbers but also in their prominence in new U.S. areas. This type of spreading is necessary as it is essential that the Lationo population grows in competitive voting districts where the Latino vote is underrepresented.

Although the number of Latinos who voted for Obama is significant, their population growth and voter turnout in key battleground states was where the Latino vote was most influential. The Latino vote becomes particularly significant during federal elections when Latinos are disproportionately located in key battleground states.[42] For the 2016 election, it is projected that only a few states with a large Hispanic population will likely be key battlegrounds for the campaigns. These states—Florida, Nevada, and Colorado—each have an electorate comprised of more than 14 percent Latinos. However, in most other key battleground states, Latinos make up less than 5 percent of eligible voters. California, Texas, and New York, the three states that make up 52 percent of Latino voters, are not likely to be competitive states for the presidential election.[43] Thus, there will have to be strong growth in regional areas not traditionally occupied by Latinos in order to maximize the impact of their large population size.

Voter Registration Has to Catch Up to Represent Total Eligible Latino Voters

About 41 percent of Latinos eligible to vote in the 2012 election did not register.[44] Newly naturalized Latinos will continue to vote in large numbers; however, more efforts at mobilizing and increasing registration of millennial Latinos will have to take place if Latino voter registration is to be reflective of the total number of Latino eligible voters. Without drastic changes in millennial engagement, the Latino vote will struggle to exert its political influence in future federal elections. As a sizable sector of the electorate, the Latino vote will have the power to sway elections if and when their voter registration and participation begins to mirror the total Latino population.

Partisan Cohesiveness

The power of the Latino vote is most felt when the group is unified and stands in support one predominant party. The decreasing Cuban support of the Republican Party can have tremendous implications on the Latino voting bloc. Although Cubans in Florida have had a long history of supporting Republican candidates, the Democratic Party has been able to court Cuban votes through a shift in their views regarding foreign policy. This once-solid GOP support group in Florida—a key battleground state—is now a toss-up group that will have a major influence on partisan cohesiveness of Latinos during federal elections.[45]

Competitive Electoral Environment

Competitive electoral environments with a significant number of registered Latino voters are key to understanding the power of the Latino vote. These areas receive much attention from the media because candidates lead aggressive campaigns in an attempt to receive endorsements and support from major voting blocs in a particular state. As more Latinos spread into new geographic regions of the United States, it is possible that "red" states will turn "blue," especially in the South. If Latinos continue to disperse into voting districts that are competitive, it is clear that we will see drastic changes in what states remain battlegrounds and in how both parties will function to ensure support of Latinos in new regions.

Extensive Campaign Outreach and Mobilization of Latinos

The political participation of Latinos is often spurred by extensive outreach efforts and in response to policies that ignite the community to mobilize. We have seen strong Latino mobilization in response to punitive policies directed toward Latinos, minorities, and anti-immigrant movements.[46] Issues regarding voter identification laws, limited voting periods, the restructuring of electoral districts, and the lack of resources made available to Latino communities about political participation still persist;[47] however, the persistence of these issues can be used to rally Latinos to mobilize and push back against inequitable voter policies.

Latino Nonvoters and the Future of the Latino Vote

As we consider the future impact of this electorate group, it is important to consider the many reasons why Latinos do not vote. As the Latino population's voting rates continue to break records, the number of Latinos who do not vote has also reached new highs. According to the Pew Research Center, despite a record turnout of Latino voters in the 2012 election, 12.1 million Latinos did not vote. This was a decline from 49.9 percent in 2008 to 48 percent in 2012.[48] This decline can be attributed to three factors: first, it is possible that the political engagement of Latinos has not caught up to the rapid population growth, as internal and external efforts to increase Latino voter participation rates are a relatively new practice; secondly, there are still barriers in place that prevent Latinos from voting, such as the 2013 Supreme Court decision that invalidated key parts of the Voter Rights Act of 1965; lastly, unaddressed issues such as comprehensive immigration reform have resulted in a disinterest and distrust of Latinos with the political process. Despite these issues, we have seen participation rates spike at times when presidential candidates have strategically targeted Latinos. Although voter turnout declined from 2008 to 2012, there was a 28 percent increase in votes cast in 2012.[49] At this time, Obama increased his vote share among Latinos from 67 percent in 2008 to 71 percent in 2012, the highest share of Latino voters since 1996, when President Bill Clinton won 72 percent of the Latino vote.[50]

In addition, there is still a significant number of legal Latino immigrants who choose not to naturalize and are unable to vote. According to the Pew Research Center, naturalization rates among legal immigrants from Latin America and the Caribbean (49%)—especially Mexican legal immigrants (36%)—trail behind the naturalization rates of those of other immigrants (72%).[51] Of those Latinos who do naturalize, one in five attribute acquiring civil and legal rights, including the right to vote, as the main reason for their decision to naturalize. This demonstrates that there is a desire to vote, but there are barriers in place that prevent this segment of the Latino population from voting. Some of these impediments include administrative costs and barriers, a lack of English proficiency, and a lack of knowledge around dual citizenship policies.[52] Although the legal inability to vote certainly explains the lack of Latino voters, it does not explain why American-born Latinos are absent at the polls.

According to the Census Bureau's survey of voters, 26.9 percent of Latinos registered to vote cite "too busy, conflicting work or school schedule" as the top reason preventing them from voting on Election Day.[53] When we consider that in 2014, 62 percent of Latino families live with incomes in or near poverty,[54] we can assume that many Latinos either prioritize work and school commitments or do not have flexibility with their work and school schedules that will allow them to participate in presidential elections. The second most common reason cited by 15.6 percent of registered nonvoting Latinos was "not interested, felt my vote wouldn't make a difference."[55] This belief, of a vote not making a difference, is not unique to Latinos. In fact, this is the second most common reason given across all racial and ethnic groups' registered voters who do not vote. One reason that may explain this belief may be lack of education and possessing a poor understanding of the political process.

Educational attainment of Latino eligible voters has steadily increased since 2000 but has not grown as quickly as the population. By the 2016 presidential campaign, about 18 percent of all Latino eligible voters will have earned a baccalaureate degree or one higher.[56] Increased educational attainment of this population is especially important, as research demonstrates that college graduates are more likely to engage in civic duties, such as voting, in comparison to high school graduates and those without a high school degree.[57] This leaves it less likely that a significant portion of Latinos who are not pursuing a postsecondary education will be exposed to the political process. Education is a key factor in dispelling voting myths such as those that lead many to believe that "their vote/one vote doesn't count." As educational attainment continues to rise, it will have a positive impact on voting rates because more Latinos will be prepared to engage in the political process and will gain a better understanding of the importance of their vote.

Latinos account for much of the diversification changes occurring in the electorate. With these changes, the importance of the Latino vote will inevitably continue to grow well into the future. Despite barriers, millennial disengagement, and lack of educational attainment, the Latino population has broken voting records election after election. The importance of the Latino vote is gaining traction; we see this as more campaigns attempt to engage in issues pertinent to Latinos. In addition, there has been a rise in Latino-led outreach efforts that are effectively leveraging social media to increase political awareness and Latino voter participation. Projections indicate that by 2060, over half of all voters will be non-White, with 31 percent of those voters identifying as Latino.[58] If these projections come to fruition, the future of the Latino vote will unequivocally play a major role in the political decisions of the country. For this reason, political leaders and presidential candidates should take heed of President Obama's efforts with the Latino population and build on his strategy of courting Latino voters.

Conclusion

As seen with the election of Barack Obama in 2008 and 2012, Latinos respond when presidential candidates make an intentional effort to mobilize and include them in their political platform. Immigration reform, education, and health policy were three major issues that brought many Latinos to vote in recent elections. Although it is important to keep in mind the diversity within Latinos, as the population continues its exponential growth within the United States, the emergence of a pan-ethnic agenda will allow the group to influence political candidates. Senator Bernie Sanders took note of this when he ran to be the Democratic nominee for the 2016 election and was credited for mobilizing millennials to be engaged in the federal election process. Given that Latino millennials make up a significant group of the Latino voting bloc and are less likely to participate in federal elections than other voters, the recent emergence of politically engaged millennials has the potential to drastically increase the influence of the Latino vote. However, increased rates of Latino millennials voting is not enough to demonstrate the importance of the Latino voting bloc. The growing population, both old and young, must disperse to new regions and become voters in competitive electoral environments in order to have the strongest influence during federal elections. When this occurs, not only will the Latino vote become a major determining factor of future political leaders, but their partisanship will also influence the policy and direction of our nation.

As we move into the future, it will be vital to ensure continued growth in the political engagement of Latino voters as they represent a sizable portion of the population. Furthermore, The slow growth of Latino voters in comparison to the number of Latino eligible voters highlights that the record-breaking numbers of Latinos at the polls has been attributed primarily to population increases and not participation increases. The power of the Latino vote will eventually become unquestionable, and we will need to ensure that Latinos are participating in the political process to push forward policies and candidates that will support the best interests of Latinos as well as other minority groups. The future of the Latino vote is powerful, and Latinos will need to be informed, educated, and prepared for the impact their collective voice will have.

Notes

1. Collingwood, Barreto, and Garcia-Rios, "Revisiting Latino Voting," pp. 632–645.
2. Krogstad et al., "Millennials Make Up Half of Latino Eligible Voters."
3. Fraga et al., "Su Casa Es Nuestra Casa," pp. 515–521.
4. Castro, Félix, and Ramírez, "The Limits of Latinidad," pp. 233–253.
5. López and Patten, "The Impact of Slowing Immigration."
6. García-Castañon, "Introduction to Mexican American Voters," pp. 193–212.
7. Castro, Félix, and Ramírez, "The Limits of Latinidad," pp. 233–253.
8. Venator-Santiago, "The Liminal Latinos," pp. 292–305.
9. López and Patten, "The Impact of Slowing Immigration."
10. Alvarez and García, "The Foundations of Latino Voter Partisanship," pp. 31–49.
11. Moreno and Wyatt, "Cuban American Partisanship," pp. 193–212.
12. Collingwood, Barreto, and Garcia-Rios, "Revisiting Latino Voting," pp. 632–645.
13. Ibid.
14. García, "Viva Kennedy."
15. Urbano, "Mexican American Group Consciousness and Partisanship," pp. 213–232.
16. Preston, "In Big Shift."
17. O'Keefe, "The Changing Union."
18. Wallace, "Latinos, President Obama, and the 2012 Election," pp. 1360–1383.

19. López and Gonzalez-Barrera, "Inside the 2012 Latino Electorate."

20. Collingwood, Barreto, and Garcia-Rios, "Revisiting Latino Voting," pp. 632–645.

21. López and Patten, "The Impact of Slowing Immigration."

22. Krogstad et al., "Millennials Make Up Half of Latino Eligible Voters."

23. Frey, "Diversity Explosion."

24. Medieros, "The Supreme Court, Health Care Reform, and Latinos."

25. Wallace, "Latinos, President Obama, and the 2012 Election," pp. 1360–1383.

26. Tesler, "The Spillover of Racialization into Health Care."

27. Obama, "A More Perfect Union."

28. Berlet, "Race and the Right."

29. Wing, "Race, the Changing Electorate and the Electoral College."

30. Wallace, "Latinos, President Obama, and the 2012 Election," pp. 1360–1383.

31. U.S. Census Bureau, "Annual Estimates of the Resident Population."

32. U.S. Census Bureau, "Projections of the population by sex, Hispanic origin, and race."

33. Bergad, "The Latino Voter Registration Dilemma."

34. Krogstad et al., "Millennials Make Up Half of Latino Eligible Voters."

35. López and Taylor, "Dissecting the 2008 Electorate."

36. Krogstad et al., "Millennials Make Up Half of Latino Eligible Voters."

37. López and Patten, "The Impact of Slowing Immigration."

38. Krogstad et al., "Millennials Make Up Half of Latino Eligible Voters."

39. Bergad, "The Latino Voter Registration Dilemma."

40. Barreto, Collingwood, and Manzano, "Assessing Latino Influence," pp. 908–921.

41. Frey, "Diversity Explosion."

42. Collingwood, Barreto, and Garcia-Rios, "Revisiting Latino Voting," pp. 632–645.

43. Krogstad et al., "Millennials Make Up Half of Latino Eligible Voters."

44. Ocampo, "Top 6 Facts on the Latino Vote."

45. Moreno and Wyatt, "Cuban American Partisanship," pp. 193–212.

46. Hero, Garcia, Garcia, Pachon, "Latino Participation, Partisanship, and Office Holding," pp. 529–534.

47. Garcia, "Introduction to Mexican American Voters."

48. Garcia, "Introduction to Mexican American Voters."

49. Collingwood et al., "Revisiting Latino Voting," 632–645.

50. López and Taylor, "Latino Voters in the 2012 Election."

51. Taylor et al., "An Awakened Giant."

52. Ibid.

53. Krogstad et al., "Millennials Make Up Half of Latino Eligible Voters."

54. Wildsmith, Hammond, and Guzman, "A National Portrait of Hispanic Children in Need."

55. Krogstad et al., "Millennials Make Up Half of Latino Eligible Voters."
56. Ibid.
57. Frey, "Diversity Explosion."
58. Taylor, "Politics and Race."

Bibliography

Alvarez, R. Michael, and Bedolla Lisa García. "The Foundations of Latino Voter Partisanship: Evidence from the 2000 Election." *The Journal of Politics* 65(1) (February 2003): 31–49.

Barreto, Matt A., Loren Collingwood, and Sylvia Manzano. "A New Measure of Group Influence in Presidential Elections: Assessing Latino Influence in 2008." *Political Research Quarterly* 63(4) (December 2010): 908–921.

Bergad, Laird W. "The Latino Voter Registration Dilemma" Center for Latin American, Caribbean & Latino Studies Latino Data Project. (January 2016).

Berlet, Chip. "Race and the Right." In *Changing the Race: Racial Politics and the Election of Barack Obama*, edited by Linda Burnham. New York: Applied Research Center, 2009.

Browning, Rufus P., Dale Rogers Marshall, and David H. Tabb. *Protest Is Not Enough: The Struggle of Blacks and Hispanics for Equality In Urban Politics*. Berkeley: University of California Press, 1984.

Castro, Lorena, Adrián Félix, and Richard Ramírez. "The Limits of Latinidad? Immigration Attitudes across Latino Origin Groups." In *Minority Voting in the United States*, edited by Kyle L. Kreider and Thomas J. Baldino (233–253). Santa Barbara, California: Praeger, 2016.

Collingwood, Loren, Matt A. Barreto, and Sergio Garcia-Rios. "Revisiting Latino Voting: Cross-Racial Mobilization in the 2012 Election." *Political Research Quarterly* 67(3) (September 2014): 632–645.

Fraga, Luis R., John A. Garcia, Rodney E. Hero, Michael Jones-Correa, Valerie Martinez-Ebers, and Gary M. Segura. "Su Casa Es Nuestra Casa: Latino Politics Research and the Development of American Political Science," *American Political Science Review* 100(4) (November 2006): 515–521.

Frey, William H., *Diversity Explosion: How New Racial Demographics Are Remaking America*. Washington, District of Columbia: Brookings Institution Press, 2015.

García, Ignacio M. *Viva Kennedy: Mexican Americans in Search of Camelot*. College Station, TX: Texas A&M University Press, 2000.

García-Castañon, Marcela. "Introduction to Mexican American Voters." In *Minority Voting in the United States*, edited by Kyle L. Kreider and Thomas J. Baldino (193–212). Santa Barbara, California: Praeger, 2016.

Hero, Rodney, Garcia F. Chris, Garcia John, and Pachon Harry. "Latino Participation, Partisanship, and Office Holding." *PS: Political Science and Politics* 33(3) (2000): 529–534.

Jones-Correa, Michael, and David L. Leal. "Becoming 'Hispanic': Secondary Pan-ethnic Identification Among Latin American-Origin populations in the United States." *Hispanic Journal of Behavioral Sciences* 18(2) (May 1996): 214–254.

Krogstad, Hens Manuel, Mark Hugo Lopez, Gustavo López, Jeffrey S. Passel, and Eileen Patten. "Millennials Make Up Half of Latino Eligible Voters in 2016." Pew Research Center. January 19, 2016. http://www.pewhispanic. org/2016/01/19/millennials-make-up-almost-half-of-latino-eligible -voters-in-2016/.

López, Gustavo, and Eileen Patten. "The Impact of Slowing Immigration: Foreign-Born Share Falls Among 14 Largest U.S. Hispanic Origin Groups." Pew Research Center. September 15, 2015. http://www.pewhispanic.org/2015/ 09/15/the-impact-of-slowing-immigration-foreign-born-share-falls-among -14-largest-us-hispanic-origin-groups/-diverse-origins.

López, Mark Hugo, and Ana Gonzalez-Barrera. "Inside the 2012 Latino Elector-ate." Pew Research Center. June 3, 2013. http://www.pewhispanic.org/2013/ 06/03/inside-the-2012-latino-electorate/.

López, Mark Hugo, and Paul Taylor. "Dissecting the 2008 Electorate: Most Diverse in U.S. History." Pew Research Center, 2009. http://www.pewhispanic.org/ files/reports/108.pdf.

López, Mark Hugo, and Paul Taylor. "Latino Voters in the 2012 Election." Pew Research Center. November 7, 2012. http://www.pewhispanic.org/files/ 2012/11/2012_Latino_vote_exit_poll_analysis_final_11-07-12.pdf.

Medeiros, Jillian. "The Supreme Court, Health Care Reform, and Latinos." Latino Decisions: Everything Latino Politics. March 30, 2012. http://www.latino decisions.com/blog/2012/03/30/the-supreme-court-health-care-re form-and-latinos/.

Moreno, Dario, and James Wyatt. "Cuban American Partisanship: A Secular Realignment." In *Minority Voting in the United States*, edited by Kyle L. Kreider and Thomas J. Baldino (254–269). Santa Barbara, California: Praeger, 2016.

Obama, Barack. "A More Perfect Union." Philadelphia, PA, March 18, 2008.

Ocampo, Lizet. "Top 6 Facts on the Latino Vote." Center for American Progress. September 17, 2015. https://www.americanprogress.org/issues/immigra tion/news/2015/09/17/121325/top-6-facts-on-the-latino-vote/.

O'Keefe, Bryan. "The Changing Union Label." American Enterprise Institute. February 28, 2008. http://www.aei.org/publication/the-changing-union -label.

Preston, Julia. "In Big Shift, Latino Vote was Heavily for Obama." *New York Times*, October 7, 2008. http://www.nytimes.com/2008/11/07/world/americas/ 07iht07latino.17612734.html?_r=0.

Segura, Gary. "impreMedia/Latino Decisions." 2012 Latino Election Eve Poll." Latino Decisions. November 7. http://www.latinodecisions.com/2012-election-eve-polls/.

Taylor, Paul. "Politics and Race: Looking Ahead to 2060." Pew Research Center. May 10, 2013. http://www.pewresearch.org/fact-tank/2013/05/10/polit ics-and-race-looking-ahead-to-2060/.

Taylor, Paul, Ana Gonzalez-Barrera, Jeffrey S. Passel, and Mark Hugo López. "An Awakened Giant: The Hispanic Electorate is Likely to Double by 2030." Pew Research Center. November 14, 2012. http://www.pewhispanic.org /2012/11/14/an-awakened-giant-the-hispanic-electorate-is-likely-to -double-by-2030/.

Tesler, Michael. "The Spillover of Racialization into Health Care: How President Obama Polarized Public Opinion by Racial Attitudes and Race." *American Journal of Political Science* 56(3) (July 2012): 690–704.

Urbano Jr., Luis J. "All for One? And One for All? Mexican American Group Consciousness and Partisanship." In *Minority Voting in the United States*, edited by Kyle L. Kreider and Thomas J. Baldino (213–232). Santa Barbara, California: Praeger, 2016.

U.S. Census Bureau, Population Division. "Annual estimates of the resident population by sex, race, and Hispanic origin for the United States: April 1, 2010 to July 1, 2014." https://factfinder.census.gov/faces/tableservices/jsf/pages/productview.xhtml?src=bkmk.

U.S. Census Bureau, Population Division. "Projections of the population by sex, Hispanic origin, and race for the United States: 2015 to 2060." https://www.census.gov/population/projections/data/national/2014/summar ytables.html.

Venator-Santiago, Charles R. "Puerto Ricans: The Liminal Latinos," In *Minority Voting in the United States*, edited by Kyle L. Kreider and Thomas J. Baldino (292–305). Santa Barbara, California: Praeger, 2016.

Wallace, Sophia J. "It's Complicated: Latinos, President Obama, and the 2012 Election." *Social Science Quarterly* 93(5) (2012): 1360–1383.

Wildsmith, Elizabeth, Marta Alvira-Hammond, and Lina Guzman. "A National Portrait of Hispanic Children in Need." National Research Center on Hispanic Children and Families, 2016. http://www.childtrends.org/wp-content/uploads/2016/02/2016-15HispChildrenInNeed.pdf.

Wing, Bob. "Race, the Changing Electorate and the Electoral College." In *Changing the Race: Racial Politics and the Election of Barack Obama*, edited by Linda Burnham. New York: Applied Research Center, 2009.

CHAPTER FOUR

African Americans, Voting, and the Republican Party

Donna L. Taylor

When President Barack Hussein Obama II was sworn in as the 44th president of the United States, he stepped into a distinctive position in history as the first African American to hold the office. Obama's campaign was fraught with challenges and concerns in relation to his inexperience on the national stage, as he had served in Congress for only two years prior to running. His ethnic background was also controversial for some, as he was of Kenyan descent, born of a white mother from Kansas. The latter proved to be an ongoing challenge, as he could not escape the lingering cloud of racism that continued to inflict itself on America.

Obama's 2008 candidacy was habitually scrutinized, as he was a political newcomer in comparison with other challengers. His opponents sought to counteract his appeal by painting him as frivolous and naive. Long-standing Senator John McCain, who ran on the Republican ticket, attempted to highlight Obama's greenness by implying that he was too progressive for the country.[1] When former Massachusetts Governor Mitt Romney ran against President Obama in 2012, his campaign used vitriolic declarations regarding Obama's class and ethnicity in an attempt to curtail his efforts in securing a second term.[2]

Examining the inherent historic relevance of the 2008 and 2012 elections mandates that the history of African Americans in the United States be explored—in order to fully appreciate the gravity of both events. The first African Americans arrived on the shores of the United States nearly 400 years ago as slaves, and since that time they have endured ongoing racism in fighting for advancement from the role of slave to the role of equal citizen. African Americans continue to struggle toward true opportunity and have persistently fought exclusion from the political process that determines their access.

The United States was founded on a principle of equality for each citizen. When the Constitution was created in 1787, and ratified two years later, the voting rights of African Americans were not stipulated. They were considered property until the Thirteenth Amendment was ratified in 1865, following the Civil War, a component of what was referred to as the Reconstruction Amendments. Forming the Reconstruction Amendments were the Thirteenth, Fourteenth, and Fifteenth Amendments, meant to imbue former slaves with previously denied rights. The Fourteenth Amendment dealt with assuring equal protection under the law, as "the Equal Protection Clause of the Fourteenth Amendment of the U.S. Constitution prohibits states from denying any person within its territory the equal protection of its laws. This means that a state must treat an individual in the same manner as others in similar conditions and circumstances."[3]

The Fifteenth Amendment focused on the rights of former male slaves in relation to their right to vote and granted them participation in the democratic process. Females did not receive the right to vote until the ratification of the Nineteenth Amendment in 1920, but at that time, voting continued to be an issue for African Americans as a whole. Racism, leftover and pervasive, continued its iron grip following the outcome of the Civil War. When the South lost, and slaves were freed, many African Americans continued to reside in or near the towns and cities in which they had been slaves. Some moved northward, but for those who remained in the South, their lives did not change rapidly. Many former slaves continued to work the properties confiscated during the war, which were merely regained by the previous landowners. Thus, it was difficult for newly "freed" slaves to consider themselves equal citizens. During the period from 1865–1866, laws known as "black codes" were enacted in order to restrict the advancement of former slaves, as well as ensure their place as a source of manual labor.[4]

The Fight for Civil Rights

The struggle for civil rights became the enduring battle for African Americans following the war. Northern politicians characteristically opposed the unfair practices imposed by southern states, and rifts that had begun before the Civil War continued to form between Americans from both sides. But as African Americans assimilated into the new America, everyday issues, in particular the act of attempting to employ their Fourteenth and Fifteenth amendments rights, continued to be problematic. In the South, especially, a much-feared white hate-group arose, known as the Ku Klux Klan (KKK), who sought to disrupt the progress of African Americans. The KKK utilized an endless barrage of fear tactics, including lynching (hanging), cross burning on the property of African Americans, torching African American–owned businesses and churches, and even resorting to murder when other methods were unsuccessful. These heinous deeds became increasingly extreme in the 1960s when African Americans attempted to exercise their right to vote. One of the most shameful, historic moments occurred in Philadelphia, Mississippi, in June of 1964.

Three young men in their early 20s, Michael Schwerner, Andrew Goodman, and James Chaney, were civil rights advocates volunteering with the Freedom Summer project, which assisted blacks with voter registration. Two of these advocates were Jewish; the other, African American, and they disappeared after being arrested, released, and then attacked outside of the small town of Philadelphia. The local police department and KKK were involved in the killings, and of the 18 persons accused, only 7 of those responsible were actually convicted. The offenders served only six years for the murders. As noted in "Murder in Mississippi," "In three cases, the jury failed to reach a verdict; one juror refused to convict a minister, and . . . after unsuccessful appeals, the convicted men entered prison early in 1970."[5]

The State of Mississippi, being part of the "Deep South," had been one of many states known for traditionally and unfailingly suppressing the voting rights of African Americans. When the Civil Rights Act of 1964 was introduced, President Lyndon Johnson—who hailed from the southern state of Texas—and a number of other southern lawmakers did not wish to originally support the legislation, given their political standing and the inevitable political ramifications. The principles of both parties had largely transformed, as the Republican Party of Abraham Lincoln had promoted the rights of African Americans, and Democrats had traditionally prevented them.

Lincoln executively ordered the Emancipation Proclamation, a document that freed slaves located in the Confederate states during the Civil War. Following this act, however, the Republican Party slowly changed from the party of positive transformation for African Americans to the party obstructing their progress. Conversely, the Democratic Party divided in the late 1940s, in response to President Truman's focus on civil rights.

Truman's desire to desegregate the military culminated in an Executive Order issued in 1948; causing conservative Southern Democrats to temporarily create their own segregationist faction, known as the "Dixiecrats."[6] Though the Dixiecrats lasted for only one year, they paved the way for the later defection of many key Democrats to the Republican Party.

Sixteen years after Truman's efforts, an originally hesitant President Johnson signed the Civil Rights Act of 1964, which was meant to end segregation and employment discrimination. Voting rights, nonetheless, were not protected, and in turn, one year later, the Voting Rights Act of 1965 was signed. The tireless actions of the Rev. Dr. Martin Luther King Jr., a young pastor in his 30s from Georgia, and a slew of other African American activists and supporters from all ethnic backgrounds, were unquestionably relevant to the process. But the deed spawned a new height of backlash against African Americans and those who stood beside them. Prior to President Johnson's signing, Dr. King and other activists had demonstrated, marched, and spoken out endlessly on the rights of African Americans.

Many times, Dr. King and his supporters were met with violence from law enforcement and others in power who had never before feared retribution. Organizations such as the National Association for the Advancement of Colored People (NAACP), the Student Nonviolent Coordinating Committee (SNCC), the Congress of Racial Equality (CORE), and the Southern Christian Leadership Conference (SCLC), in addition to African American churches and various persons, propelled the idea that the right to vote was an inherent right of all men. Dr. King himself preached a message of nonviolence, and in an effort to promote peaceful demonstration and nonprovocation, neither he nor his devotees would fight back when approached by mobs.

This practice led to many being injured or killed, unfortunately, and for a time the ideology of nonviolence was opposed by other organizations focused on African American advancement, notably the Nation of Islam. The Nation of Islam, created over 30 years before, was a black Muslim group that preached self-reliance and the promotion of the concerns of black America. The message of its rising spokesman and activist, Malcolm X, eventually fell more in line with Dr. King's, but originally, it was vehemently contradictory, as Malcolm X felt that blacks should be more defiant, and preached that Dr. King was not as militant as he should be. As found at U.S. History.org's "Malcolm X and the Nation of Islam":

As Martin Luther King preached his gospel of peaceful change and integration in the late 1950s and early 1960s, Malcolm X delivered a different message: whites were not to be trusted. He called on African Americans to be proud of their heritage and to set up strong communities without the help of white Americans. He promoted the establishment of a separate state for African Americans in which they could rely on themselves to provide solutions to their own problems. Violence was not the only answer, but violence was justified in self-defense. Blacks should achieve what was rightfully theirs "by any means necessary."[7]

After the initial Voting Rights Act of 1965 was approved, it received regular amending in order to incorporate other safeguards for illiterate Americans, English as a Second Language (ESL) populations, and the disabled. The Act was renewed in 1970, 1975, 1982, and 2006 as a means of ensuring the voting rights of all Americans subject to various discriminatory practices. The tenets of the Voting Rights Act, nonetheless, have continued to be scrutinized. Questions have been raised for years as to how much protection is still required, as many states are no longer bastions of blatant, lawless practices in relation to subduing the rights of African Americans.

Nonetheless, the primary principles remained until 2013, when Sections 4 and 5 of the Act were barred as a result of *Shelby County v. Holder*, which declared that the sections were no longer necessary because of their age. As noted in *Shelby County v. Holder*, the Supreme Court, in a 54 vote, stated that "[s]ection 4(b) of the Voting Rights Act (VRA), which was used to determine the states and political subdivisions subject to Section 5 preclearance, was unconstitutional. Section 5 is the part of the Voting Rights Act that requires certain jurisdictions to demonstrate to either the Attorney General or a federal court in Washington, D.C., that any proposed voting change is not discriminatory, before that change can be implemented."[8] This action caused many to fear that the Voting Rights Act could possibly be eviscerated for some time to come.

The Philosophy of President Reagan on African American Concerns

The act of seeking to manipulate voting rights statues, though not uncommon, was most notably attempted under President Ronald Reagan's administration. This is of particular concern because the current adaptation of the Republican Party holds a deep affection for the Reagan era. During President Reagan's first term in office, he attempted to dismantle the Voting Rights Act when renewal arrived in 1982. As explained in Andrew Cohen's "After 50 Years, the Voting Rights Act's Biggest Threat . . . The Supreme Court," which highlights author Gary May's *Bending Toward Justice:*

The Voting Rights Act and the Transformation of American Democracy, "Reagan himself had long considered the act to be unconstitutional and a 'humiliation to the South.' "[9]

Reagan's position, upon becoming president, was not surprising, as he had never been supportive of rights for African Americans, having opposed the Civil Rights Act of 1964, the Voting Rights Act of 1965, and the Fair Housing Act of 1968.[10] He further confirmed his ongoing disinterest for the plight of African Americans during the presidential campaign of 1980 when he chose to give a speech at Mississippi's Neshoba County State Fair. The county's iniquitous town of Philadelphia was a mere 10 minutes away and was the same town where the three civil rights workers had been killed 16 years before. Bob Herbert's "Righting Reagan's Wrongs," alluded to the area as an ongoing hotbed of controversy, as "[t]he case was still a festering sore at that time. Some of the conspirators were still being protected by the local community. And white supremacy was still the order of the day."[11]

Reagan spoke before a nondiverse crowd of 10,000 people, promoting his belief in "states' rights," a term which had been a code word for politicians in Southern states wishing to talk about African Americans' civil rights. Herbert points out, "He was tapping out the code. It was understood that when politicians started chirping about 'states' rights' to white people in places like Neshoba County they were saying that when it comes down to you and the blacks, we're with you."[12] Many southern politicians in the 1960s used the term to convey their disdain for the federal government's attempt at enforcing civil rights laws in their states.

One of the biggest opponents of civil rights was Governor George Wallace of the neighboring state of Alabama. Wallace was an "Old-South" Democrat, who, during his inaugural speech in January 1963, famously stated "segregation now, segregation tomorrow and segregation forever," as noted in, " 'Segregation Forever': A Fiery Pledge Forgiven, But Not Forgotten."[13] Wallace was also defiant when Alabama's state university attempted to end segregation, and went so far as to literally stand in the university's doorway, blocking black students attempting to register. President John F. Kennedy was forced to call on the Alabama National Guard in order to assist and protect the students from crowds of protestors.

Reagan's words, uttered less than 20 years after the Civil Rights Movement, offended black Southerners, many of whom had suffered injustices during that era and for whom those memories were still unsullied. During his speech at Philadelphia, Mississippi, he hinted at his stance on civil rights, and possibly the still-present loathing of many Southern whites toward desegregation. As Herbert noted, Reagan declared, "I believe that there are programs like that, programs like education and others, that should be turned back to the states and the local communities with the tax sources to fund them, and let the people . . ."[14]; the ending to his sentence was inaudible.

Though the words that followed remain unknown, he continued to foreshadow his presidency in relation to civil rights. Reagan's Philadelphia speech still reverberates as being culturally insensitive to blacks nationwide, but particularly so as it was delivered in the same county in which those three young civil rights workers were callously murdered. Republicans tout President Reagan as their standard bearer and feel he was the pinnacle of what it means to be a Conservative. But the fact that so many completely disregard his initial civil rights record and his early pandering exemplifies the Republican Party's ongoing disregard to the needs of African Americans.

During his two terms as president, not only did Reagan oppose the key civil rights issues, he also opposed the creation of a holiday for the Rev. Dr. Martin Luther King. He eventually honored the holiday, but only after he could no longer stand in opposition to Congress. President Reagan also opposed South African sanctions during apartheid, an issue which was very personal for many African Americans. Herbert called attention to the fact that Reagan "vetoed a bill to expand the reach of federal civil rights legislation."[15] These disgraceful episodes serve as further examples of Reagan's general attitude toward the needs and concerns of African Americans, which perhaps spilled into the Republican Party of today.

President Clinton, the New Democrats, and African American Engagement

When William Jefferson Clinton brought Democrats back to the White House after 12 years, he was immediately acknowledged as a unique candidate. He had served for over 10 years as governor of his home state of Arkansas and was recognized for his broad appeal to African American voters. Having grown up in the South, he was especially aware of race issues, and during his campaign, he promised to address the concerns of black Americans. On taking office in 1993, he began doing so by assembling a notably diverse staff, and placing a number of African Americans in prominent positions. Clinton's former chief speechwriter, Terry Edmonds, wrote in "President Clinton's Civil Rights Legacy: From Little Rock to the Nation," "His cabinet and White House staff did, indeed, look like America. He appointed more people of color and women than any president in history . . . of the 28 assistants to the president, the highest staff rank, 14 were either people of color, women or both—the most in history."[16]

President Clinton also became known for a poignant speech he gave in 1997 on reconciling the past issues of race and addressing the issues that had been pervasive since the Civil Rights Movement. During those volatile years, President Johnson had created a commission in order to perform studies done on race and racial incidents of the time. President Clinton summarized his own on race concerns, as pointed out by Edmonds:

> More than 30 years ago, at the high tide of the civil rights movement, the Kerner Commission said we were becoming two Americas, one white, one black, separate and unequal. Today we face a different choice: will we become not two, but many Americas, separate, unequal and isolated? Or will we draw strength from all our people and our ancient faith in the quality of human dignity, to become the world's first truly multi-racial democracy. That is the unfinished work of our time, to lift the burden of race and redeem the promise of America.[17]

President Clinton's racial sensitivity stemmed from his observations as a teen of the 1960s, at a time when President Kennedy was handling brewing racial tensions in an unraveling America. Arkansas had challenging integration issues as a result of the Little Rock Nine, a group of black students trying to attend a white high school in 1957, following the *Brown v. Board of Education of Topeka, Kansas*, ruling of 1954. The ruling effectively struck down segregation, and though it took 20 years for the country to largely desegregate its educational institutions, this event influenced Clinton's opinions on racial matters. Many presidents have spoken of their belief in civil rights, but President Clinton was proactive in advancing the needs and wants of African Americans striving for equality, exemplified in the following quotation by Edmonds:

> He strengthened civil rights enforcement and appointed a record number of African American and women judges. His policies created 22 million new jobs, leading to historically high rates of employment and income for African Americans and Hispanics. The president also launched an effort to end racial and ethnic health disparities. He took a strong stand against racial profiling and a rash of new church burnings, and he advocated "mending, not ending affirmative action."[18]

Clinton left office having deeply affected the Democratic Party and the country as a whole. In "The Clinton Presidency: Key Accomplishments," in terms of minority advancement, his presidency boasted "the lowest unemployment in 30 years . . . (and) unemployment for African Americans and Hispanics fell to the lowest on record."[19] President Clinton ushered in a Democratic Party that was more aware of the needs of average Americans, and the New Democrats, or Clinton Democrats, were touted differently from previous Democrats.

As described by Jon F. Hale in "The Making of the New Democrats," Hale pointed out that Clinton wanted to stand apart from other Democrats, outside the "line of Michael Dukakis, Walter Mondale, Jimmy Carter, and George McGovern."[20] The Democratic Leadership Council (DLC), established in 1985 to promote the presidential election of a Democrat, caused this change. In 1990, Arkansas Governor Bill Clinton assumed the role of DLC chair, and upon deciding to run for his first term in 1992, the DLC established his agenda. Hale stated, "Bill Clinton took advantage of both the ideas created within the DLC and the informal party leadership position provided by the DLC in his 1992 presidential campaign."[21]

President Clinton did not always have the support of the New Democrats, as he was more liberal than people were originally aware.[22] But the assistance of the DLC was immeasurable, and the platform of opportunity, responsibility, community, and national security became the primary idea of the party.[23] The policy of the New Democrats continued on to the presidency of Barack Obama, which began in 2009, and the audience and support system of Democrats and their beliefs were even more stalwart given the disappointing presidency of George W. Bush. President Bush's terms began with strong support following the tragedy of the September 11 terrorist attacks, but as his two-term period ended, support for his presidency had dropped from a first-term average of 62 percent to 37 percent.[24] The country was ready for a change in governing, possibly a change of party, and Barack Obama emerged to fill the needs of Americans and reconcile the inequality felt by African Americans for hundreds of years.

Obama's National Rise and Presidential Campaigns

Senator Barack Obama faced a difficult uphill battle upon beginning his quest for the presidency in 2008. He was the youngest competitor, not as well known nationally as the other candidates, and he was African American. Being a first-term senator, Obama had to prove his ability to compete on the national stage (because of his lack of political experience), in addition to being a strong enough candidate to surpass the Republican nominee. Though the country was disillusioned by the previous administration, Senator Obama received enormous support not only based on Republican pushback but also because his views were reminiscent of Democrats who came before him.

When campaigning began, Obama's appeal was broad both because he was a breath of fresh air after the presidency of George W. Bush and because he was a youthful, new face, with an appealing, young family. He garnered comparisons to President John F. Kennedy, who entered the White House around the same age, as Kennedy was 43, and a senator; and Obama, who was born the same year that Kennedy assumed the presidency, was only four years older than Kennedy had been. Endorsements came from members of the Kennedy family (in particular, long-term "liberal lion of the Senate" Ted Kennedy, who had served for nearly 50 years in Congress and whose support had been sought by, and valued by, other candidates).[25] Following Senator Kennedy's endorsement of Obama, the senator spoke at the 2008 Democratic Convention in support of the candidate he stood behind. As written at History.com's "Ted Kennedy—Facts & Summary," following the convention, the pivotal endorsement was celebrated:

> In his speech, the senator, who earlier that year had endorsed Barack Obama for president, invoked the legacy of the Kennedy family when he stated, "And this November the torch will be passed again to a new generation of Americans. . . . The work begins anew. The hope rises again. And the dream lives on."[26]

Obama not only gathered support from far-left, liberal Democrats, but he also acknowledged the support of the New Democrats, a more centrist faction, in spring 2009 after his election. While running, Obama had been careful to identify which end of the Democratic party he fell within, and he had not joined the DLC as Clinton had done. But after the election, President Obama stated that he was aligned with the New Democrats, a group known for being restrained in terms of fiscal responsibility, but broadminded in relation to social matters.[27] His appeal to Democrats as a whole had come years before, when he espoused the message of his future presidential campaign while delivering a powerful and compelling keynote address at the 2004 Democratic National Convention.

After he strode out to Curtis Mayfield's "Keep on Pushing," a song born during the Civil Rights era, he spoke in Boston that momentous evening on his multiracial family background and of a united America that does not belong to one racial group or another. The former constitutional law professor, turned state senatorial candidate, was met with rousing applause as he held the crowd with anecdotes concerning the importance of the military and the necessity of Americans working together on the behalf of one other.[28] As gathered from C-Span, "Barack Obama Speech at 2004

DNC Convention," he bellowed: "There is not a liberal America and a conservative America—there is the United States of America. There is not a black America, and a white America, and Latino America, and Asian America; there's the United States of America. The pundits . . . like to slice and dice our country into red states and blue states . . . we are one people, all of us pledging allegiance to the stars and stripes, all of us defending the United States of America."[29]

Obama went on to evoke the image of the melting pot that is the United States and made biblical allusions, appealing to the American psyche in doing so. As he ended the speech on the message of hope and change, which would become his motto upon entering the presidential race of 2008, the crowd began cheering his name. Obama's ongoing mantra illustrates how the message of a candidate can propel popularity or detract from it. True, it was for the campaigns and subsequent elections of President Barack Obama. His message propelled his initial campaign forward and spread his ability to engage with and appeal to everyman, much like President Clinton had before him. As a result, the country became aware of the persuasive candidate, and through his words and messages he gained a large-scale following, as illustrated by Marius Jucan in "Voting for Obama: The Symbols of Hope and Change in the 2008 American Presidential Campaign":

> Before long, when the first important speeches delivered by Obama captured the audience's interest, it was clear that a set of priorities for the implementation of change proper was already at hand. Due to the almost generally spread discontentment with Bush government's policies, Barack Obama's popularity took on a steady ascending slope, until it became similar to an effigy of popular culture. The unprecedented wave of sympathy helped senator Obama to unearth the anarchic state of local economic conditions, the neglecting of the civil servants' duties, the indifference and incompetence in the management of the local human and financial resources. His plan for changing America went soon past a "transitional" process from one presidency to another, reaching an ampler perspective, and implicitly a more ambitious design of the future, prompted by the severity of the crisis.[30]

The ability to form a succinct message was a skill Obama had honed while a student at Harvard Law School. Prior to his graduating from the esteemed institution, he served as editor of its law review, allowing him a significant, noteworthy accomplishment. Half of the *Harvard Law Review* editors are chosen based on scholarly achievement, and the other half are chosen through a writing contest. Once a list of viable candidates is formulated, a group of 80 editors assemble until a leader is chosen. When President Obama became head of the *HLR* in 1991, he made history as the first African American to serve in the role. When speaking on his historic accomplishment at that time, he touched on the lack of equality still present in the country, and although progress was being made, he acknowledged that black students nationwide had the aptitude to succeed in the same manner as he had, if only given the opportunity.[31]

So when crisscrossing the country years later as a presidential candidate, and reaching out to millions of Americans in an effort to promote his message of hope, he began to stand out from other hopefuls. As noted by Jucan, "The elegance of his speeches, his allusiveness to great forerunners, the critical arrows pitched at his adversaries, and chiefly the realistic analysis of the impending general impasse were transparent to any American, so that his orator's gift made clear to any good-willed citizen his political program: change."[32] Obama also emphasized issues that pertained to race as well as other concerns shared by all Americans, and the future of the country as a whole. But it was his enthusiasm and ability to energize his audiences that packed halls, stadiums, and reached millions who simply watched him on television. Jucan pointed out that, "[i]n spite of his alleged lack of experience, Barack Obama stepped on the political arena with the unflinching conviction that he was in hold of an exact plan of America's ensuing years' development."[33]

Given the history of racial aspersions cast at African Americans in the United States, Obama had to overcome opposition levied by those chiefly skeptical of his competence, based on race. African American voters were reliably nonproblematic, as many of them had never considered that an African American would reach the office of the presidency, and were excited by the prospect. But winning the support of a large population of white voters would be a necessary factor to secure the presidency, and could prove complicated. In Brian F. Schaffner's "Racial Salience and the Obama Vote," Schaffner wrote, "White voters may oppose a black candidate for different reasons. Overt racism may depress support for African American candidates if some portion of white voters refuse to support a black candidate based on skin color alone. However, white opposition to African American candidates may also arise from the stereotypes that are associated with race."[34]

Obama was well educated, with a budding senatorial career when he entered the contest, and though many thought that his race could nonetheless be an impediment, his supporters as well as his detractors based their opinions of him on more than race, which included (but were not limited to) political ideals and party affiliation. Other variables were also discovered to be vital in the decision-making process. White liberal voters were far more likely to vote for Obama than white conservatives, the former being 96 percent likely to vote for Obama versus just 6 percent for the latter. Additional factors included age, as younger voters favored Obama more than older voters did, and single voters were more likely to vote for him than married voters.[35]

The Republican Party's Disenfranchisement Strategy

Part of what appealed to African Americans about the election of President Obama was not only his race but also the ideologies of his party. Because he is a Democrat, it was expected that he would naturally appeal to African Americans, who typically do not vote Republican. This is not a new phenomenon. The Republican Party's attempts at courting black voters as well as other minorities has consistently been a failure, and their treatment of African Americans has been historically antagonistic. In Peter Beinart's "Why the Republican Push for Black Voters Is (Mostly) Doomed to Fail," this aggression was discussed:

> [T]here's a deeper problem with the GOP push to increase the number of blacks who vote Republican: It coincides with a GOP push to decrease the number of blacks who vote at all. Over the last few years, Republicans have pushed an avalanche of voter-identification and registration laws that disproportionately prevent African Americans from exercising the franchise. Since 2011, state legislatures in 14 states (11 of them entirely controlled by Republicans and only one entirely controlled by Democrats) have passed voter-ID laws, despite academic studies showing that such laws are far more likely to prevent blacks from voting than whites.[36]

As the country boasts a growing minority population, Republicans must court those populations in order to remain viable. This has proven to be tough, as the party does not have a favorable record in support of minorities, especially African Americans. Though the party does have some minority candidates and supporters, after the initial election of President Obama in 2008, the Republican Party seemed to do everything in its power to affect voting outcomes in 2012. One tactic included the ongoing disenfranchisement of thousands of voters whose voting rights had been suspended or taken away due to felonious activity.

Given that the incarceration rate is higher for minorities, not permitting felons to vote theoretically means fewer votes for Democratic candidates. The decision to suspend and then reinstate voting rights is a state's preference. This practice began after the Civil War in an effort to thwart the voting ability of newly freed slaves, after the disregarding of the Underwood Convention. The Underwood Convention was the title given to both a meeting and a doctrine created in 1870, which attempted to establish equality among "every 21-year-old male citizen, regardless of his race. . . . A set of clauses excluded only people convicted of corruption or treason, participants in duels, and 'idiots and lunatics' from voting," as noted in Matt Ford's "The Racist Roots of Virginia's Felon Disenfranchisement."[37]

Regrettably, this resolution did not last, as by the early 1900s, a movement to end the black vote was afoot. The president of the Constitutional Convention of Virginia, John Goode, spoke of the right of blacks to vote as being something that threatened the ballots' wholesomeness.[38] Goode also spoke of blacks not being fit to vote because of their lack of experience in having done so, and indicated that they were not intelligent enough to participate in the process. Other members of the convention agreed and expressed the necessity of halting the voting rights allowed by the Fifteenth Amendment. As Ford explained, the act of thwarting the progress of African Americans was a primary intention:

> "Black political suppression was neither an accident nor a mistake; it was the central purpose of the convention. Newspapers plainly reported it and politicians eagerly campaigned on it. 'I told the people of my county before they sent me here that I intended, as far as in me lay, to disenfranchise every negro that I could disenfranchise under the Constitution of the United States, and as few white people as possible,' R.L. Gordon told his fellow delegates during the suffrage debates."[39]

Other states followed with similar actions, which continued for nearly 60 years. The condition of poll taxes—fees levied against those attempting to vote—became commonplace and excluded a number of African Americans who were generally too poor to pay them. Literacy tests as well random, protracted questionnaires were used in order to halt African Americans who managed to pass the other analyses. Though many disenfranchisement procedures fell away after the Civil Rights Movement, taking away the voting rights of felons continues to be a nationwide problem.

Virginia Governor Terry McAuliffe, for example, reinstated the voting rights of over 200,000 offenders in April 2016, only to have Republican General Assembly members sue him in order to stop the progress of his action prior to November 2016's presidential election. This action could prove to be a pervasive obstacle for Democrats, as "48 states have similar restrictions, although only a handful of them include lifetime bans. The Sentencing Project estimates that almost 6 million Americans can't cast a ballot because of post-conviction restrictions imposed upon them" (as written in Laura Vozzella's "GOP Sues to Block McAuliffe Order to Let 200,000 Virginia Felons Vote").[40]

This action in Virginia was seen as purely political, as Governor McAuliffe, a Democrat, was a successful former fundraiser for President Clinton, and former head of the Democratic National Committee. Governor McAuliffe expressed his belief that the General Assembly Republicans were simply attempting to return to the behaviors of the Jim Crow era, because, as noted by Vozella, "African Americans have been disproportionately affected by felon disenfranchisement. One in four African Americans in Virginia had been banned from voting because of laws restricting the rights of those with convictions."[41] The governor further articulated the danger of this behavior being permitted, pointing out the political game playing being performed by the opposing party. "Today Republicans filed a lawsuit to preserve a policy of disenfranchisement that has been used intentionally to suppress the voices of qualified voters, particularly African Americans, for more than a century. . . . These individuals have served their time and are now living, raising families and paying taxes in our communities—this suit is an effort to continue to treat them as second-class citizens," Vozella wrote.[42]

In July 2016, Virginia's majority conservative state supreme court voted that the governor had overstepped his bounds in signing the order; thus the court attempted to thwart the voting rights recently restored. It is this behavior of the Republican Party that has affected and may continue to affect the party's future in relation to minorities, principally African Americans. Because of incidents such as this, and the Republican Party's actions historically, many believe Republicans do not typically cater to, or care about, the needs of African Americans.

2008 and 2012 Political Messaging of Republican Presidential Candidates

The messaging used to convey the beliefs and principles of a candidate can be very useful, as he or she employs those words when potentially swaying an electorate. Both positive and negative tools are used, and messages may be altered according to the expectations of the audience at hand. "Throwing meat" is not uncommon, as each candidate wants to win and sees all strategies as fair and reasonable. During the 2008 presidential campaign, though, the tools used against Obama became unusually full of propaganda, as the Republican Party's message was particularly spiteful and deceitful—spinning Obama's words into various fabrications.

On one such occasion, Senator John McCain, the Republican nominee, attempted to discredit Obama while speaking to a crowd in Ohio. As Ohio was a Republican-leaning state, McCain assumed that he would receive unquestionable support, as George W. Bush had won the state four years before. During the event, Senator McCain touted Obama as someone who would be extraordinarily liberal, raise taxes, and make America unsafe from outside forces. He also stated that Obama would diminish wealth for Americans through his financial strategies. McCain was quoted in John Dickerson's "Political Halloween": "That is what change means for Barack the Redistributor," he told a crowd of about 2000, which didn't fill the gym venue he was in. "It means taking your money and giving it to someone else."[43]

Senator McCain obtained this idea from a speech made by Obama seven years before, in which he spoke on *Brown v. Board of Education* and "the Supreme Court's reluctance to force school districts to spend money to provide equality in schools."[44] It could be discerned that Senator McCain was attempting to paint Obama as one who would take money from wealthier individuals and give it to poorer individuals. He spun Obama's quote on civil rights into a scare tactic in order to sway the predominantly white inhabitants of Dayton, Ohio, in which all minorities make up less than 20 percent of the population.[45]

Senator McCain continued to promote his beliefs across the country, and the message was generally the same. He focused on Senator Obama's lack of military, governing, and national security experience, all of which were fair points. But there were occasions when his message went too far and evoked a level of vitriol and disdain that even he had to rein in swiftly. In the fall of 2008, while campaigning in the Michigan town of Lakeville— which holds fewer than 55,000 residents and is 94 percent white—Senator McCain had to publicly disagree with a constituent who stated she could not trust Senator Obama and called him an "Arab." This was a nod to the persistent rumor that Obama was a Muslim because of his Kenyan background and his middle name, "Hussein."[46] Senator McCain, in defense of Obama, as noted in Laura Meckler's "McCain Asks Supporters to Show Obama Respect," "took the microphone from her and said, 'No, ma'am: no ma'am. He's a decent family man, citizen that I just happen to have disagreements with on fundamental issues, and that's what this campaign's all about. He's not.'"[47]

Supporters of Senator McCain had been known to describe then-Senator Obama as a potential terrorist, and hostility toward Obama had become commonplace at many McCain rallies. Not only was the message of Senator McCain overtly negative, but it was also determined by *Public Opinion*

Quarterly, a nearly 80-year-old interdisciplinary journal, that McCain's campaign darkened Obama's skin in ads, presumably in an attempt to make him seem less appealing. As described in "Bias in the Flesh: Skin Complexion and Stereotype Consistency in Political Campaigns" by Messing et al., it was discovered that "darker images were more frequent in negative ads—especially those linking Obama to crime—which aired more frequently as Election Day approached."[48]

The images of Senator Obama were darker while those of Senator McCain's were, in contrast, lighter. Individuals were quizzed with a series of words, starting with particular letters, and asked to complete the words in relation to ethnic pigeonholing. "When shown a darkened photograph of Obama, 45 percent of people responded with the common stereotype answer, while 33 percent responded that way when shown a lightened image," as noted by Wasser.[49] The behavior, though obvious, was not determined to be calculated or premeditated. But in determining whether or not these ads made a difference, they did indeed cast a negative light on Obama.

When President Obama ran in 2012 against former Massachusetts Governor Mitt Romney, a Republican who had participated in the presidential race just four years before, the message was slightly different. Governor Romney accused the president of being out of touch with the common man, and indicated the President Obama was elitist and superior. These declarations were ironic given that Romney was a millionaire businessman whose properties and expensive hobbies had come under fire, highlighting his potential inability to relate to the general electorate.

But Romney continued to hammer this message, even when it hinted at the ridiculous. At one campaign stop, after having gathered recent victories in two states and in Washington, DC, he arrogantly stated that the president "has spent years flying around in Air Force One, surrounded by an adoring staff of true believers. . . . It's enough to make you think you might become a little out of touch . . . and that's what has happened" (highlighted in Charles Riley's "Mitt Romney's New General Election Message").[50]

As had Senator McCain before him, Governor Romney failed to reach out to African Americans with any particular message, and in the end, it cost him votes from that community. Over 90 percent of the African American vote went to President Obama, partially because of the Republican Party's continued failure in courting African American voters or tailoring an agenda to fit their needs. In "Mitt Romney's Neglect of Black Americans Failed Him at the Polls," by Crystal Wright, she stated, "Even more insulting was Romney's refusal to work for the black vote beyond giving an NAACP speech and announcing a Black Leadership Council, which amounted to nothing more than cosmetic wall paper."[51] No African American events involving involvement or participation in the party were financed by the Republican National Committee.[52]

Romney's aforementioned NAACP address was clearly not one of his finest moments and was met with disdain and derision. The former governor spoke in Texas's capital city, Houston, to a crowd of hundreds at the organization's national convention. The attendees were not in favor of his critique of Obama, especially in relation to his health care plan, known as Obamacare. Philip Rucker's "Mitt Romney Met with Boos in NAACP Speech," expressed the candidate's words, "If you want a president who will make things better in the African American community, you are looking at him," Romney said. When the crowd booed and hissed, he said, "You take a look."[53] This was another instance in which Romney was accused of being out of touch and generally unable to connect with the African American audience.

Romney also made the inflammatory comment that the legitimacy of his own birth certificate had never been questioned.[54] This was a leftover claim from the 2008 campaign implying that Obama was not a true citizen. Many had asked to see his birth certificate, and even though he had produced it, many Republicans believed that it was counterfeit.

Romney's nod to that offensive accusation demonstrates how desperate his candidacy had become, and in later years he acknowledged that his lack of interaction and messaging toward minorities was his biggest mistake. In an interview from 2015, he conceded that his campaign should have advertised more with that population. As written by Raynard Jackson in "Mitt Romney's Shocking Statement About Blacks," Romney admitted his shortcoming: "[T]he real thing that I wish I had done differently is make a greater effort at communicating to minority voters in this country the policies that I think are right to help minority families and that's without question the biggest mistake I made in the campaign."[55]

Black Republicans in the Age of Obama

Republican political messaging during Obama's presidency and its impact did not always stem from those running directly against him. Other Republicans seeking to make their mark also emerged during his eight years in office, some putting a minority face on the historically dismissive party. Many of the messages emanating from these African American candidates were just as provoking and malicious toward the president as well as toward other minorities in the opposing Democratic Party. A growing concern has been the support by Republicans of African Americans who denounce African American concerns, and this behavior was particularly demonstrated with three Congressional hopefuls following the second-term election of President Obama.

Three Republican, African American Congressmen were elected prior to or during the 2014 midterms. Senator Tim Scott of South Carolina (formally elected after an initial appointment in 2013), Congresswoman Mia Love of Utah, and Congressman Will Hurd of Texas were all voted into office without any great support from African American voters, largely because of their ideologies.

The congressmen and congresswoman, though from states with divergent populations and varying interests, have in common the practice of bashing and disregarding issues that concern African Americans. They were primarily voted into office by white Republicans, and in relation to Tim Scott, in particular, he was clearly unsupported by blacks in South Carolina. An explanation was given in Jamelle Bouie's "Tim Scott Will Rise Again," stating, "Black Americans tend to hold more liberal views on government and are inclined to support Democrats, even if Republicans have a black candidate. Barring an extraordinary turn in South Carolina politics, there's little chance Scott will ever win a substantial number of black voters."[56]

Of these three elected in 2014, perhaps the most divisive message came from Congresswoman Love, a first-generation Haitian American, who, as a Mormon from Utah, had the backing and support of former Republican presidential candidate, Mitt Romney. Prior to joining Congress, she spoke passionately about her goal of dismantling the Departments of Education and Energy, and of her disdain for the Congressional Black Caucus—stating that she would "join the Congressional Black Caucus and try to take that thing apart from the inside out," as noted in Charles D. Ellison's, "Will the New Black Republicans in Congress Be Lawmakers—or Talk Show Hosts?," in which he pointed to a 2012 interview she gave to a Utah news organization.[57]

The latter declaration was found to be enormously offensive to African Americans, given that many of the CBC members are former civil rights advocates from the 1960s and 1970s, whose behaviors and sacrifices moved African Americans forward. Paradoxically and cynically, she used President Obama's 2008 messaging in reference to the CBC, when speaking to the same Utah news organization: "They use their positions to instill fear. Hope and change is turned into fear and blame. Fear that everybody is going to lose everything and blaming Congress for everything instead of taking responsibility" (as noted in Nia-Malika Henderson's "Mia Love Joins a Group She Promised to Dismantle").[58] Congresswoman Love was not thought to be naive to the histories of CBC members, but rather was seen as one taking advantage of their sacrifices while continuing to pander to her largely white electorate. Love, ironically, is the only of the aforementioned three to actually join the CBC, currently in its 45th year.

Obama's Legacy

Barack Obama's presidential aspirations garnered worldwide attention for a variety of reasons. As an African American successfully running for America's highest office, his candidacies in 2008 and 2012 were historic for that alone. Given the significance of the 2008 contest, voter turnout was understandably high. The country was invested in moving forward following the George W. Bush years, as well as coming to grips with its own views on race. Obama's elections inspired a newfound enthusiasm in the electoral process, from the African Americans community especially.

In both the 18–24 and 25–44 age demographics, African Americans outvoted every other ethnicity notably, as pointed out in Sam Roberts's "2008 Surge in Black Voters Nearly Erased Racial Gap," "[Y]ounger blacks voted in greater proportions than whites for the first time and black women turned out at a higher rate than any other racial, ethnic and gender group."[59] According to the Census Bureau, the percentages of African American's voting increased in the 2012 and "more than 66 percent of eligible blacks voted in the presidential contest. Only 64.1 percent of whites turned out to vote," as illustrated in Dan Merica's "Black Outvoted White in 2012, the First Time on Record."[60]

The election of an African American president was extraordinary given that it had taken nearly 400 years for African Americans to attain a sense of equality. After Reconstruction, the lives of African Americans had been fraught with additional dangers throughout the 19th and 20th centuries, including horrifying acts of violence and subjugation. The lack of support from various politicians during the Civil Rights Movement did not always protect or address the rights of African Americans—an ongoing practice chiefly associated with the Republican Party. The party both disrupts the progress of African Americans (through disenfranchisement policies, black Republican politicians strategizing in opposition of African Americans, and blatant ignorance of voter needs) and hampers its own progress with black voters.

The Republican party is burdened by its history of the past 50 years and will continue not to win votes when its own members continue to promote racist beliefs. In May of 2016, Linda Sorenson, the leader of Colorado's Delta County Republican Party, shared a post on Facebook in which

President Obama was compared to a monkey being bottle-fed by President Reagan. Although the head of the Rocky Mountain Black Conservatives, Derrick Wilburn is African American, but he did not support the local ministerial association and NAACP's asking her to resign. Colorado's Republican leader insisted that Ms. Sorenson would undergo sensitivity training, but refused to ask for her resignation.[61]

As the 44th president of the United States, Obama has shown the nation and the international community that an African American can attain, and preserve, the highest office in the country, and become the most powerful leader in the world. The presidency of Barack Obama brought full circle the injustices previously suffered by generations of African Americans, and conceivably changed the minds of some about the capabilities of African Americans as a whole. Though he served two terms, the maximum one can hold the office of the presidency, some are not ready to see him go, as his presence offers an immeasurable sense of awe and pride. Yamiche Alcindor, author of "Proud of Obama's Presidency, Blacks Are Sad to See Him Go," in speaking to African Americans on the legacy of Obama, stated that "what had given them hope . . . was an achievement that could never be erased even as it slips into history: that a black person can become president."[62]

Notes

1. "Barack Obama's Campaign Themes and Strategies," n.d.
2. Zeleny and Rutenberg, 2012.
3. "Equal Protection," 2014.
4. "Reconstruction," 2016.
5. "Murder in Mississippi," 2012.
6. "President Truman Issues Executive Order No. 9981 Desegregating the Military," n.d.
7. "Malcolm X and the Nation of Islam," n.d.
8. "Shelby County v. Holder," n.d.
9. Cohen, 2013.
10. Rozsa, 2014.
11. Herbert, 2007.
12. Ibid.
13. "Segregation Forever," 2013.
14. "Transcript of Ronald Reagan's 1980 Neshoba County Fair Speech," 2007.
15. Herbert, 2007.
16. Edmonds, 2011.
17. Ibid.
18. Ibid.

19. "The Clinton Presidency: Key Accomplishments," n.d.
20. Hale, 1995, p. 207.
21. Ibid., p. 225.
22. Ibid., p. 229.
23. Ibid., p. 227.
24. "Presidential Approval Ratings—George W. Bush," n.d.
25. "Ted Kennedy—Facts & Summary," 2016.
26. Ibid.
27. Lee and Martin, 2009.
28. "C-SPAN: Barack Obama Speech at 2004 DNC Convention," 2009.
29. Ibid.
30. Jucan, 2009, p. 7.
31. Butterfield, 1990.
32. Jucan, 2009, p. 9.
33. Ibid., p. 9.
34. Schaffner, 2011, p. 965.
35. Ibid., p. 976.
36. Beinart, 2014.
37. Ford, 2016.
38. Ibid.
39. Ibid.
40. Vozzella, 2016.
41. Ibid.
42. Ibid.
43. Dickerson, 2008.
44. Ibid.
45. "Race and Ethnicity," n.d.
46. Meckler, 2008.
47. Ibid.
48. Messer et al., 2015.
49. Wassner, 2015.
50. Riley, 2012.
51. Wright, 2012.
52. Ibid.
53. Rucker, 2012.
54. Sonmez, 2012.
55. Jackson, 2015.
56. Bouie, 2014.
57. Ellison, 2014.
58. Henderson, 2015.
59. Roberts, 2009.
60. Merica, 2013.
61. Salzman, 2016.
62. Alcindor, 2016.

Bibliography

Alcindor, Yamiche. "Proud of Obama's Presidency, Blacks Are Sad to See Him Go." *The New York Times.* March 12, 2016. http://www.nytimes.com/2016/03/13/us/politics/proud-of-obamas-presidency-blacks-are-sad-to-see-him-go.html?_r=0.

"Barack Obama's Campaign Themes and Strategies." ICPSR. n.d. http://www.icpsr.umich.edu/icpsrweb/instructors/setups2008/campaign-strategies.jsp. Accessed July 17, 2016.

Beinart, Peter. "Why the Republican Push for Black Voters Is (Mostly) Doomed to Fail." *The Atlantic.* February 13, 2014. http://www.theatlantic.com/politics/archive/2014/02/why-the-republican-push-for-black-voters-is-mostly-doomed-to-fail/283811/.

Bouie, Jamelle. "Tim Scott Will Rise Again." *Slate* Magazine. November 10, 2014. http://www.slate.com/articles/news_and_politics/politics/2014/11/tim_scott_won_south_carolina_s_senate_seat_the_first_black_republican_senator.html.

Butterfield, Fox. "First Black Elected to Head Harvard's Law Review." *The New York Times*, February 6, 1990. http://www.nytimes.com/1990/02/06/us/first-black-elected-to-head-harvard-s-law-review.html.

"The Clinton Presidency: Key Accomplishments." n.d. Welcome To The White House. https://clinton5.nara.gov/WH/Accomplishments/eightyears-01.html. Accessed July 21, 2016.

Cohen, Andrew. "After 50 Years, the Voting Rights Act's Biggest Threat: The Supreme Court." *The Atlantic.* February 22, 2013. http://www.theatlantic.com/national/archive/2013/02/after-50-years-the-voting-rights-acts-biggest-threat-the-supreme-court/273257/.

"C-SPAN: Barack Obama Speech at 2004 DNC Convention." YouTube. August 18, 2009. https://www.youtube.com/watch?v=eWynt87PaJ0.

Dickerson, John. "Political Halloween." *Slate* Magazine. October 27, 2008. http://www.slate.com/articles/news_and_politics/politics/2008/10/political_halloween.html.

Edmonds, Terry. "President Clinton's Civil Rights Legacy: From Little Rock to the Nation." *The Huffington Post.* December 4, 2011. http://www.huffingtonpost.com/terry-edmonds/clinton-civil-rights_b_994501.html.

Ellison, Charles D. "Will the New Black Republicans in Congress Be Lawmakers—or Talk Show Hosts?" The Root. November 17, 2014. http://www.theroot.com/articles/politics/2014/11/will_the_new_black_republicans_in_congress_be_lawmakers_or_talk_show_hosts/.

"Equal Protection." Legal Information Institute. Cornell University Law School. June 16, 2016. https://www.law.cornell.edu/wex/equal_protection.

Ford, Matt. "The Racist Roots of Virginia's Felon Disenfranchisement." *The Atlantic.* April 27, 2016. http://www.theatlantic.com/politics/archive/2016/04/virginia-felondisenfranchisement/480072/.

Hale, Jon F. "The Making of the New Democrats." *Political Science Quarterly* 110, no. 2 (1995): 207–32.

Henderson, Nia-Malika. "Mia Love Joins a Group She Promised to Dismantle." *The Washington Post*, January 6, 2015. https://www.washingtonpost.com/news/the-fix/wp/2015/01/06/mia-love-joins-the-cbc-the-group-she-vowed-to-dismantle/.

Herbert, Bob. "Righting Reagan's Wrongs?" *The New York Times*, November 13, 2007. http://www.nytimes.com/2007/11/13/opinion/13herbert.html?_r=0.

Jackson, Raynard. "Mitt Romney's Shocking Statement About Blacks." *Pittsburgh Courier,* March 30, 2015. http://newpittsburghcourieronline.com/2015/03/30/mitt-romneys-shocking-statement-about-blacks/.

Jucan, Marius. "Voting For Obama: The Symbols Of Hope and Change in The 2008 American Presidential Campaign." *Studia Universitatis Babes-Bolyai—Studia Europaea*, 2:5–24. February 2009. https://www.ceeol.com/search/article-detail?id=63483.

Lee, Carol E., and Jonathan Martin. "Obama: 'I Am a New Democrat'." Politico. February 2009. March 10, 2009. http://www.politico.com/story/2009/03/obama-i-am-a-new-democrat-019862.

"Malcolm X and the Nation of Islam." n.d. Ushistory.org. http://www.ushistory.org/us/54h.asp.

Meckler, Laura. "McCain Asks Supporters to Show Obama Respect." *The Wall Street Journal.* October 12, 2008. http://www.wsj.com/articles/SB122368132195924869.

Merica, Dan. "Blacks Outvoted Whites in 2012, the First Time on Record." CNN Political Ticker RSS. May 9, 2013. http://politicalticker.blogs.cnn.com/2013/05/09/blacks-outvoted-whites-in-2012-the-first-time-on-record/.

Messing, Solomon , Maria Jabon, and Ethan Plaut. 2015. "Bias in the Flesh: Skin Complexion and Stereotype Consistency in Political Campaigns. *Public Opinion Quarterly* 80(1): 44–65.

"Murder in Mississippi." American Experience. PBS. 2012. http://www.pbs.org/wgbh/americanexperience/features/general-article/freedomsummer-murder/. Accessed July 18, 2016.

"Presidential Approval Ratings—George W. Bush." n.d. Gallup Historical Trends. Gallup.com. http://www.gallup.com/poll/116500/presidential-approval-ratings-george-bush.aspx. Accessed July 22, 2016.

"President Truman Issues Executive Order No. 9981 Desegregating the Military." n.d. Truman Library. https://www.trumanlibrary.org/anniversaries/desegblurb.htm.

"Race and Ethnicity." n.d. Greater Ohio Policy Center—Grassroots Advocacy for Economic Growth and Improved Quality of Life—Columbus, Ohio. http://greaterohio.org/files/policy-research/race-and-ethnicity.pdf. Accessed July 24, 2016.

"Reconstruction." History.com. A&E Television Networks, 2009. July 18, 2016. http://www.history.com/topics/american-civil-war/reconstruction.

Riley, Charles. "Mitt Romney's New General Election Message." CNNMoney. April 4, 2012. http://money.cnn.com/2012/04/03/news/economy/mitt -romney-message/.

Roberts, Sam. "2008 Surge in Black Voters Nearly Erased Racial Gap." *The New York Times*, July 20, 2009. http://www.nytimes.com/2009/07/21/us/ politics/21vote.html?_r=0.

Rozsa, Matthew. "10 Real Facts About Ronald Reagan That Republicans Never Choose to Admit." Mic. March 14, 2014. https://mic.com/arti cles/85379/10-real-facts-about-ronald-reagan-that-republicans-never -choose-to-admit - .KaU5OTdAF.

Rucker, Philip. "Mitt Romney Met with Boos in NAACP Speech." *The Washington Post*, July 11, 2012. https://www.washingtonpost.com/politics/mitt-rom ney-met-with-boos-in-naacp-speech/2012/07/11/gJQAqoSBdW_story .html.

Salzman, Jason. "African American Addresses Republicans Whose Leader Compared Obama to Chimp." The Huffington Post. June 26, 2016. http://www. huffingtonpost.com/jason-salzman/african-american addresse_b_1063 5932.html.

Schaffner, Brian F. "Racial Salience and the Obama Vote." *Political Psychology* 32, no. 6 (2011): 963–988. doi:10.1111/j.1467-9221.2011.00848.x.

"'Segregation Forever': A Fiery Pledge Forgiven, But Not Forgotten." NPR. January 10, 2013. http://www.npr.org/2013/01/14/169080969/segregation- forever-a-fiery-pledge-forgiven-but-not-forgotten.

"Shelby County v. Holder." The Leadership Conference on Civil and Human Rights. n.d. http://www.civilrights.org/voting-rights/shelby-county-v- holder.html. Accessed July 20, 2016.

Sonmez, Felicia. "Mitt Romney: 'No one's ever asked to see my birth certificate.'" *The Washington Post*, August 24, 2012. https://www.washingtonpost.com/ news/post-politics/wp/2012/08/24/mitt-romney-no-ones-asked-for-my -birth-certificate/.

"Ted Kennedy—Facts & Summary." History.com. 2016. http://www.history.com/ topics/ted-kennedy.

"Transcript of Ronald Reagan's 1980 Neshoba County Fair Speech." *The Neshoba Democrat*, November 15, 2007. http://neshobademocrat.com/Content/ NEWS/News/Article/Transcript-of-Ronald-Reagans-1980-Neshoba- County-Fair-speech/2/297/15599.

Vozzella, Laura. "GOP Sues to Block McAuliffe Order to Let 200,000 Virginia Felons Vote." *The Washington Post*, May 23, 2016. https://www.washin gtonpost.com/local/virginia-politics/gop-sues-to-strip-209k-felons- from-va-voter-rolls/2016/05/23/ef2587a8-20e4-11e6-aa84-42391 ba52c91_story.html.

Wasser, Miriam. "John McCain's 2008 Campaign Darkened Barack Obama's Skin in Ads." *Phoenix New Times*, December 30, 2015. http://www.phoenixnew-times.com/news/john-mccains-2008-campaign-darkened-barack-obamas-skin-in-ads-study-finds-7930833.

Wright, Crystal. "Mitt Romney's Neglect of Black Americans Failed Him at the Polls." *The Washington Post*, November 7, 2012. https://www.washington post.com/blogs/therootdc/post/mitt-romneys-neglect-of-black-ameri cans-failed-him-at-the-polls/2012/11/07/05331e2e-28f1-11e2-96b6-8e6a7524553f_blog.html.

Zeleny, Jeff, and Jim Rutenberg. "Romney Adopts Harder Message for Last Stretch." *The New York Times*, August 25, 2012. http://www.nytimes.com/2012/08/25/us/politics/mitt-romneys-campaign-adopts-a-harder-message.html.

CHAPTER FIVE

Barack Obama and the Youth Vote

Glenn L. Starks

The election of Barack Obama to the presidency of the United States made history for many reasons. As a result of the 2008 general election, he became the first African American president in the United States. He made history again by being reelected in 2012 to a second term. His ascension to the oval office was even more profound as he was a first-term senator to the United States Congress, and only the third sitting senator in history to become president (after Warren Harding and John F. Kennedy). Running on a platform of "Change," Obama was able to galvanize youth voters in a way no other president had done, and sustain that support through two general elections and both terms in office. Harvard University election analyst Thomas Patterson spoke to the increased political participation of youth that began with opposition to the war and really grew because of Obama:

> We forget now that in the summer of 2003 that Howard Dean rocketed upward in the polls and had a lot of youthful volunteers and his message was anti-Iraq. You go back to 1992, 1996 and 2000, the youth were barely there. Barely more than a third of them participated. In 2004 it was nearly 50 percent. That's a huge turnaround. And when you look at young people and what was on their minds, Iraq was the upper most issue, . . . Since the start of this campaign in early 2007, I think what we've seen is a second source of energy for young voters and that's the Obama campaign. They

were attracted to him in the first instance by his early opposition to the war in Iraq. At the same time, he happened to have the kind of personality, the kind of message that appealed to them.[1]

Obama's winning of the 2008 and 2012 elections can mostly be attributed to support from young voters. His ability to outline the need for government changes, frame the issues of the day with enthusiasm and eloquence, and instill the need for youths to get involved in the political process were all galvanizing factors. His attraction epitomizes the characteristics of a charismatic leader with the personal appeal and attraction that drew young voters to action. Because of his influence, the enthusiasm of young Americans, their political involvement, and actual voter turnout percentages during primaries and caucuses reached historic levels even before the general election. *Time* magazine voted Obama it's 2008 "Person of the Year" and explained in its special issue:

The real story of Obama's year is the steady march of seemingly impossible accomplishments: beating the Clinton machine, organizing previously marginal voters, harnessing the new technologies of democratic engagement, shattering fundraising records, turning previously red states blue—and then waking up the day after his victory to reinvent the presidential-transition process in the face of a potentially dangerous vacuum of leadership. "We always did our best up on the high wire," says his campaign manager, David Plouffe.[2]

Obama's targeting of young voters and his ability to connect with them was reminiscent of John F. Kennedy's call to the youth in the 1960s. During his presidential inauguration address, Kennedy spoke words that epitomized a call to young Americans: "Let the word go forth from this time and place, to friend and foe alike, that the torch has been passed to a new generation of Americans."[3] Just like Kennedy, Obama was youthful, charismatic, and progressive. Alex-Assensoh (2008) also outlined Obama's ability to make a personal connection with young voters:

In commenting on then-Senator Obama's political success with the younger generation, Donna Brazile, a former political campaign strategist for Vice-President Al Gore's 2000 presidential campaign, offered the following anecdote: "Obama invited the young to become actively involved. He made them believe that they could make a difference, and he inspired them to do the impossible. Obama spoke to them as equals. They were invited into his campaign as partners who had an equal stake in the outcome. Perhaps, most importantly, Obama had the confidence in them to step back and put the youth in charge of organizing one another and to become the voice of change." . . . This philosophy of empowerment generated unprecedented levels of support among young people (66 percent) and new voters (68 percent) for Obama in the 2008 elections.[4]

Obama gained what was compared to rock-star status while on the campaign trail for the 2008 general election. At the announcement of his candidacy at the Old State Capitol in Springfield, Illinois, in 2007, some supporters wore T-shirts with the logo "Are you ready to Barack," and an estimated 15,000 supporters and over 500 journalists braved the 16-degree weather to hear Obama's speech. His campaign rallies in 2007 drew huge crowds of supporters. In February 2007, he drew 20,000 to Town Lake in Austin, Texas; a crowd of 10,000 into a plaza outside City Hall in Oakland, California, in March; 20,000 at an outdoor rally at Yellow Jacket Park in Atlanta in April; and an estimated 24,000 people to Washington Square Park, New York, in September. His rallies held in 2008 drew just as many or even more supporters around the country. On October 18, 2008, he spoke to a crowd of 100,000 people during a rally under the Gateway Arch in St. Louis.

Even before the 2008 primaries, young voters overwhelmingly supported Obama, with 29 percent polled replying they would vote for him if the primary were held that day. Comparing youth support for both Democratic and Republican contenders, 20 percent said they would vote for Hillary Clinton; 10 percent, for Rudy Giuliani; 9 percent, for John McCain; 8 percent, for Mike Huckabee; 6 percent, for John Edwards; and 5 percent, for Mitt Romney. Only 10 percent of voters were undecided. Compared to the 2004 actual primaries, youth voting increased by 103 percent, with the greatest increases in the following states:

- Iowa up by 133 percent: young Democrats from 17 percent to 22 percent
- Texas up by 301 percent: young Republicans from 9 percent to 13 percent
- Georgia up by 134 percent: young Democrats from 11 percent to 18 percent
- New York up by 160 percent: young Democrats from 8 percent to 15 percent
- Missouri up by 125 percent: young Republicans from 10 percent to 13 percent
- Oklahoma up by 188 percent: young Republicans from 9 percent to 14 percent[5]

Obama also targeted young voters, much like Bill Clinton had done when he ran for the presidency. Obama's campaign used young celebrities and political activists who became "youth directors" to go after young supporters. According to an article in *Time*:

Obama's outreach to students didn't spring from some starry-eyed principle. It started as a specific element of his early strategy in Iowa. The first-in-the-nation caucuses allow 17-year-olds to vote if they are going to turn 18 before the general election, which means most high school seniors are eligible. To win those kids, Obama did something unusual in politics: he made them a genuine priority. After his rallies in towns across the state, he met backstage with student leaders from the area—a privilege most campaigns reserve for local VIPs and fund raisers. He also hired as his youth-vote coordinator Hans Riemer, a veteran of Rock the Vote! which has been working to mobilize the student vote for years, with increasing success. Riemer extracted a promise that his work would be an integral part of the overall campaign, not a lip-serviced, photo-op'ed afterthought. His timing was perfect. The art of political organizing is in the midst of a broad philosophical overhaul that erases many of the old distinctions between young voters and their elders.[6]

The sheer excitement Obama created among youth voters overwhelmed the support given to his opposition, including his Democratic rival, Hillary Clinton. According to Von Drehle (2008b),

The excitement that created—a "tidal wave," in the words of Bill Clinton—nearly drowned the hopes of the former President's wife. But Hillary Clinton answered with her own organizational prowess, whipping up huge numbers of working-class, female and older Democrats. Only the students have kept Obama in contention: in New Hampshire, his edge among young voters was 3 to 1; in Nevada, it was 2 to 1; and in Michigan, nearly 50,000 under-30s voted "Uncommitted" because Clinton's name was the only one on the ballot.[7]

Additionally, Fisher (2010) highlighted,

Obama did significantly better among younger primary voters. While Obama won less than 40 percent of the over-60 vote in the primaries, he won more than 60 percent of the under-30 vote. For every age group, the older a voter, the less likely the voter supported Obama. The age gap between Barack Obama and Hillary Clinton during the 2008 Democratic presidential nomination contest was among the largest age gaps in American electoral history. Obama's appeal to younger voters was instrumental in his ability to pull off one of the biggest upsets in American electoral history.[8]

A whopping 6.7 million young voters took part in primaries in 2008, and the vast majority (74%) voted Democrat. Obama received 60 percent of the youth votes. They comprised 14 percent of all Democratic Party primary participants, compared to 11 percent of Republican Party primaries. John McCain received 34 percent of youth votes; Mike Huckabee, 31 percent; Mitt Romney, 25 percent; and 10 percent went to Ron Paul. From the primaries, approximately 86 percent of those who voted during the primaries said they would likely vote on November 4, and 67 percent of those would be first-time voters.[9]

Of the youth voters, the highest voter turnout rates were for those who were college educated. For example, although one in every four college-educated youths voted on Super Tuesday, 1 one in 14 out-of-college youths voted. During the general election, those without any college education comprised 24 percent of all voters 18–29. Those with no high school education only made up 4 percent of young voters. The lack of high voting for the less educated is a concern given they are the most negatively impacted by poor economic policies, lack of adequate health care, the government not investing in the nation's infrastructure, and inner-city violence. According to Rizga (2008), "There are close to 13 million 18- to 25-year-olds, who have never been enrolled in college in America. So far only about three million voted in the primaries. These non-college youths come disproportionately from lower-income backgrounds and African American and Latino communities. It is these very communities that stand to gain the most from more political power and resources, especially during the current recession."[10]

During the 2008 general election, Obama decisively won the election with 52.9 percent of the popular vote (66,882,230) and 365 electoral votes. The 2008 election saw an increase of 8,875,857 voters of all ages above those voting in 2004, 66 percent of which was attributable to an increase in voters 18–19 years old (5,585,066). McCain won 45.7 percent of the popular vote (58,343,671) and received 173 electoral votes. Eighty percent of Obama's 7.2 percent popular vote lead was due to the youth vote (6.8 million of the 8.5 million lead). The Democrats also won control of the Senate (58 seats versus 41) and the House of Representatives (257 seats versus 178). The turnout rate for voters 18–29 in 2008 was 66 percent, the highest since 18–20 year olds were given the right under the 26th Amendment in 1972 (http://www.pewresearch.org/2008/11/13/young -voters-in-the-2008-election/).[11]

An estimated 23 million youth voted, and Democrats received the greatest support from young voters as a percent of all voters in 2008 than in the preceding nine presidential elections. The only other prior election since 1972 near this 14 percent margin was in 2004 when 54 percent of youth voters supported Kerry compared to 48.1 percent of the total popular vote. One interesting poll result is that 55 percent of those polled who said race was a factor voted for Obama while approximately the same percent who said race was not a factor also voted for Obama.[12]

Based on research by Starks (2009),

> According to CNN exit polls, voters 18–29 year olds comprised 18 percent of all voters. The remaining age categories of voters were 30–44 (29 percent), 45–64 (37 percent) and 65 and older (16 percent). Obama garnered fewer percentages of votes as the age group of voters increased. Of those 18–29 years old, 66 percent voted for Obama and 32 percent for McCain (2 percent for other candidates). Within the group of voters 30–44, 52 percent voted for Obama compared to 46 percent for McCain. Approximately 50 percent of voters 45–64 voted for Obama and 49 percent for McCain, and 53 percent of those 65 and older voted for McCain and 45 percent for Obama. These statistics show a clear divide between young voters and older voters. These statistics hold true in most states. Even in McCain's home state of Arizona, 52 percent of voters 18–29 voted for Obama compared to 48 percent for McCain.[13]

Further,

> Obama received the largest percentage of votes from those who identified themselves as Democrats (89 percent) and Independents (52 percent), while McCain was overwhelmingly supported by Republicans (90 percent). Obama was also chosen by those who identified themselves as liberal (89 percent) and moderate (60 percent), while 78 percent of conservatives supported McCain. Obama was the primary choice by Blacks (95 percent), Hispanics (67 percent), Asians (62 percent) and those who identified themselves as "Other" (66 percent). The majority of White voters (55 percent) supported McCain. Interestingly, Whites comprised 74 percent of all voters. The combination of the 45 percent of White voters (particularly young White voters) and minority support led to Obama's victory. The majority of females (56 percent) also supported Obama, while 49 percent of males received his support.[14]

Obama's popularity was so unique in that he was popular for many reasons for which prior candidates actually failed to gain voter support: he was young, politically inexperienced, African American, and a political outsider who challenged the current government establishment (particularly their policies). This was a feat, given the power in both the Democratic and Republican Party establishments.

Yet, Obama's personal and political qualities were congruent to his platform mantra based on change. His personal background also epitomized the achievement of the American dream, particularly related to by Hispanic and minority youth. Many either personally relate to or just took pride in supporting a candidate who was the child of an immigrant black father (from Kenya) and American white mother (from Kansas) who separated the same year Obama born. Obama was then raised by his single mother and grandparents. From very humble beginnings he went on to graduate Harvard Law School. He was not the product of a rich family or one that was involved in politics. He spent most of his early life fighting for local causes such as increasing voter registration, tenants' rights, job training programs, civil rights, and community development. He was the complete opposite of then-President George W. Bush who grew up wealthy, spent most of his life being negatively and positively influenced by his family status, and was deeply engrained in established politics at the national level.

Along with this, the economic and social climate of the nation was congruent to Obama's mantra and what he represented in terms of a new demographic in the White House and a fresh perspective on governance. According to a poll conducted by CBS and the *New York Times* in September 2008, 81 percent of all adults believed the United States was on the "wrong track." Of those surveyed by Rock the Vote!, 69 percent agreed. For young voters, this view significantly varied by political party. Although 81 percent of young Democrats felt the nation was going in the wrong direction, 67 percent of Independent voters agreed compared to 49 percent of their Republican counterparts. By race, 67 percent of whites and Latinos agreed, compared to 82 percent of African Americans.

As stated earlier, Obama gained support not only because of his personal attraction but also because of his platform based on "change." This change addressed the social, political, and economic environment in terms of challenges the United States was facing at the time. The country was in a deep recession due predominantly to the housing market crash that began in 2007. In addition to Fannie Mae, Freddie Mac, and many private companies becoming almost insolvent, the crisis led to the largest percentage of foreclosed homes in U.S. history. As a result of the recession, the nation was dealing with very high and rising gas prices, the falling value of the American dollar, and massive layoffs by companies across the country. The government was also taking actions deemed by some economists and citizens as "socialist" such as restrictive economic policies and a massive $700 billion bailout of private companies. Youth voters supporting both parties were concerned about the economy as the U.S. unemployment rate in 2008 was the highest in 26 years and suffered the greatest downturn since the Great Depression.

The recession touched almost every sector of the economy, and particularly those areas young people cared about. Gas prices reached the highest levels in history in the years leading up to the 2008 election. In July 2008, the average national price for a gallon of unleaded gas was $4.11, and the price for a gallon of diesel was $4.84. At the same time, gas companies continued to report the highest profits in history. For example, Exxon Mobil reported $11.68 billion in profits from total revenues of $138 billion for the second quarter of 2008 (amounting to $1,485.55 a second!). As citizens became outraged, the executive branch's response was that rising prices was due to the general law of supply and demand. Congressional Democrats retorted by issuing a press release in July 2008 stating, "While oil companies are earning record profits and gas prices are soaring, the largest oil companies have invested more resources in stock buybacks than U.S. production."[15] However, Congress did nothing to address the issue beyond forging political debate where one side of the aisle blamed the other for the nation's woes.

College costs constantly increased during the decade leading up to the election. Including tuition, fees, room and board, the average 2008–09 academic year national cost for a private four-year school was $34,132; for an in-state public four-year school, $14,333; and $25,200 for an out-of-state four-year school. The cost of a private school increased 4.8 percent from 2007, 5.7 percent for in-state public schools, and 5.2 percent for public four-year schools.[16] Some students had to drop out of college because they couldn't afford it. Many of those who graduated were in debt for thousands of dollars because of student loans. According to The Project on Student Debt,

> Nationwide, average debt for graduating seniors with loans rose from $18,650 in 2004 to $23,200 in 2008, or about six percent per year. State averages for debt at graduation in 2008 ranged from highs near $30,000 to a low of $13,000. High-debt states are concentrated in the Northeast, while low-debt states are mostly in the West. At the college level, average debt varied even more, from $5,000 to $106,000. Colleges with higher tuition tend to have higher average debt, but there are many examples of high tuition and low average debt, and vice versa.[17]

This was another area many saw ignored by both Democratic and Republican Parties beyond political rhetoric. However, it was an area Obama promised to tackle if elected.

Politically, American mistrust of the government had risen after such incidents as the lack of government action after Hurricane Katrina, when approximately 2000 American citizens died due to a lack of medicine, food, water, and shelter. When the government did finally react, the city of New

Orleans was almost placed under a military and police state; this was "in the face" of all Americans because of national news coverage, and the victims of the disaster were constantly referred to as "refugees." The United States was still fighting two wars, one in Iran and one in Afghanistan, after the events of September 11, 2001. However, the general population was getting weary of these wars and the methods the administration had used to begin and sustain the wars, and wondered how and when the wars would ever end. By the end of 2008, almost 5000 American soldiers had been killed in Iraq and Afghanistan, and approximately four times as many had been wounded. As the number of deceased and wounded soldiers increased and little progress seemed to be made in ending the wars, protests and antiwar sentiment grew dramatically. According to the 2008 poll conducted by the Pew Research Center (2008):

> In Pew's latest national survey, conducted Feb. 20–24 among 1,508 adults, a 54 percent majority said the U.S. made the wrong decision in using military force in Iraq, while 38 percent said it was the right decision. Last March, 49 percent said the decision to go to war was wrong, while 43 percent said it was right. During the third and fourth years of the conflict public opinion on this question was divided, while in the war's first two years clear majorities backed the decision to use force in Iraq. The decrease in support for the decision to go to war has occurred despite a dramatically improved perception of how the effort in Iraq is going. In Pew's latest survey, as many Americans say the military situation in Iraq is going well as say it is not going well (48 percent each). In February 2007, fully two-thirds (67 percent) said the war in Iraq was not going well—the largest percentage expressing this view since the war began. The current division on this question is comparable to public perceptions through most of the second and third years of the conflict, while evaluations turned decidedly negative during the fourth year.[18]

Generally American support was also languishing for suspected terrorists being held in Guantanamo Bay, Cuba; international support for U.S. actions in the Middle East was waning and seen as another example of the United States' use of "cowboy diplomacy"; and the cost of the war was continually escalating.

Youth voters were particularly critical of the war against terrorism. By the 2008 election, over a trillion dollars had been spent with no clear plan in place to end the conflict or at least U.S. involvement. Many political experts saw opposition to the war may have been the primary factor that galvanized youth voting in 2004 and 2008. All of the aforementioned issues led to President George W. Bush losing popularity and having the lowest approval rating of any U.S. president in history except Richard Nixon during Watergate. Bush's approval rating plummeted from a high of almost 90 percent immediately after September 11, 2001, to 22 percent by the time he left office in January 2009.[19] Congress's rating was equally dismal. It fell from approximately 84 percent after September 11, 2001, to under 20 percent in 2008. Obama capitalized on this by pointing out how worse things would get if a Republican again won the election in 2008.[20] This forced contender John McCain and his vice-presidential running mate, Sarah Palin, to dub themselves as mavericks who would also bring about change. However, they failed to convince voters, and particularly failed to sway young voters from voting for Obama.

Obama's anti-establishment stance that questioned the policies that had long been espoused by both Democratic and particularly Republican office holders was directly in line with the attitudes of young voters, who themselves had grown weary of those tainted by being a part of the political establishment. For example, the recession of 2008 was seen as a direct result of policies that allowed large corporations, particularly those associated with the housing market and gas companies, to operate without sufficient government oversight to prevent corruption and unfettered greedy business practices. Wall Street was seen as the enemy of the average American due to deregulatory policies that allowed economically damaging speculation for the benefit of corporate CEOs. This sentiment by young people was accompanied by a distrust of established organizations, both in the private and public sector. Green and Roberts (2012) really highlighted this:

> Obama's campaign communication methods and message appealed to the Millennial's sense of community involvement. Obama seized the opportunity to connect with his generation and younger voters. The Millennial generation is driven by a new set of values and expectations. Schultz (1992) argued this generation manifests a postmodern world view which challenges the very assumptions of the merits of traditional organizational culture. Keough and Tobin (2001) maintained that postmodernism influences most organizations. Key postmodern traits include challenging authority, attacking conventional wisdom, tolerating ambiguity, accepting diversity, and building constructive reality. Consequently, postmodernists find themselves distrustful of institutions and hard facts. These postmodern premises attack the heart of traditional organizations, thus providing an avenue for organizational conflict between leaders and followers.[21]

Obama also took a novel approach to reach youth voters by extensively capitalizing on the use of the Internet. As discussed by Takaragawa and Carty (2012):

Again, the demographics as related to new media were significant to Obama's success. For example, in 2008, two-thirds of Internet users under the age of thirty had a social networking profile, and half of those used social networking sites to get or share information regarding the campaign and to seek out ways to participate. Twenty-seven percent of those ages 18–29 had retrieved campaign information from social networking sites, whereas just four percent of Americans in their thirties and one percent of those ages forty and older got news about the campaign that way. Among respondents under the age of thirty, eight percent said they signed up as a "friend" of one of the candidates on a website compared to three percent for those ages 30–39.[22]

According to Oshyn and Wang (2008):

A recent Harvard poll indicates that the candidates' entrees into technology to woo young voters may not be in vain—at the very least, their target audience is probably getting the message. According to virtually all of the respondents of the poll, who were between the ages of eighteen and twenty-four, the best way to contact them was via the Internet. E-mail was the number one means of access, with 84 percent saying that was the best way to reach them; Facebook came in second for those enrolled in four-year colleges (44 percent); and MySpace was second best for those not in a four-year college (34 percent).[23]

During the presidential campaign, Obama's team established a Web site called VoteForChange.com that not only provided information about his campaign but also voter registration information. After taking office, President Obama established a new Web site called www.barackobama.com. This site posted messages and blogs from the president, such as his weekly address; provided voter information; outlined extensive information on volunteering; allowed users to donate to the Democratic National Convention (DNC); and allowed users to join the site community. It also provided direct links to other Internet sites where information on the president could be found and that were used during his presidential campaign. These included Facebook, MySpace, YouTube, Flickr, Digg, Twitter, Eventful, Linkedin, BlackPlanet, Faithbase, Eons, Glee, MiGente, MyBatanga, AsianAve, and DNC Partybuilder. Even though the Obama campaign used technology extensively, they also found a way to make online communications personal. Jackson, Dorton, and Heindl (2010) highlighted this:

Obama extended and superseded Dean's strategies by using emerging digital media to release new information and form a bond with his supporters, methods that appealed to the youth audience's need to feel special, in-the-know, empowered, and connected. Perhaps the single most striking example of the Obama campaign's use of new media was the announcement of Joe Biden as his running mate, which reached the millions of his supporters in his carefully assembled digital network via text message. In addition to text messaging, the Obama campaign used MySpace, Facebook, and YouTube as tools and models for disseminating vital information directly to the public. Not only did these actions render traditional news media meaningless or irrelevant, they reaffirmed the personal connection between Obama and his supporters when a text message from Barack Obama appeared on their phones. This created a sense of "digital intimacy," the closeness one feels to another person by being near and therefore privy to his or her day-to-day activities and minutiae.[24]

The 2012 presidential election also saw very high youth voter turnout, mostly again due to the personal and political appeal of Obama. As in the 2008, Republicans in 2012 were unable to connect with young voters and again failed to address policies that were most salient to them. As outlined by Lipka (2012):

The Obama campaign deserves particular credit for the youth turnout, said John Delia Volpe, polling director of Harvard's institute. "There's no question that young people had not been nearly as engaged by almost every measure during this campaign cycle relative to four years ago," he said. "The Obama grassroots and mobilization efforts mitigated that." Young people voted overwhelmingly Democratic, with 60 percent for Mr. Obama and 37 percent for Mr. Romney. But the president clearly lost ground over the past four years. In the 2008 election, 66 percent of young voters picked him, as 32 percent did John McCain. As in 2008, the edge young voters gave to Mr. Obama proved decisive in some states. According to Circle, in the battleground states of Florida, Ohio, Pennsylvania, and Virginia, if young people had not voted or if only half of them had supported the president, Mr. Romney would have won. Exit polls published by CNN showed that in some of those states, young people favored Mr. Obama even more than they had four years ago. In Florida, for instance, 66 percent of young people voted for the president, compared with 61 percent in 2008. In Ohio, support for Mr. Obama was up to 63 percent, from 61 percent.[25]

Obama was just as aggressive in seeking youth support in 2012 as he was in 2008. During his reelection campaign, his tour included college campuses across the country. This supported his slogan to continue moving "Forward" and reaffirmed his commitment to the issues deemed most important to youth voters such as the economy and student debt. Some also cited this as a strategy to gain the support of older voters. As Ball (2012) highlighted:

> What Obama's really doing may be more about optics: the symbolic value of all those pictures and video where he's surrounded by fresh-faced, enthusiastic young adults. Every one of those images, and their repetition, drives home his association with the new generation, the future, and the transformative promise of progress—the mantle of hope that he's straining so hard to reclaim after a strenuous, wearing first term. It's of a piece with his new slogan, "Forward," and his campaign's portrayal of Mitt Romney as the candidate of the past. The cheering crowds of young people are there to serve as a stirring, hopeful sight to older voters, whether they're remembering their own youthful aspirations or thinking about the future that awaits their children and grandchildren. And it's an effect Romney can't summon, as evidenced by his appearance at an Ohio college last week: Some students appeared to struggle to remain conscious as Romney delivered a lengthy riff on office supplies.[26]

Obama's support from youth voters continued through his first term of office and during the 2012 general election. According to the Roper Center for Public Opinion Research at Cornell University (2016), 60 percent of those between the ages of 18 and 29 and 52 percent of those between the ages of 30 and 44 supported Obama over his contender Mitt Romney. Romney focused on the failed economy as his major running point, citing that Obama's policies had not succeeded. However, he failed to fully comprehend that American sentiment had not changed in blaming Republicans for the recession of 2008 and the lasting consequences. Republicans were also hampered by the low approval rating of President Bush during his terms prior to Obama's. As a result, Obama still maintained popularity. Jacobson (2013) highlighted this:

> Obama has been at least as divisive, and during the fall of 2012, partisan differences in his approval ratings exceeded Bush's previous all-time high for both an individual Gallup survey and for a quarterly average of Gallup surveys. In the individual survey, 92 percent of Democrats but only 6 percent of Republicans approved of Obama's performance, a difference of 86 points; the maximum for Bush was 83 points (94 percent approval among Republicans, 11 percent among Democrats). In the quarterly average of Gallup surveys, the comparable partisan gap was 81 points for Obama, 79 points for Bush. Party differences in evaluations of presidents always peak during the quarter in which they are on the ballot, presumably because the campaigns stir up partisan sentiments. In this instance, partisan polarization clearly served the President, for the main source of the improved

ratings that finally put Obama above 50 percent was his growing approval among Democrats, which rose from a low of about 77 percent in September 2011 to about 90 percent by the election. He also enjoyed a smaller increase in approval among independents (from 39 percent to 48 percent), while his standing among Republicans dropped from 10 percent to 8 percent.[27]

Romney gained the majority of support for those 45 and older. Robillard expounded further by pointing out:

Obama easily won the youth vote nationally, 67 percent to 30 percent, with young voters proving the decisive difference in Florida, Virginia, Pennsylvania and Ohio, according to an analysis by the Center for Research and Information on Civic Learning and Engagement at Tufts University. Obama won at least 61 percent of the youth vote in four of those states, and if Romney had achieved a 50–50 split, he could have flipped those states to his column, the study said. About half of all eligible people ages 18–29 voted in Tuesday's election, roughly the same level as 2008, according to Peter Levine, the center's director. The youth vote's share of the electorate actually increased slightly from 18 percent to 19 percent. In total, 22 million–23 million young people voted, according to the analysis. Levine and Rock The Vote President Heather Smith both said in a conference call with reporters on Wednesday that increased turnout over presidential elections in 2004, 2008 and 2012 shows high voter turnout is a "new normal" with the millennial generation, compared to less engaged voters in Generation X. In the 1990s, youth turnout was regularly less than 40 percent.[28]

Counter to Obama's direct courting of the youth and minority vote, the Republicans gave the perception they neither understood nor fully cared about the youth vote or the issues most important to them. They still clung to issues such as anti-abortion, no gun control, supporting big businesses, and anti-affirmative action policies. They were also viewed to be heavily influenced by interest groups and lobbyists at the expense of the general electorate. The efforts by Republican congressmen to combat many of Obama's key policies such as affordable health care, reducing college costs, and expanded gay rights also gave the impression Republicans were generally out of touch with current issues and the needs of young voters. Some viewed the Republican Party as being run by dinosaurs in terms of the support of issues that were based on American sentiment decades earlier. As the nation grew more diverse and tolerant, Republicans were supporting issues that seemed at times divisive and intolerant of such demographics as immigrants, women, African Americans, the poor, and the LBGT (lesbian, bisexual, gay, and transgender) community.

Obama's support was greatest among youth because of their diversity and views on the world. They supported many of the issues President Obama did, such as more rights for illegal immigrants, gay marriage and LBGT equality, and health care reform. By sticking to the promises made in both campaigns and then enacting actual policies, Obama also gained youths'. For example, he successfully ended the barring of homosexuals from joining the U.S. military in 2011. As he promised, he successful spearheaded the passing of the Patient Protection and Affordable Care Act (commonly called the Affordable Health Care Act [AHCA]) in 2010. In 2014, he issued an executive order that would grant a temporary reprieve from deportation to millions of undocumented immigrants living in the United States. As a result:

> [h]undreds of Latino activists and families gather[ed] outside of the White House the day after Obama's immigration executive order in Washington on Nov. 21, 2014. . . . The vast majority of Latinos and voters under the age of 35 support President Barack Obama's executive action last Thursday shielding between 4 and 5 million undocumented immigrants from deportation, according to new national polls. The overwhelming support from these two growing demographics may have major implications for voter turnout and party affiliation in 2016. Almost 90 percent of Latino voters say they "support" or "strongly support" Obama's executive action, according to a national poll by Latino Decisions and commissioned by two pro-immigration reform groups, Presente.org and Mi Familia Vota. Nearly three-fourths (72%) of voters under the age of 35 supported the president's action, according to a national poll by Hart Research Associates.[29]

What is remarkable is that Obama maintained the support of the youth, along with minorities, even at the end of his second term in office. This can be attributed to the policies he continued to espouse for both domestic and international issues such as immigration, tolerance, and equal rights for minorities and women. This was seen as an opportunity for Democratic presidential hopeful Hillary Clinton for the 2016 general election, although her support among youth voters was much less than Obama's. As discussed by Lederman (2015):

> Even as the public remains closely divided about his presidency, Barack Obama is holding on to his support from the so-called "Obama coalition" of minorities, liberals and young Americans, an Associated Press-GfK poll shows, creating an incentive for the next Democratic presidential nominee to stick with him and his policies. Hillary Rodham Clinton, by comparison, is viewed somewhat less favorably by the key voting groups whose

record-setting turnout in 2008 propelled Obama to the White House and will be crucial to her own success. Roughly two-thirds of Hispanics view Obama favorably, compared to just over half of Hispanics who say the same about Clinton. Among self-identified liberals, Obama's favorability stands at 87 percent, to Clinton's 72 percent. Half of Americans under the age of 30 view Obama favorably, compared to just 38 percent for his former secretary of state. The findings offer a window into the factors at play as Clinton decides how closely to embrace Obama, his record and his policies in her campaign for president. Although associating herself with Obama could turn off some independent and Republican-leaning voters, electoral math and changing demographics make it critical for Democrats to turn out high numbers of Hispanics, African Americans and young voters.[30]

According to a Gallup Poll, Obama's approval rating among those 18 to 29 years old was 69 percent as of the week of August 8–14, 2016. This is compared to 51 percent overall, 49 percent among those 30 to 49, 49 percent among those 50 to 64, and 42 percent among those over 65.[31]

Obama's influence on youth voting will have very long-term consequences, as he has been a catalyst for them becoming more politically active. This has led to other positive impacts on youth and society. Per Karlos Barrios Marcelo of the Center for Information and Research on Civic Learning and Engagement (CIRCLE) in a speech at the Foreign Press Center Briefing (2008):

This generally means they're probably involved in other activities such as following the news more carefully; maybe having closer ties with certain social groups. This is good in general because young people, what we find in the research, when they're tied to these kind of social organizations and public institutions, they have lower rates of high school dropout; there's lower violence and teen crime; there's lower pregnancy rates; so all around it's good for young people to be involved in the sort of civic part of society. And having an increasing voter turn rate is a good sign that some of that is going on right now.[32]

The support from young voters will be a major part of the legacy of President Obama. What remains to be seen is whether the Democratic Party will be able to capitalize on this support over the coming decades. To do so, candidates will have to remain technologically savvy in their communication with young voters, speak to issues that young voters are most concerned, but also pass policies to support their promises. Unlike any other time in history, young voters are now becoming more politically savvy and involved in the political process. Campaign promises alone with not be enough to retain their support.

Notes

1. Franceschi, 2009.
2. Von Drehle, 2008a.
3. Kennedy, 1961.
4. Alex-Assensoh, 2008, p. 237.
5. Rock the Vote, 2008.
6. Von Drehle, 2008a.
7. Von Drehle, 2008b.
8. Fisher, 2010, p. 296.
9. Marcelo and Kirby, 2008.
10. Rizga, 2008.
11. CNNPolitics.com, 2008.
12. Blades, 2008.
13. Starks, 2009.
14. Ibid.
15. Hargreaves, 2008.
16. Musante, 2008.
17. Reed and Cheng, 2009.
18. Pew Research Center, 2008.
19. CBS News, 2009.
20. Newport, 2012.
21. Green and Roberts, 2012, pp. 15–16.
22. Takaragawa and Carty, 2012, p. 78.
23. Oshyn and Wang, 2008.
24. Jackson, Dorton, and Heindl, 2010, p. 44.
25. Lipka, 2012.
26. Ball, 2012.
27. Jacobson, 2013, p. 6.
28. Robillard, 2012.
29. Edwards, 2014.
30. Lederman, 2015.
31. Gallup, 2016.
32. Marcelo, 2008.

Bibliography

Alex-Assensoh, Yvette M. "Change and the 2008 American Presidential Election," *Politicka Misao: Croatian Political Science Review* 45(2008): 235–243.

Ball, Molly. "The Optics of Obama's Youth Appeal." *The Atlantic*, May 4, 2012, http://www.theatlantic.com/politics/archive/2012/05/the-optics-of-obamas-youth-appeal/256748/.

Blades, Meteor. "Youth Voter Turnout Up, But Fails to Break '72 Record." *Daily Kos*, November 5, 2008, http://www.dailykos.com/story/2008/11/05/654938/.

"Bush's Final Approval Rating: 22 Percent." CBS News. January 16, 2009. 2016, http://www.cbsnews.com/news/bushs-final-approval-rating-22-percent/.

CNNPolitics.com, "Election Center 2008", November 17, 2008, http://www.cnn.com/ELECTION/2008/.

Edwards, Haley S. "Latinos, Young Voters Applaud Obama Action On Immigration, Polls Show." Time.Com, November 24, 2014. http://time.com/3602711/latinos-youth-immigration-action-polls/.

Fisher, Patrick. "The Age Gap in the 2008 Presidential Election." *Society*, 47(2010): 295–300.

Franceschi, Jela De. "Democrats Mobilize America's Youth Vote." *Voice of America* (November 1, 2009), http://www.voanews.com/a/a-13-2008-04-10-voa34/340098.html.

Gallup. Presidential Job Approval Center (2016). http://www.gallup.com/poll/124922/presidential-job-approval-center.aspx.

Green, Darryl, and Gary E. Roberts. "Transformational Leadership in a Postmodern World: The Presidential Election of Barack Obama." *Academy of Strategic Management Journal*, 11(2012): 9–25.

Jackson, Kathy M., Harold Dorton, and Brett Heindl. "A Celebration That Defined a Generation: Grant Park, New Media, and Barack Obama's Historic Victory of the US Presidency." *Journal of American Culture*, 33(2010): 40–51.

Jacobson, Gary C. "How the Economy and Partisanship Shaped the 2012 Presidential and Congressional Elections." *Political Science Quarterly*, 128(2013): 1–38.

Kennedy, John F. "Inaugural Address of President John F. Kennedy," January 20, 1961, Washington, DC. John F. Kennedy Presidential Library and Museum, https://www.jfklibrary.org/Research/Research-Aids/Ready-Reference/JFK-Quotations/Inaugural-Address.aspx.

Lederman, Josh. "Minorities, young Americans still support Obama, poll finds." PBS Newshour, July 17, 2015. http://www.pbs.org/newshour/rundown/minorities-young-americans-still-support-obama-poll-finds/.

Lipka, Sara. "Defying Expectations, Half of Young Voters Cast Ballots, 60 percent for Obama." *Chronicle of Higher Education*, 59(2012): A4.

Marcelo, Karlos Barrios. "Youth Vote 2008." Foreign Press Centers, U.S. Department of State. October 28, 2008. https://2002-2009-fpc.state.gov/111368.htm.

Marcelo, Karlo Barrios, and Emily Hoban Kirby. *Quick Facts about U.S. Young Voters: The Presidential Election Year 2008*. Medford, Massachusetts: The Center for Information and Research on Civic Learning and Engagement, 2008.

Musante, Kenneth. "College costs rise," CNNMoney (October 29, 2008). http://money.cnn.com/2008/10/29/pf/college/college/index.htm.

Newport, Frank. "Congress Approval Ties All-Time Low at 10 percent," Gallup, August 14, 2012. http://www.gallup.com/poll/156662/congress-approval-ties-time-low.aspx.

Oshyn, Kristen, and Tova Andrea Wang. "Youth Vote 2008." The Century Foundation Issue Brief (2008). http://www.whatkidscando.org/youth_on_the_trail_2012/pdf/Century%20Foundation_2008%20youthvote.pdf.

Pew Research Center. "Public Attitudes Toward the War in Iraq: 2003–2008," March 19, 2008. http://www.pewresearch.org/2008/03/19/public-atti tudes-toward-the-war-in-iraq-20032008/.

Reed, Matthew, and Diane Cheng. *Student Debt and the Class of 2008*. The Project on Student Debt (December 2009). http://ticas.org/sites/default/files/pub_ files/classof2008.pdf.

Rizga, Kristina. "Getting Out the (Rest of the) Youth Vote." *The Nation* (July 7, 2008). https://www.thenation.com/article/getting-out-rest-youth-vote/.

Robillard, Kevin. "Study: Youth vote was decisive." Politico, November 7, 2012. http://www.politico.com/story/2012/11/study-youth-vote-was-decisive-083510.

Rock the Vote! "Young Voter Turnout 2008—Primaries and Caucuses" (June 4, 2008). http://www.rockthevote.com/assets/publications/electronic-press -kit/young-voter-turnout-in-the.pdf.

Roper Center for Public Opinion Research, "How Groups Voted in 2012." Ithaca, New York: Cornell University, 2016. http://ropercenter.cornell.edu/polls/ us-elections/how-groups-voted/how-groups-voted-2012/.

Starks, Glenn L. *The Galvanization of the Young Vote in the 2008 Presidential Election: Lessons Learned from the Phenomenon*. Lanham, Maryland: University Press of America, 2009.

Takaragawa, Stephanie, and Victoria Carty. "The 2008 U.S. Presidential Election and New Digital Technologies: Political Campaigns as Social Movements and the Significance of Collective Identity." *Tamara Journal For Critical Organization Inquiry*, 10(2012): 73–89.

Von Drehle, David. "Person of the Year 2008: Why History Can't Wait." *Time*, December 17, 2008a. http://www.time.com/time/specials/2008/person oftheyear/article/0,31682,1861543_1865068,00.html.

Von Drehle, David. "The Year of the Youth Vote." *Time*, January 31, 2008b. http:// content.time.com/time/magazine/article/0,9171,1708836,00.html.

CHAPTER SIX

New Definitions of Progressivism in the Age of Obama

Linda D. Tomlinson

Ever since Barack Hussein Obama took the oath of office as the 44th president of the United States of America in January 2008, scholars, pundits, naysayers, and the like have scampered to come up with new concepts, terms, and paradigms to associate with one of the most historic events in modern times. The first person of African descent to be elected to the highest office in United States politics certainly gave cause for interpretation, speculation, and evaluation. Immediately, the media announced that America was now in a "postracial" society. This declaration came before Obama was given the opportunity to act in any official presidential capacity. The fact that the ultimate ceiling established during a bygone era of Jim Crow policies and procedures had been ameliorated caused Americans not only to celebrate victoriously but also to believe prematurely that all the country's racial problems had miraculously dissipated. Unfortunately, America was no more in a postracial society after Obama's election than South Africa was in a post-apartheid society when Nelson Mandela took office as its first black president. President Obama's ascendancy to the presidency is a mere crack in a pervasive, tightly knit web of race, class, and gender oppression in a nation which prides itself on equalitarian ideals embedded within its founding documents. What the Obama presidency did do was to precipitate renewed thinking about a new trajectory for the U.S. in the 21st century. Could this be the catalyst for a new progressivism for American politics? Historically, the progressive period occurred during times of perceived prosperity and growth. These times allow individuals to think about reforming outdated or inappropriate policies, restructuring organizations and institutions to be more inclusive, and revitalizing society for the maximum benefit of the citizens. Although Obama's election came at a time when the country was undergoing a serious economic recession resulting from the housing bubble burst, the meltdown of Wall Street financial entities, and stagnation in the U.S. automobile industry, the new president promised to bring change that the American people could believe in. For many Americans, the possibility of this kind of change appeared as a specter of a new kind of progressivism emerging. To understand how Obama's election and presidency has changed the American political landscape, we need to examine how these events have impacted ideas of progressivism. Progressivism is used here in a relatively broad sense to include actions, formal or informal, taken to affect change of government, community, or society for the betterment of the people. Throughout the last 50 years, different ideas about progressivism have arisen, mainly resulting from the technological changes occurring in the world. Individuals developed these new definitions of progressivism based on the political, economic, and social contexts they found themselves in. The election of the first president of African descent is one of those contextual circumstances. Therefore, this essay focuses on the Obama election and presidency as a catalyst in creating a landscape amenable for new definitions of progressivism to develop and flourish. Its purpose is to suggest a framework for analyzing new definitions of progressivism during the Obama presidency and beyond.

On the surface, electing a seemingly unconventional persona like Barack Obama to the presidency signaled a significant and radical change for the United States. Historically, periods of economic crisis or social upheavals are followed by reform, restructuring, and revitalization in society. Therefore, it is understandable that reform movements were prevalent during the industrial and post-industrial periods, and their adamant advocates were white, educated, middle-class men and women. These progressives were not radical in the sense that they did not vehemently advocate for the overthrow of capitalism, but instead chose to reform it to weed out corruption, make it more effective, and provide a safety net for those less fortunate.[1] This was the paradigm for the earlier progressive movement. In 2016, many ideas about reform are more radical in context and do, in some circles, include the overthrow of the corporate, capitalist system that has dominated in this period of globalization. Obama came into office with an agenda that was attractive to those who believed in more radical changes. Ideas such as enacting an Affordable Health Care Act, bringing the country out of an economic recession, keeping America safe against terrorists such as Osama bin Laden, creating positive global alliances and enacting trans-Pacific trade partners, and acting more morally responsively to our military are the very ideas that Americans found refreshing and progressive. This kind of ethos has not been evident in American society for quite some time. Since the original progressive period in the United States, the country has evolved from ideologies of conformism, liberalism, radicalism, optimism, and conservatism to feelings of pessimism and apathy.

After the restrictive conformism of the 1950s and the turbulent radical revolutions of the 1960s, the country braced for what would come in the following decades. Progressivism as defined in the earlier decades did not fit with the realities of the 1970s and beyond. During the years after 1969, identifying a coherent political, economic, and social agenda became difficult because of various interests marinating in the American landscape. Peter Filene "attacked the whole notion of a coherent progressive movement as a semantic and conceptual muddle, and declared it dead and buried."[2] If one analyzes the earlier progressive movement through a lens of coherency, it would be easy to write its obituary in a decade full of rapid changes. Daniel T. Rodgers aptly characterizes the progressive movement as a shifting era that was ideologically fluid and involved in issue-focused coalitions.[3] Similar conditions of ideological fluidity, competing multifaceted interest groups and changing technology exist for American citizens today.

In an age of social networking, Twitter feeds, snapchatting, and Instagram, the American citizenry was open for "change." Our lives exist in a constant state of change: information is relayed instantaneously; vast improvement in transportation technology makes national boundaries less daunting; and virtual communication creates opportunities for better global understanding. This is the kind of scenario that catapulted Barack Obama's mantra, "change you can believe in," into the political stratosphere. Here was an individual who not only spoke the rhetoric of technology but became a walking advertisement for technology. Obama frequently used his Blackberry and, eventually, iPhone in public, incorporated the Internet into his initial and reelection campaigns, and developed a useful rapport with the Gen X and millennial generations). Obama's pervasive use of new media was not missed by the Gen Xers and millennials, who also equated the phenomenon as progressive in their parlance. Here was a candidate who deviated from the traditional nuances of campaigning and ventured out into the world new media (it was as if the Lone Ranger reported for duty on the Enterprise).[4] Of course effective communication is vital to the success of any presidential candidate, but Obama's willingness to emerge himself into the new media and his obvious comfortableness with it indicated to some voters that he was a man of the times. Obama gave the impression of "I can be empathetic because, see, I'm just like you!" Modern voters must feel that candidates and leaders can connect with the citizenry, the people. Barack Obama presented as that type of presidential candidate in 2008 and 2012. Barack Obama's use of new media in his campaigns is not the only characteristic of a new progressivism. The ability of an action to affect and/or influence future actions is also indicative of progressivism.

Barack Obama's 2008 presidential campaign forever changed the way presidential campaigns were developed and managed. It was not only his use of the Internet and other 2.0 Web technologies but also the way the campaign raised money, how it garnered free advertising and broadened and connected to its support pool. Donations of small amounts ($5) from millions of Internet and social media contacts quickly created a substantial campaign chest. Voters, especially the Gen Xers and millennials, were very appreciative of the thank-you texts sent to them.[5] I suspect scholars will examine and analyze Obama's conscious effort to utilize the new technology in his campaign and presidency and the impact that decision has had on future campaigns.

In 2009, Obama outlined his presidency's agenda for his department heads and the American people. The change that he'd promised during the election was about to evolve from rhetoric to reality. Obama promised a "commitment to transparent, participatory, and collaborative government and making a strong link between these principles and public goods such as democracy, accountability, efficiency, effectiveness."[6] It is clear that the president hoped for a different interaction between the citizenry and its leaders. Although this is not the first time in history that an executive has offered the idea of transparency in his administration, it is the first time in history that the available technology could facilitate transparency being a reality.

The whole idea of an open government based on the technological advances available in society can be construed as progressive, especially when governments tend to reveal to the public only information it thinks relevant to the well-being of the people. This institutional behavior has engendered the general mistrust of government by the citizenry. Initially, the Obama administration seemed as if it wanted to change this mistrust scenario. In an additional memorandum on the Freedom of Information Act, the president declared that the act should be "administered with a clear presumption: In the face of doubt, openness prevails."[7] Time and intense scholarly scrutiny will decide if this assumption prevailed. Openness in government administration was only one of the lofty ideals of the Obama administration. Tackling the issue of health care in the United States was part and parcel of the change promised to the American people.

Barack Obama is not the only president in United States history who was concerned about and attempted to deal with the idea of universal health coverage. During the original progressive era, Theodore Roosevelt supported health insurance because he felt that an unhealthy nation is antithetical to a powerful nation. However, most of his work for reform on this issue occurred outside of government, in the private sector. Under Franklin Delano Roosevelt, attempts at better health insurance were included in other New Deal policies and programs. However, resistance came not only from the commercial insurance industry but also from organized labor. The issue of health care finally came to the forefront after the death of FDR, when Harry Truman gave it special attention. Truman was committed to a single universal comprehensive health insurance plan. Unfortunately, compulsory health insurance got lost in the Cold War politics of that time. Under Lyndon Johnson, Medicare and Medicaid legislation was signed into law in 1965 as part of his Great Society agenda. Baby boomers remember Bill Clinton assigning health care to First Lady Hillary Rodham Clinton. Hillary Clinton was not able to bring about a universal health care change for the nation. Historically, presidential administrations have failed to get universal health care into the American context. There was a plethora of reasons behind those failed attempts: class structure influences, ideological differences, the corporate capitalistic character of the American medical professions, dependency issues, and ideas about social responsibility. These issues and others prevented the leaders and/or government from creating an effective, viable, and sustainable universal health care system. The Obama administration came in with the intention to aggressively tackle the health care issue once and for all. Based on the noble attempts of past presidents, Obama's new determination appeared ambitious and progressive in many circles.

In the words of Obama, "Our health care crisis isn't just a problem for those worried about their coverage; it places a growing burden on the rest of us. . . . The Obama-Biden health care plan will provide affordable and accessible health coverage for every American by building on the current insurance system and leaving Medicare intact for older and disabled Americans."[8] This statement is the basis for the aggressive fight that President

Obama put up for the Affordable Health Care Act (AHCA). On March 23, 2010, President Obama signed comprehensive health care reform, the Patient Protection and Affordable Care Act, into law. Although this act has been challenged numerous times for its unconstitutionality, it remains one of the most impressive and progressive acts of the Obama administration. Opponents of this historic piece of legislation will, no doubt, continue to challenge it and/or attempt to chip away at its most significant components. The main components of that legislation that make it progressive in nature are its overall expansion of access of coverage; the requirement to have coverage; and the requirement to offer coverage. These elements make the Affordable Health Care Act tantamount to socialized medicine for some Americans and thus hark back to one of the obstacles to universal health care in the past: ideological differences. The Obama administration was temporarily successful in surmounting those roadblocks of class, ideology, industry, and labor. Furthermore, the legislation was passed by Congress, albeit by a narrow margin, and upheld by the Supreme Court of the United States. During 2015, in a 6–3 decision the Supreme Court upheld that the Affordable Health Care Act authorized federal tax credits for eligible Americans living not only in states with their own exchanges but also in the 34 states with federal marketplaces.[9] "Congress passed the Affordable Health Care Act to improve health insurance markets, not to destroy them. If at all possible we must interpret the Act in a way that is consistent with the former, and avoids the latter."[10] Even the sentiments of conservative Chief Justice Roberts are characteristic of progressive thinking and action, and indicate that progressivism is not the sole ownership of one political party. This ruling stamped a piece of Obama administration legislation with more than just a seal of judiciary approval; it also made it difficult for future legislators to get rid of it. Although Republicans generally discount the ruling, they are clearly aware that it will be harder for future presidents to reverse the interpretations of the Court. The AHCA will be become one of those progressive acts of a presidential administration that may face perpetual challenges but will find dogmatic support from among the citizenry, much like Roosevelt's Social Security Act. This is a perfect example of the Obama administration's policy actions creating an amenable climate for new definitions of progressivism to flourish. As during the Great Depression, when unemployment and lack of safety nets influenced the American population's notions of "social security," in a present-day landscape, where many Americans were uninsured because of unaffordability, unemployment, and medical insurability, health care legislation seemed possible. Even when there were clear indicators of resistance on the radar of congressional and public opinion, Barack

Obama saw a glimmer of possibility for successful passage and decided to take the risk. This trope of risk taking clearly runs through his *Audacity of Hope* and should have been a window into the mindset of this president for anyone reading it.

Another area where the Obama presidency affected new ideas of progressivism is in his economic policies. As Barack Obama became the 44th president of the United States, he also entered office at a time when the U.S. economy was teetering on the edge of a precipice (ready to tumble off). The year 2008 was a very precarious economic year, and the future years didn't appear to hold a rosier picture. The Great Recession of 2007–08 started with the bursting of an $8 trillion housing bubble that caused people to stop spending. Loss of consumer spending and fluctuations in the market precipitated stagnation in investment spending. All this stagnation leads to companies downsizing, creating high unemployment figures. To summarize this economic crisis, the United States economy found itself in a deficit web. The Economic Policy Institute puts the situation in plain terms: "In 2008 and 2009, the U.S. labor market lost 8.4 million jobs, or 6.1% of all payroll employment. This was the most dramatic employment contraction (by far) of any recession since the Great Depression."[11] Enter Barack Obama and his ideas about how to work through these economic obstacles. Like his democratic predecessor Roosevelt, Obama's various programs were intended to impact the maximum number of Americans.

The factual reality of Obama's recovery programs is that 14.1 million jobs were added; unemployment peaked at 10 percent in 2010 and then dropped to only 4.9 percent, and his economic growth was about 2 percent annually. On occasion, Obama delivered a bull market for stocks, and home prices finally began to recover. Oil production reached a 43 percent high for America, making gasoline prices very cheap, which Americans love.[12] Along with these positive results from Obama's economic policies, there were also some negative indicators that must be identified as well.

The average American expected to be much better off financially than reality has presented. Wages have remained stagnate, with increases miniscule and far between; higher education remains expensive and leaves many of its partakers in debt after graduation; and the national debt continues to soar. Racial and gender inequality persists, and a burgeoning cadre of unemployed teens threaten the social, political, and economic fabric of American society. Therefore, the dreams of total economic recovery were no more a reality for President Obama than they were for President Roosevelt. Obama's policies helped to bring the American economy back from the precipice of that economic cliff mentioned earlier, but they did not provide America with the kind of economic scenario present at the end of the Clinton administration in the 1990s. Of course, in his ascendancy to the presidency in 1992, Bill Clinton was not faced with the kind of crises that Barack Obama faced in 2009. Both Presidents Roosevelt and Obama acted in progressive ways to remedy the economic cards dealt to them, in order to improve the lives of the American people. Their reform agendas targeted the broadest swatch of individuals as possible, not a small subset or interest group.

New definitions of progressivisms must include more inclusive ideological paradigms than in the past. The progressive era of the 1920s, 1930s, and 1940s concerned itself with a specific group, such as the poor, the immigrant, or the sick. However, new definitions of progressive behavior seem to take on new characteristics. Progressivism today seems to imply reform or restructuring of a larger segment of American society. Interventions to reform health care or the economy are indicative of the new definitions about progress as a nation. In that same vein, reforming and developing new global diplomatic relationships also marks the Obama presidency as engendering a landscape for these new definitions to flourish.

Not separate from his economic agenda, Obama wished to create a different type of dialog among world powers. If some reasonable and normal standards for critiquing Obama's foreign policy are applied, one might conclude that he has done acceptably well, especially when weighed against his defined agenda. Obama's foreign policy included promises "to mend the West's breach with the Islamic world, repair the nation's image abroad, reset relations with Russia, move toward a world free of nuclear weapons, avoid 'stupid wars' while winning the 'right war,' combat climate change, and to do all this with a post-partisan style of leadership that brought Americans themselves together in the process."[13] This is indeed a very progressive, if not ambitious, undertaking for any president, let alone the first African American executive. Included in this foreign policy agenda, though not specifically stated, was a need to change the way the United States did business globally. Of course, tough rhetoric about climate change and repairing the American image globally can be directly linked to with whom and how we choose to do business with our foreign counterparts (i.e., China, Russia, the European Union).

Obama's lofty foreign policy expectations were seemingly in sync with the expectations of world leaders and their nations, especially those in the Western world. No sooner did he take the oath of office, and before he could engage in any real activities that would indicate his true stance for his foreign policy agenda, the world selected him to receive the Nobel Peace Prize. Examining these high expectations, one might tend to expect failure or at least a high degree of disappointment from advocates and critics alike. As with all progressive actions throughout history, those criticisms of policies to support the agenda exacerbated each day that Obama remained in office. The media seemed poised to be the first to announce any glitch or delay involved with foreign policy issues. Despite this climate of constant criticism and intricate teasing out of details, Obama stayed his course, remained disciplined in his foreign policy dealings, and refrained from losing sight of the big picture. He kept his eyes on the prize and remained calm, cool, and collected under pressure. His resolute and calm demeanor was evident in his plan to take out Osama bin Laden. When this event happened, most of the "regular" world had no idea that this issue was an Obama priority.

Some critics have lamented Obama's "restraint" character in foreign policy, even laying the blame of America's weakness at his feet. Although the status of America's position in the world is relative to whoever is commenting at the time, there is a prevailing belief among some sectors that the nation has lost its dominance (that it is weak). The Obama presidency cannot be characterized as acting with total restraint. Several nonpeaceful actions have been taken by his administration. Besides Osama bin Laden, other leaders have been taken out under this administration, such as Gaddafi in Libya and other high-ranking al Qaeda and ISIL leadership. When he came into office, he inherited two counterterrorism programs from George W. Bush: the rendition and harsh interrogation of terrorist suspects and the use of drone strikes to kill terror suspects outside of the United States. He signed Executive Order 13491, ensuring lawful interrogations, but decided to continue and even exacerbate the use of drones in the fight on terror.[14] Obama's legacy includes his embrace and expansion of drone technology. His use of drones outdistances that of his predecessor, George W. Bush.[15] One wonders if the Obama administration considers striking a target at a distance to make the action more humane and in line with his reformed American image around the world. Is this a more progressive national behavior? This question and its answer must be part of the discussions surrounding new definitions of progressivism.

On another side of the story, the Obama administration has worked to secure what it feels are good trade policy agreements for the nation. Primary on the list for discussion in terms of its progressive character would be the Trans-Pacific Partnership (TPP). This agreement is supposed to support more well-paying American jobs, strengthen the middle-class and advance both our interests and values abroad. Furthermore, its advocates claim it will put focus on America's small businesses to access tools that will help them to export effectively and efficiently. It supposed to put disciplines on state-owned businesses in order to create a level playing field between them and private enterprise. In a bold progressive move, it tackles the digital economy by ensuring a continued free and open Internet. President Obama said that the TPP would advance "middle-class economics—the idea that the country does best when everyone has got a fair shot, everyone is doing their fair share, everybody is playing by the same rules."[16] The president truly feels that if the U.S. does not act on this agreement, that other nations who do not share our values (i.e. China) will step in and fill the void.

Despite what is presented as a progressive administrative move, the TPP has garnered substantial criticism as well. First, many in the American population have not heard of the Trans-Pacific Partnership—they simply do not know what it is. This is not a new phenomenon for progressive policies or legislation. Historically and today, some people are too caught up in their own daily survival game. They do not have the luxury or the inclination to stay attuned to all the political sound bites occurring around them. Unlike in the past, there is more to distract and confuse the American citizenry today than in the earlier progressive era. The instantaneous access to information, although on the one hand a progressive step, can cause an "overload" scenario for some individuals. Whereas physical exhaustion was one of the distractors for industrial-age workers, today individuals are occupied with their smart devices to a level unheard of a century ago. Most of that occupation centers on entertainment as opposed to information gathering. The average citizen is not going to discuss the TPP at the dinner table, if indeed he or she even sits down to a dinner table.

The TPP has been in development for over a decade, and yet it has remained pretty obscure from the American public. Why? That is the nature of the beast (American politics). Therefore, only bits and pieces of this very important trade policy have been made available to the public for their knowledge and criticism. With the rise of rogue venues such as WikiLeaks, more restricted and/or classified information is being leaked more frequently. For example, information from WikiLeaks concerning intellectual property and environmental regulations has caused some Internet privacy rights advocates, labor unions, and environmentalists worried about the implications of TPP. There is a real concern on the part of Internet Service Providers (ISPs) that they will be forced to police their users' access. These are concerns that must be taken into account, considering technological advancements in this age. Progressive policies must be in sync with the reality of ever-changing technological advancements; those policies cannot impede technological progress. The Obama presidency was not ignorant of the nuances and complexities involved here. The administration disclosed an outline of its goals for the Trans-Pacific

Partnership agreement to assuage such groups as the Sierra Club, the World Wildlife Fund, National Resources Defense Council, and big labor—the AFL-CIO.

Organizations that support global health and believe in climate change also have their concerns about the progressiveness of TPP. Some nations feel that the agreement infringes on the idea of national sovereignty. Additionally, proponents feel that the agreement's language does not do enough to address curtailment of fossil-fuel usage. Jane Kowalski, policy director for climate change group 350.org states, "The agreement would give fossil-fuel companies the extraordinary ability to sue local governments that try to keep fossil fuels in the ground."[17] These kinds of extra-political concerns are part of the landscape in which new definitions of progressivism must develop and flourish. Not only does the political, economic, and social environment impact the kind of responsive policies the Obama administration engaged in, those same responsive policies affect how Americans define progressivism.

In conclusion, Barack Obama came into office as the 44th president of the United States with a mandate given to him by the people. That mandate was based on his campaign promise of "change you can believe in." The American people were ripe for change. They were stoked for the possibility of a new America that was more inclusive, more equitable, more gender respectful—an America morally and ethically in tune with the ideals embedded in their Declaration of Independence and the U.S. Constitution. President Obama not only viscerally indicated the possibility of change, his rhetoric and demeanor exuded that possibility also. For many, his presidency was to be the turning point for this nation whose past was infused with exclusion, inequality, racism, sexism, classicism, and corruption within its institutions. On the one hand, the expectations some Americans placed on his presidency were unprecedented, and on the other hand, so were the kind of hatred and vitriol executed against that same presidency. The Obama presidency will be intricately examined and analyzed in ways other presidencies have not been. These examinations will not be solely to tease out his legacy but also to understand where the American trajectory was during that time. We all have ideas about what it means to be on a progressive trajectory, ideas influenced by our personal experiences and our ideological frameworks. Although in some eyes, Obama engaged in an ambitious economic, social, and foreign policy agenda, it was the type of agenda necessary to bring about the change he promised during his campaign. However ambitious his policies were, they could not have been implemented if the political, social, and economic environment had not been amenable to change. Concomitantly, although his policies feed off the environmental circumstances, new ideas about progressive politics developed and flourished. Whether these new definitions of progressivism survive will depend on the American people.

Notes

1. Maier-Sarti, 2016, p. 56.
2. Filene, 1970.
3. Rodgers, 1982.
4. "The 2008 campaign was the first national campaign in which traditional media such as television, radio, and newspapers were overshadowed by new media technologies and the Internet" (Hendricks and Denton Jr., 2010, p. ix).
5. Cain Miller, 2008.
6. Obama, 2008.
7. Ibid.
8. Obama-Biden Plan, 2008.
9. de Vogue and Diamond, 2015.
10. Barnes, 2015.
11. "The Great Recession," 2016.
12. Long, 2016.
13. Indyk, Lieberthal, and O'Hanlon, 2013.
14. Obama, 2009.
15. President Bush authorized approximately 50 drone strikes that killed 296 terrorists and 197 civilians in Yemen, Pakistan, and Somalia. President Obama 506 drone strikes, killing 3040 terrorists and 391 civilians. According to Micah Zenko, this is an attempt on the part of the Obama administration to normalize the practice of using drone strikes. See Zenko, 2016.
16. Obama, 2016.
17. Kowalski, 2015.

Bibliography

Barnes, Robert. "Affordable Care Act Survives Supreme Court Challenge." *Washington Post*. Courts and Law section, June 25, 2015. https://www.washingtonpost.com/politics/courts_law/obamacare-survives-supreme-court-challenge/2015/06/25/af87608e-188a-11e5-93b7-5eddc056ad8a_story.html.

Cain Miller, Claire. "How Obama's Internet Campaign Changed Politics," *New York Times*, November 7, 2008. https://bits.blog.nytimes.com/2008/11/07/how-obamas-internet-campaign-changed-politics/?_r=0.

de Vogue, Ariane, and Jeremy Diamond. "Supreme Court Saves Obamacare." *CNN Politics*, June 25, 2015.

Filene, Peter G. "An Obituary for 'The Progressive Movement.'" *American Quarterly* 22 (1970): 20–34.

"The Great Recession." *The State of Working America.* The Economic Policy Institute. http://stateofworkingamerica.org/great-recession/. Accessed August 2, 2016.

Hendricks, John Allen, and Robert E. Denton Jr., eds. *Communicator-in-Chief: How Barack Obama Used New Media Technology to Win the White House.* New York: Rowman and Littlefield, 2010.

Indyk, Martin S., Kenneth G. Lieberthal, and Michal O'Hanlon. "Bending History: Barack Obama's Foreign Policy." Brookings Institute, September 4, 2012.

Kowalski, Jane. policy director for climate change, https://350.org/press-release/350-org-tpp-text-confirms-a-handout-to-fossil-fuels/.

Long, Heather. "Key Truths about the Obama Economy." *CNNMoney,* July 28, 2016.

Maier-Sarti, Wendy. "From Progressivism to the 1920s." *Annual Editions: United States History, Vol. 2: Reconstruction through the Present.* New York: McGraw Hill Education, 2016.

Obama, Barack. "Memorandum for the Heads of Executive Departments and Agencies on Transparency and Open Government." Office of Management and Budget. December 8, 2008. http://www.whitehouse.gov/the_press_office/TransparencyandOpenGovernment.

Obama, Barack. Executive Order #13491, Ensuring Lawful Interrogations. White House. January 22, 2009.

Obama, Barack. "The Trans-Pacific Partnership: What You Need to Know About President Obama's Trade Agreement." https://www.whitehouse.gov/issues/economy/trade. Accessed October 28, 2016.

Obama-Biden Plan. *Journal of American Medicine Association (JAMA)* 3000(16) October 22/29, 2008.

Rodgers, Daniel T. 1982. "In Search of Progressivism." *Reviews in American History* 10(4) December: 113–132. The Johns Hopkins University Press.

Zenko, Michael. "Obama's Embracing Drone Strikes Will Be a Lasting Legacy." *New York Times,* January 12, 2016. http://www.nytimes.com/roomfordebate/2016/01/12/reflecting-on-obamas-presidency/obamas-embrace-of-drone-strikes-will-be-a-lasting-legacy.

CHAPTER SEVEN

You Can't Call That Mentoring: The Fallacy of Mentoring in Obama's My Brother's Keeper

Torie Weiston-Serdan and Arash Daneshzadeh

Jordan, an assured and strident Black youth, excitedly enters a room full of young Black men. The room is bustling, full of movement and full of a palpable eagerness. Much of this eagerness comes from the fact that all of the young men in the room have been specially selected to experience a "day of mentoring" from two of the community's most lauded celebrities. In addition, the day is meant to begin a yearlong program of mentoring that the school district is implementing in conjunction with President Obama's My Brother's Keeper initiative. Jordan isn't sure how this will be different from what he's seen before, but he knows that the first Black president of his country is pushing it, and he is hoping that this is an opportunity for his voice and the voices of people like him to be heard. Jordan, a 16-year-old living in urban America, has had his fair share of mentoring experiences. Most of them are similar to the event he is eager to attend now, but with much less fanfare. These mentoring days, often headed by local community groups or educators, bring a group of adult "experts" in to inspire and motivate the young people in the room. Typically very boring and often quite presumptuous, the adults stand in front of large groups of "needy" and "at-risk" youth and offer life advice. Although

Jordan isn't entirely sure what these terms mean, he knows that they are often imposed on him and mostly by folks outside of his community. The advice typically includes "focus on your work"; "perform well in school"; "listen to your teachers"; "your grades are important"; "your test scores are important"; "make sure you present yourself well"; "pull up your pants"; "learn how to tie a tie"; and other pieces of advice these adults think youth might find useful. Most often these mentoring days end with pictures of the adults helping young people to tie a tie and a group picture that proves they helped such a needy group. Jordan is hoping that today's experience isn't like the other days of mentoring he has had to endure. Jordan has a community mentor he has been matched with by the local community center. They meet weekly but mostly talk about Jordan's school performance. Jordan likes his mentor but doesn't feel all that connected to him, and he wishes he could have conversations with him about deeper issues. It seems the meetings are so wrapped up in making sure that Jordan stays out of trouble and "school talk" that it leaves little room to discuss anything else. And Jordan has questions; he has concerns; he has fears; he is angry about the condition of his neighborhood; so on and so forth.

Given that today's mentoring experience will be full of celebrity, Jordan is hoping to get some real advice and answers to some of his most pressing questions. He even prepared a list of questions he might ask should he be called upon. He is particularly eager to hear about how the two celebrities "mentoring" them for the day have been able to become so successful. As two thriving Black men, who appear to have personal, professional, and financial success, Jordan is hoping to learn more about what he should do to rise to the level of prominence he wants for himself. He has heard the basics before, understands the conversations about grades and such, but he is looking for something else. He wants to learn how to overcome the challenges facing him as a young Black man, how he too can thrive, how he might be able to feel whole and happy when so much is working against him. Jordan has been on this search for as early as he can remember. Since the age of 10, he recounts being less connected to teachers, less interested in academic lessons and more targeted by his school. Jordan is academically bright and capable, and knows this but seems unable to connect his interests to the content presented in his classrooms and often gets bored. Jordan has always dreamed of being an audio engineer. He is obsessed with acoustics, sound, space, and musical gadgets. He studies to understand how sound travels and in different spaces and mediums. He builds instruments and plays them on his YouTube channel. But neither his teachers nor the adults "mentoring" him have bothered to ask about any of this.

Cheers erupt as the two celebrities hit the stage. The audience's eyes are fixed as the celebrities talk about the traveling they have done, the people they have met and how much communities of color are in disrepair. They emphasize their work in these communities and highlight examples of having turned young people around and in the direction of success. While much of this talk sounds familiar to Jordan, he waits with a patient assurance that he will receive some useful and uplifting information. After some talk from the celebrities on stage, representatives from the military are introduced, and they too talk about the pursuit of success. Embedded in their pitch to the young men in the crowd is the importance of being disciplined, focused, and clean-cut. Jordan immediately begins feeling uncomfortable. "What do they mean by clean cut?" he wonders. At 13, Jordan started growing dreadlocks, an act that required meaningful negotiation with his parents, who feared he might be viewed as a "drug dealer" or "hoodlum." Jordan recalls his mother's sincere care and concern, her pleas to maintain a look that would keep him "safe." But for Jordan, the look was an authentic expression of self, and he felt good when his locks began to grow out, allowing him the freedom to style them in different ways.

After some time, the celebrities are ready to take individual questions from the audience. Young men line up to ask questions, and soon one of the young men in the audience asks a question about how to become successful. The celebrities and their other guests on stage are eager to take on this issue. They immediately begin with advice on how to perform in ways that ultimately make you "successful." One of the celebrities notes the look and style of the military men on stage and references the fact that they are "kempt." They define *kempt* as being clean-cut, wearing clothes that fit, and having one's pants pulled up. This "kempt" look includes "dressing for success," or wearing suits, button-up shirts, and ties, to project a "business" look. Not only do the celebrities and their guests speak about the need to project a "kempt" look, they begin to encourage the young men in the audience to look at themselves and to question whether they fit the standards they have described. A wave of sound and movement takes over the audience as the young men begin looking at one another, pointing, and discussing whether their hair or clothing fits the description of "kempt." One of the military guests announces that they will provide free haircuts "on the spot today" for any young man who is ready to make a move in the direction of success. Young men begin to volunteer. Jordan looks around cautiously. He is proud of his dreadlocks; it's a style that makes him feel good about himself, but he signed up for this to learn about how he can become successful, and it seems the men on stage have that figured out, and none of them is wearing dreadlocks. While Jordan ponders this, several more of his peers volunteer, and the military man on stage is now ordering up help from men who will cut their hair. The event is taking a turn; it almost has the feeling of a Sunday morning in church, where folks are catching the spirit everywhere you look. Chairs and barbers are lined up beside the stage, and young men begin receiving haircuts. While this is happening, the two celebrities headlining the event are speaking to young men about the courage they have summoned to "clean up" and take the first steps to getting their lives together. Jordan feels the pressure mounting. He has to decide—and fairly quickly—if he will receive this "mentoring moment" and follow the advice of the celebrity mentors on stage. Several young men at his table, having already grappled with the concept, have entered the haircut line. Jordan decides to participate, stands up, and accompanies several of his peers in line. But unlike the excitement the others seem to feel, Jordan finds that once he settles in the barber's chair, hears the buzz of the clippers, and feels the release of the first cut, he immediately regrets his decision. He can't say why yet, but he feels violated. Most of the adults in the room celebrate; one of the celebrity hosts even shakes Jordan's hands, applauding him as "a smart young brotha." Jordan leaves the event with no resources, no materials, and no dreadlocks.

Jordan isn't the only young man of color who had this type of experience. In fact, the afore-described encounter, though fictional, is drawn from real-life events, one in particular that has gained a considerable amount of controversy and attention. The debate, noted here, began in June of 2016, when Dr. Steve Perry—head of the all-male Capital Preparatory Magnet School in Hartford, Connecticut, took to a social media site (Twitter) and released the following statement: "I witnessed 200 boys VOLUNTARILY cut dreads, braids & unkept frosh bc @IAMSTEVEHARVEY and @USARMY connected aesthetics with to success. Powerful."[1] The firestorm that ensued brought fierce opponents of respectability politics out in droves.[2] At the heart of the response was the idea that hairstyles, which grow naturally for Black people, cannot be considered "unkept frosh." Opponents also argued that these hairstyles were a direct illustration of Blackness so that the forced or encouraged elimination of them was one of many forms of anti-Black racism. As this chapter is being written, a "dreadlock ban" during the hiring process is major news. This issue is not demarcated by gender. Young women of color find themselves in these situations as well. In a book about how Black girls are criminalized, Monique Morris highlights a familiar problem in mentoring practice for girls. She specifically recounts a school-based mentoring program in which same-gender matches and dress-up days impose gender normative expectations on female protégés. Furthermore, she highlights the normative ways in which adults in the programs expect young women to perform their gender-oppressing alternative ways for young women to express themselves. In fact, the war waged on natural hairstyles among women and girls is still ongoing now.[3] The plaintiff at the heart of the "dreadlock ban" case is a women. Incidents like these are illustrative of a larger problem with mentoring models. The idea that mentoring has been provided to youth to force them to adhere to normative structures and systems is being debated and challenged, albeit against a long-standing pattern of "traditional" mentoring strategy.[4] If mentoring relationships are supposed to represent safe spaces that help young people to build self-love and resilience, then they should not be centering on the anti-Black practices that are plaguing communities in the first place.

Few presidential administrations have done more to advance mentoring programming, especially for youth of color, then the Obama administration. However, the expansion of programming that is often rooted in deficit perspectives and assimilationist values is more harmful than helpful for youth of color. This begs the question of whether the advocacy touted by Obama's My Brother's Keeper is advocacy young people of color need or can trust.

My Brother's Keeper and the Obama Legacy

Beginning in 2011, when Michelle Obama attended the National Mentoring Summit in Washington, D.C., and culminating in the introduction and facilitation of My Brother's Keeper, the Obama administration has shown interest in and support for mentoring programs. Mentoring rhetoric reached a fever pitch since the Obama administration launched it's My Brother's Keeper initiative. Increased attention by the Obama administration, coupled with the funding support of generous corporate sponsors and donors has meant that the creation of mentoring programs serving the youth of color has attracted a significant number of nonprofit dollars.[5] It has also meant that the mentoring and youth development market finds it particularly appealing to pander to communities of color. This work, which appears progressive on one end; highlighting data that illustrate the Black male experience as particularly daunting in comparison to its White counterpart, is somewhat insubstantial when it comes to altering mentoring praxis so that it can be better utilized to confront this experience. And this isn't just true of the mentoring happening in the MBK space; this applies to mentoring for Black youth in most spaces. There is a call to action, a request for mentors to engage in providing support systems for these young people, but that call to action is couched in civil discourse about respectability. The call often focuses on helping young people make "right" decisions, helping them dress well, helping to cultivate the resilience we think they'll need to survive in this America. This mentoring ignores systemic inequality, but it also encourages mentors to engage in a process to "un-other" Black youth, and it all smacks of a certain anti-Blackness. To be fair, this critique of Obama's My Brother's Keeper is not a critique of individual practitioners utilizing the funding and attention to provide healing spaces for young men and boys of color. No, this work examines the conceptual leanings of the My Brother's Keeper as a policy initiative rooted in anti-Blackness, as well as how the policy has been used by the power elite to impose respectability on the lower classes via acculturation and respectability.

Mentoring programming, a significant aspect of the My Brother's Keeper initiative, has become, like other initiatives dealing with young people, part of the neoliberal education reform agenda, resulting in its exponential growth and support. Neoliberalism has impacted mentoring and youth development programs in much the same way as it has the field of education; a focus on individual responsibility and normative standards fueled by increased privatization and corporate funding.[6] The My Brother's Keeper Web site, citing two years of MBK work, notes that "independent private sector support for grants and in-kind resources has more than doubled to more than $600 million."[7] Although much of the attention paid to mentoring has bolstered economic support for a necessary and helpful process, it has also created controversy, as the call for increased mentoring for young men and boys of color comes with questions and concerns regarding the systemic and institutional treatment of these youth and how mentoring practice can best be altered to address those issues.[8] Although the My Brother's Keeper initiative has been rolled out by a Black president and at a time of increased racial tensions in the country, there is still a debate as to whether mentoring will involve processes like the ones described in the narrative, by both Black and "other" folks under the auspices of White supremacist frames, engaging in anti-Black and oppressive structures in an effort to encourage assimilation among young people of color. Obama, being the first Black president, has had his own challenges being accepted by mainstream American society. For example, the birther controversy, which was a debate regarding whether the president was even born here in the United States, questioned his legitimacy as a U.S. citizen, not to mention his presidency, and made the country painfully aware that our first Black president would have an uphill battle to climb. This almost eight-year-long battle is symbolic of the idea that anti-Blackness is so deeply rooted in our society, our first Black president has to be "something else" from "somewhere else." In 2014, Michael Jeffries, professor of American studies at Wellesley, discusses America's reckoning with its anti-Blackness in an opinion editorial about happenings in Ferguson. His definition of anti-Blackness encapsulates the complexity of the term: "It is not merely about hating or penalizing Black people. It is about the debasement of Black humanity, utter indifference to Black suffering, and the denial of Black people's right to exist."[9] Utilizing this definition allows us to see the anti-Blackness of mentoring at work. Most folks who support or are involved in Obama's MBK mentoring wouldn't identify themselves or the structures they operate in as anti-Black, and yet the very ways in which mentoring is approached, especially in the MBK space, exemplifies the sentiment. According to the MBK Web site, one of the initiative's goals is to "take important steps to connect young people to mentoring, support networks and the skills they need to find a good job or go to college and work their way into the middle class."[10] Again, a seemingly harmless goal, but the implications here are based on deficit notions: the assumptions that these youth don't already exist in the middle class and that they lack necessary skills to earn a middle-class salary. Furthermore, the connection between attaining middle-class status and the notion of "success" draw us back to the conversation about the kinds of looks and behaviors (read: normative) required to earn that status; not to mention the fact that these youth are still only relegated to middle-class status, not beyond.

Mentoring based on hierarchical notions, goals of respectability, and aspirations of assimilation become an avenue for erasing the Blackness of our young people and aligns with the aspects mentioned above of "indifference to Black suffering, and the denial of Black people's right to exist."[11] This mentoring doesn't critically acknowledge context, doesn't speak to negative racialized experiences, and doesn't center on or value the beauty of Black existence. What it does is to "make youth over" so that they are more acceptable to dominant society and, as a result, justifies the harm done to them by actions fueled by anti-Blackness. This "un-othering" devalues the spectacular beauty of the cultural currency these young people possess: their Blackness. As grown folks needlessly justify this encouragement to assimilate, to normalize, to "un-other" young people, they can call it many great things, but they cannot call it mentoring.

A Brief History of Mentoring

Mentoring is said to have its roots in ancient Greece; in the Odyssey, Odysseus, leaves his son, Telemachus, under the guidance and tutelage of

Mentor. Rooted in an age-old concept and with a complex and nuanced history, youth mentoring has evolved to become a popular and mainstream youth development strategy. The mentoring literature defines the concept as a caring relationship focused on the consistent support and positive development of a child or youth. Mentoring has gained a lot of popularity and attention over the years and has been studied to illustrate its practical significance and impact. So much of this research has been helpful to its very expansion, justifying the validity of the practice. The My Brother's Keeper initiative has bolstered the popularity of mentoring further, especially as a strategy for addressing the needs of underserved minority youth. Consequently, funding for mentoring programs, especially those serving marginalized youth, has swelled. Because youth mentoring has a long and relatively positive social history, it is accepted widely and is said to "resonate with mainstream cultural values."[12] The fact that it resonates so strongly with the mainstream may, in fact, be one of its problems, especially when it comes to the context, of young men and boys of color, the very youth the program is dedicated to serving.

Mentoring has always reflected an attempt to inculcate White and middle-class values into youth, although originally mentoring programs existed to serve poor and urban White children who were "victims" of an industrial America. When Big Brothers of America was founded in 1904, racial segregation was the law and reality in the country.[13] Marian Wright Edelman (1999), a Black activist for children's rights, suggested that mentoring was alive and well in segregated America, but that minority youth were much more likely to be engaged in naturally occurring mentoring relationships. Natural mentoring relationships happen outside of formal program structures, that is, in relationships with extended family and close neighbors.[14] Although poor and urban White children were initial targets of assimilationist mentoring programs, social constructions have shifted to focus on non-White groups, so that now, the primary image of mentoring programming includes young people of color. Given the history of mentoring, it is understood that mentoring, as a construct, was not originally intended to serve those considered racialized by today's standards.

The anti-Blackness found in Obama's mentoring initiative results from a combination of neoliberal idealism, which supports the expansion of a mentoring and youth development "free" market; individualist ideals and a "pull-yourself-up-by-your-bootstraps" ideology; and acritical perspectives that fail to address systemic and institutional challenges disproportionately facing young people of color. This dangerous blend of perspectives presents a seemingly helpful process (read: mentoring) that gives rise to efforts to destroy the "otherness" (read: assimilation) of Black and other youth of color.

Surviving White Respectability: Blackness as a Theatrical Prop

Black childhoods are under duress. The role of hyper-surveillance and draconian disciplinary policies comprise a well-documented deposition in the indictment of schools. At the epicenter of this vast body of research is a continuum of academic confinement and epistemological suicide that aims to relegate youth context as in need of intervention and gross reconstruction. The deficit lens in which Black youth are framed embodies the parasitic underside of school. In this regard, schools function as a hyper-objectifying body of concentric rubrics, curricula, and evaluations that commodify the intellectual and physical labor of youth according to post-colonial norms for achievement. The function of these subtractive school practices, described by Angela Valenzuela (1999), is a potent erasing of student context; both the socioecological and the cultural. The genealogy of the "school's investment in [student] cultural and linguistic divestment" spans over generations in America, watermarked by atrocities perpetuated by school-based apartheid.[15] Schools in America have always played a complementary and active part in the barbaric advancement of global conquest by European settlers. The legacy of historical subjugation emerges in the anti-indigenous and chattel anti-Blackness imbued within contemporary values, artifacts, and collective mores materialized by school leadership and organizational design.[16] Schools are surrogates of power on behalf of our balkanized society. Since the inception of early schools by colonial settlers, dominant culture has homogenized pedagogical spaces around a binary nomenclature of superiority. One proxy for school-sanctioned imperialism is access, particularly the triangulated relationship between access to spaces of formalized schooling, cultural awareness, and literacy.

The participation of schools in the advancement of colonial rule is marred by geopolitics. Historically, education laws have targeted subpopulations in order to pathologize the subculture of youth as in need of restoration. The political origins of school-sanctioned assaults were espoused by dominant imperial rule and enacted through laws, like literacy bans throughout the southern United States, which criminalized the teaching of writing and reading to any enslaved Africans; and Carlisle Indian Boarding schools, which are traced to the kidnapping and forced assimilation of thousands of First Nation youth by White school administrators in an effort to "cleanse" them of their native intellectual ancestry.[17] The legacy of schools today upholds an ethos of domination. Angela Valenzuela (1999) explains that today's incarnation of postcolonial schooling promotes a conception of achievement that grounded in a priori framing of Black and Brown youth as "needy" students. Valenzuela unpacks the racial calculus associated with objectifying academic potential of youth. One looming consequence of schooling that "deprives youth of historically derived understandings" and the "interpretive skills with which to assess these intergenerational cross-currents" is further division between mentoring curricula and student context.[18] Valenzuela and other scholars believe that without interrogating the conditions and values of mentoring strategies, anglo-normative rubrics will reproduce colonial vestiges. These values are exploited by school systems and mentoring firms alike to justify a domain of positivist intervention strategies like the "pull-your-pants up" bromides promulgated by Steve Perry.

Mentoring that solely focuses on the cosmetic application of decorum (i.e., bowties, hiked pants, haircuts) fails to recognize the preexisting contributions of schooling apparatus in centralizing the tenets of "appropriate behavior" while amplifying a monolithic narrative about the lives of Black children. A mentoring strategy unilaterally driven by stereotypical perceptions of urban youth abdicates schools from modifying the negatively pathological associations with hoodies, sagging pants, and afros. These associations reduce the intergenerational trauma meted by a matrices of domination, including postcolonial schooling, to a superficial matter of attire. Similarly Trayvon Martin, the unarmed, 17-year-old Black high school student from Sanford, Florida, murdered by a self-appointed neighborhood watchman—George Zimmerman—who stalked the teen from his vehicle and deemed Trayvon as "suspicious" as he walked home in his own neighborhood. During the infamous court case, George Zimmerman's defense team argued that Zimmerman's suspicion of Martin was justified given Trayvon's hooded sweatshirt, popularly called a "hoodie." In this regard, the criminogenic lens in which Blackness and urban youth culture are scrutinized is left unexamined while a narrative of respectability politics was upheld as legal justification for execution. Not only are Black youth, like Trayvon Martin, socialized to blame themselves for trauma they have endured, but they are led to believe that their very identity must be unlearned if they are to assuage the delicate White supremacist fears about their universalized image of the "young Black hoodlum" as an ontological threat. Rather than unearthing centuries of anti-Black rhetoric exorted and activated by structures that criminalize opportunities for literacy and culturally inclusive pedagogical climates, mentoring programs peddle a conception of academic "underachievement" that essentialize Blackness—in all

social milieus—as educationally stunted. This narrative obstructs meaningful discussion around the historical significance of coloniality, White
supremacy, and commodified Black labor in creating vacuums that usurp
opportunity for educational spaces in predominantly Black communities.
As Barbara Ransby and Tracye Matthews (1993) assert about prescriptive
mentoring programs targeting Black youth, "[P]rogress is predicated upon
the notion that the main problems confronting the African American community and diaspora at this historical juncture are internal to the Black
community itself. The problems are defined as cultural, behavioral, and
psychological, not as political, economic or structural. In other words—
our problem is us."[19]

Dissonance of Monocultural Schooling in Multicultural Spaces

When Dr. Steve Perry tweeted his celebration of the demise of Black hair,
his underlying assumption was that redemption for the systemic quarantine
of Black boys is a matter of theatrical performances of gender, class, and
race. Perry promotes a shortsighted vision of social progress that relegates
the trauma endured by cutting the natural hair of Black children to a
teachable lesson. That is, identity is something to be given to, rather than
self-defined by, youth. This lesson packages a singular model of Black male
identities like a bank transaction. Rather than encouraging youth to pivot
away from the White racial frames of dangerous and maladaptive Blackness, Perry and Harvey insist that youth embrace these norms as a form
of self-preservation and even advancement. The focus of youth liberation,
according to corporatized and monocultural mentoring programs is not
on divestment from oppression. To sanitize Black boys of themselves is to
free them from a historical anvil that only grounds them in suffrage. Capitulation is conflated as transformation. Perry has not publically discussed
reconditioning the social etymology and binary constructs that define
Black childhoods, but continues to belabor shifts in attitude and performance. These self-imposed changes demand that children reconstruct any
conspicuous demarcations (i.e., hair, clothes, speech) of their Black boy
identities.

As pedagogical sites like schools and mentoring programs police masculinity and race, Black youth are left with an intractable feat. They are
impossibly charged with taking ownership over the development of their
identities while confined by external pressures to conform. These sites
operate as enclosure that leave no opportunity for self-exploration, by denying youth an unsanctioned space, or Third Space, in which discovery and
autonomous reflection can occur.[20] Sanctions can materialize as grades,

attendance rates, grants, or other capital-driven dividends that reinforce a child's behavior. But schools that sanction have also been proven to be rife with bias against the agency and outright humanity of Black children. Goff, Jackson, and Di Leone (2014) found that Black youth are more likely to be associated with apelike qualities and thus dehumanized as untamed and illegible specimens rather than human children.[21] As Michael Dumas and Joseph Nelson (2016) further explain, this deficit lens encloses Black childhoods, reimagining youth, gender, and race as fungible mistakes that must be "fixed." Dumas and Nelson are correct in that the social imagination of youth is chained to a historical amalgamation of commodification that reifies a political economy embedded by Western colonization. This phenomenon is particularly constraining for Black youth because:

> [f]or Black boys, anti-Black prejudice and, perhaps more so, dehumanization are compounded by the tenuous position of Black boys and girls within the already fragile and troubled social conception of childhood. . . . Further, the "crisis" focus of the public discourse on Black males—in which young men and boys become constructed as "problems" in themselves—prevents us from seeing Black boys outside of public fears and anxieties about their future lives as adults and locates crises within Black male bodies rather than the political economy and racial order that heavily determine the living conditions and life chances of Black males from boyhood on.[22]

In his seminal work, George Herbert Mead (1934) describes the "Parliament of Selves,"[23] a sufficient allegory for the mental gymnastics and political negotiations subjected upon Black youth whose very existence is weaponized against them by mentoring programs that aim to erase casual harbingers of culture. Researchers can also play a fundamental role in shifting the dialectic about Black boys. According to Tyrone Howard (2013), in order to cultivate a nondeficit, unsanctioned bedrock of mentoring that does not uphold the dehumanizing constructs of postcolonial capitalism, academics must explore how Black youth are "navigating difficult terrain, and how they address the life challenges inside and outside of school."[24] In this regard, what is deemed by schools widely as misbehavior is reoriented as reasonable behavior given the conditions of schools. The dialogical comparison is paramount, as we shift the academic lens from pathologizing Black youth to disrupting and interrogating the architecture of Black identity formation—which Feagin (2013) asserts as the "social glue" for a larger fabric of White Supremacy.[25] By employing an ecological lens to deconstructing empirical work, mentoring programs and scholars can synthesize a new narrative that affirms Black youth as autonomous participants in the process of self-definition.

A New Way of Mentoring

Telling Jordan's story is an attempt to communicate the unnecessary harm done to youth of color when anti-Blackness and assimilationist values undergird mentoring programming. Obama's MBK and similar programming, work to undermine liberation movements that motivate young people to address the systemic and institutional White supremacy blighting their daily existence. America eats it babies. We see the evidence in unaddressed and systemic poverty, urban gentrification, health and medical disparities and most importantly, education. But the mentoring processes that focus on the victims of these social problems never address these systems. There is little to no discussion about the concept of gentrification, pervasive and systemic poverty, failed education reform or the carceral police state. Instead, the conversations focus on how young people can adapt to these failed systems, forcing them to adjust and align with the toxicity of them. Aligning perfectly with neoliberalism and acritical, color blind approaches to education, mentoring in the age of Obama, props up systems that damage the most vulnerable young people among us. Furthermore, major initiatives like MBK often incentivize the very corporations tied to many of these social problems, and provides them with tax breaks and positive public relations when they "chip-in" to help. In this way, corporations benefit from both the problems and the solutions.

If mentoring, the very practice which has been touted as positive youth development is not a process or space for the unconditional love and support of children of color, and the Black president who posits the largest youth of color mentoring initiative in the country's history engages an assimilationist framework for that mentoring, arguably harmful for youth of color, what systems and people exist to do the necessary work? Much of the reason traditional mentoring has not changed is for lack of imagination and lack of structure. As pointed out early in the chapter, mentoring was never meant to address the needs of a population marginalized in ways youth of color are. In 2009 and again in 2014, researchers pointed out that race and ethnicity played a significant role in mentoring relationships, but that there were "limited research-based guidelines in the practice field regarding how race/ethnicity should be considered." They also note that the major document establishing standards for mentoring practice in the field, the Elements of Effective Practice, "pay little attention to the role of race and ethnicity in mentoring programs."[26] The document at the center of their critique was never intended to provide insight on race and ethnicity; it was instead a guiding document of standards-based practice. Its sole purpose was to establish a set of streamlined standards that mentoring programs could follow. A few critical voices implementing mentoring programs in the MBK space realized that these standards would not meet the needs of the population they were serving, noting that these youth required more support and more space to process the trauma and racism they have endured. None of them expressed a problem with young people's ability to assimilate; they expressed a problem with traditional mentoring methods that did not support a critical or liberatory process.

Critical mentoring is one way to address the critique. Focusing first on mentoring work happening in the MBK space and then on mentoring work writ large, critical mentoring sought to move mentoring practice and research into a larger discourse around the critical examination of race, ethnicity, class, gender, and sexuality. The concept also provided tools for practitioners and researchers to begin challenging deficit-based notions of protégés, limited metrics that ignore metanarratives and protégé adaptation to dominant ideologies. Furthermore, the concept allowed for liberatory processes that push both the mentor and the protégé to trigger critical consciousness and an ongoing and joint struggle for transformation. Critical mentoring establishes a way to "clap back," or contest the idea that mentoring needs to change the young person. In fact, it encourages mentors and protégés to push against the very systems that victimize them. And this is what mentoring praxis should look like.

In practice, critical mentoring processes aren't just part of the mentoring relationship, but part of the organization and programming model. It has to be a part of how the organization and program "do business." In practice that includes the following:

- Mentoring that fully considers race, ethnicity, gender, class, and sexuality when building the infrastructure for programs, including recruiting of mentors, training of mentors, support of mentoring relationships, mentoring activities, and finally, target outcomes; mentoring that is focused on critical consciousness and transformation rather than assimilation and adaptation
- Mentoring that places emphasis on the whole community, the whole protégé, rather than just parts of the whole
- Mentoring that includes, from its very inception, the needs of the community and the needs of the youth in the community
- Mentoring that promotes and supports mentor/protégé partnerships for community transformation

- Critical mentoring work that also informs how mentoring is studied as well
- Mentoring research that utilizes critical frameworks, that is, critical race theory, critical pedagogy, and so on, for the analysis of mentoring relationships, mentoring outcomes, programmatic structures and outcomes, and so forth
- Mentoring evaluation that moves beyond standard evaluative strategy and utilizes evaluative strategy that empowers the protégés and highlights programmatic outcomes beyond statistical ones, for example, empowerment evaluation, photovoice, and so on
- Challenges to the mentoring metanarrative with new and critical forms of research

Very little of this transformative language can be found in Obama's My Brother's Keeper policy. In order for the My Brother's Keeper initiative to include the love of young men and boys of color, it must be radically altered.

Immediate ways to implement more critical practices for MBK programs include examining and reworking program goals, focusing on recruiting and retaining diverse program staff and mentors, and providing critical training for every person involved in the planning and implementation of mentoring programming. It has been said "nothing about us without us," and the saying is fitting for MBK mentoring programs working within and hopefully with communities of color. MBK mentoring programs should immediately survey their program goals. If these program goals have not been developed or reworked in collaboration with the community, and most especially the youth being served, they must be changed. Doing work with young people of color means giving them voice and extending them meaningful opportunities to participate in building their programming. Also, if the program goals aren't connected to overarching issues of race, class, gender, and sexuality, issues that must be addressed when doing transformational work in minoritized and marginalized communities, they must be reworked.

Mentoring organizations often cite lack of volunteerism as a problem in communities of color. MBK has had success with bringing together a community of supporters. Still, recruiting and retaining diversely is something else all together. This may be even more important for MBK mentoring programs that run the risk of mistaking men of color as one homogenous group. MBK mentoring programs should be recruiting a variety of ages, sexualities, class standing, ability, and so on. Bettina Love cites the mentoring connections masculine women often have with young men and boys, noting that most overlook the importance of the connection because of traditional gender biases.[27] Also, when considering program goals, the work must be relevant and meaningful to the community being served.

This must be discussed with community members, and having them within the organization means they should actively inform the work.

Training is one of the most important components of attaining critical mentoring status. Programs must have all persons in the organization train on issues of race, class, gender, and sexuality in their training modules. Programs working with Black males need to include training modules that help mentors address the unique needs of Black males; programs working with LGBTQ youth should do the same; and so forth. Programs that do not discuss issues of race, class, gender, and sexuality risk setting up mentors for failure and alienating the youth they aim to support. More importantly, they expose young people like Jordan to mentors who can't fully address their needs. To discount the context of youth of color and force them to choose alternate and often oppressive ways of being harms them, renders the mentoring relationship useless, and undermines the work the program may be trying to do. If MBK is to be truly transformative, it must be reassessed for the sake of young people who have already been so problematized that mentoring is the only safe space they may find. This could have made all the difference in Jordan's experience.

You Can't Call That Mentoring

Jordan's walk home was a long one. Feeling despondent, tricked, and dejected, he slowly meanders through his urban neighborhood—a neighborhood replete with boarded windows, cracked concrete, and temporary fencing, long abandoned by most celebrities and attractive only to the military because of the desperate youth who dream of adventures beyond here. This neighborhood has never seen a president of the United States, and the image of the man in the oval office is one relegated to a television screen. Policies and initiatives aren't something Jordan has a deep understanding of, but he knows that programs for youth like him come and go. His neighborhood, the schools in them, and the hopelessness of it all remains. Jordan has very little understanding of what research says about mentoring, but he knows the programs in his neighborhood don't feel like welcoming and accepting spaces for Black boys and girls. Still trying to make sense of the day, Jordan chokes back tears, though he doesn't understand why they are there. Jordan's confusion and sadness isn't solely about his hair, but about the fact that he has lost more than his dreadlocks; he has lost a sense of self and a hope that, until today, he held onto firmly. Although so much of the external messaging Jordan received, especially from school, was negative, Jordan was resilient enough to seek out mentors he thought would be positive. Even so, his mentoring experiences, most especially this last one, was not only disappointing, but heartbreaking.

Jordan's experience illustrates the trauma and violence visited upon young people who enter MBK mentoring spaces expecting transformational praxis and receiving anti-Black pathology. Young people like Jordan should not have to have these experiences, especially not in the context of a mentoring relationship and not in the name of "providing opportunities" if those opportunities require him and others like him to be stripped of their most natural and beautiful characteristics. The language, ideas, and intent at the heart of Obama's My Brother's Keeper initiative cannot be rightfully called mentoring. In solidarity with young people like Jordan, we must reclaim the term, the structure, the relationships, and the purpose of mentoring so that it can no longer be used to devalue and traumatize young people by stripping them of their culture. There are opportunities to make My Brother's Keeper the initiative it should be, but it must first be rid of it's anti-Blackness properties and shift toward a critical mentoring perspective and approach. Our young people can no longer afford to leave MBK mentoring spaces with no resources, no materials, and no dreadlocks.

Notes

1. Perry, 2016.
2. Hart, 2016.
3. Morris, 2016.
4. Ellis, 2014.
5. Foundation Center, 2015.
6. Hillman, 2016.
7. White House, 2016.
8. Ellis, 2014; Daneshzadeh and Weiston, 2016.
9. Jeffries, 2014.
10. White House, 2016.
11. Ibid.
12. Keller, 2010, 23.
13. Baker and Maguire, 2005.
14. Spencer, 2010.
15. Valenzuela, 1999, 226.
16. Schein, 1992; Rankin and Reason, 2005.
17. Adams, 1997; Fear-Segal, 2007.
18. Valenzuela, 1999, p. 226.
19. Ransby and Matthews, 1993, p. 58.
20. Gutierrez, Baquedano-Lopez, and Tejeda, 1999.
21. Goff, Jackson, and Leone, 2014.

22. Dumas and Nelson, 2016.
23. Mead, 1934.
24. Howard, 2013, p. 78.
25. Feagin, 2013, p. 126.
26. Sanchez et al., 2014.
27. Love, 2016.

Bibliography

Adams, David W. "The Federal Indian Boarding School: A Study of Environment and Response, 1879–1918." (Dissertation) Indiana University Press, 1997.

Baker, David, and Colleen Maguire. "Mentoring in Historical Perspective." In *Handbook of Youth Mentoring*, edited by David L. DuBois and Michael J. Karcher. Thousand Oaks: Sage Publications, 2005.

Browne, Simone. *Dark Matters: On the Surveillance of Blackness.* Durham, NC: Duke University Press, 2015.

Coles, Ann. "The Role of Mentoring in College Access and Success." *Pathway to College Network* 2011, 1–11.

Corasaro, W. A. (2015). *The Sociology of Childhood* (4th ed.). Thousand Oaks, CA: Sage.

Daneshzadeh and Weiston, 2016. Obama '08. Retrieved http://www.nytimes.com/packages/pdf/politics/factsheet_healthcare.pdf.

DuBois, David L., Nelson Portillo, Jean E. Rhodes, Naida Silverthorn, and J. C. Valentine. "How Effective Are Mentoring Programs for Youth? A Systematic Assessment of the Evidence." *Psychological Science in the Public Interest,* 2011.

DuBois, David L., Bruce E. Holloway, Jeffrey C. Valentine, and Harris Cooper. "Effectiveness of Mentoring Programs for Youth: A Meta-Analytic Review." *American Journal of Community Psychology* 30, no. 2 (2002): 157–97.

DuBois, David L., and Michael J. Karcher. "Youth Mentoring in Contemporary Perspective." In *Handbook of Youth Mentoring*, edited by David L. DuBois and Michael J. Karcher, 2nd ed., 3–13. Thousand Oaks: Sage Publications, 2014.

Dumas, Michael J., and Joseph Derrick Nelson. "(Re)imagining Black Boyhood: Toward a Critical Framework for Educational Research." *Harvard Educational Review,* 86, no. 1 (2016): 27–47.

Edelman, Marian Wright. *Lanterns: A Memoir of Mentors.* New York: HarperCollins, 1999.

Ellis, Antonio. "Rethinking President Obama's My Brother's Keeper Initiative." *Diverse Issues in Higher Education,* July 2014. http://diverseeducation.com/article/65942/.

Feagin, Joseph R. *The White Racial Frame: Centuries of Racial Framing and Counter-Framing.* 2nd ed. New York: Routledge, 2013.

Fear-Segal, Jacqueline. *White Man's Club: Schools and the Struggle of Indian Accul-turation.* Lincoln, NB: Nebraska University Press, 2007.

Foundation Center. "Quantifying Hope: Philanthropic Support for Black Men and Boys," 2015. http://bmafunders.org/wp-content/uploads/2015/04/quantifying-hope-web-final.pdf.

Goff, Phillip Atiba, Matthew Christian Jackson, and Brooke Allison Lewis Di Leone, Carmen Marie Culotta, and Natalie Ann DeTomasso. "The Essence of Innocence: Consequences of Dehumanizing Black Children." *Journal of Personality and Social Psychology* 106, no. 4 (2014): 526–45.

Gutierrez, Kris D., Patricia Baquedano-Lopez, and Carlos Tejeda. "Rethinking Diversity: Hybridity and Hybrid Language Practices in the Third Space." *Mind, Culture, and Activity* 64, no. 4 (1999): 286–303.

Gutierrez-Morfin, Noel. "U.S. Court Rules Dreadlock Ban During Hiring Process Is Legal." *NBC News*, September 2016. http://www.nbcnews.com/news/nbcblk/u-s-court-rules-dreadlock-ban-during-hiring-process-legal-n652211?cid=sm_fb.

Harris, Frederick. *The Price of the Ticket: Barack Obama and Rise and Decline of Black Politics.* Oxford: Oxford University Press, 2014.

Hart, Carl. "'Crazy Baldheads' Seek to Eliminate Dreads." The Root, June 2016. https://www.theroot.com/articles/culture/2016/06/carl-hart-dreadlocks-steve-perry/.

Heitzeg, Nancy A. *The School-to-Prison Pipeline: Education, Discipline, and Racial-ized Double Standards.* Santa Barbara, CA: Praeger, 2016.

Hillman, Matty. "Youth Mentorship as Neoliberal Subject Formation." *International Journal of Child, Youth and Family Studies* 7, no. 3/4 (2016): 364–80.

Homer, and Robert Fagles. *The Odyssey.* New York: Penguin Group, 1996.

Howard, Tyrone C. "How Does It Feel to Be a Problem? Black Male Students, Schools, and Learning in Enhancing the Knowledge Base to Disrupt Deficit Frameworks." *Review of Research in Education* 37 (2013): 54–86.

Jeffries, Michael. "Ferguson Must Force Us to Face Anti-Blackness." *Boston Globe*, November 2014. https://www.bostonglobe.com/opinion/2014/11/28/ferguson-must-force-face-anti-blackness/pKVMpGxwUYpMDyHRWPln2M/story.html.

Keller, Thomas E. "Youth Mentoring: Theoretical and Methodological Issues." In *The Blackwell Handbook of Mentoring: A Multiple Perspectives Approach Handbook of Mentoring: A Multiple Perspectives Approach*, edited by Tammy D. Allen and Lillian T. Eby, 23–47. Malden, MA: Blackwell Publishing, 2010.

Love, Bettina. "'She Has a Real Connection with Them': Reimagining and Expanding Our Definitions of Black Masculinity & Mentoring in Education through Female Masculinity." *Forthcoming*, 2016.

Mead, George. *Mind, Self and Society.* Chicago: The University of Chicago Press, 1934.

Morris, Monique W. *Pushout: The Criminalization of Black Girls in Schools.* New York: New Press, 2016.

Nelson F. L., and Sadler T. (2013). A Third Space for Reflection by Teacher Educators: A Heuristic for Understanding Orientations to and Components of Reflection. *Reflective Practice*, 14 (1): 43–57.

Nocella, Anthony J., Priya Parmar, and David Stovall. *From Education to Incarceration: Dismantling the School-to-Prison Pipeline.* New York: Peter Lang, 2014.

Perry, Steve. Twitter Post, June 11, 2016, 11:51 p.m., http://twitter.com/DrSteve Perry.

Rankin, Susan R., and Robert D. Reason. "Differing Perceptions: How Students of Color and White Students Perceive Campus Climate for Underrepresented Groups." *Journal of College Student Development* 46, no. 1 (2005): 43–61.

Ransby, B., and Matthews, T. (1993). Black Popular Culture and the Transcendence of Patriarchal Illusions. *Race & Class*, 35 (1): 57–68.

Rhodes, Jean. "The Real Mentoring Gap—and What to Do about It." *The Chronicle of Evidence Based Mentoring*, 2015. http://chronicle.umbmentoring.org/the-real-mentoring-gap-what-to-do-about-it/.

Sanchez, Bernadette, Yari Colon-Torres, Rachel Feuer, Katrina Roundfield, and Luciano Berardi. "Race, Ethnicity, and Culture in Mentoring Relationships." In *Handbook of Youth Mentoring*, Second, 145–58. Thousand Oaks: Sage Publications, 2014.

Schein, Edgar H. *Organizational Culture and Leadership.* 2nd ed. San Francisco: Jossey-Bass, 1992.

Spencer, Renée. "Naturally Occurring Mentoring Relationships Involving Youth." In *The Blackwell Handbook of Mentoring: A Multiple Perspectives Approach*, edited by Tammy Allen and Lillian T. Eby, 97–117. Oxford: Blackwell Publishing, 2010.

Tarter, Brent. *The Grandees of Government: The Origins and Persistence of Undemocratic Politics in Virginia.* Charlottesville: University of Virginia Press, 2013.

Tierney, William G. "Models of Minority College-Going and Retention: Cultural Integrity versus Cultural Suicide." *Journal of Negro Education* 68, no. 1 (1999): 80–91.

Valenzuela, Angela. *Subtractive Schooling: U.S.-Mexican Youth and the Politics of Caring.* Albany: State University of New York Press, 1999.

Wallace, David A. *Education for Extinction: American Indians and the Boarding School Experience 1875–1928.* Lawrence: University of Kansas Press, 1997.

Weiston-Serdan, Torie. "5 Things Every Mentor Should Know about Working with Black Youth." *For Harriet*, 2015. http://www.forharriet.com/2015/07/5-things-every-mentor-needs-to-know.html#axzz3gk4k85fV.

Weiston-Serdan, Torie. "Critical Mentoring: A Definition and Agenda." *Blog*, 2015. https://wordpress.com/post/62521172/221/.

Weiston-Serdan, Torie, and Arash Daneshzadeh. "Critiquing the Anti-Blackness in Mentoring." *Diverse Issues in Higher Education*, August 2016.

White House. "My Brother's Keeper Initiative," 2016. http://www.mentoring.org/my_brothers_keeper.

CHAPTER EIGHT

The Great Divider: Obama's Influence on Trust in Government and Racial Attitudes[1]

Clarissa Peterson and Emmitt Y. Riley III

The 2008 Presidential Election and the False Hope of a Postracial America?

"Obama's presidency represents the paradox of American representation. Obama represents for all of us because he stands as the symbol of America to the world. He also represents to the American citizenry proof of progress in a nation that has never before embraced a black commander in chief. Yet a third sense of representation has a racial tinge, because Obama is also a representation of a black populace that, until his election, had been excluded from the highest reach of political representation."

—Michael Eric Dyson, *The Black Presidency*[2]

Since 2008, scholars have debated the degree to which race has impacted vote choice among whites and their job approval rating for America's first

African American President. Although scholars have yet to reach a consensus on how the Obama presidency has reshaped the political landscape, the empirical research has provided important insights on the links between white support for Barack Obama and his policies, racial resentment, polarization, and how the election of Barack Obama has caused scholars of black politics to revisit some of its core assumptions. Despite several studies examining the relationship between white support for Barack Obama and racial resentment, we still know very little about how the Obama presidency may have influenced levels of trust in government among citizens.

A significant amount of research suggests that trust in government is a prerequisite for a healthy democracy. Since the early 1970s, scholars have noted a significant decline in levels of trust in government. This decline is exasperated when scholars investigate political trust in government by race. Prior research on descriptive representation contends that African American political representation may have a positive impact on citizens' attitudes toward politicians and governmental institutions.[3] The findings of these studies may have profound political implications for the influence of America's first African American on levels of trust in government. In 1968, the National Advisory Commission on Civil Disorders found an important link between African American distrust in government and the lack of African American political representation.

Although political scientists have devoted a significant amount of attention to examining whether white Americans would vote for Barack Obama, very little attention has been sought to investigate the impact of race on racial resentment and levels of trust in government within the context of the Obama presidency. With so much scholarly attention focusing on vote choice among whites, scholars have missed a significant opportunity to examine how the descriptive representation of America's first African American president may have influenced levels of trust in government and racial resentment among blacks and whites.

In this chapter, we investigate how African American political representation affects trust in government and racial attitudes. Specifically, we ask: What impact has Barack Obama's presidency had on racial attitudes within the United States when measured in terms of racial resentment, and to what degree did America's first phenotypically black president impact levels of trust in the United States government? Using survey data collected by the American National Election Studies (ANES) from 2004–12, we find that the Obama's presidency has had a dividing impact on both levels of racial resentment and trust in government by race. Although levels of racial resentment and trust in government seem to be similar in 2008 among blacks and whites, we find significant racial divides in subsequent years following Barack Obama's election and reelection.

2008: The Hopeful Optimism of a Postracial Society

The historic election of Barack Obama in the 2008 presidential election marked a very important moment in American politics in that the United States of America elected its first African American president. In 2008, "the United States became the only advanced industrialized democracy to have elected as its head of government an individual from a minority racial-ethnic group."[4] The election of Barack Obama as the 44th president of the United States resulted in many political pundits, analysts, and news anchors arguing that America has entered into "a postracial society." In the view of these individuals, the symbolic election of a black man to the nation's highest political office represented a transition from an era when race served as a political barrier that prevented blacks from being elected to political offices outside of majority black districts. Several scholars suggest that race did not play a factor in the 2008 election. These scholars suggest that the 2008 election had "no visible scars of racism attached to the nation or the Republican Party."[5] As further evidence that race was not a factor, Abigail Thernstrom used the 2008 presidential election of Barack Obama as an opportunity to argue that white voters no longer use race to evaluate black candidates. She is quoted as saying that the election of America's first phenotypically black president "will allow black parents to tell their children, it really is true: the color of your skin will not matter."[6] On November 5, 2008, *The New York Times* advanced this postracial narrative by publishing the following headline: "Obama: Racial Barrier Falls in Decisive Victory,"[7] highlighting Barack Obama's Electoral College victory of 353 votes over Senator John McCain's 185.

Immediately following the 2008 presidential election, the postracial narrative continued to dominate the political discourse in American politics. Members of both the black and white communities interpreted the descriptive representation of Obama's election as evidence that the past vestiges of racism were no longer prevalent. Robert Franklin, president of Morehouse College, a prominent historically black college, appeared on a talk show and stated the following:

> Oh, I'll tell you, it was an amazing theme that began to emerge that can be summarized in two words: no excuses. I mean, one after the other they got up and said, "You know, after this election it means there're no excuses for our academic underperformance, for our irresponsible behavior—no

excuses. And one of the young men looked at the rest of the students and said, "You guys, there are a few of you who come to class late, a few of you who are not prepared for class—no excuses." So it's interesting the way in which the sense that Obama has achieved this, we are now able to achieve. America permits achievement.[8]

The ideas depicted in the above assertion suggest that the election of Barack Obama eradicated discrimination and that blacks should somehow stop using excuses and pull themselves up by their own bootstraps. What is shortsighted about Dr. Franklin's comments is that he ignores the systemic nature of racism and places the onus solely on the individual behavior of African Americans. Even though the election of Barack Obama was indeed historic, his election did very little to change the discriminatory practices in employment, housing, education, income, wealth, and the criminal justice system. In many ways, Dr. Franklin's comments embrace the politics of respectability and racial conservatives' assessments of the predicament of African American people. These same arguments contend that many of the disparities facing African Americans are a result of laziness and individual bad decision-making.

Shortly after the 2008 and 2012 presidential elections, racial tension in the United States increased dramatically. From the unprecedented opposition faced by the Obama administration to the murders of several unarmed black teens, America's reaction to the Obama presidency revealed that the country is anything but postracial. In *Black Presidency: Barack Obama and the Politics of Race in America*, Dyson notes:

> Obama has faced levels of resistance that no president before him has confronted. No president has had his faith and education questioned like Obama. No other president has had his life threatened as much. No other president has dealt with racial politics in Congress to the extent of being denied an automatic raise in the debt ceiling, causing the nation's credit rating to drop. No other president has had a representative shout "You lie!" during a speech to Congress. No other president has been so persistently challenged that he has had to produce a birth certificate to settle questions of his citizenship.[9]

As early as his first term, scholars noted the spillover effects of racial attitudes into opposition to President Obama's signature policy achievement—the American Affordable Healthcare Act. Michael Tesler argues that strong racial attitudes against President Obama have the potential to prime white opposition not only to Obama but to his policies as well. Additionally, scholars have found racial resentment to be a strong predictor of his job performance and white political behavior. In fact, scholars such as Michael Tesler found that President Obama's association with issues like health care polarized public opinion by racial attitudes and race in ways that were unprecedented. Not only have scholars found massive levels of polarization, they have also found Barack Obama's presidency to be a strong predictor of old-fashioned racism. Under this framework of white racism, African Americans are lazy and lack intelligence. Further dispelling the fallacy of the notion of America's postracialism, Vincent L. Hutchings finds "scant evidence of a decline in the racial divide . . . blacks and whites remain as far apart on racial policy matters in 2008 as in 1988."[10]

Although the current scholarship examining the Obama presidency has taken different approaches, many of the themes suggest that the Obama presidency has certainly changed the political landscape in a number of ways. The Obama candidacy has changed the way we think about campaigns, winning strategies, and building winning coalitions in national campaigns. From a symbolic perspective, President Obama represents racial progress and just how far the nation has come since the 1960s. On the flip side, Barack Obama's presidency has reminded America that the United States has yet to grapple with deep vestiges of race and racism. As historic as Obama's presidency has been from a symbolic standpoint, its impact on racial polarization in America has been baffling. To use the words of one scholar, "Mass politics had become more polarized by racial attitudes since Barack Obama's rise to prominence. That is, the election of President Obama helped usher in a most-racial political era where racially liberal and racially conservative Americans were more divided over a whole host of political positions than they had been in modern times."[11]

Linking Descriptive Representation and Political Trust in Government

The academic literature has missed an important opportunity to examine the degree to which Barack Obama's election as president of the United States has impacted levels of trust in the federal government. The extant literature concerning descriptive representation provides important theoretical conjectures that are useful in understanding Obama's influence on trust and racial attitudes among blacks and whites. One of the core themes of the prior literature suggests that descriptive representation may have a positive impact on how citizens view public officials and political institutions. Descriptive representation refers to the degree to which elected officials share identities such as race and gender with their constituencies. For example, Barack Obama descriptively represents African Americans. A substantial body of political science research examines the extent to which descriptive representation yields substantive representation. The implications of this body of work suggest that an increase in African American representation may be associated with an increase in trust in government among members of the African American community. Implicit in these studies is the idea that African American politicians will use their political power to advance issues that are important to African Americans, thereby creating a sense of political inclusion, which may increase political trust.

Defining Political Trust

Before moving into a deep exploration of the academic literature on political trust, it is important to establish what is meant by the term *trust*. Scholars such as Arthur Miller have characterized political trust as a combination of both positive and negative assessments of the national government.[12] Under this conception, political trust captures how citizens evaluate both trust in politicians and the overall function of and process of government. According to Mangum, "Political trust is mainly concerned with expectations and their relationship to the outcomes of government's actions."[13] It is important to note that scholars disagree about how to interpret low levels of political trust. For example, Citrin argues that declining levels of trust in government represent negative evaluations of politicians and policies, whereas Miller suggests that low levels of trust represent an indictment of the system.[14]

Determinants of Political Trust

Although scholars have examined trust in government from a variety of different perspectives, the empirical record demonstrates that since the 1970s Americans generally have become more distrusting of government. Early studies on political trust explored whether decreases in political trust were results of disaffection with the overall performance of the government[15] or dissatisfaction with political leaders. Social scientists have cited several factors from cultural to political that influence trust. Several scholars have linked trust in government to the performance of the national economy. These studies predict that an increase in negative beliefs about the economy's performance is associated with increased levels of distrust. Other scholars suggest that societal issues such as scandals, corruption, crime, and poverty all influence levels of trust. In addition to the economic and societal factors, scholars have found citizens' evaluations of political institutions and politicians to be significant predictors of distrust.[16]

Even though scholars tend to agree that a lack of descriptive representation is linked to African American distrust in government, much of the current scholarship has neglected an opportunity to interrogate Barack Obama's influence on political trust. Mangum provides a compelling theoretical examination of political trust among African Americans by empirically investigating the psychological involvement, policy stratification, and reference group models. He finds that each of these models significantly influences African American trust in government. Although his study has contributed to our understanding of the dynamics of political trust among African Americans by using the 1996 National Black Election Study, he is unable to investigate whether the descriptive representation of America's African American President has had any impact on African American trust in government. In fact, his analysis only includes African Americans; thus he is unable to compare levels of trust in government among African American and whites. Shayla C. Nunnally also shows that African Americans are less trusting of government. She argues that because African Americans have suffered from a long legacy of disenfranchisement, violence, intimidation, and the failure of the United States government to provide equal protection under the law, African American trust in government has been breached, resulting in substantially lower levels of trust in American democracy. Like Mangum's seminal work, Nunnally's work does not address Barack Obama's influence on trust.

Theories of Political Trust

Several theories have been used to explain political trust. A widely accepted assumption within political science suggests that the more citizens trust their government, the better democracy functions; yet African Americans have long maintained strong levels of distrust for government. Many scholars examining trust in government among African Americans have linked distrust to several theories that deal with the political conditions of African Americans, descriptive representation, and public policy. Although the study at hand does not test each of these theories, we contend that several of them provide important theoretical contributions in scholarly understandings of trust and distrust in the American electorate within the context of the Obama presidency.

Mangum's most profound critique regarding the academic literature on political trust is that it lacks theoretical development. In an attempt to fill this void, he applies three theoretical frameworks to explain political trust among African Americans. The frameworks he uses are as follows: the psychological model, the policy satisfaction model, and the reference group model.

Psychological Involvement Theory of Political Trust

The psychological involvement model is concerned with capturing the political, social, and economic position of African Americans within the United States. Simply put, the psychological involvement model is predicated on political efficacy, that is the degree to which individual citizens believe that they can impact the actions, decisions, and policy outputs of government. According to Mangum, "Lacking a voice in, or some control over, the decision-making process causes people to become skeptical about the political outcomes."[17] Under this model, if citizens believe that they do not have political power and influence, they are likely to exhibit negative feelings toward government. Additionally, the psychological involvement model posits that if citizens perceive that the government is not responsive to their concerns, they may be less likely to trust government and government leaders. African Americans within the United States have historically been victims of discrimination. From slavery to Jim Crow, African Americans have and continue to face a plethora of challenges in their efforts to be treated equal. Given that there is a massive body of academic literature that suggests that political efficacy has had a profound impact on the political behavior of African Americans, it is highly likely that political efficacy may be linked to lower levels of political trust.

The Policy Satisfaction Theory of Political Trust

The policy satisfaction model rests on the assumption that political trust is linked to the degree to which citizens are satisfied with the policy outputs of government.[18] Democratic theorists argue that a healthy democracy rests on the notion of popular sovereignty, that is, the ability of citizens to exercise control over the decisions of government. According to Citrin, citizens' trust for politicians and political institutions is conditioned on how well politicians are able to serve as problem solvers. Many empirical studies show that when citizens are satisfied with the policy outputs of government, they tend to exemplify stronger levels of trust in government.[19] Marc Hetherington suggests that when citizens perceive that the policies produced by the government are effective, they are likely to have stronger levels of trust in government than those who do not see the policy outputs as effective.

But how might this particular theory apply to African Americans? Because African Americans have historically faced disenfranchisement and discrimination, the policy outputs of government are important. In many instances, politicians have refused to directly take on race-based policy initiatives. According to Maurice Mangum, "government's ability or willingness to address this problem should impact African Americans' trust in government."[20] At its core, this model assumes that African American trust in government is a function of whether African Americans believe the government is taking meaningful steps to eradicate discrimination. Simply put, if African Americans believe that progress is being made to address discrimination, they may be more likely to trust government; if they do not believe that progress is being made, they will be less likely to trust government.

The Group Reference Theory of Political Trust

The reference group model deals directly with descriptive representation and references to characteristics such as political party among political leaders. This particular model associates political trust with increased levels of descriptive representation. One scholar argues that "given the amount of descriptive representation for African Americans at the national levels of government, the actual political reality is their lack of descriptive representation."[21] This model raises important questions about the intersections of political trust, the descriptive characteristics of politicians, and heuristics. For example, in the absence of African American political representation, what cues do African Americans use to assess their levels of trust for politicians that are not of the same race? Scholars suggest that in the absence race, an individual's affinity toward a group's political party has the ability to serve as an important cue.[22] For example, if Republicans are in control of the government and individuals have positive feelings toward the Republican Party, then the individuals should be more likely to have positive evaluations of the government.

Racial Attitudes and the Obama Presidency

Another important element that this chapter investigates is President Obama's influence on racial attitudes. There is an extensive literature on how racial attitudes have primed opposition to President Obama and his policies. Many were quick to label the election of Barack Obama as the start of a postracial society. Yet exit polling and ANES data seem to suggest that the election and candidacy of Barack Obama led to perhaps the strongest impact of racial attitudes on presidential evaluations and the 2008 vote choice in the history of such measures. Political scientists for several years have sought to explain white resistance to African American candidates. These studies consistently demonstrate that high levels of racial resentment are linked to opposition of African American candidates and race-targeted policies.

The racial resentment thesis is predicated on the notion that older forms of racism such as overt racism (i.e., Jim Crow) has evolved into a new form of racism known as symbolic racism or racial resentment. Although Jim Crow rests on the idea that blacks are morally inferior and are therefore not worthy of sharing the same public facilities and residential areas, symbolic racism, also known as racial resentment, is based on "a blend of anti-black affect and the kind of traditional American moral values embodied in the Protestant Ethic."[23] Racial resentment contends that prejudice in the evaluation of black candidates stems from the denial of the continued struggle for equality among African Americans. The opposition from whites who are racially resentful rests in symbolic racism rather than a realistic threat to white political interest.[24] Sears asserts that racial resentment is "a mixture of anti-black feelings with the finest and proudest of traditional American values, particularly individualism."[25]

The framework of symbolic racism was first introduced by Kinder and Sears in a 1981 study that investigated the impact of white racial attitudes on vote choice in the Los Angeles mayoral election of 1969. Kinder and Sears argue that symbolic racism is developed early in life, which stems from negative ideas toward African Americans intersecting with conservatism. Additionally, several studies have found that symbolic racism is a strong predictor of white opposition to black candidates and is indirectly related to nonracial issues such as welfare, busing, and crime.[26]

Critiques of Racial Resentment

Although racial resentment has been found to be a predictor of white political behavior, the meaning and measurements of this theory have not gone without their share of critics. Scholars have questioned its validity and whether it is a manifestation of racism and not just simply conservatism.[27] Despite this criticism, many of the studies challenging the racial resentment model have been rebutted and scholars have found the conceptualization of racial resentment to be empirically valid.

Many scholars recently created additive scales to capture racial resentment. This has resulted in a number of criticisms against racial resentment both empirically and theoretically. Tarman and Sears outline and address each of the four major criticisms against the racial resentment model. They note that racial resentment has been challenged in the following ways: (1) having been conceptualized and measured inconsistently over time; (2) that it may not be a single, internally consistent and coherent belief system; (3) that it may generate repressed strong associations with racial policy preference because of content overlap between measures of the independent and dependent variables; and (4) is racial resentment a distinctive belief system in its own right or does it simply reflects various other familiar constructs.[28]

Tarman and Sears contend that while some empirical analyses have certainly been inconsistent with measuring racial resentment, overall studies have been consistent in measuring racial resentment.[29] In measuring racial resentment, scholars have examined the following themes: (1) the denial of continued discrimination for blacks; (2) blacks should try harder; (3) blacks should work their way up without any special favors; and (4) blacks have received more than they deserve.[30]

In addressing the question of racial resentment, a single internally consistent belief system, Tarman and Sears note, "The theory represents these four themes as a logically consistent view of black's place in society and the polity: blacks are no longer much discriminated against, so remaining disadvantages must result mostly from their own lack of effort."[31] Racial resentment has also been criticized by scholars citing that it has a strong association with white racial policy preferences only because the items used to capture both concepts are similar in content.

The major questions concerning critics of racial resentment center on the question, is racial resentment a "distinctive and independent belief system or is it merely redundant with older concepts that have traditionally been used to explain racial attitudes, such as political conservatism, old fashion racism, individualism, or anti egalitarianism?"[32] The empirical test does not support this critique; in fact, Tarman and Sears find that in both the 1986 and 2000 ANES data, the items used to measure racial resentment are due to a factor other than ideology and party identification.

Essentially, symbolic racism has faced a number of critics; however, as Tarman and Sears suggest, these criticisms are not supported empirically. Despite such critics, the measures of racial resentment have been found to be predictors of a number of political attitudes and behaviors.[33] Scholars have even controlled for a number of other variables in multivariate analyses, and racial resentment remains a significant predictor of attitudes and behaviors. The extant literature reveals that racial resentment continues to shape attitudes on racial and nonracial attitudes, attitudes toward African

American candidates, attitudes toward the Confederate flag, and partisan identification among Southern whites and vote choice.

For many African Americans, the Obama presidency symbolizes an important mark in American politics. Historically African Americans have always exemplified strong levels of distrust in government. One of the benefits of descriptive representation is the idea that it presents under-represented groups with a sense of inclusiveness. The Obama presidency presents an ideal opportunity to empirically interrogate the impact of race on racial resentment and trust in government. Previous studies have not examined how the Obama presidency might have impacted racial resent-ment between both blacks and whites, and these studies have also neglected to investigate how race might have impacted levels of trust in government as a result of the Obama presidency. Political scientists who do study racial resentment have not given much thought as to what it means when Afri-can Americans exemplify strong levels of racial resentment.

Because America has never had an African American president, it is log-ical to expect that the excitement and apprehension in 2008 for an Obama presidency might have impacted both levels of racial resentment and trust in government among blacks and whites. We suspect that to several Amer-icans the Obama presidency might have symbolized this fictional postra-cial moment in America when African Americans no longer face racial barriers. If this is the case, then there may be an expectation that his presi-dency in 2008 might have activated stronger levels of racial resentment within both groups. However, it is important to note that one must account for the political climate. Shortly after the 2008 election, many Americans were exposed to the realities of the Obama presidency and repeated acts of blatant racism. It is these realities that have the potential to cause whites and blacks to react differently. Once Americans witnessed the realities of the Obama presidency and how society at large responded to America's first African American president, one can reasonably argue that in 2012 both whites and blacks would have responded differently to racial resent-ment and level of trust in government.

We suggest that blacks and whites may have interpreted Barack Obama's election differently. For African Americans, his election may have been seen as an opportunity for a black man to utilize his political office to address issues important to the African American community. It is this hopeful optimism that we contend may lead to temporary increased levels of politi-cal trust among African Americans. Additionally, we assert that if African Americans believed that the election of Barack Obama symbolized the breaking down of racial barriers, then African Americans may embrace the notion that African Americans no longer have reasons for excuses and therefore may have more attitudes that could be characterized as racially resentful. For many white Americans, we contend that Barack Obama's rise to political power represents a threat to the white political power and therefore may activate strong levels of racial resentment and decrease political trust.

Data and Methods

The data for this empirical analysis were taken from the ANES Survey covering the years 2004, 2008, and 2012, a data source that has consistently been used to explain racial attitudes. Although it does not provide a strong enough sample to investigate black attitudes alone, we believe it is sufficient for making the kind of comparisons and generalizations we make below. It is important to examine the 2004, 2008, and 2012 elections so that the impact of race on political attitudes can be compared. The following are the two models we test.

Political trust $= \beta_0 + \beta_1$ Race $+ \beta_2$ Obama feelings $+ \beta_3$ Education $+ \beta_4$ Income $+ \beta_5$ Ideology $+ \beta_6$ Past vote $+ \beta_7$ Feelings about the economy $+ \varepsilon$

Racial resentment $= \beta_0 + \beta_1$ Race $+ \beta_2$ Obama feelings $+ \beta_3$ Education $+ \beta_4$ Income $+ \beta_5$ Ideology $+ \beta_6$ Past vote $+ \beta_7$ Feelings about the economy $+ \varepsilon$

Measuring Racial Resentment and Trust

We are interested in explaining two specific variables in this analysis: racial resentment and trust in government. Racial resentment is measured on a scale ranging from 3 to 15. Using the measures created by Kinder and Sanders, three items were taken from the ANES data and used to create a racial resentment index. ANES researchers asked white respondents to indicate whether they agreed or disagreed with the following statements:

1. Generations of slavery and discrimination have created conditions that make it difficult for blacks to work their way out of the lower class.
2. It's really just a matter of some people not trying hard enough; if blacks would only try harder they could be just as well off as whites.
3. Irish, Italian, Jewish, and many other minorities overcame prejudice and worked their way up. Blacks should do the same without any special favors.

The racial resentment index was created by taking the responses to the above questions and recoding them in a way such that lower scores mean the respondent had less racial resentment and higher scores indicate the respondents harbor more racially resentful attitudes.[34]

Trust in government measures the level of trust the respondent has for the federal government to do what is right. Government trust is coded so that higher numbers mean the respondent has less trust in the federal government (1=trust just about always, 2=trust most of the time, and 3=trust some of the time or never).

When looking at both of these measures, blacks and whites had very different attitudes regarding racial resentment and trust in government prior to the election of Barrack Obama. This is most notable at the extremes (see Figure 8.1). Figure 8.1 displays how blacks and whites answered the first measure of racial resentment in 2004, 2008, and 2012. The first bar within each group represents the percentage of whites; the second bar

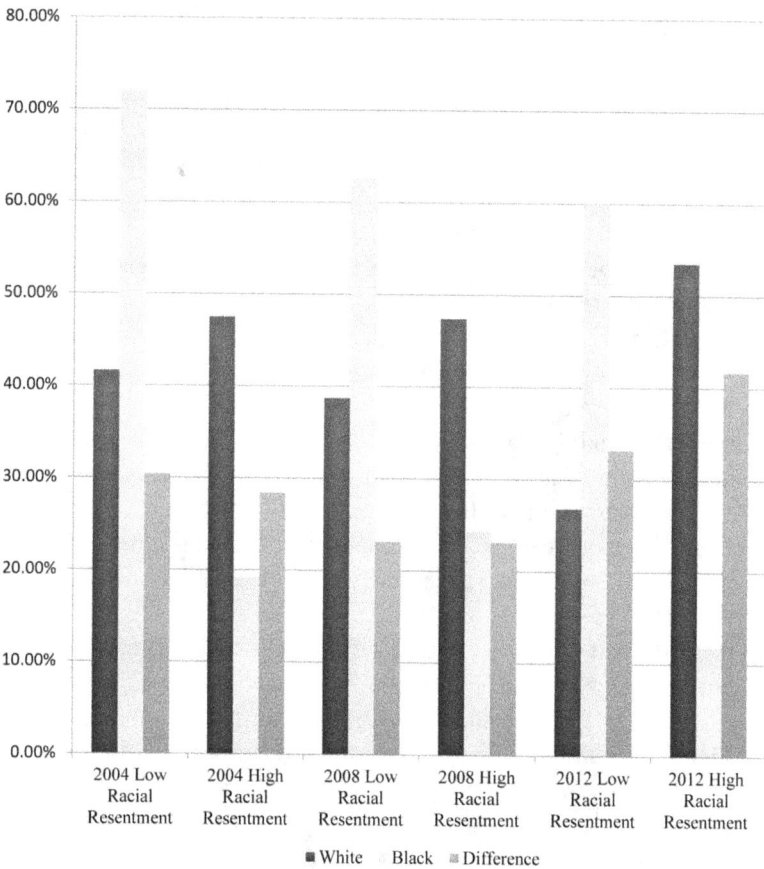

Figure 8.1   Denial of continued discrimination.

represents the percentage of blacks; and the last bar represents the percentage difference between the two groups. When asked about the denial of continued discrimination in 2004, the table shows there is a 30 percent difference between blacks and whites, with blacks being much more likely than whites to take the position of low racial resentment, 72 percent and 41.69 percent, respectively. The opposite is true at the highest racial resentment category. Whites are much more likely than blacks to take a position of high racial resentment, 47.5 percent to 19.1 percent, respectively. These positions represent a 30.4 percentage point difference in the least resentful category and a 28.4 percentage difference in the most resentful category.

Initially the Obama election seems to have had a diminishing effect on these attitudes. The 2008 attitudes suggest that there was a smaller gap between blacks and whites among these attitudes. Black support for the least resentful categories dropped to 62.6 percent while their support for the most resentful positions rose to 24.3 percent. The differences among the least resentful attitudes between the two groups decreased from 30.4 percent in 2004 to 23.9 percent in 2008, and among the most resentful it decreased from 28.4 percent in 2004 to 23 percent in 2008. These data suggest that the election of a black president may have created some degree of convergence of the two groups.

After the country had more experience with its first black president, we begin to see the attitudes reflecting this reality and possibly reacting to it. The black–white differences regarding opinions on the denial of continued discrimination illuminate the pervasive divisions that exist between these two groups. Blacks and whites seem to return to their previous views about blacks, with even more of a difference between the two. Figure 8.1 shows that now more than half (53.5%) of whites expressed views that were more resentful. At the same time, almost two-thirds (60%) of blacks expressed views that were least resentful. In the least resentful attitudes, the differences between the groups soared to 33.2 percent, and in the most resentful they soared to 41.7 percent. These differences are even *larger* than those observed in 2004.

A similar pattern is observed with each of the individual measures of racial resentment (see Figures 8.2 and 8.3). The differences in the least resentful attitudes for *Blacks should try harder* are 19.1 percent in 2004, 12.1 in 2008, and 31.3 in 2012. The most resentful attitudes show racial differences of 13.6 percent in 2004, 8.7 percent in 2008, and 27.9 percent in 2012. When asked whether *Blacks should work their way up*, we notice the low-resentment attitudes having differences of 25.2 percent in 2004, 12.3 percent in 2008, and 26.5 percent in 2012. The differences between

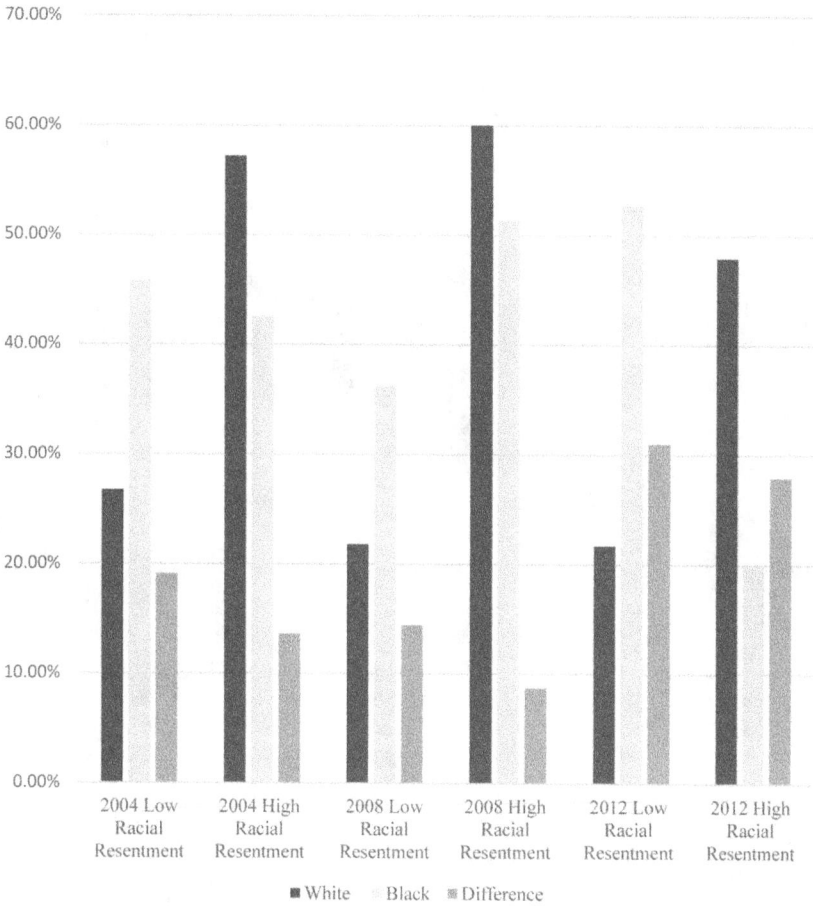

Figure 8.2 Blacks should try harder.

blacks and whites who are most resentful are 29.1 percent in 2004, 15.5 percent in 2008, and a substantial 43.6 percent in 2012.

The 2012 differences when looking at the attitudes regarding the denial of continued discrimination and blacks' ability to work their way up should not be overlooked. These measures show a difference of 41.7 percent and 43.6 percent among the most resentful respondents. Almost half (47.5 percent) of whites show racial resentment by denying the continued discrimination of blacks, and only 19.1 percent of blacks feel that way. Almost two-thirds of whites (62.7%) believe that blacks should work their way up like other groups. Again, only 19 percent of blacks share that attitude.

There is clearly a widening gap between the attitudes of whites and blacks when asked about issues of racial resentment. Although these

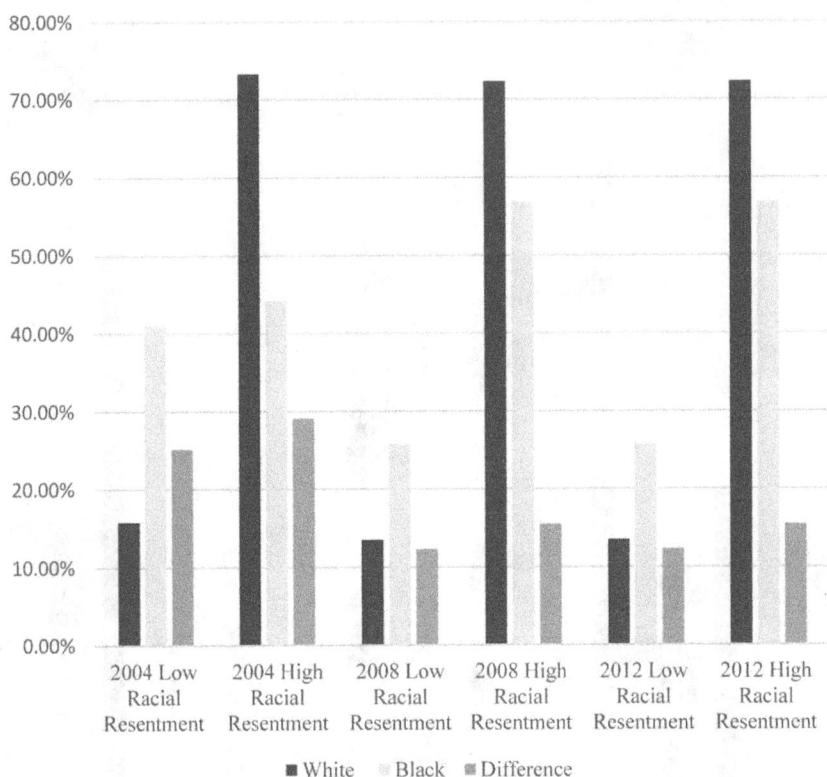

Figure 8.3   Blacks should work their way up.

showed some signs of lessening in 2008, that gap reemerged in 2012 with an even greater gap between whites and blacks. More rigorous testing of the role that race plays in these attitudes is necessary to support our claims.

Our main concern here is that we are specifically interested in the differences between how blacks and whites have responded to Obama's presidency. Race is defined as "black," "white," and "other." Anyone who identified as multiracial was coded as "other." We believe attitudes toward Obama are the main driver toward racial resentment attitudes in 2012. This variable is measured by asking respondents to rate their feelings toward Barack Obama.

We use a number of controls in addition to the explanatory variables above. Abramowitz and Knotts and Abramowitz and Saunders found *political ideology* to be an indicator of vote choice; therefore, it is also important to control for this variable.[35] Ideology is measured on a seven-point scale from extremely liberal to extremely conservative. One of the criticisms against racial resentment is that it is simply a cleavage of ideological preferences and attitudes.[36] It is important to note that ideology as conceptualized in these studies is measured as policy preferences of voters, using a number of social and political issues. The model also includes a measure of the respondent's vote in the previous election.

The national economy was at the center of the political debate during the 2008 presidential election; as a result, this analysis controls for *economic conditions*. The ANES data asked respondents if they believed economic conditions were better or worse. This variable is recoded as 0 if the respondent thought the economy was better and 1 if the respondent thought the economy was worse. Fiorina asserts that voters will engage in retrospective voting during times of economic hardship, and that this behavior has the capacity to trump partisan identification and racial attitudes.[37]

Several other variables that have been found to have a significant impact on political attitudes were also included in the model. Stonecash, Brewer, and Mariani suggest that levels of *educational attainment* also impact vote choice; in order to test his assertion, we include a measure of levels of education.[38] This variable records the number of years of formal education a person has had. We also control for income, measured by household income, and vote in previous presidential election. The following hypotheses are tested below.

H_1: *Race will be a greater predictor of racial resentment attitudes in 2012 than in the previous years.*

H_2: *Race will be a greater predictor of trust in the government in 2012 than in previous years.*

H_3: *Respondents who dislike President Obama will be more likely to show racial resentment.*

Findings and Analysis

We use multiple regression to more thoroughly investigate the relationships that influence racial resentment and political trust. Tables 8.1 and 8.2 show the results of the determinants of racial resentment and political trust. Table 8.1 displays the models across 2004, 2008, and 2012. The evidence is quite supportive of the hypotheses outlined above.

H_1: *Race will be a greater predictor of racial resentment attitudes in 2012 than in the previous years.*

Table 8.1   **Determinants of Racial Resentment**

	R^2 0.30	R^2 0.29	R^2 0.30
	2004	**2008**	**2012**
	(SE)	(SE)	(SE)
Constant	13.89** (1.21)	14.09** (0.80)	8.89** (0.67)
Race	−0.272 (0.20)	−0.332** (0.14)	−0.42** (0.14)
Obama feelings	−0.012* (0.01)	−0.04** (0.00)	0.651** (0.09)
Economy	−0.207** (0.09)	0.012 (0.12)	0.39** (0.14)
Ideology	0.704** (0.1)	0.226** (0.07)	0.26** (0.08)
Past vote	0.092 (0.11)	0.029 (0.08)	0.19 (0.228)
Income	−0.005 (0.03)	−0.01 (0.02)	0.03 (0.02)
Education	−0.390** (0.06)	−0.44** (0.06)	−0.25** (0.05)

[a]There were no questions on Barack Obama in 2004. Instead, respondents were asked to rate their feelings about Kerry on a scale from 0 to 100, with 0 being "cold" and 100 being "hot."
*Indicates significance at the 0.10 level.
**Indicates significance at the 0.05 level.

Our regression analysis shows that race did have a greater impact on racial resentment in 2012 than in the previous years (see Table 8.1). Race is a significant predictor of racial resentment in 2008 and 2012, but not in 2004. Because race is coded with low numbers representing whites, these values tell us that whites are more likely to have the most racial resentment attitudes across 2008 and 2012. When controlling for other factors, race has a negative influence on attitudes of racial resentment. A closer look at the values indicates that race has a greater influence from 2008 to 2012 (−0.33 to −0.42). Notice that race was not a significant predictor in 2004 and was a weaker predictor in 2008 than in 2012. This is support for our first hypothesis.

H_2: *Race will be a greater predictor of trust in the government in 2012 than in previous years.*

Our second hypothesis is moderately supported by our analysis. Similar to our findings with racial resentment, race is not a significant predictor when explaining trust in 2004, but is a significant predictor in 2008 and 2012 (see Table 8.2). These models indicate another complexity that had occurred in the racial resentment models. The model has more explanatory power in 2012 (with the R^2 equal to 0.09 in 2004, 0.01 in 2008, and

Table 8.2 Determinants of Trust

	R² 0.09	R² 0.01	R² 0.19
	2004	2008	2012
	(SE)	(SE)	(SE)
Constant	1.93** (0.24)	2.17** (0.25)	2.28** (0.11)
Race	0.06 (0.04)	0.09** (0.04)	−0.06** (0.02)
Obama feelings	0.00 (0.00)	−0.00* (0.00)	0.09** (0.01)
Economy	0.06** (0.02)	0.09** (0.04)	0.39 (0.14)
Ideology	−0.05** (0.02)	0.02** (0.02)	0.01 (0.01)
Past vote	0.01 (0.02)	0.00 (0.02)	0.00 (0.04)
Income	0.00 (0.00)	−0.00 (0.01)	−0.00 (0.00)
Education	0.04** (0.01)	0.01 (9.02)	0.01 (0.01)

ᵃThere were no questions on Barack Obama in 2004. Instead, respondents were asked to rate their feelings about Kerry on a scale from 0 to 100, with 0 being "cold" and 100 being "hot."

*Indicates significance at the 0.10 level.

**Indicates significance at the 0.05 level.

0.19 in 2012), and the parameter value changes from positive in 2008 to negative in 2012. Because higher numbers indicate less trust, this indicates that whites were more likely to trust the government in 2008 and *less* likely to trust the government in 2012. We believe this indicates that whites were frustrated by the Obama presidency and reacted negatively by taking that frustration out in their views of the national government. Unfortunately, the continued attacks on the president's character and policies reinforced this pessimistic view. Although we do not believe this evidence conclusively indicates there is a greater racial impact in 2012 than there was in 2008, we do believe there is an important impact that race has on political trust.

H_3: *Respondents who dislike President Obama will be more likely to show racial resentment.*

Our third hypothesis is also addressed in Table 8.1. According to this table, feelings toward Obama (toward Kerry in 2004) were important in each year. In 2004, people with lower feelings toward Kerry were more likely to have attitudes that reflected racial resentment. The 2008 and 2012 values show that those who are more unfavorable toward Obama are more likely to have attitudes showing racial resentment. This finding supports our hypothesis that disliking Obama influenced racial resentment.

Conclusion

This analysis reveals that even though the United States has elected its first African American president, the American society is anything but postracial. In fact, the implications of this analysis suggest that race remains a significant predictor of racial resentment and trust in government. The candidacy and subsequently election of Barack Obama marked a milestone in the history of the United States of America; despite this historic moment, scholars such as Tesler, Sears, Knuckey, Ford, Maxwell, and Shields have emerged, arguing that the candidacy of Barack Obama activated strong racial attitudes among white voters and that those attitudes influenced the 2008 vote choice unlike any other election in the history of such measures.

This analysis finds that race is a significant predictor of racial resentment and trust in government. This analysis contributes to the literature in several ways. First, it is important to note that racial issues did not dominate the campaign in the 2008 election; therefore, the findings of this analysis suggest that despite having few overt references to race, there is something unique that subjects African American candidates to racial evaluations. The implications of this study suggest that the presence of an African American candidate is enough to activate strong racial attitudes, and limits white support for African American candidates. In addition, this analysis suggests that race is a strong predictor of racial resentment and trust in government. This study adds to the growing body of literature concerning the impact of race on racial resentment and trust in government by taking advantage of the one of the first opportunities to employ data over multiple years to analyze the political attitudes of whites and nonwhites in a presidential election. One of the major contributions of this analysis is that it is one of the first studies to examine the impact of descriptive representation at the presidential level to investigate the impact of race on racial resentment and trust in government. Research in political science has not given much thought about how to interpret racial resentment among blacks. In fact the racial resentment has been a model primarily applied to whites. This analysis seeks to engage this void in the academic literature.

It is ironic that many incorrectly attribute the social divisions within the United States to President Obama. Rather than finding that Obama divided the American people, we find the American people to be divided because of their reluctance to purge themselves of racism. President Obama violated their beliefs about the possibilities of blackness, but rather than reaching a new plateau, American racism required people to find new ways to continue racist beliefs. In the end, Barrack Obama was not "The Great Divider." Good old-fashioned racism deserves that title.

Notes

1. A previous version of this paper was presented at the 2016 Southern Political Science Association Annual Meeting in San Juan, Puerto Rico.
2. Dyson, 2016, p. 3.
3. Gay, 2002.
4. Knuckey, 2011, pp. 1–2.
5. Ibid., p. 2.
6. Thernstrom, 2008, p. 2.
7. Quoted in Nagourney, 2008, p. 1.
8. Quoted in "Spiritual Voices on Obama Administration," 2009, p. 1.
9. Dyson, 2016, p. 12.
10. Hutchings, 2009, p. 917.
11. Tesler, 2016, p. 3.
12. Miller, 1979.
13. Mangum, 2012, p. 3.
14. Citrin, 1974; and Miller, 1979.
15. Ibid.
16. Hetherington, 1998.
17. Mangum, 2012, p. 5.
18. Ibid.
19. Hetherington, 1998.
20. Mangum, 2012, p. 6.
21. Ibid., p. 8.
22. Abney and Hutcheson, 1981.
23. Ibid., p. 419.
24. Henry and Sears, 2002.
25. Sears, 1988, p. 102.
26. Peffley and Hurwitz, 2007.
27. Sniderman and Hagen, 1985.
28. Ibid.
29. Ibid.
30. Kinder and Sears, 1981.
31. Tarman and Sears, 2005, p. 733.
32. Ibid., p. 752.
33. Kinder and Sears, 1981.
34. For example, a respondent who is racially sympathetic is assigned a racial resentment score of 1, whereas a person who is extremely racially resentful is assigned a score of 5.
35. Abramowitz and Knotts, 2006; Abramowitz and Saunders, 1998.
36. Sniderman and Hagen, 1985.
37. Fiorina, 1981.
38. Stonecash, Brewer, and Mariani, 2003.

Bibliography

Abney, Glenn, and John D. Hutcheson Jr. 1982. "Race Representation and Trust Changes in Attitudes after the Election of a Black Mayor." *Public Opinion Quarterly* 45(1): 91–101.

Abramowitz, Alan I. 2006. "Ideological Realignment in the American Electorate: A Comparison of Northern and Southern Voters in the Pre-Regan and Post-Reagan Eras." *Politics and Policy* 34(1): 94–108.

Abramowitz, Alan I. 2008. "Forecasting the 2008 Presidential Election with the Time-for-Change Model." *Political Science and Politics* 41(4): 691–95.

Abramowitz, Alan I., and Kyle L. Saunders. 1998. "Ideological Realignment in the U.S. Electorate." *Journal of Politics* 60(3): 634–52.

Bartels, Larry M. 2000. "Partisanship and Voting Behavior 1952–1996." *American Journal of Political Science* 44(1): 35–50.

Bobo, Lawrence, and James R. Kluegel. 1993. "Opposition to Race-Targeting: Self-Interest, Stratification Ideology, or Racial Attitudes?" *American Sociological Review* 58: 443–64.

Caesar, James W., Andrew E. Busch, and John J. Pitney. 2009. *Epic Journey The 2008 Election and American Politics.* Princeton, NJ: Princeton University Press.

Citrin, Jack. 1974. "Comment: The Political Relevance of Trust in American Government." *American Political Science Review* 68(3): 973–72.

Citrin, Jack, Donald P. Green, and David O. Sears. 1990. "White Reactions to Black Candidates: When Does Race Matter?" *Public Opinion Quarterly* 54(1): 74–96.

Curry, Tom. 2008 "How Obama Won the White House." MSNBC. November 11, 2008. http://www.nbcnews.com/id/27540321/ns/politics-decision_08/t/how-obama-won-white-house/# V2iwIldRfdk.

Dyson, E. Michael. 2016. *The Black Presidency Barack Obama and the Politics of Race in America.* New York: New York.

Easton, David A. 1965. *Systems Analysis of Political Life.* New York: New York Wiley.

Ford, Pearl K., Angie Maxwell, and Todd Shields. 2010. "What's the Matter with Arkansas? Symbolic Racism and the 2008 Presidential Candidate Support." *Presidential Studies Quarterly* 40(2): 286–302.

Fiorina, Morris. 1981. *Retrospective Voting in American Elections.* New Haven: Yale University Press.

Gay, Claudine. 2002. "Spirals of Trust: The Effect of Descriptive Representation on the Relationship Between Citizens and Their Government." *American Journal of Political Science* 46(4): 717–33.

Henry, P. J., and David O. Sears. 2002. "The Symbolic Racism Scale." *Political Psychology* 23(3): 253–83.

Hetherington, Marc. 1998. "The Political Relevance of Political Trust." *American Political Science Review* 92(4): 791–808.

Highton, Benjamin. 2004. "White Voters and African American Candidates for Congress." *Political Behavior* 26(1): 1–25.

Howell, Susan E. 1994. "Racism, Cynicism, Economics, and David Duke." *American Politics Quarterly* 22(2): 190–207.

Hutchings, Vincent. 2009. "Change or More of the Same: Evaluating Racial Attitudes in the Obama Era." *Public Opinion Quarterly* 72(5): 917–42.

Jackman, Simon and Lynn Vavreck. 2010. "Obama's Advantage: Race, Partisanship, and Racial Attitudes in Context." Annual Meeting of the Midwest Political Science Association. April 21, 2010.

Kinder, Donald R., and Lynn M. Sanders. 1996. *Divided by Color: Racial Politics and Democratic Ideals.* Chicago: University of Chicago Press.

Kinder, Donald R., and David O. Sears. 1981. "Prejudice and Politics: Symbolic Racism versus Racial Threat to the Good Life." *Journal of Personality and Social Psychology* 40(2): 414–31.

Knuckey, Jonathan. 2005. "Racial Resentment and the Changing Partisanship of Southern Whites." *Party Politics* 11(1): 5–28.

Knuckey, Jonathan. 2011. "Racial Resentment and Vote Choice in the 2008 U.S. Presidential Election." *Politics & Policy* 39(5): 555–82.

Knuckey, Jonathan, and Byron Orey. 2000. "Symbolic Racism in the 1995 Louisiana Gubernatorial Election." *Social Science Quarterly* 81(4): 1027–35.

Krysan, Maria. 2000. "Prejudice Politics and Public Opinion Understanding the Sources of Racial Policy Attitudes." *Annual Review of Sociology* 26(3): 35–168.

Lewis-Beck, Michael, Charles Tien, and Richard Nadeau. 2010. "Obama's Landslide: A Racial Cost." *Political Science and Politics* 43(1): 69–75.

Mangum, Maurice. 2012. "Explaining African-American Political Trust Examining Psychological Involvement Policy Satisfaction, and Reference Group Effect." *International Social Science Review* 87(1): 3–18.

Mansbridge, Jane. 1999. "Should Blacks Represent Blacks and Women Represent Women: A Contingent 'Yes?'" *The Journal of Politics* 61(3): 628–57.

McConahay, John B., and J. C. Hough 1976 "Symbolic Racism." *Journal of Social Issues* 43(1): 69–76.

Miller, Arthur. 1974. "Political Issues and Trust in Government 1964–1970." *American Political Science Review* 68(3): 951–72.

Miller, Arthur H. 1979. "Type-Set Politics Impact of Newspaper on Public Confidence." *American Political Science Review* 73(1): 67–84.

Miller, Arthur H., and Stephen Borrelli. 1991. "Confidence in Government during the 1980s." *American Politics Quarterly* 19(3): 147–73.

Nagourney, Adam. 2008. "Obama Elected President as Racial Barrier Falls." *New York Times,* November 4, 2008. http://www.nytimes.com/2008/11/05/us/politics/05elect.html_r=0.

Nunnally, Shayla. 2012. *Trust in Black America Race Discrimination and Politics.* New York, NY: University Press.

Orey, Byron. 2001. "A New Racial Threat in the New South: A Conditional Yes." *American Review of Politics* 22(2): 233–329.

Orey, Byron. 2004. "Racial Attitudes and Support for the Mississippi State Flag." *American Politics Research* 32(1): 102–16.

Peffley, Mark, and John Hurwitz. 2007. "Persuasion and Resistance Race and the Death Penalty in America." *American Journal of Political Science* 51(7): 996–1012.

Peffley, Mark, Todd Shields, and Bruce Williams. 1996. "The Intersection of Race and Crime in Television News Stories: An Experimental Study." *Political Communications* 13: 309–27.

Pitkin, Hanna F. 1972. *The Concept of Representation*. Los Angeles, CA: University of California Press.

Reeves, Keith. 1997. *Voting Hopes or Fears White Voters Black and Racial Politics in America*. New York: Oxford University Press.

Sears, David O. 1988. "Symbolic Racism." In *Eliminating Racism Profiles in Controversy*, edited by Phyllis A. Katz and Dalmas A. Taylor. New York: Plenum: 53–84.

Sears, David O., Jack Citrin, and Rick Kosterman. 1987. "Jesse Jackson and the Southern White Electorate." In *Blacks in Southern Politics*, edited by Laurence W. Moreland, Robert P. Steed, and Todd A. Baker. New York: Praeger, 209–25.

Sears, David O., and P. J. Henry. 2005 "Over Thirty Years Later: A Contemporary Look at Symbolic Racism and Its Critics." *Advances in Experimental Social Psychology* 37(3): 95–105.

Sears, David O., and Donald R. Kinder. 1971. "Racial Tensions and Voting in Los Angeles." In *Los Angeles Viability and Prospects or Metropolitan Leadership*, edited by Werner Z. Hirsch. New York: Praeger, 51–88.

Sears, David O., Colette Van Laar, Mary Carrilllo, and Rick Kosterman. 1997. "Is it really Racism? The Origins of White Americans' Opposition to Race-Targeted Policies." *Public Opinion Quarterly* 61(1): 16–53.

Sniderman, Paul M., and Michael G. Hagen. 1985. *Race and Inequality: A Study in American Values*. Chatham, NJ: Chatham House.

Sniderman, Paul M., and Thomas Pizza. 1993. *The Scar of Race*. Cambridge: Harvard University Press.

Sniderman, Paul M., and Philip E. Tetlock. 1986. "Symbolic Racism Problems of Motive Attribution in Policy Analysis." *Journal of Social Issues* 42(2): 129–50.

"Spiritual Voices on the Obama Administration." *Religion and Ethics Newsweekly*, January 16, 2009. http://www.pbs.org/wnet/religionandethics/2009/01/16/january-16-2009-spiritual-voices-on-obama-administration/1991/.

Steele, Shelby. 2008. "Obama's Post-Racial Promise." *The Los Angeles Times*, November 5, 2008. http://www.latimes.com/opinion/opinion-la/la-oe-steele5-2008nov05-story.html.

Stonecash, Jeffrey M., Mark D. Brewer, and Mack D. Mariani. 2003. *Diverging Parties Social Change Realignment and Party Polarization*. Boulder, CO: Westview Press.

Tarman, Christopher, and David O. Sears. 2005. "The Conceptualization and Measurement of Symbolic Racism." *Journal of Politics* 67(3): 731–61.

Tesler, Michael. 2012. "The Spillover of Racialization into Health Care: How President Obama Polarized Public Opinion by Racial Attitudes and Race." *American Journal of Political Science* 56(3): 690–704.

Tesler, Michael. 2013. "The Return of Old Fashioned Racism to White Americans' Partisan Preferences in the Early Obama Era." *Journal of Politics* 75(1): 110–23.

Tesler, Michael. 2016. *Post Racial or Most Racial? Race and Politics in the Obama Era.* Chicago, IL: University of Chicago Press.

Tesler, Michael, and David O. Sears. 2010. *Obama's Race: The 2008 Election and the Dream of a Post Racial America.* Chicago, IL: Chicago University Press.

Thernstrom, Abigail. 2008. "Great Black Hope: The Reality of President-Elect Obama." National Review Online, November 6, 2008. http://www.national review.com/articles/2264/great-black-hope/nro-symposium.

United States. 1988. The Kenner Report for the National Advisory Commission on Civil Disorders in 1968. New York: Pantheon Books.

Valentino, Nicholas A,. and David O. Sears. 2005. "Old Times They Are Not Forgotten: Race and Partisan Realignment in the Contemporary South." *American Journal of Political Science* 49(3): 672–88.

Walton, Hanes. 1972. *Black Politics: A Theoretical Structural Analysis.* Philadelphia: J. B. Lippincott.

Weisberg, Herbert F., and Christopher J. Devine. 2009. "Racial Attitude Effects of Voting in the 2008 Election." *Typescript.* Columbus, OH: The Ohio State University.

William, Gamson. 1968. *Scandal The Crisis of Distrust in American Politics.* Homewood, IL: Dorsey Press.

Coalition Building, Social Media, and Political Messaging

CHAPTER NINE

Body Cameras and Policing: From Ferguson to Baltimore

MaCherie M. Placide

How the Obama Administration's Response to the Uprisings in Ferguson and Baltimore Shaped the Overall Discussion on Policing and the Use of Body Cameras

The 21st century has introduced a diffusion of technological innovations that have influenced the amount of information citizens have at their fingertips. Through the use of smartphones, a new generation is now swept into a digital life in which lots of information can be transmitted and is available at the push of a button. This new way of communication continues to change the policy landscape in the United States, impacting law enforcement agencies and policing.

This use of social media has caused firestorms from Ferguson, New York, and Baltimore, in which the public has viewed law enforcement officers visually brutalizing African American men and women. The measure of brutality has been witnessed by citizens with smartphones, who immediately post the misconduct on various social media apps for the public to view. The scenes of televised brutality only prove that law enforcement agencies are not transparent or accountable, and these poor interactions increase public distrust.

Needless to say, law enforcement agencies are challenged with improving their interactions with communities and reducing the amount of misconduct among people of color. With the incorporation of new technology, there have been discussions with law enforcement executives, community leaders, and elected officials on the use of body-worn cameras (BWCs) to assist in the reduction of misconduct complaints and instances of unnecessary use of force while increasing officer professionalism and training. President Obama and his administration, via the U.S. Justice Department, have not only taken steps to fiscally support the use of BWCs within law enforcement agencies but also to holistically examine policing and create measureable best practices.

This chapter examines the law enforcement operations, including the use of BWCs as a tool to monitor the actions of law enforcement officers in the field. Moreover, it addresses President Obama's response to the uprisings, from Ferguson to Baltimore, and how his administration has helped shape the overall discussion of law enforcement operations in the United States.

Police Operations

Police operations are those activities conducted in the field by law enforcement officers, including patrol, traffic, investigation, and general calls to service communities, which they "serve and protect."[1] The role of the police officer is integrative: concerned with keeping the peace as well as the law in the communities they serve.

Democracy in the United States possesses a monopoly of the legitimate use of force over citizens. The legitimate use of force is unquestioned provided that it is done within the law and maintains a level of defined social order. Yet in recent years, the use of force by the police has come under question when it has been used on minority ethnic and racial groups. In October 2014, a Chicago police officer shot Lacquan McDonald 16 times; the incident was recorded by police dash cams. In November 2014, Tamir Rice, 12 years old, was fatally shot by police officer in Cleveland when it was reported he was holding a gun—that was found to be a toy.

In July 2014, Eric Garner, 43, was placed in a chokehold by a New York City police officer, Daniel Pantaleo, for a petty misdemeanor. Because of Garner's asthmatic condition, the choking led to his death, with the coroner calling his death a homicide. The New York Police Department has a policy prohibiting chokeholds.

In August 2014, a Ferguson police officer gunned down Michael Brown, 18 years old. Brown's hands were up at the time of the shooting. In North

Charleston, South Carolina, on April 2015, Walter Scott, 50 years old, was shot eight times in the back, running away from police officer Michael Slager. A bystander captured the entire shooting, including the officer's attempt to plant a stun gun next to Scott's body.

In the same month, Freddie Gray, 25 years old, of Baltimore, Maryland, was allegedly arrested for possessing a switchblade. A witness reports that police officers were beating Gray with police batons. Two bystanders recorded on video Gray screaming in pain as he was handcuffed and dragged to the police van. Although the circumstances are unclear as to what caused Gray to fall into a coma, he died seven days later from ascribed spinal cord injuries. Six police officers were charged with murder after the medical examiner ruled Gray's death a homicide. In each of these cases, the men were unarmed, and their fates were recorded by bystanders with smartphones or by the officers' own dash cams, verifying the brutality and misconduct of law enforcement officers. So far, the police officers involved in these events have been exonerated of any charges, even with verifiable video evidence of their misconduct.[2] These actions have caused major public resentment and community pressure, sparking law enforcement leaders, public officials, and community groups to address the issues of racial profiling and police brutality.

A Brief History of Policing in the United States

Before the Industrial Revolution, Americans shared the English's belief that members of a community had a duty to help maintain order; therefore, they adopted the offices of English constable, sheriff, and night watchman. The watch system was the main means of maintaining order and catching criminals. Each citizen was required to be a member of the watch, but paid watchmen could not be hired as replacements. Over time, cities began to hire paid, uniformed watchmen to deal with crime.

Since this nation's founding, various forms of policing have been part of its society. However, the English can be credited with establishing the foundation for a formal set of policing rules that was adopted by America in the 19th century. During the Industrial Revolution, citizens in America experienced physical uncertainty and insecurity that would be considered intolerable in the 21st century. As Monkkonen notes, "[I]t wasn't uncommon to hear that people drowned in shallow water, unable to swim, or that trains mutilated and killed pedestrians. Wagons hit children and injury meant death."[3]

In England, the constable and watch were responsible for the policing duties of the village. In the 15th century, the police function was vested in the office of constable, a part-time peacekeeper who conducted the watch and initiated the "hue and cry,"[4] a tactic used by the constable to give alarm with loud outcries or clamor when in the pursuit of a felon or an offender. A subordinate to the justice of the peace, the constable arrested those who broke the "King's peace," from bakers cheating on the weight of bread, to the whole community neglecting to provide for the poor.[5]

The development of a money economy and the expansion of a greater urban community reduced the watch to a poorly employed force paid a minimal wage that began as a fee-based scheme of buying substitutes for watch duty. Monkkonen describes the "posse comitatus," a group composed of males over the age of 15 in the county, called up by the sheriff to pursue an offender until caught; its members were usually notified by the shouts and screams of a crime victim. He goes on to note that poor pay, the uneducated and unskilled personnel, and the nature of the legal obligation were reasons for the ineffectiveness of the position and the beginning of the concept of community policing.

In the United States, according to Monkkonen, the position of the colonial constable was elected and paid by fees assigned by the court or justice of the peace. In England the position was an uncompensated voluntary position designated as a night watch. Constables, sheriffs, or marshals did little law enforcement or patrolling of the town. In contrast to the John Wayne *Rio Bravo* concept of law enforcement, where deputies patrolled the streets and performed night watch duties, it was marshals who were given these tasks, which included reporting fires, raising the alarm when criminal offenses were discovered, and arresting and detaining suspicious and disorderly persons. Monkkonen also notes:

> In Boston, the watch had a statutory obligation to examine all persons, whom they had reason to suspect of unlawful design; to walk the rounds in and about the streets; to report fires and suppress riots and disturbances; and to maintain and light the streetlamp.[6]

Monkkonen says that Sir Robert Peel articulated the precept of modern policing in 1829. Sir Robert was not new to the concept of law enforcement. Prior to becoming England's home secretary, Sir Robert created and administered the police of Ireland. His experience working with the rebellious Irish helped him to overcome England's political and philosophical resistance to a uniformed police, as well as to structure a new kind of police force.

In many areas in England (before the concept of modern policing), the military were used to preserve order. During a time in England when pickpocketing, gambling, and theft were commonplace among the criminal element, the military did not have the capacity to handle such criminal activity. To resolve the problem, Sir Robert introduced legislation in the British Parliament setting out the structural terms of a police force, which was to operate within the City of London.

Monkkonen indicates that Sir Robert separated policing and the judiciary. He believed that the police should be responsible for one facet of the law, that being the prosecution phase. The trial, conviction, and punishment phase would be placed in the hands of the judiciary; today, this concept remains the same.

The New Westminster Police Service found that Sir Robert suggested the following nine principles that would govern the English police force:

1. To prevent crime and disorder, as an alternative to their repression by military force and by severity of legal punishment.

2. To recognize always that the power of the police to fulfill their functions and duties is dependent on public approval of their existence, actions, and behavior.

3. To recognize always that to secure and maintain the respect and approval of the public means also to secure the willing co-operation of the public in the task of their observance of laws.

4. To recognize always that the extent to which the co-operation of the public can be secured diminishes proportionately with the necessity of the use of physical force and compulsion for achieving police objectives.

5. To seek and preserve public favor, not by pandering to the public opinion, but by constantly demonstrating absolutely impartial service to law, in complete independence of policy and without regard to the justice or injustices of the substance of individual laws. By ready offering of individual service and friendship to all members of the public without regard to their wealth or social standing. By ready exercise of courtesy and friendly good humor, and by ready offering of sacrifice in protecting and preserving life.

6. To use physical force only when the exercise of persuasion, advice and warning is found to be insufficient to obtain public co-operation to an extent necessary to secure observance of law or to restore order. To use only the minimum degree of physical force which is necessary on any particular occasion for achieving a police objective.

7. To maintain at all times a relationship with the public that gives reality to the historic tradition that the police are the public and that the public are the police. The police being only members of the public who are paid to give full-time attention to duties which are incumbent on every citizen, in the interests of community welfare and existence.

8. To recognize always the need for strict adherence to police executive functions and to refrain from ever seeming to usurp the powers of the judiciary or avenging individuals of the state, or authoritatively judging guilt and punishing the guilty.

9. To recognize always that the test of police efficiency is the absence of crime and disorder, and not the visible evidence of police action in dealing with them.[7]

Sir Robert's efforts led to the establishment of the Metropolitan Police of London. This model of the new London police force also became a model for the United States' police system. There was an important parallel in the origins of Sir Peel's metropolitan force—staffed by "Peelers" or "Bobbies"—and the constable watch system, which it replaced. Both arrangements were designed to control dissident and rebellious populations. But Sir Robert's genius lay in his ability to see both the need for legitimacy of some sort and the ineffectiveness of continual military presence as a successful means of social control. Sir Robert's principles created a new kind of bureaucracy located in a social space midway between an outside military force and the group of people to be controlled. The Metropolitan Police were considered neither civilian nor military, and this was reflected in the uniforms that they wore—using blue instead of the traditional military red. The legitimacy of the Metropolitan Police was represented through the English Constitution; their behavior and demeanor were bound by rules of law and decorum and, most importantly, by avoiding political factionalism.

The Metropolitan Police provided a workable model across England, but in America the British model gave rise to much controversy and resistance. The process of unifying the day constable and one night watch into an uniformed police took 20 years to fully complete in the United States. Proponents of the new police argued that the traditional system could no longer adequately cope with crime and disorder because of its inefficiency, lack of control, incompetent and/or corrupt personnel, fragmented organization, and inability to prevent disorder and crime. On the other hand, opponents to the new police claimed that the order threatened traditional civil liberties and freedom, the English pointing at the evil French police of Fouché and the Americans at the monarchical and antidemocratic English.

James W. Gerard is credited with bringing the concept of the London model to the United States in 1853. On a visit to London, the new tactics of policing by the Metropolitan Police fascinated Gerard. Gerard wanted to transform the New York Police, and his argument for its implementation was twofold—moral and physical efficiency. The physical efficiency came from better organization and greater numerical strength per capita, but the moral efficiency came from the character of the police, which was symbolized and actualized by the uniform. Gerard states that:

> the great *moral* power of the policeman of London in preventing crimes lies in his coat. This moral power operated by striking fear and dread in the hearts of the 'criminally disposed population . . . by their well-known intelligence, activity, unflinching firmness, and incorruptible *honesty*.' . . . The dress is respectable, and they *feel* respectable . . . their costume is a sure guarantee that they will never disgrace it; they know that they are known by it and, therefore, while they are watching others, that they are watched themselves. They take good care, therefore, not to enter tipling shops, or visit any places or do any acts which will disgrace their uniform.[8]

Though the policemen wearing the uniform were not to disgrace the attire, the supposed connection between the uniform and the professionalism of the newly formed police was lacking in the United States; the uniform did not ward off political corruption. According to Carte and Carte, incompetence and brutality were common within police departments, especially in the larger cities—Boston, New York, and Chicago. Many police officers were haphazardly selected, poorly trained, and underpaid.[9]

After the formation of the federal government in 1789, police power remained with the states, again in response to fear of centralized law enforcement. However, the American police developed under conditions that were different from those in England. Police in the United States had to deal with ethnic diversity, local political control, regional differences, the exploration and settling of the West, and a general violent society.

Cole and Smith described three historical periods in American policing: the political era (1840–1920), the professional model era (1920–1970), and the community model era (1970–present).[10]

The period between 1840 and 1920 is known as the political era because of the close ties that were formed between police and local political leaders. In cities across the country, the police worked for the mayor's political party rather than for the citizens. Political machines recruited and maintained the police, and the police helped the machine leaders get out the vote for favored candidates. Ranks in the police force were often for sale to the highest bidder, and many officers were "on the take."[11]

The growth of cities in the United States led to pressures to modernize law enforcement. Social relations in cities were different from those in rural areas. Between 1830 and 1879, there was much civil disorder in the large cities. Ethnic conflict, hostility toward nonslave blacks and abolitionists, mob actions against banks during economic declines, and violence in settling questions of morality, such as the use of alcohol—all these factors contributed to fears that a stable democracy would not survive.

By the 1850s, most major cities had created police departments organized on the English model. Departments were headed by a chief appointed by the major and council. The city was divided into precincts, and full-time, paid patrolmen were assigned to each. Early police forces sought to prevent crimes and keep order through the use of foot patrols. The officer on the beat dealt with crime, disorder, and other problems as they arose— using reactive tactics to deal with law and order.

Additionally, police performed a number of service functions such as caring for derelicts, operating soup kitchens, regulating public health, and handling medical and social emergencies. In cities across the country, the police provided beds and food for the homeless. In station houses, overnight lodgers might sleep on the floor or sometimes in clean bunkrooms.

Police developed differently in the South due to the existence of slavery and the agrarian nature of that region. Where white owners feared slave uprisings, police agencies were developed with full-time officers in cities with large numbers such as Charleston, New Orleans, Savannah, and Richmond), to reinforce white supremacy among slaves.

Westward expansion in the United States produced conditions that were different from those in the East or the South. The frontier was settled before order could be established. Thus, those who wanted to maintain law and order often had to take matters into their own hands by forming vigilante groups.

One of the first official positions created in rural areas westward was that of sheriff. Compared to the 17th-century England "shire reeves," the American sheriff was elected and had broad powers to enforce the law. As elected officers, sheriffs had close ties to local politics. They also depended on the men in the community for assistance through the "posse comitatus" in which local men above the age of 15 were required to respond to the sheriff's call for assistance, forming a body known as a posse.

After the Civil War, the federal government appointed United States marshals to help enforce the law in the Western territories. Some of the best-known folk heroes of American policing were U.S. Marshals Wyatt Earp, Bat Masterson, and Wild Bill Hickok, who tried to bring law and order to the "Wild, Wild, West."[12]

During the 20th century, all parts of the country became increasingly urban causing a blur over some regions in defining policing. In the early 20th century, growing criticism of the influence of politics on the police led to efforts by progressive reformers to make police more professional and to reduce their ties to local politics.

The Professional Model Era: 1920–1970

Reformers during the progressive movement greatly influenced policing in America. Reformers looked to achieve two goals: more efficient government and more governmental services to assist the less fortunate. A related goal was to reduce the influence of party politics and patronage (favoritism in handing out jobs) on government. The Progressives saw a need for professional law enforcement officials who would use modern technology to benefit society as a whole, not just local politicians.

August Vollmer, chief of police of Berkeley, California, from 1909 to 1932, was one of the leading advocates of professional policing. He initiated the use of motorcycle units, handwriting analysis, and fingerprinting. Vollmer urged that the police be made into a professional force, a nonpartisan agency of government committed to public service. This model of professional policing has six elements:

1. The force should stay out of politics.
2. Members should be well trained, well disciplined, and tightly organized.
3. Laws should be enforced equally.
4. The force should use new technology.
5. Personnel procedures should be based on merit.
6. The main task of the police should be fighting crime.[13]

Shifting the police's paradigm from maintaining order to crime control broke many ties that the police had developed with the communities they served. By the end of World War I, police departments had greatly reduced their involvement in social services. Instead, police officers became crime fighters.

O. W. Wilson, a student of Vollmer, became a leading advocate of professionalism among police officers. He promoted the use of motorized patrols, efficient radio communication, and rapid response. He hypothesized that one-officer patrols were the best way to use personnel and that the two-way radio allowed for supervision by commanders. These new procedures and technologies would allow police officers to be more efficient.

By the 1930s, the police were using new technologies and methods to combat serious crimes. They became more effective against crimes like murder, rape, and robbery; this was an important factor in gaining citizen support. By contrast, efforts to control victimless offenses and to strictly maintain order often aroused citizen opposition. According to Moore and Kelling, the clean and bureaucratic model of policing put forth by the reformers could be sustained only if the scope of police responsibility was narrowed to crime fighting.[14]

During the turbulent 1960s, the Civil Rights Movement, protests against the Vietnam War, urban riots, and rising crime rates challenged the many assumptions of the professional model. In their attempts to maintain order during public demonstrations, the police in many cities were more concerned with maintaining the status quo. During this period, police officers found themselves enforcing laws that discriminated against African Americans and the poor. With America's growing numbers of low-income racial minorities living in the inner cities, the professional style isolated the police from the communities they served. In the eyes of the inner-city residents, the police were an occupying army keeping them at the bottom of society rather than public servants helping all citizens.

Although the police continued to portray themselves as crime fighters, citizens became aware that the police were not effective in this role.

The Community Policing Model Era: 1970–Present

Because crime rates increased for many offenses, and the police were unable to change the perception that the quality of urban life was declining, there was a call for a move away from the crime-fighting focus and toward greater emphasis on keeping order and providing services to the community.

In 1992, Sparrow, Moore, and Kennedy reported research findings that undermined the acceptance of the professional crime-fighter model:

1. Increasing the number of patrol officers in a neighborhood was found to have little effect on the crime rate.
2. Rapid response to calls for service did not greatly increase the arrest rate.
3. It is difficult to improve the percentage of crimes solved.[15]

Critics of the professional style argued that it isolated the police from the community and reduced their knowledge about the neighborhoods they served, especially when police patrolled in cars. Use of the patrol car prevented personal contacts with citizens. Instead, it was argued, police should get out of their cars and spend more time meeting residents. This would permit the police to help people with a range of problems and, in some cases, would prevent problems from arising or growing worse.

The "Broken Windows" policing strategy that was pioneered by New York City police and used by law enforcement agencies across the country was theorized by James Q. Wilson and George L. Kelling, who believed that policing should work more on "little problems" such as maintaining order, providing services to those in need, and adopting strategies to reduce the fear of crime.[16]

Wilson and Kelling based their approach on three assumptions:

1. Neighborhood disorder creates fear. Areas with street people, youth gangs, prostitution, and drunks are high-crime areas.
2. Just as broken windows are a signal that nobody cares, and can lead to more serious vandalism, untended disorderly behavior is a signal that the community does not care. This also leads to more serious disorder and crime.
3. If the police are to deal with disorder and thus reduce fear and crime, they must rely on citizens for assistance.[17]

The community policing approach urged greater use of foot patrols so that officers will become known to citizens, who in turn will cooperate with the police. It is believed that through attention to little problems, the police may not only reduce disorder and fear but also improve public attitudes toward policing. When citizens respond positively to police efforts, the police will have improved bases of community and political support.

Using a problem-oriented approach to policing means that officers must be prepared to handle a range of problems, from noisy teenagers to battered spouses, to accident victims. In doing so, police officers can reduce disorder and fear of crime.

In "Broken Windows," Wilson and Kelling call for strategies to restore order and reduce crime in public spaces in U.S. communities. In cities across the country, from Baltimore to New York, San Francisco, and Seattle, police are paying greater attention to "quality of life crimes"—by arresting subway fare-beaters, rousting loiterers, and panhandlers from parks, and aggressively dealing with those obstructing sidewalks, harassing, and soliciting.

By dealing with the "little crimes," the police not only help restore order but also often prevent more serious crimes. In New York, for example, searching fare-beaters often yielded weapons; questioning a street vendor selling hot merchandise led to a fence specializing in stolen weapons; and arresting a person for urinating in a park resulted in discovery of a cache of weapons.

Reformers argue for a greater focus on order maintenance and service; they do not call for an end to the crime-fighting role. Instead, they want a shift in emphasis. The police should pay more attention to community needs and seek to understand the problems underlying crime, disorder, and incivility. However, citizen videos in the 21st century prove that community needs are not being met, and the Broken Windows theory is actually broken.

Dash Cameras, Body Cameras, and Police Officers

Clearly, the recent events of senseless killings of unarmed African Americans by police officers has caused citizen groups to pressure for more best practices and transparency of local police departments. The development of policy and implementation of body cameras has begun a debate between the police and communities, and the debate of their effectiveness. Yet, in review of the many tools used by police departments to fight crime and maintain a level of professionalism, dash cams (cameras mounted on police dashboards) have been a constant consideration for many local and state law enforcement departments.

Historically, the first recorded use of a camera was in 1939, in which a test car mounted with a camera measured the speed of trucks and private cars.[18] Over time, police departments began using dash cameras to film car chases, traffic violations, and drunk drivers as well as to gather evidence of committed crimes and arrests. Dash cams became popular in the 1990s after lawsuits were filed for racially based traffic stops by state police across the United States. In many of these civil cases, the courts confirmed that racial profiling had occurred, thus decreasing the public's confidence in the police.

The U.S. Department of Justice's Office of Community Oriented Policing Services (COPS) offered a motivation to police departments with the In-Car Incentive Program. The program gave financial aid to state and highway patrols to install in-car cameras in their vehicles. Forty-seven states and the District of Colombia received $21 million in federal assistance for the purchase of dash cameras. According to a study conducted by the International Association of Police Chiefs, the number of in-car camera systems grew from 3400 to 17,500 in a three-year period after the COPS In-Car Incentive Program.[19]

In a 2010 study by the U.S. Department of Justice, 66 percent of local police departments expanded their use of dash cams in vehicles. The use of video cameras in patrol cars increased from 55 percent in 2003 to 71 percent in 2007, becoming a common tool used by police departments.[20] The impact of the dash cams showed an improvement in professionalism and courtesy, with 96 percent of officers exonerated of allegations and complaints.[21]

The new tool of debate, body cameras, is following the same path as the introduction of dash cams. The Obama administration, through the Department of Justice, has created an incentive program for law enforcement agencies to implement body cameras. Similarly to a dash cam, the body camera is considered to increase transparency and accountability, improve police and citizen behavior, provide efficient way of examining evidence, expedite prosecution of civil lawsuits, and improve police training. The U.S. Department of Justice awarded $23 million in grants to local police departments in a pilot program to measure the impact of body-worn cameras (BWCs).[22] Thirty-two states are participating in the pilot program. Of the 285 grant applicant submissions, 73 grants have been awarded to large, medium, and small agencies as well as expansion programs.[23]

Table 9.1   Body Camera Grants Awards 2015

State	Locality	Federal Award
AL	Andalusia	$87,224
AZ	Glendale	$449,986
AZ	Peoria	$53,170
AZ	Salt River Pima-Maricopa Indian	$193,596
CA	Imperial County Sheriff's Office	$74,770
CA	Los Angeles Police Department	$1,000,000
CA	Pasadena	$250,000
CA	Richmond	$150,000
CA	Sacramento	$599,756
CA	San Bernardino	$546,502
CO	Colorado Springs	$600,000
CT	New Haven	$90,000
CT	Stamford	$600,000
DC	Metropolitan Police Department	$1,000,000
FL	Apopka Police Department	$43,000
FL	Miami-Dade County	$1,000,000
FL	Orlando	$497,000
FL	Pensacola	$64,500
GA	Newton County Sheriff's Office	$89,199

(continued)

Table 9.1 (*continued*)

State	Locality	Federal Award
GA	St. Mary's Police Department	$69,000
GA	Wilkinson County	$9,523
IA	Dubuque	$61,230
ID	Twin Falls	$90,000
IL	Chicago	$1,000,000
IL	Elgin	$250,000
IL	Lake County Sheriff's Department	$73,000
IN	Fort Wayne	$126,585
KS	Dodge City	$45,205
KS	Wichita	$250,000
KS	Wyandotte County/Kansas City	$352,500
LA	New Orleans Police Department	$237,000
MI	Dearborn	$59,571
MI	Detroit Police Department	$1,000,000
MN	Leech Lake Band of Ojibwa	$41,967
MN	Minneapolis Police Department	$600,000
MN	St. Paul Police Department	$600,000
NC	Fayetteville	$530,000
NE	Omaha	$67,500
NJ	Cherry Hill Police Department	$82,525
NM	Albuquerque Police Department	$250,000
NV	Las Vegas Metropolitan PD	$250,000
NY	Albany	$133,305
NY	Rochester	$600,000
NY	Spring Valley	$11,905
NY	White Plains	$31,638
OH	Akron	$367,478
OH	Hamilton County Sheriff's Office	$139,500
OK	Tulsa	$599,200
OR	Beaverton	$150,000
OR	Eugene	$249,000
PA	Carlisle, Borough of	$43,500

(*continued*)

Table 9.1   (*continued*)

State	Locality	Federal Award
PA	Central Bucks Regional Police Department	$52,805
PA	Johnstown	$63,000
PA	Pittsburgh	$250,000
SC	Charleston	$25,264
SC	Greenville	$93,750
SC	Spartanburg	$184,500
TX	Corpus Christi	$125,000
TX	Laredo Independent School District	$46,499
TX	New Brunsfels	$31,745
TX	San Antonio	$1,000,000
TX	Webb County	$18,959
UT	Salt Lake	$181,540
VA	Dinwiddie County	$16,200
VA	Fairfax	$28,878
VA	Lynchburg	$205,486
VA	Newport News Sheriff's Office	$209,486
VA	Waynesboro	$36,445
WA	Seattle Police Department	$600,000
WI	West Allis	$75,000
WV	Ranson	$45,000

Source: U.S Department of Justice/Bureau of Justice Assistance: 2015 Grant Award.

The Bureau of Justice Assistance (BJA) reported that of the 55,000 camera requests, 22,000 body-worn cameras have been purchased by localities. In order to monitor the effectiveness of the awards, the BJA will provide the oversight, training, and evaluation.

The jury is still out on the use of BWCs. Cities participating in the BWC pilot implementation program must measure the effectiveness of their program. For example, the Orlando Police Department, in conjunction with the University of South Florida, has developed a pilot project in which the use of BWCs is measured. The project examined officer-use-of-force complaints, injuries (officer or citizen), officer attitudes, and perceptions of key stakeholders.

Two groups participated in a 12-month study: 50 officers with BWCs and 50 officers without cameras. Preliminary results indicate that officers with BWCs experienced a 29.7 percent reduction in complaints against officers, a 7.7 percent decline in use-of-force incidents. The study, by Lynch, Jennings and Fridall, further reported that officers with BWCs had a decrease in "take downs" by 86 percent; however, the use of chemical agents increased by 80 percent.[24]

The Orlando Police Department is proactively updating its procedures to include the use of BWCs for all its officers; while their results provide a snapshot of its effectiveness, the study is continual. The use of body cameras on police officers may not reduce police misconduct. Although they may visually verify an action of brutality by an officer, this does not mean that a charge—an indictment or a conviction—will prevail.

There are advantages and disadvantages to the use of BWCs by law enforcement agencies. The eInvestigator reports the following advantages:

1. Minimizes citizen complaints about police officer behavior, which includes unnecessary use of force
2. Provides video evidence of decisions made by officers in a highly intense situation
3. Provides protection for officers against false accusations of misconduct or abuse
4. Increases transparency and accountability of officers
5. Supports the de-escalations of confrontational situations between officers and civilians
6. Provides evidence in obtaining accurate witness and victim statements
7. May help expedite court proceedings by providing indisputable proof of a situation[25]

On the other hand, the disadvantages to BWCs include the following:

1. The equipment and upkeep is expensive, which includes maintenance and storage of recorded data and footage collected. Additional costs include cataloging and retrieving footage in response to subpoenas, investigations, and public information agencies.
2. To operate the device, officers must physically activate the camera when they exit their patrol car. Most importantly, in interactions with civilians, it is up to an officer's discretion to activate or deactivate a recording.
3. There are privacy issues for both officers and civilians.
4. Technological issues related to the functioning of the camera—that is, a dead battery, damaged components, obstructed lens, and other problems—resulting

in missing important witness statements or crucial behavior by officers or citizens.

President Obama's Impact on Policing

Since the events that exposed fractures in the relationship between the local police and communities, President Obama has signed an executive order establishing a Task Force on 21st Century Policing.[26] This presidential task force was charged with identifying best practices and recommendations on how policing practices can promote effective crime reduction while building public trust within communities they serve. The recommendations identify six pillars of best practices, which include: (a) Building Trust and Legitimacy; (b) Policy and Oversight; (c) Technology & Social Media; (d) Community Policing and Crime Reduction; (e) Training and Education; (f) Officer Wellness and Safety.[27]

Building Trust and Legitimacy

The foundation to good relationships between law enforcement and communities rests on trust. That trust builds confidence, which creates legitimacy.

According to the McCarthy confidence in law enforcement has been flat among people of color. Comparatively, whites have always had a higher level of confidence in law enforcement than people of color, because it has been the poor and people of color who have experienced the greatest injustice in arrest and imprisonment. As the task force indicates, decades of research and practice support the premise that people are more likely to obey the law when they believe that those who are enforcing the law have legitimate authority.[28] However, legitimate authority is conferred only on those believed to be acting in a just way. Mazerolle et al. identify four central principles of procedurally just behavior:

1. Treating people with respect and dignity
2. Giving individuals "voice" during encounters
3. Being neutral and transparent in decision-making
4. Conveying trustworthy motives[29]

When communities believe that officers are unbiased, benevolent, honest, and lawful, they are more likely to feel obligated to follow the law and the dictates of the authorities—being more willing to cooperate and engage with authorities.

Policy and Oversight

In order for trust and legitimacy to exist between law enforcement and communities, there must be consensus on the policies reflecting on the values of the two groups. Clear and comprehensive polices on law enforcement operations, which may include use of force; training on de-escalation for mass demonstrations and for situations involving gender identification or racial profiling; external and internal investigations; and prosecution of officer-involved shootings may help to build trust between law enforcement and communities. Demographic data as well as aggregate data should be made publicly available. The Obama administration supports the creation of a mechanism for the U.S. Department of Justice to investigate complaints and issue sanctions regarding the inappropriate use of tactics and equipment during mass demonstrations.

In addition, law enforcement should establish periodical review of policies and procedures, conduct peer review of critical incidents separate from criminal and administrative investigations, and establish civilian oversight mechanisms with communities. Not all agencies are the same in size or demographics—larger law enforcement agencies have the advantage of more resources than smaller sized agencies. Therefore, smaller agencies should take advantage of technical assistance and incentive funding provided by the U.S. Department of Justice for Community Oriented Policing Services and the Office of Justice Programs.

Technology and Social Media

The Obama administration recognizes that the use of technology can improve best practices of policing and reinforce community trust and legitimacy. However, the use of technology must have an established framework with specific goals that are clearly defined. The use of new dash cameras, BWCs, unmanned aircraft, and social media apps can improve policing practices and, again, build trust and legitimacy with communities.

However, the speed of technology changes faster than established policy frameworks, which can move at an incremental pace. It will be important for law enforcement agencies to have continued assessment and evaluation of new technology and comply with changes as they occur. The continual identification of changes in new technology will only reinforce policy oversight, giving way to improvements in effective and efficient policing practices. However, Miller and Toliver note that BWCs can offer benefits; they raise serious questions about how the technology will change the relationship between police and communities.[30] BWCs create concerns about the public's privacy rights as well as how officers interact with people in the community.

The Obama administration has encouraged the broadening of federal standards to include research and development of new technology. Although not advocating for a one-size-fits-all approach for law enforcement agencies, the Obama administration encourages interoperability and compatibility both within law enforcement agencies and across agencies and jurisdictions. This interconnection supports the preservation of civil and human rights protections.

Community Policing and Crime Reduction

The crux of community policing is to support organizational strategies that support the use of problem-solving techniques to address the immediate conditions that give rise to public safety issues such as crime, social disorder, and fear of crime. The Eric Garner case is a prime example of the failure of community policing. According to the Federal Bureau of Investigation, for 2013 the rates of violent and property crime have dramatically dropped in the United States.[31]

Along with creating a strong framework for the adoption of new technology, law enforcement agencies should develop strategies that reinforce community engagement. Community policing means law enforcement agencies create collaborative partnerships with agencies beyond law enforcement, for example, Eagle County, Colorado's Law Enforcement Immigrant Advisory Committee, which was developed in collaboration with Catholic Charities to help immigrant communities.

Most importantly, community policing is about problem solving, which may lead to prevention. This means solving problems in partnership with the community to effectively address chronic crime and disorder. Elkins explains, "that it is about teaching new recruits that law enforcement is more than cuffing 'perps'—it's understanding why people do what they do."[32]

The Obama administration is taking steps to support research and funding to examine the factors that lead to strategies of crime reduction in communities and is encouraging an infusion of nondiscriminatory policing. In addition, the administration is collaborating with other agencies to develop and disseminate baseline models of crisis intervention, that is, using a team approach that can be adapted to localities.

Training and Education

Delattre explains that all police and law enforcement executives want to recruit candidates of good character and to encourage the best in them.[33] Bill Gillespie, executive director of the Minnesota Police and Peace Officer Association, which represents more than 7000 licensed officers in the state, asked, "How do police departments get qualified people, regardless of their race, gender, or ethnicity, involved in law enforcement?"[34]

The United States is pluralistic in its citizen makeup, and the scope of law enforcement must expand its responsibilities to better meet the needs of the communities they serve. Officers today encounter challenges that include domestic and international terrorism, changing laws, new technologies, new cultural mores and immigration, and mental health crises. Thus, law enforcement agencies must establish standards for hiring, training, and education.

Law enforcement requires education at a higher level, including continual training. The presidential task force discussed and recommended basic recruitment and in-service training development that should include the following:

- Community policing
- Interpersonal and communication skills
- Bias awareness
- Scenario-based, situational decision-making
- Crisis intervention
- Procedural justice and impartial policing
- Trauma and victim services
- Mental health services
- Analytical research and technology
- Languages and cultural responsiveness[35]

The Obama administration supports the development of partnerships with training facilities nationwide in order to promote consistent standards for high-quality training and establish training innovation hubs. The presidential task force further recommends that training hubs should establish partnership with academic institutions to develop rigorous training practices, evaluation, and development of curricula based on evidence-based practices.

Officer Wellness and Safety

Without debate, the job of law enforcement is one in which officers place their lives on the line. Encountering life-threatening situations is part of the regular routine of law enforcement. The tragedy of Sandy Hook Elementary School and that scene of carnage will stay with law enforcement officers for the rest of their lives. Some officers are physically injured carrying out their duties, but in any case, law enforcement officers face physical, mental, and emotional injuries. These injuries carry over to permanent physical or mental damage and, sometimes, eventual death.

However, a large number of officer deaths are a result of poor physical health due to poor nutrition, lack of exercise, sleep deprivation, and substance abuse. An officer whose capabilities of judgment and behavior are adversely affected by poor psychological or physical health is of little use to a community he or she is assigned to serve. This diminished capacity is a danger to the community and to other officers. As task force member Tracey Meares explains, "Hurt people can hurt people."[36]

In many large and medium-sized law enforcement agencies, there is a mechanism to identify law enforcement officers who may have a propensity to or are engaged in behavior that falls outside of the mission and vision of the department. Conroy and Bostrom define these Early Warning Systems (EWSs) as tracking strategies that gather data on officers such as the following:

1. Number of arrests by an officer—location, gender, ethnicity, and reason
2. Number of accidents by an officer in a three-month period
3. Number of citations submitted by an officer—location, gender, ethnicity, and reason
4. Number of shootings in which an officer was involved
5. Number of internal affairs complaints by an officer in a specific time period
6. Number of disciplinary reviews conducted on an officer
7. Use of sick time or leave time by an officer[37]

The use of the EWS captures and flags specific instances of notable activity by an officer who may be experiencing unusual behavior. An EWS can be a valuable tool for human resource departments as well as employee assistance programs to remedy problems with law enforcement officers.

The Obama administration supports the promotion of safety and wellness within law enforcement agencies. The administration further supports the funding of research to measure the efficacy of annual mental health assessments for officers, as well as fitness, resilience, and nutrition. Research funding should extend to examining the efficiency of limiting the total number of hours an officer should work within a 24- to 48-hour period. Most law enforcement shifts go beyond a regular eight-hour day, extending to 10- to 12-hour period.

Most importantly, the administration is expanding efforts to collect and analyze data not only on officer deaths but also on injuries and "near misses." The presidential task force strongly recommends that law enforcement agencies should adopt policies that require officers to wear seat belts and bulletproof vests, and provide training to raise awareness of the consequences of failures to do so.

It will take time to be able to measure the results of the use of BWCs and the changes to policing. From its established beginnings in the 18th-century policing in the United States has slowly evolved, adapting to the changing demographic landscape. Policing's role is rooted historically in a hierarchical, authoritarian system, but the expectations and demands of modern society require much more of officers today than was required of their forbearers. Obama's tenure in office has extraordinarily challenged the status quo in America. The change has been difficult and is evident in the tragic death of those killed at the hands of incompetent law enforcement officers.

But it is also clear that this country's democratic process works to counteract incompetency and force policy changes for the better.

Notes

1. Hess and Wrobleski, 1993.
2. Police officers in the Freddie Gray, Walter Scott, and Lacquan MacDonald cases.
3. Monkkonen, 1981, p. 1.
4. Lycos, 2002.
5. New Westminster Police Service, 2002.
6. Monkkonen, 1981, p. 39.
7. New Westminster Police Service, 2002, pp. 1–2.
8. Monkkonen, 1981, p. 41.
9. Carte and Carte, 1975.
10. Cole and Smith, 1999.
11. Ibid.
12. Calhoun, 1990.
13. Monkkonen, 1981, p. 23.
14. Kelling and Moore, 1987.

Body Cameras and Policing: From Ferguson to Baltimore 193

15. Sparrow, Moore, and Kennedy, 1992, p. 57.
16. Wilson and Kelling, 1982.
17. Ibid., p. 30.
18. "Camera Car," 1939.
19. International Association of Police Chiefs (IAPC), 2002.
20. U.S. Department of Justice, 2010.
21. IAPC, 2002.
22. The awarded grants include $19 million to purchase body-worn cameras, $2 million for training and technical assistance, and $1.9 million to survey the impact of the BWCs.
23. Bureau of Justice Assistance (BJA), 2015.
24. Lynch, Jennings, and Fridell, 2015.
25. eInvestigator, 2014.
26. Office of Community Oriented Policing Services, President's 21st Century Task Force on Policing, 2015.
27. U.S. Department of Justice, Office of Community Oriented Policing Services, 2015.
28. U.S. Department of Justice, Office of Community Oriented Policing Services, 2015.
29. Mazerolle et al., 2013, p. 45.
30. Miller and Toliver, 2014.
31. Federal Bureau of Investigation, 2014.
32. Elkins, 2014.
33. Delattre, 2002.
34. Post-Bulletin, 2004.
35. Office of Community Oriented Policing Services, President's 21st Century Task Force on Policing, 2015, p. 51.
36. Office of Community Oriented Policing Services, President's 21st Century Task Force on Policing, 2015.
37. Conroy and Bostrom, 2002.

Bibliography

Baker, W. "The Impact of Video Evidence on Modern Policing (NIJ grant# 2001-CK-WX-0157)." *IACP report to National Institute of Justice* (2004).
Berman, Mark, Wesley Lowery, and Kimberly Kind. 2015. "South Carolina Police Officer Will Be Charged With Murder After Shooting." *The Washington Post.* April 7. www.washingtonpost.com/news/post-nation/wp/2015/04/07/south-carolina-police-officer-will-be-charged-with-murder-after-shooting/?utm_term=.bc3bdboec61b.
Bureau of Justice Assistance (BJA). 2015. "Bureau of Justice Assistance Fact Sheet 2015 Awards for Body-Worn Camera Pilot Implementation Program." *U.S. Department of Justice.* February 1. www.bja.gov/bwc.

Bordua, D., and J. Reiss. 1966. "Command, Control, Charisma: Reflections on Police Bureaucracy." *The American Journal of Sociology*, 72: 68–70.

Calhoun, F. 1990. *The Lawmen*. Washington, D.C.: Smithsonian Institute.

"Camera Car Gets Dope on Fast Drivers." 1939. *Popular Science*, April 1: 54.

Carte, G., and E. Carte. 1975. *Police Reform in the United States: The Era of August Vollmer, 1905–1932*. Berkeley, CA: University of California Press.

Cole, G., and C. Smith. 1999. *Criminal Justice*. Belmont, CA: Wadsworth Publishing.

Conroy, Dennis, and MaCherie Placide. 2002. *Promoting Cooperative Strategies to Reduce Racial Profiling Initiative*. Technical Assistance, St. Paul: Office of Community Oriented Policing Services.

Cooper, Anderson. *Freddie Gray Witness Speaks*. CNN. Atlanta, GA, April 23, 2015.

Cumming, E., I. Cumming, and L. Edell. 1965. "Policeman as Philosopher, Friend, and Guide." *Social Problems*, 12(3): 276–286.

Davey, Monica, and Mitch Smith. 2015. "Chicago Braces After Video of Police Shooting Is Released." *The New York Times*, 11(24): 3.

Delattre, E. 2014. *Character and Cops: Ethics in Policing*. Washington, D.C.: AEI Press, 2002.

Elkins, Faye. "Five COPS Office Directors Look Back and Think Forward at the 20th Anniversary Celebration." *Community Policing Dispatch*, 8(1) (January).

Federal Bureau of Investigation. 2014. "Crime Statistics for 2013: Decrease in Violent Crimes and Property Crimes." *Federal Bureau of Investigation*. November 10. http://www.fbi.gov/news/stories/2014/november/crime-statistics -for-2013-released/crime-statistics-for-2013-released.

"Finding Qualified Candidates Tough, Police Official Say." (2004, January 12). *Post-Bulletin*, p. 4B.

Goldstein, H. 1975. *Police Corruption: A Perspective on Its Nature and Control*. Washington DC: The Police Foundation.

Graham, David. 2015a. "The Atlantic." *The Mysterious Death of Freddie Gray*. April 22. www.theatlantic.com/politics/archive/2015/04/the-mysterious -death-of-freddie-gray/391119.

Graham, David. 2015b. "Probable Cause in the Killing of Tamir Rice." *The Atlantic*. June 11. www.theatlantic.com/politics/archive/2015/06/tamir-rice-case -cleveland/395420.

Hess, K., and H. Wrobleski. 1993. *Police Operations*. St. Paul, Minnesota: West Publishing.

International Association of Chiefs of Police. 2002. "The Impact of Video Evidence on Modern Policing: Research and Best Practices." *International Association of Chiefs of Police*. April 1. www.theiacp.org/portals/0pdfs/IACPin -CarCameraReport.pdf.

Jonsson, Patrik. 2014. "Eric Garner Ruled Victim of Chokehold." *Christian Science Monitor*. August 2. www.csmonitor.com/USA/Justice/2014/0802/Eric -Garner-ruled-victim-of-chokehold-homicide-should-a-grand-jury-indict -video.

Kelling, George L., and Mark Harrison Moore. *From Political to Reform to Community: The Evolving Strategy of Police.* Program in Criminal Justice Policy and Management, John F. Kennedy School of Government, Harvard University, 1987.

Lycos. *Meaning of Hue and Cry.* 2002. http://infoplease.lycos.com/ipd/A0481509.html.

Lynch, Mathew, Wesley Jennings, and Lorie Fridell. 2015. *Body-Worn Cameras in Policing: Preliminary Results from Orlando.* Whitepaper, University of South Florida, Miami: University of South Florida.

Mazerolle, Lorraine, Sarah Bennett, Jacqueline Sargeant, Elise Davis, and Matthew Manning. 2013. "Legitimacy in Policing: A Systematic Review." *The Campbell Collection Library of Systematic Reviews,* 9. https://www.campbellcollaboration.org/library/legitimacy-in-policing-a-systematic-review.html.

Miller, Lindsay, and Jessica Toliver. 2014. "Implementing a Body-Worn Camera Program: Recommendations and Lessons Learned." *Office of Community Oriented Policing Services.* December 1. http://ric-zai-inc.com/Publications/cops-p296-pub.pdf.

Monkkonen, E. *Police in Urban America 1860–1920.* New York, New York: Cambridge University Press, 1981.

New Westminster Police. 2002. "Sir Robert Peel's Nine Principles of Policing." *New West Police.* June 21. www.newwestpolice.org/peel.html.

Office of Community Oriented Policing Services. 2015. *President's Task Force on 21st Century Policing.* Task Force, U.S. Department of Justice, Washington, D.C.: Office of Community Oriented Policing Services, 116.

"Police Body Cameras: Do They Reduce Complaints of Officer Misconduct?" 2014. *eInvestigator.com.* December 29. www.einverstigator.com.

Sparrow, Malcolm, Mark Moore, and D. Kennedy. 1992. *Beyond 911: A New Era for Policing.* New York: Basic Books.

Tyler, Tom, Jonathon Jackson, and Ben Bradford. 2014. "Procedural Justice and Cooperation." In Gerben Bruinsma and David Weisbud, eds. *Encyclopedia of Criminology and Criminal Justice* (4011–4024). New York: Springer.

U.S. Department of Justice. 2015. "U.S. Department of Justice Report Regarding the Criminal Investigation Into the Shooting Death of Michael Brown By Ferguson, Missouri Police Officer Darren Wilson." *United States Department of Justice.* March 3. www.justice.gov/sites/default/files/opa/press-releases/attachments/2015/03/04/doj__report__onshooting__of__michael__brown__1.pdf.

Westphal, Lonnie. "The In-Car Camera: Value and Impact." *The Police Chief,* June 1, 2016: 13.

Wilson, J.Q., and G. L. Kelling. "Police and Neighborhood Safety: Broken Windows." *Atlantic Monthly,* March 1, 1982.

CHAPTER TEN

President Obama: Code-Meshing and the Power of Speech in Racial Politics

Cassandra Chaney and Kyomi Gregory

Introduction

As the 44th president of the United States, Barack Hussein Obama (born on August 4, 1961) is a unique figure in American history. In addition to being one of the few men in this country to hold this office, Obama is the first African American to hold the office, as well as the first president to be born outside of the continental United States. As a native Hawaiian, Obama later graduated from Columbia University and Harvard Law School, and was a community organizer in Chicago before earning his law degree. As a civil rights attorney, he became especially knowledgeable about the challenges of African Americans and other marginalized residents of the United States, and served three terms representing the 13th District in the Illinois Senate from 1997 to 2004. When he accepted the Democrat nomination for president of the United States on August 28, 2008, Obama had already demonstrated a keen ability to connect with his audience through speech. Throughout his tenure as president, Obama has built a platform on hope, and he mentions painful historical realities as the impetus for current change.[1]

This chapter examines President Barack Obama's use of code-meshing in changing racial politics. This ability has served as a useful tool to connect with a diverse population of Americans. His speeches are of special interest to linguists because he interweaves aspects of African American English (AAE) with his own "Black preacher style." His language has played a role in changing the dynamic of racial politics and has greatly influenced how society perceives politicians. This chapter explores Obama's use of various AAE characteristics in his speeches and his communication style, and the impact of his communication style in social media. This is done by analyzing 15 speeches that were given over a 12-year period of time, from 2004 to 2015. This work is significant because we are aware of no scholars that have examined Obama's use of code-meshing and how his communication style has impacted social media.

In the subsequent sections, we provide a brief critique of President Obama's communication style. After this, we provide key scholarly works related to what AAE is, as well as its historical development and contemporary use. Furthermore, we discuss code-meshing. Specifically, we define code-meshing and provide examples related to how Obama has effectively used this form of communication throughout his career.

President Obama's Communication Style

Extant scholarship over the past eight years has examined various aspects of Obama's presidency. For example, researchers have qualitatively examined the extent to which Obama and his wife can increase low marriage rates among African Americans as well as how the parenting style of the POTUS and first lady influence Black parents to be more engaged in their children's lives. In addition to the aforementioned aspects of his personal life, Obama is considered by many to be an impassioned and effective orator. According to White House spokesman Bill Burton, "His speeches can go for pages without applause lines, making comprehensive arguments about particular issues. And though people may not remember particular lines or phrases from every speech, when he is done speaking, people always get a sense of who the president is and exactly where he is coming from." In addition, Adam Frankel, presidential speechwriter who started writing for President Obama when he was a candidate, said this: "I think there are memorable lines in certain speeches (by President Obama), but what makes him unique as a speaker is not necessarily a single line, but the overall story he tells, the seriousness with which he tells it, and the trust he puts in people to understand a complicated argument." Although words are influential, they are never more important than clearly presenting to the world the man behind those words. This reality was stated by Jeff Shesol, who wrote speeches for President Bill Clinton: "I think it's very important for people to remember the words. Words have power. A successful speech will resonate and phrases will provide a kind of power in the near term and the longer term. But, ultimately, it's important to any president to be able to make continually clear who he is, what he believes and where he wants to go."[2]

African American English (AAE)

Because a large part of Obama's early community activism occurred in the large urban city of Chicago, his communication style was undoubtedly influenced by elements of AAE. But what is AAE? Over four decades ago, William Labov defined the "Black English Vernacular" as the relatively uniform dialect spoken by the majority of Black youth in most parts of the United States today, especially in the inner city areas of New York, Boston, Detroit, Philadelphia, Washington, Cleveland, Chicago, St. Louis, San Francisco, Los Angeles, and other urban centers. It is also spoken in most rural areas and used in the casual, intimate speech of many adults.[3] Linguists define Black English as a hybrid language containing elements of Euro-American English ("standard English") and elements of West African languages (surviving Africanisms from Yoruba, Ibo, Ewe, etc.). AAE is a rule-governed non-mainstream American English dialect. The vocabulary of the new language is fairly easy to master, but the syntactical structure and idiomatic rules require considerable time and practice to master. Although all languages change over time, the structure of a language remains relatively rigid and fixed. It is important to note that the greatest differences between Black and White English are on the level of grammatical structure.

However, more recent work has found the uniform ways that people of African descent generally speak is not merely due to racial segregation. More recently, Walt Wolfram associated several factors for the development of this uniform dialect among Blacks. For one, historically, urban AAE was established because of transplant dialect communities, or Southern rural speakers who moved to non-Southern cities during the early waves of the Great Migration in the first half of the 20th century. Although there was great residential mobility to areas where many African Americans currently reside, "[t]he increasing number of African American in-migrants in these urban contexts, the shared Southern rural cultural heritage, the segregated living conditions, and the bi-racial ideology characteristic of most Northern urban cities certainly provided an ideal context for nurturing ethnolinguistic distinction."[4]

There are several elements that make AAE different from other varieties of English. One of the most distinguishable aspects of AAE from other varieties of English is the verb phrase. This form of communication includes the use of tense, mood, and aspect.[5] One of the most prominent aspects of AAE is the use of the form *be* as a main verb. An example would be: "If you don't be quiet, I won't get a thing done."[6] In addition to African American's prominent use of the form *be*, members of this group demonstrate two aspects of speech that make their communication processes distinctly different from other races.

According to Joycelyn Landrum-Brown, there are two dimensions of Black speech: language and style. Language involves sounds, grammar and structure, and words. On the other hand, style involves the way speakers put sounds and grammatical structure together to communicate meaning in a larger context. In particular, style involves what an individual does with the words as well as the incorporation of the total expression, for example, using Black "songified" rhythmic speech, voice inflections, and tonal patterns. Tonal Semantics, or the use of voice, rhythm, and vocal inflection to convey meaning, gives Black speech its "songified," or musical, quality and Black rappers and preachers frequently use word sound to communicate deep emotions that words alone cannot convey. Examples of tonal semantics include shouting; intonational contouring; and the use of rhyme, repetition, and alliterative word play. From a strictly linguistic view, Smitherman (1975) indicates West African languages are tone languages, and the speakers of these languages generally rely on the tone with which they pronounce syllables, sounds, and words to convey meaning.

Code-Meshing—What Is It? How Does President Obama Do This Effectively?

Code-meshing is the blending or meshing of language varieties; it simply means the blending of two dialect variations as opposed to keeping them separate. Code-meshing eliminates the idea of "linguistic segregation" and promotes an integrationist model for combining language dialects in oral language. In contrast, "code-switching" indicates the concept of bi-dialectalism that individuals must switch from one dialect to another in oral language. This term indicates choosing one dialect over the other. Over the past decade with the use of social media, we can see the inclusiveness of a variety of dialect variations across mass media that utilizes oral language that combines dialect variations. Code-meshing is the blending of oral language in which the first dialect breaks through and is combined with the second dialect.

President Obama has served as an excellent example of mastering "code-meshing" throughout his two-term presidency. One example is in 2012, when he was offering a conventional handshake to a White assistant coach for the USA's basketball team before immediately dapping two of the African American players, and greeting one player by saying "What's sup, champ?"[7]

Another example is in 2008, with his delivery of a speech to a predominantly African American crowd in South Carolina, where he was firing up the audience by walking slowly across the stage throughout the speech.[8] He then utilized a phrase said by Malcolm X: "They're tryna bamboozle you." This resulted in the "Black preacher–style" tradition of "call and response" from the audience. The audience screamed "Yes!" President Obama responded by saying, "It's the same old okey-doke." The audience responded, "That's right!" President Obama said, "Ya'll know about the okey-doke."

Code-meshing has been done seamlessly by President Obama throughout his interactions with the public and throughout his speeches. He has successfully changed the racial politics of American English. President Obama's speech has successfully provided a connection between language and racial politics and has helped to give us a better understanding of the impact of "code-meshing" and its connection to culture and people.

The Approach Used in This Investigation

For this chapter, we used a qualitative approach that examined contextual themes present in Barack Obama's speeches.[9] The speeches were a large cross-section of public addresses that began when Barack Obama was a senator of Illinois to his presidency of the United States. This method involved three steps. The first step involved examining the content of 300 speeches made by President Obama. These speeches were obtained from the following website: http://www.americanrhetoric.com/barackobama speeches.htm. This website contains the delivery date of the speech and the speech title as well as the audio and portable for the speech. (See Table 10.1 for the delivery date, speech title, audio, and portable of select speeches over a 12-year period, or from 2004 to 2016).

The second step was to extract from those 300 speeches the ones in which Obama specifically focused on the African American race and/or historical events that directly affected the lives of African Americans. This selection criteria was directly related to our focus on Obama's use of AAE.

Table 10.1   Delivery Date, Speech Title, Audio, and Portable Format of Barack Obama's Speeches

Delivery Date	Speech Title	Audio	Portable
July 27, 2004	Democratic National Convention Keynote Speech	mp3	PDF
June 4, 2005	Knox College Commencement Speech	mp3	PDF
January 31, 2006	Senate Speech on the Passing of Coretta Scott King	mp3	PDF
August 1, 2007	Woodrow Wilson Center Speech	mp3	PDF
March 18, 2008	"A More Perfect Union" speech	mp3	PDF
January 18, 2009	Lincoln Memorial pre-inaugural speech	mp3	PDF
January 17, 2010	Martin Luther King Jr. Remembrance Day speech	mp3	PDF
October 16, 2011	Address at the Martin Luther King Jr. Memorial dedication	mp3	PDF
November 7, 2012	Second presidential election victory speech	mp3	PDF
February 27, 2013	Address dedicating Rosa Parks statue	mp3	PDF
April 10, 2014	Keynote address at the Civil Rights Summit	mp3	PDF
August 27, 2015	Hurricane Katrina 10-year anniversary address	mp3	PDF
May 27, 2016	Address at the Hiroshima Peace Memorial	mp3	PDF

The third step was to identify those speeches in which Obama greatly relied on an AAE communication style. The final step involved examining the context of these speeches. Words and phrases were the unit of analysis. In addition, we determined whether the event at which Obama spoke was a eulogy, an acceptance speech, an acknowledgement of a historical person and/or event, or an event in which he advised the public regarding his current plans as president.

Content of President Obama's Speeches

Of 300 speeches, we identified 15 speeches in which Obama specifically focused on an African American historical figure and/or an event that specifically affected the lives of African Americans. These speeches occurred from 2005 to 2015. One speech was in 2005; two speeches were in 2006; three speeches were in 2008; one speech was in 2009; one speech was in 2010; one speech was in 2011; one speech was in 2012; one speech was in 2013; one speech was in 2014; and one speech was in 2015. In addition, two speeches were related to Martin Luther King Jr.; two speeches were related to Rosa Parks; one speech was related to the 50th Anniversary of the March on Selma; one speech was related to the renewal of the Voting Rights Act; one speech was related to his first presidential election; one speech was related to his second presidential election; one speech was related to race and the presidential campaign; and one speech was related to the 10th anniversary of Hurricane Katrina. (See Table 10.2 for a list of the speeches that were analyzed. This table includes the delivery date, speech title, and focus of delivery).

Qualitative examination of Obama's speeches from 2005 to 2015 reveals four aspects of his communication style. First, he frequently uses repetition in his speeches.[10] Second, the president uses powerful metaphors that speak to historical difficulties and current triumphs. Specifically, these metaphors encourage racial unity among his listeners. Third, Obama uses tone, namely syllables, sounds, and words to convey meaning.[11] Finally, Obama uses a hybrid communication style that blends standards of Standard American English (SAE) with a "Black preacher style"[12] to connect with his audience.

Repetition

Through this story, Obama juxtaposes the insurmountable oppression of racial pain with eventual triumph. Obama declares (http://2008election.procon.org/pdf/Obama20080120.pdf):

And there are many lessons to take from this passage, just as there are many lessons to take from this day, just as there are many memories that fill the space of this church. As I was thinking about which ones we needed to remember at this hour, my mind went back to the very beginning of the modern Civil Rights era. Because before Memphis and the mountaintop, before the bridge in Selma and the march on Washington, before Birmingham and the beatings, the fire hoses, and the loss of those four little girls, before there was King the icon and his magnificent dream, there was King the young preacher and a people who found themselves suffering under the yolk of oppression. And on the eve of the bus boycotts in Montgomery, at a time when many were still doubtful about the possibilities of change, a time when there were those in the black community who not only mistrusted

Table 10.2 Delivery Date, Speech Title, and Focus of Delivery of Barack Obama's Speeches From 2005–2015

Delivery Date	Speech Title	Focus of Delivery
October 25, 2005	Death of Rosa Parks Senate floor Statement[i]	Rosa Parks
January 31, 2006	Senate speech on the passing of Coretta Scott King	Coretta Scott King
July 20, 2006	Senate speech on Voting Rights Act renewal	Voting Rights Act renewal
January 20, 2008	Eulogy for former pastor of Ebenezer Baptist Church[ii]	Eulogy
March 18, 2008	A More Perfect Union speech[iii]	Race and the presidential campaign
June 15, 2008	Speech to Apostolic Church of God in the South Side of Chicago, Father's Day[iv]	Father's Day
August 28, 2008	Democratic National Convention presidential nomination acceptance[v]	Presidential nomination acceptance
November 4, 2008	First presidential election victory speech[vi]	1st presidential election
January 18, 2009	Lincoln Memorial pre-inaugural speech	Lincoln Memorial
January 17, 2010	Martin Luther King Remembrance Day speech	Martin Luther King Jr.
October 16, 2011	Address at the Martin Luther King Jr. Memorial dedication	Martin Luther King Jr.
November 7, 2012	Second presidential election victory speech	2nd presidential election
February 27, 2013	Address dedicating Rosa Parks statue	Rosa Parks
April 10, 2014	Keynote address at the Civil Rights Summit	Civil rights
August 27, 2015	Hurricane Katrina 10-year anniversary address	Hurricane Katrina anniversary

[i] Obama Speech: Death of Rosa Parks Senate Floor Statement (October 25, 2005), http://obamaspeeches.com/034-Death-of-Rosa-Parks-Obama-Speech.htm.

[ii] Ebenezer Baptist Church Address (January 20, 2008), http://www.americanrhetoric.com/speeches/barackobama/barackobamaebenezerbaptist.htm.

[iii] Obama, B. (March 18, 2008) Transcript of Obama speech, http://www.politico.com/story/2008/03/transcript-of-obama-speech-009100.

[iv] Barack Obama's Father's Day Speech (June 15, 2008), http://frankwarner.typepad.com/free_frank_warner/2008/06/barack-obamas-f.html.

[v] Obama, B. (August 28, 2008) Barack Obama's Acceptance Speech, http://www.nytimes.com/2008/08/28/us/politics/28text-obama.html?_r=0.

[vi] "Transcript: 'This is your victory,' says Obama" (2008), http://edition.cnn.com/2008/POLITICS/11/04/obama.transcript/.

each other, but mistrusted themselves—King inspired with words not of anger, but of an urgency, a fierce urgency that still speaks to us today. "Unity," he said, "is the great need of the hour." "Unity is the great need of the hour." Unity is how we shall overcome.[13]

By using the word *unity* three times, Obama stresses to his audience the need to disregard personal partisanship and strive for racial and societal harmony. Furthermore, through the use of alliterative word-play, the POTUS compares seemingly impossible racial barriers as "the mountain-top" and "a yoke of oppression" that "inspired," led to "a fierce urgency" that impels current change.

Powerful Metaphors

Obama uses symbols to convey broad meanings. For example, he compares prejudice and bigotry to trees that once produced "bad fruit" that eventually resulted in progress, namely, his recognition of the nation's willingness to elect the first African American president of the United States. He states (http://latimesblogs.latimes.com/washington/2010/01/obama-church-text.html):

> We enjoy the fruits of prejudice and bigotry being lifted—slowly, sometimes in fits and starts, but irrevocably—from human hearts. It's that progress that made it possible for me to be here today; for the good people of this country to elect an African American the 44th President of the United States of America.[14]

Tone

Obama changes the tenor of his voice to stress certain words. For example during the Senate floor speech honoring the life of Coretta Scott King on January 31, 2006, Obama stresses the word *four* to remind his audience of the selfless actions of Ms. King. He said (https://www.congress.gov/congressional-record/2006/1/31/senate-section/article/s376-1?r=15):

> With no time to even cry or mourn, to wallow in anger or vengeance, Coretta Scott King took to the streets just four days after the assassination and led 50,000 through the streets of Memphis in a march for the kind of justice that her husband had given his life for.[15]

AAE and the Black Preacher Style

Obama uses a hybrid communication style that blends standards of SAE with a "Black preacher style" to connect with his audience. A part of this connection involves his appropriation and secularization of commonly used church terms to connect with his audience, but particularly African Americans who have historically valued religion and spirituality. For example, Obama uses the biblical phrase "my brother's keeper" as a reminder for Americans to actively seek ways to help and build one another up (http://www.nola.com/katrina/index.ssf/2015/08/transcript_of_president _obamas.html):

> These Americans live the basic values that define this country—the value we've been reminded of in these past 10 years as we've come back from a crisis that changed this city, and an economic crisis that spread throughout the nation—the basic notion that I am my brother's keeper, and I am my sister's keeper, and that we look out for each other and that we're all in this together.[16]

During his eulogy of the former pastor of Ebenezer Baptist Church, Obama began his address with a scriptural reference regarding when Joshua and the Israelites went against Jericho (http://www.simplysteno.com/010obama .pdf):

> Scripture tells us that when Joshua and the Israelites arrived at the gates of Jericho, they could not enter. The walls of the city were too steep for any one person to climb. They were too strong to be taken down by brute force. And so, the people sat for days, unable to pass on through; but God had a plan for His People. He told them to stand together and march together around the city, and on the seventh day he told them that when they heard the sound of the ram's horn, they should speak with one voice. And, at the chosen hour when the horn sounded and a chorus of voices cried out together, the mighty walls of Jericho came tumbling down. That's what scripture tells us.[17]

(See Table 10.3 for the speech title, focus of delivery, supporting example, and communication style that Obama demonstrates in each speech.)

The Pragmatic Language

Obama's use of language in conversation, nonverbal cues, and intonation patterns plays a crucial role in his communication. Cultural practices are manifested through pragmatics, and these elements play a crucial role in the daily lives of all communicators.[18] President Obama has been seen doing the fist bump across the world with Michelle Obama, the "dap" to a basketball player, and the head nod with the comment "Nah, we straight."

Table 10.3 Speech Title, Focus of Delivery, Supporting Example, and Communication Style

Speech Title	Focus of Delivery	Supporting Example	Communication Style
Death of Rosa Parks Senate floor statement	Rosa Parks	Her life, and her brave actions, reminded each and every one of us of our personal responsibilities to stand up for what is right and the central truth of the American experience that our greatness as a nation derives from seemingly ordinary people doing extraordinary things.	Powerful metaphors
Senate speech on Voting Rights Act renewal	Voting Rights Act	The arc of the moral universe is long, but it bends toward justice. That's because of the work that each of us do [sic] that it bends toward justice. It's because of people like John Lewis and Fannie Lou Hamer and Coretta Scott King and Rosa Parks—all the giants upon whose shoulders we stand—that we are beneficiaries of that arc bending toward justice. That's why I stand here today. I would not be in the United States Senate had it not been for the efforts and courage of so many parents and grandparents and ordinary people who were willing to reach up and bend that arc in the direction of justice.	Powerful metaphors; tone
Eulogy for former pastor of Ebenezer Baptist Church	Eulogy	Scripture tells us that when Joshua and the Israelites arrived at the gates of Jericho, they could not enter. The walls of the city were too steep for any one person to climb. They were too strong to be taken down by brute force. And so, the people sat for days, unable to pass on through; but God had a plan for His People. He told them to stand together and march together around the city, and on the seventh day he told them that when they heard the sound of the ram's horn, they should speak with one voice. And, at the chosen hour when the horn sounded and a chorus of voices cried out together, the mighty walls of Jericho came tumbling down. That's what scripture tells us.	AAE and the Black preacher style; tone

"A More Perfect Union" speech	Race and the presidential campaign	This moment in history because I believe deeply that we cannot solve the challenges of our time unless we solve them together—unless we perfect our union by understanding that we may have different stories, but we hold common hopes; that we may not look the same and we may not have come from the same place, but we all want to move in the same direction—toward a better future for of children and our grandchildren.[i]	Powerful metaphors; tone
Senator Barack Obama's speech to Apostolic Church of God in the South Side of Chicago, Father's Day	Father's Day	We keep faith that our Father will be there to guide us, and watch over us, and protect us, and lead His children through the darkest of storms to light of a better day. And that's my prayer for all of us on this here on Father's Day. That's my hope for this country in the years to come. And I hope that all of you feel that same faith, that same possibility that I do. Because if we rise up, if we have faith in the Lord, if we're working hard, if we do what we must do as fathers, and as mothers and grandfathers and grandmothers, if we're looking after our children, then I promise you, better days are ahead. God's going to lead us in a bright direction. God is going to lead us in a better direction. God bless you all. Thank you, Apostolic. I appreciate it. Thank you.	AAE and the Black preacher style; powerful metaphors
First presidential election victory speech	Victory speech	This is our time, to put our people back to work and open doors of opportunity for our kids; to restore prosperity and promote the cause of peace; to reclaim the American dream and reaffirm that fundamental truth, that, out of many, we are one; that while we breathe, we hope. And where we are met with cynicism and doubts and those who tell us that we can't, we will respond with that timeless creed that sums up the spirit of a people: Yes, we can.	Repetition; tone

207

(continued)

Table 10.3 (*continued*)

Speech Title	Focus of Delivery	Supporting Example	Communication Style
Lincoln Memorial pre-inaugural speech	Lincoln Memorial	On the ground below is a tribute to a generation that withstood war and depression—men and women like my grandparents who toiled on bomber assembly lines and marched across Europe to free the world from tyranny's grasp. Directly in front of us is a pool that still reflects the dream of a King, and the glory of a people who marched and bled so that their children might be judged by their character's content. And behind me, watching over the union he saved, sits the man who in so many ways made this day possible.	Powerful metaphors; tone
Martin Luther King Jr. Remembrance Speech	Martin Luther King Jr.	But let me tell you—during those times it's faith that keeps me calm. It's faith that gives me peace. The same faith that leads a single mother to work two jobs to put a roof over her head when she has doubts. The same faith that keeps an unemployed father to keep on submitting job applications even after he's been rejected a hundred times. The same faith that says to a teacher even if the first nine children she's teaching she can't reach, that that 10th one she's going to be able to reach.	AAE and the Black preacher style; powerful metaphors
		The same faith that breaks the silence of an earthquake's wake with the sound of prayers and hymns sung by a Haitian community. A faith in things not seen, in better days ahead, in Him who holds the future in the hollow of His hand. A faith that lets us mount up on wings like eagles; lets us run and not be weary; lets us walk and not faint.	

Address at the Martin Luther King Jr. Memorial dedication	Martin Luther King Jr.	So let us hold fast to that faith, as Joshua held fast to the faith of his fathers, and together, we shall overcome the challenges of a new age. Together, we shall seize the promise of this moment. Together, we shall make a way through winter, and we're going to welcome the spring. Through God all things are possible. We've inherited the progress of unjust laws that are now overturned. We take for granted the progress of a ballot being available to anybody who wants to take the time to actually vote. We enjoy the fruits of prejudice and bigotry being lifted—slowly, sometimes in fits and starts, but irrevocably—from human hearts. It's that progress that made it possible for me to be here today; for the good people of this country to elect an African American the 44th President of the United States of America.	Powerful metaphors; tone
Second presidential election victory speech	Victory speech	America, I believe we can build on the progress we've made, and continue to fight for new jobs, and new opportunity, and new security for the middle class. I believe we can keep the promise of our founding—the idea that if you're willing to work hard, it doesn't matter who you are, or where you come from, or what you look like, or where you love—it doesn't matter whether you're black or white, or Hispanic or Asian, or Native American, or young or old, or rich or poor, abled, disabled, gay or straight—you can make it here in America if you're willing to try.	Tone
Address dedicating Rosa Parks statue	Rosa Parks	Three hundred and eighty-five days after Rosa Parks refused to give up her seat, the boycott ended. Black men and women and children re-boarded the buses of Montgomery, newly desegregated, and sat in whatever seat happen to be open. And with that victory, the entire edifice of segregation, like the ancient walls of Jericho, began to slowly come tumbling down.	AAE and the Black Preacher Style; Powerful Metaphors

(continued)

Table 10.3 *(continued)*

Speech Title	Focus of Delivery	Supporting Example	Communication Style
Keynote address at the Civil Rights Summit	Civil rights	Because of the Civil Rights movement, because of the laws President Johnson signed, new doors of opportunity and education swung open for everybody—not all at once, but they swung open. Not just blacks and whites, but also women and Latinos; and Asians and Native Americans; and gay Americans and Americans with a disability. They swung open for you, and they swung open for me. And that's why I'm standing here today—because of those efforts, because of that legacy.	Powerful metaphors; repetition; tone
"Remarks by the President at the 50th Anniversary of The Selma to Montgomery Marches"[1]	Selma to Montgomery marches	The Americans who crossed this bridge, they were not physically imposing. But they gave courage to millions. They held no elected office. But they led a nation. They marched as Americans who had endured hundreds of years of brutal violence, countless daily indignities—but they didn't seek special treatment, just the equal treatment promised to them almost a century before.	Powerful metaphors; tone
Hurricane Katrina 10-year anniversary address	Hurricane Katrina anniversary	These Americans live the basic values that define this country—the value we've been reminded of in these past 10 years as we've come back from a crisis that changed this city, and an economic crisis that spread throughout the nation—the basic notion that I am my brother's keeper, and I am my sister's keeper, and that we look out for each other and that we're all in this together.	AAE and the Black preacher style; tone

[1] "Remarks by the President at the 50th Anniversary of the Selma to Montgomery Marches," The White House, Office of the Press Secretary, March 7, 2015, https://www.whitehouse.gov/the-press-office/2015/03/07/remarks-president-50th-anniversary-selma-montgomery-marches.

Understanding the Communication Style of President Obama

The communication style of President Barack Obama is uniquely different from former presidents. Even though former leaders publicly acknowledged influential African Americans such as Dr. Martin Luther King, Coretta Scott King, and Rosa Parks, Obama's genetic connection to African Americans allows him to more deeply relate to his audience and their collective struggles and triumphs.[19] Although his speeches are generally devoid of AAE elements, he strategically uses this dialect in contexts that speak to the majority of working-class people and educated individuals that frequently code-mesh. For example, although Senate Majority Leader Harry Reid observed that Mr. Obama spoke "with no Negro dialect, unless he wanted to have one," Obama told a Black cashier at Ben's Chili Bowl (a popular eatery in Washington) days before his 2009 inauguration, "Nah we straight" when this individual tried to give him his change. Through his subtle use of AAE and Black slang, Obama was perceived to be more relatable, likeable, and have more "personality" than his former Republican challenger, Mitt Romney. Although Romney was castigated for being inauthentic, Obama has been praised for his poise, skill, and great mastery over AAE.

Most noted, when Obama speaks about social issues that greatly affect Black people, he earns a credibility, validity, and respectability not experienced by former presidents. For example, because African Americans are the least likely racial group to marry and the racial group most likely to rear children as single parents,[20] Obama's call to Black fathers to be more involved in their children's lives was especially powerful. Essentially, by publicly sharing that his father was not actively involved in his life, he purposefully becomes the voice of a generation of Black children whose Black fathers are largely MIA (missing in action) from the lives of their children. However, at the end of this speech, Obama reminds his audience that if they care for their children "as fathers, and as mothers and grandfathers and grandmothers," God will lead them "in a better direction." Of note, Obama emphasizes faith, religion, and God when he discusses the need for social change.

The historical and contemporary salience of religion has been noted by several scholars[21] and over forty years ago, Robert Staples recognized religion as one of the racial hallmarks of Black families. Therefore, Obama places contemporary realities within a historical context by providing examples in which seemingly ordinary individuals' accomplished extraordinary things. In general, it was not the educated, wealthy, and powerful that effected national change but rather the uneducated, poor, and powerless that stood firmly and unapologetically demanded change. Subtly, by discussing race and the negative effects of racism, our commander in chief connects equitable treatment with the American dream of "life, liberty, and the pursuit of happiness." In addition, Obama recognizes structural issues that impact people of color. For example, even though Blacks make up approximately 13 percent of the United States population, they and Hispanics comprise 60 percent of individuals incarcerated.[22] Thus, although former presidents have provided pardons for former criminals, according to ProPublica, Blacks are substantially less likely than Whites to receive these pardons.[23] Because Obama shares the same phenotypical characteristics of African American men that are currently incarcerated, his computation of prison releases poignantly acknowledges the silent pain experienced by the incarcerated and aligns beautifully with religion's foundational belief in forgiveness.[24]

Impact of President Obama's Communication Style on Social Media

President Obama's communication style has greatly influenced and been influenced by social media. In fact, several political critics noted Obama's use of social media in his political campaigns, including podcasting, Twitter, MySpace, Facebook, and YouTube, has been compared to the adoption of radio, television, MTV, and the Internet in catapulting his presidential campaign to success. In fact, during the 2008 presidential campaign Barack Obama had more "friends" on Facebook and MySpace and more "followers" on Twitter than his opponent John McCain. Currently, Obama has 75.2 million Twitter followers,[25] which speaks to his popularity, accessibility, and likeability.

Limitations of the Current Analysis

The current analysis had several limitations. For one, although our focus on Barack Obama was the methodological foundation of the current examination, we cannot generalize his way of speaking to other presidents. So, even though presidents build their platforms on certain core issues that are of interest to the general population, Obama has a unique way of code-meshing that deeply resonates with his audience. In addition, our focus on President Obama in no way is meant to minimize the communication style of Vice-President Joe Biden or First Lady Michelle Obama. However, because presidential speeches are the most viewed and critiqued, our focus on President Obama supported the overarching goals of the analysis, which was his use of AAE. Finally, the methodology of this examination necessitated that we implement a purposive sampling strategy and focus on speeches in which race and or racial politics were the focus. Although some may consider this a limitation, this systematic way of conducting research acknowledged how Obama's unique racial position as president has given him a certain credibility when discussing race. Thus, these represent inherent strengths of the current work.

Ways to Build on Our Examination of President Obama's Speeches

There are three ways that individuals can build on our examination of President Obama's speeches. First, future scholars can explore the current and future president's level of engagement with social media. Because Twitter, MySpace, Facebook, and YouTube are relatively recent forms of social media, future work in this area can examine the content of current and future presidents' postings. Such work in this area may reveal the extent to which president's influence and are influenced by those who were previously in their position. Second, future scholars can qualitatively examine how individuals in the United States and abroad have been influenced by the communication style of Obama. Future work in this area may make known the specific personality characteristics and public delivery that make Obama's speeches especially memorable. Finally, future scholars can also examine the speeches of Vice-President Joe Biden as well as those of First Lady Michelle Obama. Future work in his area may reveal similarities and differences between how Obama and these key individuals in his life communicate.

Conclusion

As we reflect on the presidential tenure of President Barack Obama, the world will forever be reminded of his historical place among the nation's presidents as well as the ways in which he communicated with the public. Through repetition, he makes the main points of his message clear. Through metaphors, he creates strong symbolic pictures to convey the ability of seemingly insignificant people creating significant social change. Through tone, he encourages Americans to contemplate painful aspects of their history as well as the need to create a future ripe with hope and change. Through a Black preacher style, he validates the historical salience of religion among African Americans as well as those who hold firmly to faith during trying times. Fundamentally, through the stories that he told, the world clearly understood Obama's values, his faith, and his hope for a better world. During his two-term presidency, he extended the call for peace and unity that was first made by the late Dr. Martin Luther King Jr.[26] While the nation has a new president, one thing is certain; Although President Obama is no longer in the White House, the world will forever understand who he is.

Notes

1. Hayden, 2015.

2. USA Today, 2010.

3. Labov, 1972, p. xii.

4. Wolfram, 2004; Charity, 2008; Hyter, Rivers, and DeJarnette, 2015.

5. Fasold, 1972; Labov, 1972; Labov, 1998; Dayton, 1996; Baugh, 1983; Rickford, 1999.

6. Fasold, 1969, p. 764.

7. "Behind the Scenes with President Obama & Team USA Basketball," You-Tube video, 2:38, posted by "Infomisa," September 6, 2012, https://www.youtube.com/watch?v=a7fjQHdMqY4.

8. "Barack Obama in Sumter, SC," YouTube video, 2:29, posted by "Barack Obama.com," January 23, 2008, https://www.youtube.com/watch?v=gh69Zi2rV-U.

9. King, Keohane, and Verba, 1994.

10. "Presidential Speeches," April 23, 2009. https://africanamericanenglish.com/2009/04/23/presidential-speeches/.

11. Smitherman, 1975.

12. Alim and Smitherman, 2012.

13. Remarks of Senator Barack Obama: The Great Need of the Hour, January 20, 2008. Retrieved from: http://2008election.procon.org/pdf/Obama20080120.pdf.

14. Barack Obama's Address at the Martin Luther King Memorial Dedication, October 16, 2011. Retrieved from: http://latimesblogs.latimes.com/washington/2010/01/obama-church-text.html.

15. Barack Obama's Senate Floor Speech Honoring the Life of Coretta Scott King on January 31, 2006. Retrieved from: https://www.congress.gov/congressional-record/2006/1/31/senate-section/article/s376-1?r=15.

16. Transcript of President Obama's Katrina speech, Given on August 27, 2015, Retrieved from: http://www.nola.com/katrina/index.ssf/2015/08/transcript_of_president_obamas.html.

17. Barack Obama's Eulogy of the Former Pastor of Ebenezer Baptist Church, Retrieved from: http://www.simplysteno.com/010obama.pdf.

18. Hyter, Rivers, and DeJarnette, 2015.

19. Frederick, 1970.

20. African American Healthy Marriage Initiative, http://www.aahmi.net/focus.html.

21. Chaney, 2008a; Chaney, 2008b; McAdoo, 1974.

22. Kerby, 2012.

23. LeFleur, 2011.
24. "Remarks by the President on Commutations of Prison Sentences," The White House, Office of the President, March 17, 2016, https://www.whitehouse.gov/the-press-office/2016/03/30/remarks-president-commutations-prison-sentences.
25. Twitter@BarackObama. https://twitter.com/barackobama?lang=en.
26. Robinson, Moore, and Williams-Black, 2015.

Bibliography

Adjaye, Joseph K., and Adrianne R. Andrews, eds. *Language, rhythm, & sound: Black popular cultures into the twenty-first century.* Pittsburgh, PA: University of Pittsburgh Press, 1997.
African American Healthy Marriage Initiative. n.d. Retrieved on June 4, 2016 from: http://www.aahmi.net/focus.html
Alim, H. Samy, and Geneva Smitherman. *Articulate While Black: Barack Obama, Language and Race in the U.S.* Oxford: Oxford University Press, 2012.
Alim, H. Samy, and Geneva Smitherman. "Obama's English." *The New York Times,* September 8, 2012. http://www.nytimes.com/2012/09/09/opinion/sunday/obama-and-the-racial-politics-of-american-english.html?_r=0.
"Barack Obama in Sumter, SC." YouTube video, 2:29, posted by "BarackObama .com," January 24, 2008. https://www.youtube.com/watch?v=gh69Zi2rV-U.
"Barack Obama's Acceptance Speech." *The New York Times,* August 28, 2008. http://www.nytimes.com/2008/08/28/us/politics/28text-obama.html?_r=0.
Baugh, John. "A survey of Afro-American English." *Annual Review of Anthropology* 12 (1983): 335–354.
"Behind the Scenes with President Obama & Team USA Basketball." YouTube video, 2:38, posted by "Infomisa," September 6, 2012. https://www.youtube.com/watch?v=a7fjQHdMqY4.
Chaney, Cassandra. "The benefits of church involvement for African Americans—The perspectives of congregants, church staff and the church pastor." *Religion and Society* 10 (2008a): 1–23.
Chaney, Cassandra. "Religiosity and spirituality among members of an African American church community: A qualitative analysis." *Journal of Religion and Spirituality in Social Work: Social Thought* 27 (2008b): 201–234.
Chaney, Cassandra, and Colita Nichols Fairfax. "A change has come: The Obamas and the culture of black marriage in America." *Ethnicities* 13, no. 1 (2012): 20–48.
Chaney, Cassandra, and Colita Nichols Fairfax. "The Obamas and the culture of black parenting in America." *Journal of Pan African Studies* 5, no. 10 (2013): 20–50.
Charity, Anne Harper. "African American English: An overview." *Perspectives on Communication Disorders and Sciences in Culturally and Linguistically Diverse Populations* 15, no. 2 (2008): 33–42.

Dandy, Evelyn Baker. *Black communications: Breaking down the barriers.* Chicago, IL: African American Images, 1991.

Dayton, Elizabeth. "Grammatical categories of the verb in African-American Vernacular English." (1996). Scholarly Commons. Penn Libraries, University of Pennsylvania. http://repository.upenn.edu/dissertations/AAI9712915.

Delgado, Richard. "Why Obama: An Interest Convergence Explanation of the Nation's First Black President." *Law & Inequity* 33 (2015): 345–369.

Fasold, Ralph W. "Tense and the form be in Black English." *Language* 45, no. 4 (1969): 763–776.

Fasold, Ralph W. "Tense Marking in Black English. A Linguistic and Social Analysis." *Urban Language Series*, no. 8. (1972).

Hayden, Tom. *Long Sixties: From 1960 to Barack Obama.* New Brunswick, NJ: Routledge, 2015.

Hyter, Yvette D., Kenyatta O. Rivers, and Glenda DeJarnette. "Pragmatic Language of African American Children and Adolescents." *Topics in Language Disorders* 35, no. 1 (2015): 8–45.

Kerby, Sophia. "The Top 10 Most Startling Facts about People of Color and Criminal Justice in the United States." Center for American Progress. (March 13, 2012). https://www.americanprogress.org/issues/race/news/2012/03/13/11351/the-top-10-most-startling-facts-about-people-of-color-and-criminal-justice-in-the-united-states/.

King, Gary, Robert Keohane, and Sidney Verba. *Designing Social Inquiry: Scientific Inference in Qualitative Research.* Princeton, New Jersey: Princeton University Press, 1994.

Kochman, Thomas. *Black and white styles in conflict.* Chicago, IL: University of Chicago Press, 1981.

Labov, William. "Co-existant systems in African-American vernacular English." *African American English: Structure, History and Use* (1998): 110–153.

Labov, William. *Language in the inner city: Studies in the Black English vernacular,* vol. 3. Philadelphia, PA: University of Pennsylvania Press, 1972, p. xii.

Labov, William. *Sociolinguistic patterns* no. 4. Philadelphia, PA: University of Pennsylvania Press, 1972.

LeFleur, Jennifer "How ProPublica Analyzed Pardon Data." ProPublica. (December 3, 2011). https://www.propublica.org/article/how-propublica-analyzed-pardon-data.

Lehrman, Robert, and Andrew S. Crines. "The Oratory of Barack Obama." In *Democratic Orators from JFK to Barack Obama* (pp. 261–282). London: Palgrave Macmillan, 2016.

Major, Clarence. "Dictionary of Afro-American Slang." New York, NY: International Publishers, 1970.

McAdoo, Harriette Pipes, ed. *Black families.* Thousand Oaks, CA: Sage Publications, 2006.

McWhorter, John. "We Should Celebrate Our Bilingual President." The Root. (October 5, 2011). http://www.theroot.com/we-should-celebrate-our-bilingual-president-1790866163.

Obama, Barack. "Death of Rosa Parks Senate Floor Statement." Best Speeches of Barack Obama through his 2009 Inauguration. (October 25, 2005). http://obamaspeeches.com/034-Death-of-Rosa-Parks-Obama-Speech.htm.

Obama, Barack. "Ebenezer Baptist Church Address." January 20, 2008, Ebenezer Baptist Church, Atlanta, GA. American Rhetoric Online Speech Bank. http://www.americanrhetoric.com/speeches/barackobama/barackobamaebenezerbaptist.htm.

Obama, Barack. "Father's Day Speech." Apostolic Church of God, South Side, Chicago, IL, June 15, 2008. Free Frank Warner. June 17, 2008. http://frankwarner.typepad.com/free_frank_warner/2008/06/barack-obamas-f.html.

Obama, Barack. "Transcript: 'This is your victory,' says Obama." CNN Politics. (2008) http://edition.cnn.com/2008/POLITICS/11/04/obama.transcript/.

Obama, B. "Transcript of Obama speech." Politico. (March 18, 2008). http://www.politico.com/story/2008/03/transcript-of-obama-speech-009100.

Powery, Luke A. "Embodying the Sermon." *Ways of the Word: Learning to Preach for Your Time and Place* 64, no. 4 (2016): 183.

"Presidential Speeches." Word. (April 23, 2009). https://africanamericanenglish.com/2009/04/23/presidential-speeches/.

"Remarks by the President at the 50th Anniversary of the Selma to Montgomery Marches." The White House, Office of the Press Secretary. (March 7, 2015). https://www.whitehouse.gov/the-press-office/2015/03/07/remarks-president-50th-anniversary-selma-montgomery-marches.

"Remarks by the President on Commutations of Prison Sentences." The White House, Office of the Press Secretary (March 17, 2016). https://www.whitehouse.gov/the-press-office/2016/03/30/remarks-president-commutations-prison-sentences.

Rickford, John R. "Carrying the New Wave into Syntax: The Case of Black English BIN[1]." In *Analyzing Variation in Language: Papers from the Second Colloquium on New Ways of Analyzing Variation*, vol. 2, p. 162. Georgetown University Press, 1975.

Rickford, John Russell. *African American vernacular English: Features, evolution, educational implications*. Hoboken, NJ: Wiley-Blackwell, 1999.

Robinson, Nichelle Boyd, Virginia J. Moore, and Thea H. Williams-Black. "Has the Dream Been Fulfilled? Dr. Martin Luther King, Jr. & President Barack Hussein Obama." *Multicultural Education* 23, no. 1 (2015): 59–63.

Smitherman, Geneva. *Black language and culture: Sounds of soul*. New York, NY: Harper & Row, 1975.

Smitherman, Geneva. *Talkin and testifyin: The language of Black America*, vol. 51. Detroit, MI: Wayne State University Press, 1977.

Staples, Robert. "The black family revisited: A review and a preview." *Journal of Social and Behavioral Sciences* 20 (1974): 65–78.

"Speech Critics Address Obama's Oratory." USA Today. (January 24, 2010). http://usatoday30.usatoday.com/news/washington/2010-01-24-obamaorations_N.htm.

Williams, Frederick, ed. *Language and Poverty: Perspectives on a Theme*. Chicago, IL: Markham Publishing, 1970. Review by J. L. Dillard, *Language* 48, no. 2 (June 1972): 479–487.

Wolfram, Walt. "The grammar of urban African American vernacular English." *Handbook of Varieties of English* 2 (2004): 111–132.

Young, Vershawn Ashanti, Rusty Barrett, Y'Shanda Young-Rivera, and Kim Brian Lovejoy. *Other People's English*. New York, NY: Teacher's College Press, 2014.

CHAPTER ELEVEN

The Duplicitous Commodification of the Obama Presidency: Interrogating Barack Obama's Sociopolitical Assent and Relevance through a Conscious Hip-Hop Pedagogy

Ahmad R. Washington, Belema Idoniboye, and Marta N. Mack-Washington

Introduction

The meteoric rise of Barack Hussein Obama from relative obscurity in the U.S. Senate to ubiquitous visibility, as the first Black president of the United States is nothing short of remarkable. Although a cadre of political insiders sensed Obama's educational pedigree, impeccable credentials, charisma, and oratorical abilities would make him a viable and formidable presidential candidate in four to eight years, should he choose to run, the general public, in retrospect, was largely unaware of the Chicago senator; that is, until he delivered the keynote address at the 2004 Democratic National Convention in Boston, Massachusetts.

Having been selected to deliver the keynote address in the spring of 2004, then–Illinois Senator Obama—a man who had served the South Side of Chicago as a grassroots organizer after matriculating through the prestigious Harvard Law School under the tutelage of the preeminent Critical Race Scholar Dr. Derrick Bell—rendered an eloquent and energizing address that injected his name into public and political discourse. With Curtis Mayfield's "Keep on Pushing" serving as his introductory musical accompaniment, Senator Obama sauntered to the lectern to articulate a speech replete with idyllic anecdotes about American exceptionalism, a narrative that was ostensibly affirmed by his very presence on that stage. Gone from Obama's rhetoric was any forthright semblance of race cognizance or, more importantly, an acknowledgement that racism continues to constrict the life opportunities for non-Whites in this country; Senator Obama's speech spoke of an America where hard work, ingenuity, and resilience, rather than racial identification, overwhelmingly determined one's station in these United States of America.[1] Senator Obama would leverage this watershed occasion for his own pursuit and eventual achievement of the office of President of the United States.

Although his speech at the Democratic Convention was integral in catalyzing his presidential chase, Obama's proximity to hip-hop culture in 2008 and 2012, through his affiliations with hip-hop icons (i.e., Beyoncé, Jay Z, P. Diddy, etc.), appropriation of lyrics or references to caricatured tropes (i.e., Pookie from *New Jack City*), were also instrumental in galvanizing voters, including millennials, and African American millennials most especially.[2] Political benefit notwithstanding, Obama's calculated association with hip-hop culture, one could argue, reflects the harsh ontological reality hip-hop culture and the would-be president both experience because of their proximity to Blackness in a vehemently anti-Black society. Throughout his candidacy and presidency, Obama, the son of a Kenyan immigrant, was repeatedly marked as a suspicious, perpetual foreigner because of his Blackness and ethnic name; as a consequence, his words and actions were hyper-surveilled, dissected, and subjected to intense scrutiny. Similarly, because of its anchoring in the counterhegemonic aspirations and boisterous articulations of Black and Latino youths from poor and working-class communities, hip-hop culture has historically been framed as nihilistic, morally bankrupt, irresponsible, and untrustworthy.

Mitigating this suspicion was of paramount importance for Obama, which meant renouncing his affiliation with radical thinkers who had mentored him, most notably, Rev. Jeremiah A. Wright Jr. Analogously, the process of making hip-hop more palatable and less threatening to "middle America" was facilitated through globalization and corporatization, which helped fashion a facsimile of hip-hop culture for popular culture. This hypermediated and commercialized hip-hop—a hip-hop which is necessarily divorced from its nonconformist, radical, and counter-hegemonic underpinnings—mimics a neoliberal ideology that ascribes tremendous importance to capital and economic prosperity, asset accumulation, and gratuitous conspicuous consumption while also espousing a universalizing, class-focused, postracial discourse.[3]

Although a bevy of hip-hop's most prominent and economically prosperous figures (i.e., Jay Z, P. Diddy, etc.) used their platforms to endorse Obama during his initial and reelection campaigns, other artists harkened back to hip-hop's tradition of radical social commentary in their critiques of Obama for how he had buttressed a militaristic, corporate-friendly, politically moderate regime by pivoting away from his campaign mantra of *Hope* and *Change*. This chapter seeks to contribute to the discourse within hip-hop pedagogy by examining the complex, symbiotic relationship between hip-hop culture and America's first hip-hop president. This chapter explores President Obama's political ideology and how it has vacillated since his speech in 2004. The focus then shifts to how hip-hop was used to help then-Senator Obama forge a path, albeit tumultuous, to the White House. The chapter concludes with an analysis of various hip-hop artists who have used their talents to chastise Obama for how he has been complicit in domestic and foreign militarism that endangers the lives of Black and Brown communities.

Barack Obama's Personal Narrative and Racial Politics

Barack Hussein Obama's uniquely neoliberal White-fragility-centered, cosmopolitan-themed life story phenomenally connects him to contemporary neoliberal American politics but simultaneously disconnects him from a most intimate connection with the plight of most African Americans as well as the tradition of radical Black leftist politics in the United States. Born in 1961 in Honolulu, Hawaii, to a White American mother and a Black Kenyan father in the midst of the 20th-century American Civil Rights mass movement, Barack Hussein Obama II was the progeny of White bourgeoisie liberalism and African bourgeoisie conservatism. Honolulu, Hawaii, was far removed from the mainland United States, where the clash between White domination and Black resistance was the most brutally intense. By any standards of that era, his parents' relationship and marriage could be viewed as a radical demonstration of resistance to the openly prevailing ideologies of that time regarding interracial marriage, but their lack of demonstrated civil rights activism or outspokenness on race during the height of the Civil Rights mass movement perhaps also reveals their aloofness to the movement.

Growing up in Hawaii and, for a period of time, in Indonesia, and being raised by an upper-middle class White mother and grandparents, largely divorced Barack Obama from the day-to-day brutality of segregation and racial animus many mainland African Americans encountered. Obama's childhood was much different from most African Americans of his time, as he was shrouded daily with White love and provided an elite cosmopolitan education. Obama's identity was largely tied to his middle-class White family despite his olive-skinned complexion. His parents effectively separated shortly after his birth and divorced in 1964, when the future president was still a toddler. Obama did not have a healthy relationship with his father, only seeing him once during his childhood. This strained relationship unfortunately did not improve before Obama Sr.'s tragic death in an automobile accident in 1982. President Obama has noted on several occasions that this immense void during his childhood caused much of his self-destructive behavior and often left him feeling incomplete and unaware of who he was and what his purpose was in life. It was not until the latter part of his teenage years that Obama found his purpose in life and rededicated himself fully to learning, which opened up the pathway toward his long-time marriage to radical Black liberation politics.

In 1979, Obama graduated from high school and began his collegiate studies at Occidental College in Los Angeles. By his own admission, Obama was not a serious or stellar student, but it was during this time that he became actively involved in the anti-apartheid movement, giving his first public political speech. Obama was also heavily influenced during this time by radical Black students on campus. In 1981, he transferred to Columbia University as an incoming junior. During his time in New York City, he was heavily influenced by the tremendous wealth disparities and plight of inner city minorities. It was also during this time that he first made serious connections to his paternal relatives. After graduating in 1983, Obama spent two more years in New York City, working at Business International Corporation and then the New York Public Interest Research Group. During this time, Obama was actively involved in activism, particularly the May Day movement to improve the dangerous and squalid conditions of the New York City subway.

In 1985, Obama was hired as director of Developing Communities Projects, a faith-based communal organization on Chicago's predominantly African American South Side. Among his primary responsibilities as a community organizing director were overseeing job and educational tutoring programs and educating low-income tenants about their tenant rights. It was during this time that Obama honed his rhetorical skills and was able to directly capture the narratives of the Black proletariat.

In 1988, Obama was accepted to and enrolled in Harvard Law School (HLS). During his time at HLS, he served as a research aide to iconic liberal constitutional law professor Laurence Tribe and was heavily influenced by critical race theorist Professor Derrick Bell, who eventually left HLS after the school failed to hire any African American woman professors. Obama received his first douse of national media attention when he made history in 1990 by becoming the first Black president of the *Harvard Law Review*, the nation's most prestigious legal academic journal.

After graduating in 1991, Obama accepted a two-year fellowship at the University of Chicago Law School to work on his seminal autobiography *Dreams from My Father*. During this time, Obama also served as director of a voting registration campaign and then as a civil rights attorney for a small Chicago-based law firm.

Barack Obama's Political Leanings and the Plight of African Americans

I mean, you got the first mainstream African American who is articulate and bright and clean and a nice-looking guy. I mean, that's a storybook, man.[4]

—Joseph R. Biden Jr. (January 31, 2007)

Understanding Barack Obama's meteoric rise in American politics, which led him in just four short years to go from an unheralded inner-city Illinois state senator to his political party's standard bearer and the 44th president of the United States, requires just as much devoted reflection on how his uniquely neoliberal, White-fragility-centered, cosmopolitan-themed life story and presidential campaign tapped into a broad multiracial cohort's multifaceted and diverging emotional aspirations, as it did on the unique global challenges America faced at the time of his election.[5] As the result of an extremely dire global economic crisis and two extremely costly and controversial wars in Afghanistan and Iraq, the latter of which Mr. Obama openly and vehemently opposed from its conception, the success of his two historic presidential campaigns ultimately congealed around a unique convergence of racial interests perhaps unprecedented for any American presidential candidate.[6] Remarkably, Obama and his presidential campaign shrewdly capitalized on this unprecedented opportunity through a masterful blending of Black performance art with popular culture multiculturalism; this blending not only projected and reinforced Obama's eruditeness, youthfulness, mixed ancestry, and refreshing presence on the international political scene but concomitantly attracted millions of millennials, first-time voters, and important swing voters to his presidential campaigns.[7] Indeed, racial interest convergence and Obama's populist appeals to a war-weary public worked in tandem to temporarily sweep aside America's sordid legacy of race and racism and propel him to the White House as America's first African American president.[8]

In analyzing Obama's masterful mixing of Black performance art with popular culture multiculturalism, it is very important to keep in mind multicultural sociopolitical paradigms within the context of Americanism are, and always have been, centered on White consensus notions of aesthetic beauty, assimilationist respectability, and White fragility.[9] Taken together, these impulses and perceptions that many, if not most, White people are guided by in judging non-White people of color fold into a single word then-Senator Joseph Biden used in 2007 to describe his then–junior colleague: "mainstream."[10] In 2010, Senate Majority Harry Reid (D–Nevada) found himself in hot water when it was discovered that he had more clearly articulated this reasoning in private during the 2008 presidential race, noting that Obama could be a successful presidential candidate because he is "light-skinned with no Negro dialect, unless he wanted to have one."[11]

For neoliberal African American politicians seeking elective office at the national or statewide level (which invariably requires them to attract a significant percentage of White voters), there is a seeming necessity for these politicians to successfully place themselves within the politically advantageous box of "mainstreamness" while not completely alienating their Black roots or their perpetually marginalized, but always euphoric, Black base constituency.[12] It is a tough and delicate balancing act that is always expected to pay big dividends for Black candidates; but since the Civil War Reconstruction, with the exception of President Obama, one state attorney general, two Black governors, and four other Black U.S. senators (one of whom is a moderate Republican), never has a Black candidate won statewide election. If elected, it is not trite to say that governing under this paradigm is equally as complicated.

Although Barack Obama's ability to dance on the outer boundaries of "mainstreamness" explains how he was able to appeal to many first-time voters, White millennials, and record numbers of African Americans, this observation still does not escape a reckoning with America's time-honored, insidious ploy of shrewdly granting semblances of Black sociopolitical advancement only when this advancement converges with the interests of White Americans in salvaging America's global hegemony and racially disparate paradigm of capitalism.[13] What is more, this interest convergence is always subsequently revised and repackaged as some nationalistic display of a newfound, collective, revolutionary, altruistic White morality on race relations.[14]

This time-honored tradition does not contradict the effectiveness of the Obama campaigns' masterfully blended media outreach. In fact, it goes hand in hand with it because the Obama campaign, and later his administration, went to great lengths to absolve White guilt, primarily among older and more conservative Whites, by shrewdly using aspects of Afrofuturism.[15] Afrofuturism is defined as "an intersection of imagination, technology, the future and liberation."[16] Because Afrofuturism is primarily forward looking, Obama's employment of it allowed him to divorce himself from the real-time bitterness tied to the lingering history and everpresent displays of Black oppression, and concurrently center his race rhetoric on an imaginative faultless society built on peace, inclusiveness, and equality.[17] This was neatly summed up in his "color-blind" campaign slogans, such as "Yes We Can" and "Hope," and his statement during his reelection campaign that he was "not the president of Black America."[18] None of these slogans directly called for tolerance of the plight and pathology of the oppressed. This was also clarified as Obama moved to distance himself from his radical Black leftist past and condemning statements of his one-time pastor and Black liberation theologian Rev. Dr. Jeremiah A. Wright; and eventually, he distanced himself from his one-time academic mentor, critical race theorist Professor Derrick A. Bell. Obama later resigned from Wright's Chicago-based Trinity United Church of Christ. Nevertheless, many in the Black community saw these moves as the price of the ticket and clung to hopes that a President Obama would be empowered by his historic election and guided in his policies by his deep understandings of legal history, critical race theory, Black liberation theology, and Afropessimism, as expressed in his bestselling autobiography *Dreams from My Father: A Story on Race and Inheritance.*

Once the chances of this dissipated in Obama's first term, despite having a Democratic-controlled U.S. House of Representatives and 60-seat filibuster-proof majority in the U.S. Senate for the first half of his first term, Blacks put their faith in the chances that a term-limited President Obama would embrace the radical Black leftist agenda. However, despite his continued evasions of the radical Black leftist agenda, Obama remains highly popular in the African American community because of his masterful use of Black performance art, such as hip-hop, R&B, and even gospel music, to signal to his loyal base that he remains connected to them. This effective use of Black performance art is steeped in America's sordid history of race when African Americans could only give voice to their political malcontent through art, not the ballot, and when petitions for redress fell on deaf ears. However, it also serves as a contemporary means for liberal politicians to smooth Black communal discontent about a politician or his or her political party's hostility toward or lack of political fortitude regarding the radical Black leftist agenda. This was a highly effective technique for President Obama and before him, President Bill Clinton. The aesthetic value of Secretary Hillary Clinton being closely connected to President Obama as a cabinet official during his first term may be partly if not largely responsible for her overwhelming support from African Americans during the 2016 Democratic Party primaries despite being challenged from the left by Senator Bernie Sanders, a democratic socialist, who ideologically was much closer to the views of many of the radical Black leftists who inspired a younger Barack Obama.

Unsurprisingly, Obama's coerced concessionary race rhetoric and actions during his presidential campaign perversely became assets for scores of "color-blind" White conservatives and "discount justice" neoliberal revisionists after his 2008 election. Claims of a "postracial" American society emerged from both of these ideological stains immediately after Obama's election, only further undermining the Black radical leftist agenda and preempting any substantive personal perspective on race from Obama. Thus it should have come as no surprise that soon after his 2009 inauguration, President Obama proclaimed that he was not the president of "Black America" and later walked back statements he made in the aftermath of Harvard University sociologist Dr. Henry Gates Jr.'s controversial arrest. Many in the Black community, particularly the neoliberal Black petite bourgeoisie, were caught in the baffling paradox of needing to appear publicly supportive of the nation's first Black president and knowing that holding back necessary criticisms of the president were doing nothing to advance the Black agenda and were in fact perpetuating harm on the Black bottom proletariat.

Devoid of this context, what is often lost or ignored in the aftermath of these episodic moments of coerced Black sociopolitical advancement is the fact that the deep rhetorical concessions made by the African American community and their leaders along with America's continued evasions of robust and unfettered reparatory justice for African Americans perversely advances disparate White hegemonic sociopolitical and economic power.

Moreover, these concessions and evasions perpetuate the commodification of systemic anti-Black racism. Interconnected to this communal capitulation and anti-Black perpetuation is the cyclical inevitability that the interest convergence phenomenon, which brought about the episodic moment of seeming Black sociopolitical advancement, will dissipate as soon as economic stability is reobtained. This is termed *White backlash*. This theory best explains the birth of the racially tinged neoconservative political movement called the Tea Party; the dramatic rise in the extrajudicial killings of Black Americans by law enforcement, terrorists, and vigilantes; and how a narcissistic fascist demagogue, whose claim to fame includes White nativist and supremacist rhetoric about President Obama's citizenship and religion, can capture the Republican nomination while receiving the most primary votes in the history of that party's primary process.

In light of all this, perhaps it is fair to say that critical race theory views the presidential elections of Barack Obama, the biracial, Black-identifying, contradictory antiwar capitalist, as a convergence of interests between many neoliberal Whites and many non-White people of color, particularly Blacks, as a means to salvage American capitalism, end an overly expansive hegemonic war that was costing the lives of thousands of Americans (mostly White Americans), and to realize long-held Black aspirations to be governed by a progressive Black leader (a Black messiah) even if that meant absconding Black radical ideals of Black nationalism, unfettered reparatory justice, and complete atonement. Taken together, as historic as Barack Obama's elections were in the context of American and African American history, his election also demonstrated the continued will of the majority of Black Americans to concede to counterrevolutionary realpolitik and to abandon Martin King's clarion call for a true revolution of values as long as solace can be found in this through the incorporation of Black performance art and popular culture multiculturalism. Because Obama had so convincingly incorporated Black performance art and popular culture multiculturalism, it is important to turn our attention to the mode of Black performance art that was integral in securing his initial election—hip-hop culture.

Hip-Hop Culture

Any serious engagement with hip-hop culture must, first, contextualize the culture by situating it on a genealogical continuum of radical social resistance movements spearheaded by Black and Brown youth. These youth were intent on dramatically recalibrating the repressive racial, political, and economic social order, particularly in urban cities, as it was being experienced during the crescendo, plateau, and subsequent decline of the competing ideologies of the Civil Rights era.[19] Therefore our examination must include a discussion of the sociohistorical factors that precipitated the exodus of millions of African Americans from the agricultural South to the industrial West, Midwest and North; the politics that circumscribed social mobility and economic empowerment and self-determination within poor and working-class Black and immigrant Latino communities; and how hip-hop culture represented a discursive practice—effervescent, defiant, and liberatory in its orientation—and not simply a conduit for lamenting the disenfranchisement people of color were facing.[20]

The Move Northward

The African American Great Migration, an epoch occurring at the turn of the 20th century, saw nearly six million African Americans relocate from an existence in the agricultural South to densely populated northern, Midwestern, and Western enclaves. Rightly, historians point out the consequential social and economic incentives that compelled numerous African Americans to trek to cities like Philadelphia, Detroit, Chicago, and New York. In the South, deeply entrenched abject poverty, unrepentant political disenfranchisement, and blatant and unrelenting White racial animus and violence were all justifications for Blacks leaving the South en masse.[21]

Quickly, though, African Americans migrating from the South soon realized that although the physical terrain had changed, the differences between White vitriol in the North, Midwest, and West and what they experienced in the south were virtually imperceptible. Housing discrimination in the North and Midwest, whether discrete or blatant, denied countless African Americans access to decent housing. Prevented from purchasing homes in White suburbs, African Americans were often relegated to residential squalor in densely populated urban ghettos. In places like Detroit or Chicago, when Blacks were able to procure housing, they habitually faced anti-integration White mobs who congregated around homes to impose physical violence or inflict property damage; these practices essentially locked African Americans almost completely out of home ownership, robbing them of the ability to accrue valuable equity, from the 1930s until the 1960s.[22]

Youth-Driven Voice of Dissent

By the late 1960s, the South Bronx had been decimated by the departure of industrial and manufacturing jobs, stable employment opportunities that provided decent wages for manual laborers and their families.[23] Not surprisingly, Whites, who were unshackled by racism, made expeditious exits from the Bronx; so too did many middle-class African Americans who possessed sufficient streams of requisite economic and social capital. Economically self-interested politicians and capitalists were all too eager to abandon those that could not afford to exit the Bronx by allowing the borough to plummet into abysmal conditions.[24] The eventual construction of the Cross Bronx Expressway, which enabled economically and racially privileged suburbanites to traverse the cities for work and leisure activities without having any meaningful contact with the blighted Bronx, was emblematic of the abandonment imposed on people living in the Bronx.[25]

Youth coming of age in the Bronx at this time were justifiably despondent and upset; responding with livid discontent after being treated as disposable is certainly understandable. Youth had various channels through which they could express their frustration and resentment. In the Bronx, gangs burgeoned as young people sought affiliation and protection. Violent clashes were frequent; bones were broken and lives were lost. Although political organizations like The Black Panthers and The Young Lords were present as viable alternatives that enabled disaffected youth to organize in solidarity with one another, intense government repression from organizations like COINTELPRO (Counterintelligence Program) and the assassinations of seminal revolutionary leaders like Fred Hampton, Malcolm X, and Dr. King in the late 1960s destabilized these organizations, leaving their members in disarray.

This political consciousness returned in 1971 after a young man named Cornell Benjamin aka "Black Benji" was killed as he attempted to negotiate a peace treaty between rival gangs. Rather than retaliate, these young men and women, who had been cast aside repeatedly as worthless by agents of the dominant ruling class, decided to organize to resist the oppression they all faced on the basis of their race and class.[26] This race and class consciousness, forged in the context of discernible indifference and perpetual societal alienation, would be the galvanizing force that would come to inform political rap for years to come. Moreover, this political stream of thought that would later inspire artists like Queen Latifah, Chuck D, and others was also present in the work of other Black and Afro-Latino performers. Radical poets like Nikki Giovanni, The Last Poets, and Gil Scott-Heron, who verbalized the rage, hopes, and aspirations of Blacks and derided the exploitive racial and economic policies that wreaked pain and havoc on impoverished people, here and abroad, are often considered the progenitors of what is considered political rap. In other words, the collision of hip-hop and the American political discourse is far from uncommon.

Hip-Hop and the Path to the Presidency

At the time of Obama's path to the presidency, many within hip-hop were overcome with a veritable deluge of euphoria, pride, and irrepressible glee. Although divergent responses to Obama proliferated following his election and reelection, here special attention is paid to how more prominent and economically viable hip-hop artists gestured toward Obama and how he strategically reciprocated the acknowledgement.

"Obama on the text . . ."

The ability to access the president on a whim connotes power and prestige; this is precisely what Jay Z was meaning to communicate to listeners in 2009 when he uttered this line. Though Jay Z is insanely rich and a global icon in his own right, this accessibility to Obama, whether we can prove it or not, is meant to stamp him as someone to be taken seriously in social and political spaces that people affiliated with hip-hop are often barred from entering. Because Obama had made it, many inside and outside of the industry opined "that the election represents an important step forward for Blacks."[27]

To many, Obama symbolized the coming to fruition of the dreams and aspirations of the Civil Rights Movement, and signaled the definitive ushering in of a postracial democratic society where opportunities for upward mobility were available to all those who were willing to work for them.[28] Further, by subordinating race-specific ameliorative policies and prioritizing color-blind initiatives to stabilize the precarious economic plight of working and middle-class Americans, irrespective of race, not only did Obama reflect the money-over-everything ethos that proliferated in popular hip-hop at the time, he also endeared himself to Americans who had grown weary with a Republican administration that seemed incapable of defibrillating a stagnant economy and uninterested in ending costly wars in Iraq and Afghanistan that it had surreptitiously initiated.

Countless other rappers, including Jadakiss, Nas, and Talib Kweli, offered support of candidate and President Obama. There was a resounding message of racial and class reconciliation within many of these songs.[29] Mostly offering uncomplicated analyses of racial and class oppression, these songs fashion Obama as a panacea, a magical elixir for the toxic racism and elitism that has ailed this country.

Obama's Political Passivity, Racial Uplift Ideology, and Handling of Domestic Dilemmas and Affairs

Although there were a few faint voices from the margins of the hip-hop community that were critical of President Obama at the very beginning of his campaign for presidency, he was able to leverage his popular appeal in the media as the first hip-hop president after procuring the early endorsements of respected artist such as Talib Kweli, Jay Z, and Nas. The dissenting voices from the margins of the hip-hop community included Afro Latina hip-hop activist Rosa Clemente, who criticized Obama for *using* hip-hop to captivate the American youth. She called on the hip-hop community and its youth to see through his $750 million marketing campaign. She was adamant that Obama was not the first hip-hop president and that the label hip-hop president should emerge from within the hip-hop community—not via the pop-culture, mass-media machine. She went on to say, "The few times he was pressed on his association to Hip Hop, he spoke about offensive rap lyrics and Black men having respect for themselves by pulling up their pants."[30] In other words, by policing a counterculture that defined itself in opposition to mainstream White American culture and Black respectability the President evidenced that he was not "hip-hop."

Some hip-hop artists gradually became more vocal—specifically those positioned outside the industry's mainstream—and their voices reached a fever pitch toward the end of the president's tenure in office. In what follows, we utilize moments where he directly engages African Americans (e.g., conferences, commencement ceremonies, etc.) to frame our analysis of Obama's use of political passivity, racial uplift, and Black respectability to allay the voices of the next generation of Black activists. Events such as "The Beer Summit," the Howard University commencement speech (2016), his public indictment of the #BlackLivesMatter movement, and his participation in Senator Pinckney's funeral services following the 2015 Charleston Massacre all serve to contextualize Obama's tone-deaf and sometimes insensitive engagement with Black Americans in public discourse.

President Obama's participation in constructing narratives regarding Black life and grief—specifically *how* Black Americans have responded to social inequalities, during an era of heightened sociopolitical unrest and economic uncertainty—are couched in political passivism, racial uplift, and Black respectability. Moreover, the paternalistic tone and tenor of Obama's speeches when he is addressing African American communities or speaking about its experiences is far too often available for public consumption. These are opportunities that he never seems to miss, although many members of this community wish quietly that he would. What does it mean for the first president to sacrifice Black realities (in political discourse) on the altar of bipartisanship and the American myth of meritocracy? What does it mean for a U.S. Black president to help perpetuate the tropes that facilitate an anti-Black reality?

We can conceptualize the ways that President Obama engages African Americans (in discourse) through what Evelyn Brooks Higginbotham defined as the politics of respectability. In her analysis of the women's movement in the Black Baptist Church, Higginbotham characterized the politics of respectability as a belief held by African Americans, from post-reconstruction through the era of the New Negro Movement, that "equated public behavior with individual self-respect and with the advancement of African Americans as a group. They felt that certain 'respectable' behavior in public would earn their people a measure of esteem from White America."[31] The politics of respectability is not confined to this era of American history, but has become a part of the ways in which victim-blaming political strategies are imposed on Black Americans to circumvent focusing on systemic changes that need to be made within society. One of the places where we can observe ways in which Obama fuses Black respectability politics (as a mechanism of racial uplift) and political passivity is through his commencement speeches at Morehouse College (2013) and Howard University (2016), and his criticism of #BlackLivesMatter movement as disorganized noise—suggesting that they "can't keep yelling."[32]

#BlackLivesMatter

On April 23, 2016, *The New York Times* carried an article where Obama made an interesting pivot from questions suggesting that his administration had not taken racial profiling in airports seriously, and focused his energies toward the Black Lives Matter movement. Obama took Black Lives Matter to task, noting that they can't just keep yelling (at politicians) and that they needed a plan. Obama told the European audience that the #BlackLivesMatter movement was "effective in bringing attention to problems," but said young activists should be more willing to work with political leaders to craft solutions instead of criticizing from outside the political process." Obama went on to say that once a movement has brought an issue forward, "and elected officials or people who are in a position to start bringing about change are ready to sit down with you, then you can't just keep yelling at them." "And you can't refuse to meet because that might compromise the purity of your position," he also noted that, "The value of social movements and activism is to get you at the table, get you in the room, and then to start trying to figure out how is this problem going to be solved."[33]

Obama met with members affiliated with #BlackLivesMatter in 2014; however, when some activists at that meeting said they felt that their voices were not being heard, Mr. Obama replied, "You are sitting in the Oval Office, talking to the President of the United States." We cannot know is if the young people affiliated with the #BlackLivesMatter movement missed an opportunity to broker opportunities for change with the President. What we do know, however, is that the #BlackLivesMatter movement was founded upon experiences that are at best skeptical that any agent of the State or a State agency (including the office of the President) would seek justice for Black Americans.

Obama . . . Don't Do It: Commencement Speeches

Two weeks later Obama offered the commencement address at Howard University—one of the oldest historically Black colleges and universities—and continues his critique of #BlackLivesMatter movement.

> Number three, you have to go through life with more than just passion for change; you need a strategy. I'll repeat that. I want you to have passion, but you have to have a strategy. Not just awareness but action. Not just #hashtags, but votes. You see change requires more than righteous anger. It requires a program and it requires organizing. At the 1964 Democratic convention, Fannie Lou Hammer—all five-feet-four-inches tall—gave a fiery speech on the national stage. But then she went back home to Mississippi and organized cotton pickers. And she didn't have the tools and technology where you can whip up a movement in minutes. She had to go door to door. And I'm so proud of the new guard of black civil rights leaders who understand this. Its thanks in large part to the activism of young people like many of you, from Black Twitter to Black Lives Matter that America's eyes have been opened—white, black, Democrat, Republican—to the real problems, for example, in our criminal justice system.[34]

After recounting the historical significance of Howard University, the president stood before hundreds of young African American graduates and their families—decedents of enslaved Africans—and asked them to "expand our moral imaginations to understand and . . . empathize with all people who are struggling." A statement leading up to a request to sympathize with the middle-aged White man, who you may think has all the advantages, but over the last several decades has seen his world upended by economic and cultural and technological change, and feels powerless to stop it. You got to get in his head too.[35]

Christina Sharpe, in an interview with Selamawit Terrefe for Rhizomes, a cultural studies online journal, offers and instructive point about an analogous moment that occurred during Rev. Pinckney's funeral, that may help clarify the audience's silence after hearing Obama ask an African American audience, many of whom had come to witness relatives who were the first college graduates in their families, to sympathize with White men whose lives have changed economically and culturally in the past few decades. Sharpe's reaction is worth quoting at length.

I don't know if you saw it, but Savion Glover performs a tap dance and in that dance was the sound of mourning and joy and presence and it was all there. It was completely gorgeous and moving and life giving. As I watched the funeral for Rev. Pinckney, Baraka's funeral was somewhere in the back of my mind, disturbing my mind. Of course, Pinckney's service was religious and Baraka's was secular; I knew why Barack Obama delivered the so-called eulogy for Rev. Pinckney's funeral and I say so-called eulogy because it wasn't a eulogy, it was a political speech. . . . But I really wanted him not to deliver that speech. I wanted him, if he was going to be there, to stay in the audience to greet the family, to comfort the family, and to sit in the audience and listen, but of course he didn't. When he took the stage he gave the same one note performance that I think he always gives when it comes to Black people. It's the sort of note that sutures Black suffering to romance and redemption. The note of a more perfect union, the note of unhearable Black suffering. The note of romance of empire. There's a moment when I watched—and I didn't want to watch, but I was compelled to watch the funeral, to watch his eulogy—there was this moment as I watched his face that looked as if he was deciding what he was going to do next and then it became clearer to me that, oh my god, he's going to sing. And that line from Invisible Man kept going through my head, "the Brother does not sing!" I tweeted that because I could and couldn't believe he was actually going to do that. And then, of course, when he sings it's the opposite of Glover's tapping. For that reason, it seemed to me that he had to sing "Amazing Grace" because "Amazing Grace" is precisely that . . . unhearable Black suffering. It's precisely that song of romance and redemption because we know John Newton's history, that he keeps working on the slavers after his conversion and it's only later that he writes "Amazing Grace."[36]

These words brings into sharp relief the ways in which Obama uses his adulation among many members in the Black community, just as he had with the hip-hop youth,[37] to give him the latitude needed to draw upon the politics of respectability to police Black grief and assuage Black rage. The politics of respectability also facilitate a space for blunting the possibility for social unrest in the Black community by rushing them to forgiveness; while on the one hand they are asked to remember; on the other hand they are also actively encouraged to begin forgetting. In his critique of the polices that emerged from the Reagan administration, Killer Mike likened Obama to Reagan, as evidence that presidents are all figureheads and that the President's position is somewhat ceremonial who work on behalf of the real power brokers of this country. He noted,

> Ronald Reagan was an actor, not at all a factor. Just an employee of the country's real masters. Just like the Bushes, Clinton and Obama. Just another talking head telling lies on teleprompters.[38]

This is to say that some segments of the Black community read Obama's comments differently. He isn't speaking as a local community organizer; he is speaking as the President of the Unities States. Although Black Americans have grown accustomed to the discursive violence that often emerge from the State. It feels different—violent even—when our country's first Black President buttresses these narratives.

Notes

1. Cho, 2009; Gosa, 2012.
2. Spence, 2015.
3. Ibid.
4. Biden, 2014.
5. Harris, 2014.
6. Bell, 2009.
7. Alim and Smitherman, 2012; Simba, 2009.
8. Simba, 2009.
9. Alim and Smitherman, 2012; Nelson, 2009.
10. Robinson, 2007; Young, 2009.
11. Young, 2009; Zeleny, 2010.
12. Marable, 2009.
13. Bell, 2009.
14. Cho 2009.
15. Greer, 2009.
16. Womack, 2013.
17. Greer, 2009.
18. Ibid.; Dingle, 2012.

19. Chang, 2007.
20. Ibid.; Love, 2012; Ogbar, 2007; Rose, 1994; Rose, 2008.
21. Browne-Marshall, 2013.
22. Ibid.; Bell, 2015; Coates, 2014; Chang, 2007.
23. Rose, 2008.
24. Chang, 2007.
25. Ibid.
26. Ibid.
27. Gosa, 2012.
28. Asukile, 2008.
29. Adaso, 2016.
30. Clemente, 2008.
31. Higginbotham, 1993.
32. Shear and Stack, 2016.
33. Ibid.
33. Obama, 2016.
34. Terrefe, 2016.
35. Obama, 2016.
36. Terefe, 2016.
37. Clemente, 2008.
38. Render, 2012.

Bibliography

Adaso, H. (2016). Top 10 Obama rap songs. About.com. Retrieved from http://rap.about.com/od/songs/tp/ObamaRapSongs.htm.

Alim, H. Samy, and Geneva Smitherman. *Articulate while Black: Barack Obama, language, and race in the US.* Oxford: Oxford University Press, 2012.

Asukile, Thabiti. "The Barack Obama new era: Race matters more than ever in America." *The Black Scholar* 38, no. 4 (2008): 41–43.

Bell, Derrick. "On celebrating an election as racial progress." *Human Rights* 36 (2009): 2.

Bell, Jeannine. "Can't We Be Your Neighbor? Trayvon Martin, George Zimmerman, and the Resistance to Blacks as Neighbors." *Boston University Law Review* 851 (2015): 95.

Browne-Marshall, Gloria J. "Stop and Frisk: From Slave-Catchers to NYPD, A Legal Commentary." *Trotter Review* 21, no. 1 (2013): 9.

Chang, Jeff. *Can't stop won't stop: A history of the hip-hop generation.* New York, NY: Macmillan, 2007.

Cho, Sumi. "Post-racialism." *Iowa Law Review* 94 (2009): 1589.

Clemente, Rosa A. "Why President Elect Barack Obama is not the first Hip Hop President." Green Institute. 2008, http://www.greeninstitute.net/clemente_obama.

Coates, T. "The case for reparations." *The Atlantic*, June 2014. https://www.the
    atlantic.com/magazine/archive/2014/06/the-case-for-reparations/361631/.

Dingle, Derek T. "Oval Office Interview with President Barack Obama." *Black
    Enterprise* 6 (2012). http://www.blackenterprise.com/mag/president-obama
    -interview-small-business-unemployment-exclusive/.

Gosa, Travis L. "The Audacity of Dope." *The Iconic Obama, 2007–2009: Essays on
    Media Representations of the Candidate and New President* (2012): 85.

Greer, O. "'Yes We Can': (President) Barack Obama and Afrofuturism." *Anamesa*
    7 (2009): 34–42.

Harris, Fredrick. *The price of the ticket: Barack Obama and the rise and decline of
    Black politics.* (Transgressing Boundaries: Studies in Black Politics and
    Black Communities). Oxford: Oxford University Press, 2014.

Higginbotham, Evelyn Brooks. *Righteous discontent: The women's movement in the
    Black Baptist church, 1880–1920.* Cambridge, MA: Harvard University Press,
    1993.

Love, Bettina L. *Hip-hop's li'l sistas speak: Negotiating hip-hop identities and politics
    in the new South.* New York: Peter Lang, 2012.

Marable, Manning. "Racializing Obama: The enigma of post-black politics and
    leadership." *Souls* 11, no. 1 (2009): 1–15.

Nelson, Camille. "Racial Paradox and Eclipse: Obama as a Balm for What Ails
    Us." *Denver University Law Review* 86 (2009): 743.

Obama, Barack. "Remarks by the President at Howard University Commence-
    ment." The White House. Office of the Press Secretary. May 7, 2016. https://
    obamawhitehouse.archives.gov/the-press-office/2016/05/07/remarks
    -president-howard-university-commencement-ceremony.

Ogbar, Jeffrey Ogbonna Green. *Hip-hop revolution: The culture and politics of rap.*
    Lawrence, KS: University Press of Kansas, 2007.

Render, M. (2012). Reagan. [Recorded by Michael Render (Killer Mike)]. On
    R.A.P. Music. Atlanta, GA: Williams Street Records.

Robinson, Eugene. "An Inarticulate Kickoff." *Washington Post* 2 (2007). http://www
    .washingtonpost.com/wp-dyn/content/article/2007/02/01/AR2007020
    101495.html.

Rose, Tricia. *Black noise: Rap music and black culture in contemporary America.* Mid-
    dletown, CT: Wesleyan University Press, 1994.

Rose, Tricia. *The hip-hop wars: What we talk about when we talk about hip-hop—and
    why it matters.* New York, NY: Basic Civitas Books, 2008.

Shear, Michael D., and Liam Stack. "Obama Says Movements Like Black Lives
    Matter 'Can't Just Keep on Yelling.'" *The New York Times*, April 23, 2016.
    https://www.nytimes.com/2016/04/24/us/obama-says-movements-like
    -black-lives-matter-cant-just-keep-on-yelling.html?_r=0.

Simba, Malik. "The Obama campaign 2008: A historical overview." *Western Jour-
    nal of Black Studies* 33, no. 3 (2009): 186.

Spence, Lester K. *Knocking the hustle: Against the neoliberal turn in black politics.*
    Brooklyn, NY: Punctum Books, 2015.

Terrefe, Selamawit. "What Exceeds the Hold?: An Interview with Christina Sharpe." *Rhizomes: Cultural Studies in Emerging Knowledge* (2016). http://www.rhizomes.net/issue29/terrefe.html.

Thai, Xuan, and Ted Barrett. "Biden's description of Obama draws scrutiny." CNN.com. (February 9, 2007). http://www.cnn.com/2007/POLITICS/01/31/biden.obama/.

Womack, Ytasha. *Afrofuturism: the world of Black sci-fi and fantasy culture*. Chicago, IL: Chicago Review Press, 2013.

Young, Vershawn Ashanti. "Momma's memories and the new equality." *Present Tense: A Journal of Rhetoric in Society* 1, no. 1 (2010): 6.

Zeleny, Jeff. "Reid Apologizes for Remarks on Obama's Color and 'Dialect.'" *The New York Times*, January 9, 2010. http://www.nytimes.com/2010/01/10/us/politics/10reidweb.html.

CHAPTER TWELVE

Black Women as Agents of Social Change during the Obama Presidency

Melissa Brown

When Barack Obama won the nomination as the first Black president of the United States in 2008, some declared his victory evidence the United States had entered a "postracial" era, as if his presidency alone ended racial stratification, the unequal distribution of resources based on a socially constructed racial hierarchy. As Obama's presidency proceeded, however, the narrative of a postracial America started to unravel. Critiques from political conservatives about Obama's ability to lead echoed the racial essentialism that undergirds White supremacist notions of Black inferiority. For instance, the "birther" movement demanded Obama's birth certificate. Despite all evidence to the contrary, they alleged Obama identified as a Kenyan Muslim and called for his impeachment on the premise that Obama did not have a constitutionally protected right to the presidency.

Such logic implies non-Whites do not meet the criteria for the full extension of their constitutional right to citizenship by birth in the United States because "White people are able to define Whiteness as normality and to position themselves as full citizens whilst pushing non-White people (including migrants and indigenous people) to the margins or even outside of the boundaries of citizenship."[1] In addition to the birther movement, the years of Obama's presidency contained many events that brought racial stratification to light. In particular, the 2012 extrajudicial killing of a Black teenager in Sanford, Florida, catalyzed the formation of #BlackLivesMatter, an antiracist social movement organization aimed at eliminating police violence against Blacks worldwide.

#BlackLivesMatter started in response to the 2013 acquittal of George Zimmerman, a neighborhood watchman, in the shooting death of 17-year-old Trayvon Martin. Alicia Garza, a grassroots activist from California, took to Facebook to share her disappointment with the verdict with the words "Black lives matter." Her message had a simple, yet profound point:

> Garza knew that the criminal justice system was not going to address this problem. . . . [S]he and her friends Patrisse Cullors and Opal Tometi founded #BlackLivesMatter to spark nationwide discussion of the way black lives are consistently undervalued in America and what people can do to change that. "We really felt like there needed to be a space that people could relate to that didn't blame black people for conditions we didn't create," explains Garza.[2]

Although Trayvon Martin's death catalyzed the creation of #BlackLivesMatter, its expansion into an international social movement started with the extrajudicial shooting of 18-year-old Michael Brown by a White police officer in Ferguson, Missouri. Michael Brown's death sparked protests worldwide, including "die-ins," in which activists occupied public space and lay down for the amount of time Michael Brown's corpse remained exposed in the middle of a road, shedding light on how Black death remains a public spectacle. Like previous antiracist social movements, #BlackLivesMatter seeks to rectify the oppression of people of color. Unlike previous movements, #BlackLivesMatter emerged during the first time a Black man held the U.S. presidency. This illuminates the contradictions of color-blind rhetoric used to obscure the reality of racial stratification in the United States.

Though the civil unrest that Michael Brown's death initiated echoed the strategies of prior antiracist social movements, a significant portion of its success relied on its insistence on remaining decentralized and connected through activism on social media. The rise of #BlackLivesMatter within this unique political context not only relied on social media activism, but also on the politics of Black feminism. Black feminism aims to empower Black women with new and critical ways of thinking centered on how racism and sexism work together to create Black women's social issues and inequalities that arise from mutually constructed systems of oppression. #BlackLivesMatter incorporates Black feminism in three ways: "#Black-LivesMatter does not exclude people due to their race, sex, and/or class; #BlackLivesMatter acknowledges the divergence in experiences of White women and women's of color; and #BlackLivesMatter acknowledges intersectionality shapes the oppression of Black women."[3]

Thus, Black women used social media activism within a social atmosphere where modern illusions of "color blindness" fly in direct contradiction to the experiences of police brutality documented by #BlackLivesMatter. #BlackLivesMatter in many ways reflects the history of grassroots activism and societal critique advanced by Black feminist foremothers like Ida B. Wells, Sojourner Truth, and Maria W. Stewart. Thus, an understanding of #BlackLivesMatter requires acknowledging and assessing the role of Black women in the movement and the Black feminist ideology that guides them.

A Brief History of Black Feminism

Black women have advocated for their rights since slavery in an effort to give voice to their experiences. In the 18th century, Phyllis Wheatley, a West African woman enslaved in Massachusetts, used poetry to give voice to enslaved Black women in the era after the American Revolution. Women like Sojourner Truth exemplify Black feminist activism in the 19th century. In 1851, Sojourner Truth gave a speech at a women's rights convention in which the women's rights advocate and abolitionist challenged both racism and sexism faced by Black women when she asked, "Ain't I a Woman?" Her speech interrogated the way society disavowed Black women of their liberties by failing to acknowledge the humanity of Black women.

In 1892, another Black woman, Anna Julia Cooper, published *A Voice from the South*, a book in which she described the importance of the voices of Black women for social change. Another exemplary Black feminist, Ida B. Wells, an activist and journalist, led a crusade against lynching during the 1890s. The work of these and other Black women shows how Black community politics laid the foundation for social justice toward sexism from Black men, marginalization from White feminists, and disenfranchisement under White male privilege.

A significant aspect of Black feminism is intersectionality. Intersectionality refers to the way gender, race, and other social categories interact to influence an individual's life outcomes. Black women sought to create safe space for their experiences and struggles after the Civil Rights and women's rights movements of the mid-twentieth century, which centered on Black men and White women, respectively. For instance, in the 1970s, a group of Black women formed the Combahee River Collective. These Black feminists saw intersectionality as integral to the distinction between their movement and that of White feminism because "[t]he major source of difficulty in our political work is that we are not just trying to fight oppression on one front or even two, but instead to address a whole range of oppressions."[4] During the latter years of the 20th century, Black women remained active in social justice as Black feminism. Black women scholars, politicians, and educators like sociologist Patricia Hill Collins, critical race scholar Kimberlé Crenshaw, and writer bell hooks used intersectionality to expand academic and professional discourse.

Intersectionality remains an important part of Black feminism in the 21st-century antiracist social movements, which reflects how Black women join theory and action to form critical praxis. For instance, three Black women founded #BlackLivesMatter, an antiracist social movement to bring attention to racialized police violence. Their activism centers not just on Black men, but also Black women, Black queer people, Black people with disabilities, and other groups within the Black community. Like the Black feminists before them, these women work to uplift not only Black women but all people, because the guiding principles of intersectionality emphasize inclusivity, solidarity, and coalition building. Still, the women of #BlackLivesMatter and other Black women activists face erasure as marginalized voices within the antiracist and feminist struggles during Obama's presidency.

Black Feminism in the Age of Obama

Despite the importance of Black women within antiracist and feminist social movements, few scholars have examined how or why they used social media to mobilize during the Obama presidency. This section reveals how the persistence of #BlackLivesMatter reflects both the political climate of the Obama presidency and the significance of Black feminist politics in negotiating and challenging color-blind racism. The strategies of #BlackLivesMatter exemplify the use of social media and digital activism by Black women operating within grassroots movements in the 21st century. These include not only #BlackLivesMatter but also #SayHerName, a movement that responds to the co-optation of the #BlackLivesMatter narrative that occurred in mainstream media and institutions, by centering on Black women and girls specifically. Lastly, #BlackLivesMatter exhibits how Black women seek to confront structural inequality by challenging rape culture on predominantly Black campuses. Additionally, Black women confront structural inequality at the federal level by advocating for White House initiatives and federal policies that seek to empower Black women and girls.

Ultimately, an analysis of the role of Black women in #BlackLivesMatter, #SayHerName, and other calls to action demonstrates demonstrate that Black women continue to act as agents of social change in a society that has often taken their labor and knowledge for granted. Their activism reflects how some Black women do not view the Obama presidency as an indicator of a postracial America. Instead, the years of the Obama presidency led by Black women to verbalize dissatisfaction with the effects of racialized criminalization and divestment from poor and predominantly Black communities in a neoliberal advanced capitalist society.

Why Black Feminism: The Significance of Black Women in Contemporary Social Movements

Black women have organized against racism and sexism since the colonial era. During slavery, the objectification of enslaved Black women relied on notions of Black femininity that likened them to animals requiring restraint, making them little more than the "mules" of slave labor. Women like Sojourner Truth and Harriet Tubman exemplify the crucial role Black women played in challenging the institution of slavery. Maria W. Stewart and Harriet Jacobs used writing, speeches, and teaching to advocate the end of the institution of slavery. During the women's suffrage movement, Sojourner Truth, Anna Julia Cooper, and Ida B. Wells made efforts to convince the government to give all women the right to vote. These activists gave voice to Black women in antiracist and feminist movements that rendered the unique experience of Black womanhood invisible through a monolithic portrayal of antiracism as a Black men's cause and feminism as a White women's struggle. Black feminism, then, seeks to empower Black women by bringing attention to the unique oppression they face at the intersection of race and gender. Modern Black feminism uses the legacy of these and other Black women activists as a foundation in order to pursue these goals.

Concepts and strategies developed by Black women during the late 20th century guide the work of contemporary Black feminism. During this time period, Black feminists pursued spaces that centered on Black women in an effort to develop an antiracist feminism with inclusiveness and solidarity as an organizing principle. The Combahee River Collective, a

Black feminist and lesbian organization formed in the 1970s, exemplifies the politics of Black feminism:

> The most general statement of our politics at the present time would be that we are actively committed to struggling against racial, sexual, hetero-sexual, and class oppression, and see as our particular task the development of integrated analysis and practice based upon the fact that the major systems of oppression are interlocking. The synthesis of these oppressions creates the conditions of our lives. As Black women we see Black feminism as the logical political movement to combat the manifold and simultaneous oppressions that all women of color face.[5]

The current movements for Black lives build on these principles and demonstrate the important influence Black feminism had during Obama's presidency. For instance, the national chapter of #BlackLivesMatter names collective value as significant to their work: "[A]ll Black lives, regardless of actual or perceived sexual, gender identity, gender expression, economic status, ability, disability, religious beliefs or disbeliefs, immigration status or location [matter]."[6] Likewise, in their report on police brutality against Black women, #SayHerName states its intention to bring to light violations against "pregnant women, profiling and abusive treatment of lesbian, bisexual, transgender, and gender nonconforming Black women."[7]

Understanding the diversity of experiences for Black women and the resultant oppression remains central to Black feminist organizing within social movements. During the Obama presidency, Black feminism exemplified intersectionality as a form of critical praxis built on the grassroots efforts of Black women whose work has culminated into networks of anti-racist feminist activists across the globe.

Black Feminism in Action: Intersectionality as Critical Praxis

Black feminism relies on intersectionality as a form of critical praxis to generate social change. Intersectionality as critical praxis frames the actions of Black feminist community organizers and social movement organization leaders alike. This grassroots approach confronts the social problems that affect the Black community and includes recognition of how systems of oppression intersect to compound the effects of systemic disadvantage due to gender, class, and sexuality:

> Local, grassroots, small-scale, and/or temporary groups that draw upon intersectionality to guide their critical praxis can often escape public notice.

Typically, these groups are composed of society's overlooked populations, specifically the young, women, people of color, and poor people. Yet groups such as these have a vested interest in drawing upon intersectional frameworks to address social inequalities.[8]

In the age of digital technology and the Internet, intersectionality as critical praxis includes online advocacy for social change through social media and other Web-based platforms. In 2007, Black women used blogs and email campaigns to protest the NAACP's support of a group of teenagers accused of sexually assaulting a Black mother and child in West Palm Beach, Florida. They advocated for a display of solidarity that centered on the trauma experienced by Black women and children victimized by sexual assault. In 2016, as a means to bring to light how police brutality against women often includes sexual violence, the African American Policy Forum (AAPF) hosted a series of webinars on Black women and police violence during the trial of Daniel Holtzclaw, a police officer accused of sexually assaulting a number of Black and lower-income women in Oklahoma.

The Black feminism of the social movements during the Obama presidency exemplified how intersectionality as critical praxis brings attention to a wide range of oppressions. Furthermore, it also exemplifies how agents of social change rely on their personal networks in absence of the institutional support afforded social movement organizations. The students at Spelman College, a historically Black university for women, took to social media with the hashtags "@RapedAtSpelman" and "#RapedByMorehouse" to bring attention to how institutions like their brother institution Morehouse College protect men accused of sexual violence; in addition, they held protests on campus, thus building on the work of critical race scholar Kimberlé Crenshaw:

> Although the rhetoric of both agendas formally includes Black women, racism is generally not problematized in feminism, and sexism, not problematized in antiracist discourses. Consequently, the plight of Black women is relegated to a secondary importance: The primary beneficiaries of policies supported by feminists and others concerned about rape tend to be white women; the primary beneficiaries of the Black community's concern over racism and rape, Black men. Ultimately, the reformist and rhetorical strategies that have grown out of antiracist and feminist rape reform movements have been ineffective in politicizing the treatment of Black women.[9]

In addition to sexual violence, Black women advocated for more knowledge and access in regards to reproductive health. A group of Black women organized Black Breastfeeding Week to resolve the racial disparity in infant nursing. They build their public health advocacy on the knowledge that Black mothers face high infant mortality rates and diet-related diseases in addition to the structural disadvantage of lack of access to quality food. Overall, bodies represented a significant site of advocacy for Black women as an effort to challenge how the oppression limits Black women's sexual agency during Obama's presidency.

Black Transwomen's Lives Also Matter

The Black feminism that informs current antiracist social movements departs from the politics of previous civil rights struggles that wedded Black liberation to ideals associated with the Black heterosexual men. Black feminism espouses a politics of inclusion that gives critical attention to people who live within the margins of Blackness. Such a perspective serves as the foundation for intersectionality as critical praxis as people work from the knowledge that the effects of multiple systems of oppression manifest in their lives. During the Obama presidency, movements informed by Black feminism maintained a vocal stance on support for queer and transgender women as part of their efforts toward social justice for people who do not benefit from Black male privilege.

For instance, #SayHerName draws attention to the death of Mya Hall in its 2015 report on violence against Black women. Black transwomen represent a vulnerable population that lack institutional and social support. #SayHerName highlights the lack of visibility about the deaths of Black transgender women relative to Black men:

> Just before Freddie Gray's case grabbed national attention, police killed unarmed Mya Hall—a Black transgender woman—on the outskirts of Baltimore. Alleged to be driving a stolen car, Hall took a wrong turn onto NSA property and was shot to death by officers after the car crashed into the security gate and a police cruiser. No action has been taken to date with respect to the officers responsible for her death.[10]

#SayHerName recognizes the ways silence on violence against Black transgender women results from systems of power that disenfranchise them, creating barriers to a safe and productive life. This attention to the social barriers Black transgender women confront daily represents a queering of Black feminism:

> In the context of black feminist/queer of color critique, here "queering" signifies the insistence that the politics of difference—a politics that

emphasizes multiplicity and heterogeneity of identities—insists upon a strident disinvestment in both black heteronormativity and white homonormativity in order to build an alternative culture of political empowerment for all black people.[11]

Like the Combahee River Collective, #SayHerName recognizes the relative silence about the violence Black women face, particularly if they identify as queer or transgender. Thus, Black feminism in the Obama era continues in the legacy of an ideology that recognizes how oppression intersects at the level of race and sex to create barriers to sexual agency unique to Black women.

Social Media and Digital Activism: How Digital Technology Facilitates Black Cyberfeminism

The previous section outlined how Black feminism informed antiracist social movements that transpired while the nation's first Black president took office. Although some alleged society had arrived at a postracial pivotal point in America's history, the extrajudicial killings of Black men and women that occurred throughout Obama's presidency paint a different picture of the state of American political affairs. Dissatisfaction with political outcomes reinvigorated the mobilization of Black women and intersectionality as Black feminist praxis. Thus Obama's presidency served as the political backdrop to the continuation of a historic antiracist and feminist social movement.

Although the activism of Black women during the Obama presidency echoed the history of Black freedom struggles in the United States, how Black women activists pursue mobilization and solidarity incorporated innovative digital technology. This section includes several points about social media activism, the marriage of social networking sites and political advocacy, in the antiracist movements spurred by police violence during Obama's presidency. First, social media activism is defined and contextualized through a digital sociology and social movement lens. Second, the use of digital technology in addition to Black feminist activism represents the most recognizable distinction between antiracist social movements during the Obama presidency and those that occurred during the late 20th century. Specifically, the social media activism enables Black cyberfeminism. Cyberfeminism "refers to a range of theories, debates, and practices about the relationship between gender and digital culture,"[12] and Black cyberfeminism incorporates intersectionality in its praxis. Third, this section concludes with a discussion of three events in which Black women joined social media activism with Black cyberfeminism to engage in feminist and antiracist activism during the Obama presidency.

Social Media Activism: The Digital Sociology of 21st-Century Social Movements

Social media activism refers to the use of social network Web sites and apps as a platform for political organization, engagement, and protest. Although social media activism represents a portion of the antiracist and feminist activism led by Black women during Obama's presidency, social media activism served a purpose in a number of other protests prior to Obama's presidency and continues to do so throughout the 21st century. Furthermore, activists use social media with modes of protest associated with earlier Black freedom struggles. For instance, a picture of group of Howard University students with hands held in the air included the words "#HANDSUPDONTSHOOT" as a meme shared on Twitter in the months after Michael Brown's death in Ferguson, Missouri.

Black Cyberfeminism: Digital Technology and Intersectional Critical Praxis

The uniqueness of the antiracism during Obama's presidency incorporates Black cyberfeminism through activism on social network sites like Facebook and Twitter. This specific approach serves as a form of cyberfeminist practices that include "experimentation and engagement with various Internet technologies by self-identified women across several domains."[13] Cyberfeminist practices, like feminism in general, includes a number of approaches informed by a wide range of feminist theoretical perspectives in order to make known "a feminist theory of how gendered bodies and relations shape technologies and how we interact with them." Black cyberfeminism adopts intersectionality as a framework to further inform the theory, dialogues, and practices associated with digital technology. Through the synthesis of research on Black feminist thought and feminist technology studies, it interrogates the reproduction of social inequality in the digital sphere.

Digital sociologist Tressie Cottom builds on Kishonna Gray's Black cyberfeminist framework in an explanation of the threefold concerns of Black cyberfeminism. First, Black cyberfeminism examines the way society's structure oppresses marginalized groups in relation to technology and virtual space: "Black cyberfeminism would interrogate how social relations of dominance are translated through digitally-mediated relationships with technology, the interests that produce it and the processes that resist them." Second, Black cyberfeminism looks at how oppression intersections shape experiences because of digital technology: "The second theme argues that structural oppression is translated through technologies and reproduces different individual and categorical experiences by race, class, gender." Lastly, Black cyberfeminism concerns the distinct form identity takes in the digital sphere: "unmarked categories of race, class and gender operate in specific ways. And, the specificity of those categories can be marked, or revealed, theoretically, when Black cyberfeminism's focus on power relations is centered in analysis."[14] Taken together, the Black cyberfeminist framework calls for the use of intersectionality to understand the relationship among social inequality, social identity, and digital technology.

Obama's presidency represents a political era in which Black cyberfeminism brought attention to violence against Black men and women through activism with digital technology as a means to pursue political goals. In lieu of a comprehensive history, this section focuses on three moments of activism that exemplify Black cyberfeminism. These include #BlackLivesMatter, #SayHerName, and @RapedAtSpelman. Although #BlackLivesMatter and #SayHerName spoke to state-sanctioned violence against Black men and women, @RapedAtSpelman centered on intraracial violence. Specifically, @RapedAtSpelman gave voice to Black women victims of sexual violence by male peers at historically Black colleges and universities.

Black Feminist Politics in the Digital Age: #BlackLivesMatter and Grassroots Organizing

Black feminism emerges through Black community politics accomplished through grassroots organizing and civic engagement to resolve the marginalization of Black people. The importance of civic engagement and grassroots organizing among members of the Black community reflects the historic efforts of political groups during earlier Black freedom struggles. These efforts included protests; voter registration drives; community policing; and nutritional support through community gardens as well as feeding the public. Thus, Black community politics emphasizes local space as the stage for political engagement.

Public perception of #BlackLivesMatter holds that the antiracist movement lacks leadership; however, this criticism reveals a bias toward a certain vision of leadership rather than a reality of how the movement formed. Black women established and lead many of the #BlackLivesMatter chapters formed within the cities and suburbs of the United States. A number of these women reference their prior knowledge and lived experience in community organizing as a foundation for the work that they do with #BlackLivesMatter. For instance, Mary Hooks of Southerners on New Ground joined Dre Propst, a Black male community organizer, to form the Atlanta chapter of #BlackLivesMatter in 2015. A group of Black women, current and former educators and activists, also lead the #BlackLivesMatter in the tri-state area of DC, Virginia, and Maryland. Black women in particular act as agents of social change, bringing their lived experience to their role as representatives of #BlackLivesMatter within their community.

#BlackLivesMatter also functions as a "call to action," quite often invoked through the digital sphere on social media. The Pew Research Center conducted a 2016 analysis of activity on Twitter between 2013 and 2016. Findings revealed 38 percent of tweets associated with the hashtag showed support to the movement, while 11 percent expressed criticism of the movement. Additionally, #BlackLivesMatter was used eight times as often on the Web site Twitter than the phrase #AllLivesMatter between 2013 and 2016.

#BlackLivesMatter demonstrates the breadth of antiracist social media activism that occurred during the second term of Obama's presidency. Still, the role of Black women in social movements gets constrained in the digital sphere as well. Though Alicia Garza first used #BlackLivesMatter initially, Missourian activist Netta Johnson was the only Black woman to appear in the top 10 most retweets of users who shared the phrase #BlackLivesMatter on Twitter. Additionally, other than Sandra Bland, few tweets that included the phrase #BlackLivesMatter referred to women victims of police violence. #SayHerName sought to fill that void.

#SayHerName: Recognizing Black Women Victims of Police Violence

In May 2015, a team of scholars led by Kimberlé Crenshaw, professor of law at University of California, Los Angeles (UCLA) and Columbia University, published a report online titled "Say Her Name: Resisting Police Brutality Against Black Women." After Sandra Bland, a Black woman in Texas, died in police custody in July of that year, they updated the report to include her death in a series of profiles of Black women and girl victims of police violence. The authors expressed a Black feminist stance in their motivation to provide the report:

> Say Her Name sheds light on Black women's experiences of police violence in an effort to support a gender-inclusive approach to racial justice that centers all Black lives equally. It is our hope that this document will serve as a tool for the resurgent racial justice movement to mobilize around the stories of Black women who have lost their lives to police violence.[15]

With a paragraph summary as a unique glimpse into the circumstances of each woman's death, the profiles of these victims within the report included pictures, their name, date of birth, and the city in which they died. Beyond that, the report featured statistical data about the sex-related crimes of police officers as well as images from a #SayHerName vigil held in New York in May 2015. From their "intersectional, Black feminist perspective," the authors of this report "demand[ed] the inclusion of Black women, and girls, transgender and not transgender, lesbians, bisexual, and heterosexual in the dominant discourse around police violence."[16]

@RapedAtSpelman: Finding Feminism as a Reprieve from Heterosexism

Whereas initiatives like #BlackLivesMatter and #SayHerName speak to the antiracist politics of Black feminism toward police violence, @Raped-AtSpelman speaks to grassroots organizing against sexual violence from Black male perpetrators. According to a 2010 study, 14.2 percent of women reported experiencing either attempted or completed sexual assault after entering college:

> Victims of forced sexual assault were also more likely to be on a date with the assailant at the time of assault. Incapacitated sexual assaults, on the other hand, were more likely to be perpetrated by a member of a fraternity and to involve more than one assailant.[17]

Antiracist discourse often avoids the topic of sexual violence in the Black community while feminist discourse tends to racialize sexual violence, perpetrating the myth of the Black male beast and the fragile White victim.[18] Black feminism responds to this silence by creating space that gives voice to the experiences of women of color who have suffered sexual assault. In the case of @RapedAtSpelman, these women were members of all-woman HBCUs who intended to shed light on encounters with men at their brother school.

The call to action provided by @RapedAtSpelman echoed those of Black women at Spelman who had previously alleged a member of their brother institution had sexually assaulted her. One student by the name of Melanie spoke to the online publication Buzzfeed about how her university responded to her sexual assault claim:

> After all, Morehouse had handed off Melanie's case to an independent investigator based in Massachusetts who, without ever meeting her in person, concluded she hadn't been raped, despite the fact that both parties agreed Melanie had said "no" repeatedly. Later, she'd learn that the college also classified her reported rape as a case of "simple battery."[19]

Women like Melanie do not have many choices as sexual assault victims because their all-women school had no jurisdiction over the male students they accused. Thus, Melanie echoed the sentiment of many Black women victims, reporting to the online publication Mic that she "felt that administrators failed to generate 'urgency and attention to sexual assault cases' or pursue 'justice for their students,' prioritizing its relationship with brother school Morehouse College instead."[20]

The perceived complacency of the institution-inspired student activism against sexual violence thus included a list of demands released by students at the Atlanta University Center that would require institutions to provide better support for women and LGBTQIA (lesbian, gay, bisexual, transgender, queer, intersex, asexual) students.

Social media activism gave voice to these Black women through the Twitter handle "@RapedAtSpelman," which documented an anonymous account of one woman's difficulties receiving institutional support in light of her experience. Response to these tweets generated a response from the surrounding HBCU community. This included a protest near the campus where the alleged assault occurred and a statement of support from the university's president. Protestors used social media to document their protest, which included an image of a young Black woman bearing a sign that read "You can never say Morehouse has their sister's back if they're just going to force her on it."[21] Black women used social media and protest to bring attention to sexual violence due to a perceived failure of institutions to provide adequate support for victims.

Talking Back to Political Power: Black Feminist Politics in the Age of Obama

The previous sections examined how Black feminism emerged as a powerful political force in antiracist and feminist struggles during Obama's presidency. The Black feminists of the Obama era built on the legacy of the Black women activists that came before them. Through the efforts of women who joined grassroots organizing with social media activism, Black feminist activism during the Obama presidency brought significant attention to police violence experienced by Blacks in the United States. Whereas the previous sections referenced the ways that Black feminism shifted social and cultural aspects of U.S. society, this section draws on examples of the Black feminist activism that disrupted political processes and institutions.

Although some questioned the direction of movements like #BlackLivesMatter, Black women inspired to action took the political stage in the latter years of Obama's presidency, setting the tone for the rhetoric that took shape around race and policing. This section centers on Black women activists who did the work of confronting long-standing biases in political institutions.

Where My Girls At?: Black Feminists Respond to My Brother's Keeper

In 2014, Obama formed the My Brother's Keeper (MBK) Task Force as an effort on the part of the federal government to "address persistent opportunity gaps faced by boys and young men of color." Funds allotted for the program included "more than $600 million in private sector and philanthropic grants and in-kind resources" as well as "$1 billion in low-interest financing have been committed in alignment with MBK."[22] Although initiated at the federal level, the MBK Task Force incorporated its efforts to close opportunity gaps at the state and local levels of government in addition to the private sector. These efforts included opening national labs to local youth, providing teens and young adults for jobs, and enrolling high school students from low-income backgrounds in college prep courses.

In a series of blog posts at *Salon*, *The New York Times*, and *The Washington Post*, Kimberlé Crenshaw, Brittney Cooper, Nia-Malika Henderson, and other Black feminists applauded Obama's MBK Task Force but also offered a poignant critique of its inattention to women and girls of color. In June of 2014, the AAPF released a document titled "Why We Can't Wait: Women of Color Urge Inclusion in 'My Brother's Keeper.'" The document urged President Obama to reconsider the effectiveness of a program that centered only on boys and men:

> The need to acknowledge the crisis facing boys should not come at the expense of addressing the stunted opportunities for girls who live in the same households, suffer in the same schools, and struggle to overcome a common history of limited opportunities caused by various forms of discrimination.[23]

This criticism of the MBK Task Force represented a call for the federal government to adopt intersectionality in its intentions to create opportunity for people of color. Thus, Black feminism responded directly to Obama's actions as a president because it recognized that "women and girls of color are not doing fine, and until they are, men and boys will not be doing fine either."[24]

The efforts of these Black feminists did not go unnoticed. In November of 2014, the White House Report on Women and Girls of Color released a report that centered on what the administration had done to "reduce barriers to success for everyone including women and girls of color"[25] during the first six years of Obama's presidency. This report included a call to action to form a working group that would continue to develop opportunities for girls of women and color. A year later, the same council released a report titled "Advancing Equity for Women and Girls of Color." They suggested five areas for the continued development of women and girls of color. In addition to reforming school discipline, they recommended support for sexual assault survivors, inclusive STEM (science, technology, engineering, and mathematics) education, continued reduction of teen pregnancy rate, and job creation.

The same month they released the report, the White House Report on Women and Girls of Color held a forum to discuss the report and made a commitment of $118 million to support women from low-income backgrounds. Although this dollar amount pales in comparison to the amount supplied to the MBK initiative, the response from the White House represents a turning of the tide in federal level support for girls and women of color.

Calls to action used grassroots organizing, including Black cyberfeminism through the use of blogs and online petitions. Black women activists during the Obama presidency made use of digital tools to leverage visibility for women and girls of color. The formation of an initiative specifically for women of girls and color represents how intersectionality confronted structural inequality during Obama's presidency.

The MBK Task Force appeared to reveal the administration's understanding structural inequality, as it provides opportunities for men and boys of color to exit the school-to-prison pipeline. Black women activists, operating in the legacy of Black feminists like Ida B. Wells and Fannie Lou Hamer, spoke directly to institutional power by making the case that adequate federal support required attention to women and girls of color. Building on their efforts, including their participation in the forum, Obama extended his legacy as the first Black president of the United States to incorporate an intersectional approach to White House initiatives for people of color.

Taking the Political Stage: Black Women and the 2016 Political Climate

Bree Newsome exemplifies the courage of Black women to demonstrate directly within the political arena. Days after a White man killed several members of a historically Black church in Charleston, South Carolina, people across the nation called for the state house to remove the Confederate flag poised over the dome. The debate presented in the media about the flag took two opposing stances: on the one hand, people saw the Confederate flag as symbolic of a Southern heritage. On the other hand, people viewed the Confederate flag with far more wariness, and Bree Newsome in particular decided to take action:

> And yet the flag, for many a symbol of hatred, racism, and division, con-tinued to fly over South Carolina's statehouse grounds in Columbia, as it had since 1961 when it was raised in commemoration of the centennial anniversary of the Civil War. It remained there until a young activist named Bree Newsome scaled the 30-foot flagpole on June 27, 2015, declaring "This flag comes down today" as she ripped it from its hooks.[26]

Bree Newsome's actions are emblematic of Black women as agents of social change. Risking their bodies and lives, their protest shakes the very foun-dation on which institutions of power construct their identity. The ability of Black women to disrupt political stages during the Obama presidency shifted the narrative of a business-as-usual democratic practice, particu-larly as candidates for the 2016 presidential election started to campaign.

On August 8, 2015, Marissa Johnson and Mara Willaford, a pair of Black women who self-identified as members of #BlackLivesMatter, took the stage during then Democratic presidential candidate Senator Bernie Sanders at a rally in Seattle, Washington. With microphone in hand, Johnson extended a welcome to the campaigning senator, offering a history of the purported liberal oasis, culminating with the words "We are located in King county where the silhouette of Martin Luther King reigns high while we spend $210 million building a new jail to imprison Black children." Willaford, embodying an air of resistance next to her, Johnson let the crowd know: "We will fight for Black lives no matter what it takes."[27]

A year after they took the stage, Marissa Johnson reflected on her expe-rience in *The Root*, a digital publication that largely centers on news about and by Blacks from across the diaspora. In her own words, Johnson saw the legacy of Black feminist activism in her work as a grassroots activist:

> Black women rising, with ample conviction and without fear, is a type of resistance that undoes the very fabric of American society. It defies the logic of every system in America that was designed to restrain and suppress black, poor and female bodies. Black women rising strikes fear into America because we are the foundation on which she built her empire. There is no doubt that we have endured enough deserving of angry resistance in response.[28]

Pushback from the status quo had come severely and swiftly for Johnson and Willaford. Those who denounced their protest argued that Bernie Sanders had a history of involvement in the Civil Rights Movement. Such strategies of silencing, however, are not new and represent a reinforcement rather than reduction of White supremacy, as research on White antiracism suggests.[29]

As in the past, activism on behalf of Black Americans paralleled an increasing conservatism and racial myopia among White Americans. The actions of these Black women activists represent an unwillingness to ignore the way racism and sexism shaped the political climate as Obama's presidency came to an end. However, their work does not end with or start with this presidency, but rather reflects a historical commitment to Black feminism.

Black Feminist Futures: Envisioning the Trajectories of Black Women's Activism

Black feminism defines much of the antiracist activism that has transpired during the Obama presidency. Movements like #BlackLivesMatter and #SayHerName gained momentum through similar grassroots organizing strategies used by Black feminist activists like Ida B. Wells and Fannie Lou Hamer. The Black feminists in these movements have also made use of a unique form of activism through the use of social media in addition to organizing marches and protests. This social media activism allowed members of these movements to build transnational coalitions and document police violence through the 21st-century digital technology of smartphones and social network sites. Through the efforts of Black women on social media, dialogue about race and identity in America reached center stage on several occasions throughout Obama's presidency. Often, the dialogue on social media led by Black women transcended the digital space to bring about mainstream media attention and real change within well-established predominantly White institutions.

Scholars agree that Black feminism in these contemporary antiracist social movements represents a long-standing model of intersectionality as critical praxis in Black women's activism. They also argue that Obama's presidency created a particular social climate that preceded the emergence of #BlackLivesMatter. Obama's presidency revealed the contradictions of the color-blind rhetoric of a "postracial" America. These contradictions include the increasing militarization of the police, the routine failure of the justice system to prosecute the perpetrators of extrajudicial killings of Blacks, and the general silence of the administration on matters of race, including the treatment Obama faced from political conservatives.

Reflecting the diffuse nature of online communities themselves, the emphasis on decentralization that characterizes these contemporary civil rights movements does not indicate they lack leadership. Historian Marcia Chatelain pushes back against this description of #BlackLivesMatter in a 2015 an interview for *Dissent* magazine, stating, "I think women are leading without suggesting they are the only leaders or that there is only one way to lead."[30] Thus, the leadership of #BlackLivesMatter takes on the structure of Black community politics as practiced by Black feminists who center grassroots organizing in their work. Chatelain further reveals that the Black feminist approach to movements has always faced criticism as "leaderless":

> Across history, any time a movement has had black women at its helm or in its leadership—from Ida B. Wells and the Niagara movement to Ella Baker in the civil rights movement—there have been sexist and racist attempts to undermine them. The most damaging impact of the sanitized and oversimplified version of the civil rights story is that it has convinced many people that single, charismatic male leaders are a prerequisite for social movements. This is simply untrue.[31]

Therefore, the decentralized approach of #BlackLivesMatter not only has historical precedence but has also faced criticism before due to the societal belief that men who meet the ideals of hegemonic masculinity embody leadership.

There are three topics that warrant further study of Black women's role in the current movement for Black lives. First and foremost, these movements start within local networks. Black women leverage their activism through social capital leveraged within family and peer relationships. #BlackLivesMatter, for example, houses several chapters across the United States in addition to a national chapter. This decentralized approach, with all its merits, distorts the relevance the labor of women at the local level in the public eye.

Second, the labor of Black women who operate outside of prominent social movement organizations also gets rendered invisible. Many existing social movement organizations for and led by Black women predate the movement for Black lives and for Black women. For instance, SisterSong has pursued reproductive justice for women of color since 1997. The Ida B. Wells Society for Investigate Reporting aims to diversify the newsroom, calling for ethical journalism in the legacy of the Black woman who used her writing to expose lynching in the late 19th-century United States.

Finally, Black women who espouse a certain type of social and cultural capital continue to remain the face of these movements. Poor and Working class Black women remain invisible, aside from when they lose their lives to violence. Questions remain about what poor and working class Black women as activists during Obama's presidency. Similarly, activism centered on queer Black women remains under examined, despite the role of queer Black women leading this current movement, as Chatelain states:

> It isn't a coincidence that a movement that brings together the talents of black women—many of them queer—for the purpose of liberation is considered leaderless, since black women have so often been rendered invisible.[32]

This reflection on antiracist social movements during the Obama presidency produces the following conclusion: Black women act as agents of social change through the use of intersectionality as critical praxis. Beyond that, Black women who make intersectionality an aspect of their social media activism defy conceptualizations of Black people as lacking access or ability with digital technology. Indeed, digital technology expands the action repertoire of Black feminist activism, offering a means to document police violence and a tool to maintain the identity of their collective. In this way, digital technology amplified the power of the grassroots organizing of Black women.

Through social media, Black women influence the narrative of contemporary antiracist social movements, unencumbered by inequitable access to mainstream media like print and television journalism. Digital technology provides multiple avenues to the creation of content independent of mainstream media: videos on YouTube, blogs on WordPress, and the potential to go viral. The digital sphere, then, gives Black women a stage to innovate and strategize toward a society that incorporates rather than ignores intersectionality in its approach to reduce violence against Black women. Black women's social media activism builds on a legacy of Black feminism that responds to contemporary social issues. Their efforts peeled back the disingenuous claim of Obama as a "postracial" president.

Notes

1. Lovell, 2007.
2. Pleasant, 2015.
3. Bridewell, 2016.
4. Combahee River Collective, 1983.
5. Ibid.; Collins, 2000.
6. #BlackLivesMatter, n.d.

7. Crenshaw et al., 2015.
8. Collins, 2015.
9. Crenshaw, 1991.
10. Crenshaw et al., 2015.
11. Isoke, 2014,
12. Daniels, 2009, p. 102.
13. Ibid., p. 103.
14. Cottom, 2016.
15. Crenshaw et al., 2015, p. 2.
16. Ibid., p. 30.
17. Krebs, Lindquist, and Barrick, 2010.
18. Crenshaw, 1991; White, 2001.
19. Badejo, 2016.
20. Zeilinger, 2015.
21. Izadi, 2016.
22. The White House, n.d.
23. AAPF, 2014.
24. The White House Report on Women and Girls of Color, 2014.
25. Chism, 2016.
26. Basu, 2015.
27. O'Brien, 2009; Hughey, 2010; Hughey, 2012.
28. Johnson, 2016.
29. Chatelain and Asoka, 2015, p. 60.
30. Ibid.
31. Ibid.
32. Ibid.

Bibliography

#BlackLivesMatter. n.d. "Guiding Principles." Retrieved March 10, 2016. http:// blacklivesmatter.com/guiding-principles/.

Allers, Kimberly Seals. 2014. "Top Five Reasons We Need a Black Breastfeeding Week." Black Breastfeeding Week: August 25–31. August 19. http://black breastfeedingweek.org/why-we-need-black-breastfeeding-week/.

Anderson, Monica, and Paul Hitlin. 2016. *Social Media Conversations About Race.* http://www.pewinternet.org/2016/08/15/social-media-conversations -about-race/.

Badejo, Anita. 2016. "'Our Hands Are Tied Because of This Damn Brother-Sister hood Thing.'" Buzzfeed. January 21. https://www.buzzfeed.com/anitaba dejo/where-is-that-narrative?utm_term=.kgNwXkLgL-.yv9180VlV.

Basset, Mary. 2015. "#BlackLivesMatter—A Challenge to the Medical and Public Health Communities." *New England Journal of Medicine* 363(1): 1–3. http:// www.nejm.org/doi/full/10.1056/nejmp1500529#t=article.

Basu, Tanya. 2015. "Black Lives Matter Activists Disrupt Bernie Sanders Speech." Time.com. August 9. http://time.com/3989917/black-lives-matter-protest -bernie-sanders-seattle/.

Beyerlein, Kraig, and Kenneth T. Andrews. 2008. "Black Voting during the Civil Rights Movement: A Micro-Level Analysis." *Social Forces* 87(1): 65–93. http://www.jstor.org/stable/20430850.

Black Lives Matter Atlanta. n.d. "About." http://www.blacklivesmatteratl.org/ about.html. Retrieved March 10, 2017.

Black Lives Matter DMV. n.d. "Who Is Black Lives Matter DC?" http://www.black livesmatterdmv.org/about/. Retrieved March 10, 2016.

Bonilla, Yarimar, and Jonathan Rosa. 2015. "#Ferguson: Digital Protest, Hashtag Ethnography, and the Racial Politics of Social Media in the United States." *American Ethnologist* 42(1): 4–17.

Brah, Avtar, and Ann Phoenix. 2004. "Ain't I a Woman? Revisiting Intersection-ality." *Feminist Challenges: Crossing Boundaries* 5(3): 75–86.

Bridewell, Analexicis. 2016. "Black Lives Matter: Why Black Feminism?" *First-Gen Voices: Creative and Critical Narratives on the First-Generation College Expe-rience* 5(1): Article 13.

Byrne, Dara N. 2007. "Public Discourse, Community Concerns, and Civic Engage-ment: Exploring Black Social Networking Traditions on BlackPlanet.com." *Journal of Computer-Mediated Communication* 13(1): 319–40.

Charles, Dorothy, Kathryn Himmelstein, Walker Keenan, and Nicolas Barcelo. 2015. "White Coats for Black Lives: Medical Students Responding to Rac-ism and Police Brutality." *Journal of Urban Health: Bulletin of the New York Academy of Medicine* 92(6): 1007–10.

Chatelain, Marcia, and Kaavya Asoka. 2015. "Women and Black Lives Matter." *Dissent* 62(3): 54–61. https://muse.jhu.edu/content/crossref/journals/dis sent/v062/62.3.chatelain.html.

Chism, Rachel. 2016. "Bree Newsome on Racial Injustice and Why She Tore down the Confederate Flag." *The Hub.* April 28. http://hub.jhu.edu/2016/04/28/ jhu-forms-on-race-in-america-bree-newsome/.

Cho, Sumi, Kimberlé Williams Crenshaw, and Leslie McCall. 2013. "Toward a Field of Intersectionality Studies: Theory, Applications, and Praxis." *Signs* 38(4): 785–810. http://www.jstor.org/stable/10.1086/669608.

Chun, Jennifer Jihye, George Lipsitz, and Young Shin. 2013. "Intersectionality as a Social Movement Strategy: Asian Immigrant Women Advocates." *Signs: Journal of Women in Culture and Society* 38(4): 917–40. http://www.scopus .com/inward/record.url?eid=2-s2.0-84880385840&partnerID=40&md 5=7d4fb78302229fb6ac40eda530c9e427.

Clark, Meredith D. 2014. "To Tweet Our Own Cause: A Mixed-Methods Study of the Online Phenomenon 'Black Twitter.'" PhD dissertation, University of North Carolina at Chapel Hill, Durham, NC.

Collins, Patricia Hill. 2000. *Black Feminist Thought: Knowledge, Consciousness, and the Politics of Empowerment,* 2nd ed. New York: Routledge.

Collins, Patricia Hill. 2015. "Intersectionality's Definitional Dilemmas." *Annual Review of Sociology* 41: 1–20.

Combahee River Collective. 1983. "The Combahee River Collective Statement." In *Home Girls: A Black Feminist* Anthology, edited by Barbara Smith (272–82) New Brunswick, NJ: Rutgers University Press.

Cooper, Brittney C. 2014. "'Not Going to Lie Down and Take It': Black Women Are Being Overlooked by This President." *Salon.* June 17. http://www.salon.com/2014/06/17/not_going_to_lie_down_and_take_it_black_women_are_being_overlooked_by_this_president/.

Cottom, Tressie McMillan. 2016. "Black CyberFeminism: Intersectionality, Institutions and Digital Sociology." In *Digital Sociologies*, edited by J. Daniels, K. Gregory, and T. M. Cottom. Bristol: Policy Press.

Crenshaw, Kimberlé Williams. 1991. "Mapping the Margins : Intersectionality, Identity Politics, and Violence Against Women of Color." *Stanford Law Review* 43(6): 1241–99. http://www.jstor.org/stable/1229039.

Crenshaw, Kimberlé Williams. 2014. "The Girls Obama Forgot." *The New York Times.* http://www.nytimes.com/2014/07/30/opinion/Kimberl-Williams-Crenshaw-My-Brothers-Keeper-Ignores-Young-Black-Women.html?_r=0.

Crenshaw, Kimberlé Williams, Andrea J. Ritchie, Rachel Anspach, Rachel Gilmer, and Luke Harris. 2015. *Say Her Name: Resisting Police Brutality Against Black Women.* New York: African American Policy Forum, Center for Intersectionality and Social Policy Studies.

Daniels, Jessie. 2009. "Rethinking Cyberfeminism(s): Race, Gender, and Embodiment." *Women's Studies Quarterly* 37(1/2): 101–24. http://www.jstor.org/stable/27655141.

Eaton, S. C., J. N. Livingston, and H. P. McAdoo. 2008. "Cultivating Consciousness Among Black Women: Black Nationalism and Self-Esteem Revisited." *Journal of Black Studies* 40(5): 812–22. http://jbs.sagepub.com/cgi/doi/10.1177/0021934708320012.

Einwohner, Rachel L. 2002. "Bringing Outsiders in: Opponents Claims and the Construction of Animal Rights Activists' Identity." *Mobilization* 7(3): 253–68. http://mobilizationjournal.org/doi/abs/10.17813/maiq7.3.x726315p10013277?code=hjdm-site.

Eltantawy, Nahed, and Julie B. Wiest. 2011. "Social Media in the Egyptian Revolution: Reconsidering Resource Mobilization Theory." *International Journal of Communication* 5: 1207–24. http://ijoc.org/index.php/ijoc/article/view/1242.

Ems, Lindsay. 2014. "Twitter's Place in the Tussle: How Old Power Struggles Play out on a New Stage." *Media, Culture & Society* 36(5): 720–31.

Everett, Joyce E., J. Camille Hall, and Johnnie Hamilton-Mason. 2010. "Everyday Conflict and Daily Stressors: Coping Responses of Black Women." *Affilia: Journal of Women and Social Work* 25(1): 30–42.

Freelon, Deen, Charlton D. McIlwain, and Meredith D. Clark. 2016. "Beyond the Hashtags : #Ferguson, #Blacklivesmatter, and the Online Struggle for

Offline Justice." Washington, DC: Center for Media and Social Impact. http://www.cmsimpact.org/sites/default/files/beyond_the_hashtags _2016.pdf.

Garunay, Melanie. 2015. "Expanding Opportunities for Women and Girls of Color." The White House Blog, November 13. https://www.whitehouse. gov/blog/2015/11/13/expanding-opportunities-women-and-girls-color.

Gerbaudo, Paolo, and Emiliano Treré. 2015. "In Search of the 'We' of Social Media Activism: Introduction to the Special Issue on Social Media and Protest Identities." *Information, Communication & Society* 18(8): 865–71. http:// www.tandfonline.com/doi/full/10.1080/1369118X.2015.1043319.

Giddings, Paula. 1984. *When and Where I Enter: The Impact of Black Women on Race and Sex in America.* New York: W. Morrow.

Henderson, Nia-Malika. 2014. "1,000 Women of Color Want Women and Girls Included in 'My Brother's Keeper.'" *The Washington Post,* June 18. https:// www.washingtonpost.com/blogs/she-the-people/wp/2014/06/18/ 1000-women-of-color-want-women-and-girls-included-in-my-brothers -keeper/.

Hughey, Matthew W. 2010. "The (Dis)similarities of White Racial Identities: The Conceptual Framework of 'Hegemonic Whiteness.'" *Ethnic and Racial Studies* 33(8): 1289–1309. http://www.tandfonline.com/doi/abs/10.1080/ 01419870903125069.

Hughey, Matthew W. 2012. *White Bound: Nationalists, Antiracists, and the Shared Meanings of Race.* Stanford: Stanford University Press.

The Ida B. Wells Society for Investigative Reporting. n.d. "About." http://idab wellssociety.org.

Isoke, Zenzele. 2014. "Can't I Be Seen? Can't I Be Heard? Black Women Queering Politics in Newark." *Gender, Place & Culture* 21(3): 353–69. http://www .tandfonline.com/doi/abs/10.1080/0966369X.2013.781015.

Izadi, Elahe. 2016. "Spelman, Morehouse Investigate Gang-Rape Allegations Posted by Anonymous Twitter Account." *The Washington Post,* May 5. https://www.washingtonpost.com/news/grade-point/wp/2016/05/05/ spelman-morehouse-investigate-gang-rape-allegations-posted-by-anony mous-twitter-account/.

Johnson, Marissa. 2016. "1 Year Later: BLM Protestor Who Interrupted Bernie Sanders' Rally Discusses the Moment and the Movement." The Root. August 9. http://www.theroot.com/1-year-later-blm-protester-who-interru pted-bernie-sand-1790856353.

Joseph, Peniel E. 2008. "Reinterpreting the Black Power Movement." *OAH Magazine of History* 22(3): 4–6. https://www.jstor.org/stable/i25162176.

Krebs, C. P., C. H. Lindquist, and K. Barrick. 2011. "The Historically Black College and University Campus Sexual Assault (HBCU-CSA) Study." Ann Arbor, MI: Inter-university Consortium for Political and Social Research. http://doi.org/10.3886/ICPSR31301.v1

Lee, Jennifer, and Frank D. Bean. 2010. "Theoretical Perspectives on Color Lines in the United States." In *The Diversity Paradox: Immigration and the Color Line in Twenty-First Century America.* New York: Russell Sage Foundation.

Lindsey, Treva B. 2015. "Post-Ferguson: A 'Herstorical' Approach to Black Violability." *Feminist Studies, Inc.* 41(1): 232–37. http://www.jstor.org/stable/10.15767/feministstudies.41.1.232.

Lovell, Melissa. 2007. "Settler Colonialism, Multiculturalism and the Politics of Postcolonial Identity Settler Colonialism, Multiculturalism and the Politics of." Australasian Political Studies Association Conference, September 23–26, Monash University, Melbourne.

Markham, T. 2014. "Social Media, Protest Cultures and Political Subjectivities of the Arab Spring." *Media, Culture & Society* 36(1): 89–104. http://mcs.sagepub.com/cgi/doi/10.1177/0163443713511893.

O'Brien, Eileen. 2009. "From Antiracism to Antiracisms." *Sociology Compass* 3(3): 501–12. http://doi.wiley.com/10.1111/j.1751-9020.2009.00206.x.

Pleasant, Liz. 2015. "Meet the Woman Behind #BlackLivesMatter—The Hashtag That Became a Civil Rights Movement." *Yes Magazine*, May 1. http://www.yesmagazine.org/issues/make-it-right/meet-the-woman-behind-black-lives-matter-the-hashtag-that-became-a-civil-rights-movement.

Rainey, Shirley A., and Glenn S. Johnson. 2009. "Grassroots Activism: An Exploration of Women of Color's Role in the Environmental Justice Movement." *Race, Gender & Class* 16(3/4): 144–73. http://www.jstor.org/stable/41674682.

Rapp, Laura, Deeanna Button, Benjamin Fleury-Steiner, and Ruth Fleury-Steiner. 2010. "The Internet as a Tool for Black Feminist Activism: Lessons From an Online Antirape Protest." *Feminist Criminology* 5(3): 244–62.

Ray, Rashawn. 2011. *Race And Ethnic Relations In The Twenty-First Century: History, Theory, Institutions, and Policy.* San Diego, CA: Cognella.

Savali, Kirsten West. 2016. "African American Policy Forum Demands Justice for Holtzclaw Survivors." The Root. January 19. http://www.theroot.com/articles/culture/2016/01/days_of_accountability_and_visibility_african_american_policy_forum_demands/.

Silverleib, Alan. 2011. "The Birther Movement: Immune to Facts?" CNN. April 28. http://www.cnn.com/2011/POLITICS/04/27/birthers.evidence/index.html.

Sister Song. n.d. "Our History." http://sistersong.net. Retrieved March 10, 2016.

Smith, Lydia. 2014. "Eric Garner and Michael Brown 'Die-In' Demos: When Did Lying down Become a Form of Protest?" *International Business Times.* December 11. http://www.ibtimes.co.uk/eric-garner-michael-brown-die-demos-when-did-lying-down-become-form-protest-1479124.

Springer, Kimberly. 2002. "Third Wave Black Feminism?" *Signs: Journal of Women in Culture and Society* 27(4): 1059–82.

The White House. n.d. "My Brother's Keeper." Retrieved March 10, 2016. https://www.whitehouse.gov/my-brothers-keeper.

"White House Report: Women and Girls of Color: Addressing Challenges and Expanding Opportunities." 2014. White House, Office of the Press Secretary. November 12. https://obamawhitehouse.archives.gov/the-press-office

/2014/11/12/white-house-report-women-and-girls-color-addressing
-challenges-and-expan.

Tremayne, Mark. 2014. "Anatomy of Protest in the Digital Era: A Network Analysis
of Twitter and Occupy Wall Street." *Social Movement Studies* 13(1): 110–26.
http://dx.doi.org/10.1080/14742837.2013.830969/.

Wells, Veronica. 2016. "@RapedAtSpelman Exposes Protection of Black Men at
the Expense of Black Women on HBCU Campuses." Madame Noire.
May 4. http://madamenoire.com/695637/raped-at-spelman/.

White, E. Frances. 2001. *Dark Continent of Our Bodies: Black Feminism and the Politics of Respectability.* Philadelphia, PA: Temple University Press.

White House. 2016. *My Brother's Keeper 2016 Progress Report: Two Years of Expanding Opportunity and Creating Pathways to Success.* Washington, DC: The
White House.

"Why We Can't Wait: Women of Color Urge Inclusion in 'My Brother's Keeper.'"
2014. African American Policy Forum. June 17. http://www.aapf.org/recent
/2014/06/woc-letter-mbk.

Yamahtta-Taylor, Keeanga. 2016. *From# BlackLivesMatter to Black Liberation.* Chicago, IL: Haymarket Books.

Zeilinger, Julie. 2015. "These Challenges Are Why Sexual Assault at HBCUs Isn't
Talked About Enough." Mic. December 11. https://mic.com/articles/129
658/these-challenges-are-why-sexual-assault-at-hbcus-isn-t-talked
-about-enough#.3PDxxjZPX.

CHAPTER THIRTEEN

The Black President and the Black Body: The Intersection of Race, Class, Gender, and Violence in America

David O. Fakunle, Calvin J. Smiley, and Marisela B. Gomez

Introduction

The destruction of Black life at the hands of law enforcement is unfortunately endemic to the Obama legacy as the 44th president of the United States. On January 1, 2009, 19 days before President Obama was sworn into office, Oscar Grant was shot in the back by a Bay Area Rapid Transit (BART) police officer while handcuffed in Oakland, California. This killing was captured on cell phone video by onlookers and became the inaugural case of viral footage showing police violence exacted on the Black body. Oscar Grant's death and the many more subsequent deaths of Black people increased the legitimacy of Black communities' historic call for justice from overuse and extrajudicial force by law enforcement. In other words, to quote a recent statement by actor Will Smith, "Racism isn't getting worse, it's getting filmed."[1] Video surveillance, smartphones, and other recording devices have opened the door to a national discourse on police brutality in Black communities. Simply known as #BlackLivesMatter (BLM), this movement, comprised of multiracial and gender-inclusive activists, has continued to call for action to stimulate police reform, specifically; and broadly, to address social, political, and economic inequalities in the United States and internationally.

This chapter addresses several aspects of the response by President Obama and his administration to the increased social media evidence of harassment and death of Black victims during interactions with law enforcement and other forms of pseudo-vigilantism. First, we look at the role of social media and the #BlackLivesMatter movement. Then we use a historical lens to explore the meaning of Black life in America and how that shapes the current context of the #BlackLivesMatter movement. We then look more specifically at cases of Black death and how the government responded, if at all. It is here we are invested in understanding the context and content of why different but similar cases of law enforcement violence enticed or spurned response by President Obama. What are the differing media and political angles that emphasize various aspects of mainstream media involvement? Next, we discuss various campaigns and policies that the Obama administration has introduced that would aid, hinder, or remain stagnant in the fight for equality. Finally, our conclusion is an analysis of President Obama and how his legacy has shaped or reshaped the meaning of Black life in America.

Social Media and #BlackLivesMatter

The #BlackLivesMatter movement has utilized social media sharing applications, such as Facebook, Twitter, and Instagram, to publicize events of brutality against the Black body and hold law enforcement accountable. For example, the death of Eric Garner was captured on a cell phone, showing six police officers tackling Mr. Garner to the ground and an officer choking him while he exclaimed, "I can't breathe." The video also caught the aftermath of police and other agents not administering any life-saving techniques. Additionally, the New York City medical examiner ruled that Mr. Garner's death was a homicide, specifically caused by neck compressions from the officer who utilized the chokehold banned by the New York Police Department (NYPD). Despite eyewitnesses, clear video footage, and medical reports, none of the officers, including Officer Daniel Pantaleo, who physically choked Mr. Garner, were charged with any wrongdoing.

This case, along with others such as the deaths of John Crawford, Rekia Boyd, Tamir Rice, Sandra Bland, Freddie Gray, Korryn Gaines, and more, all ended in the same or a similar manner: no charges; non-indictments; and, rarely, indictments without convictions. This treatment of the Black community is indicative of the historic legacy of Blackness seen as "other," "invisible," and "insignificant" in America's long legacy of racist injustice.

Furthermore, the visceral racism embedded in American society has recently manifested in a petition to have the #BlackLivesMatter movement labeled as a "hate" group. This petition had over 141,000 signatures, once again reinforcing the concept that Black lives *do not* matter in the United States. The White House gave a public response stating, "We are not able to address the formal request of your petition."[2] Although the White House does not designate who are considered domestic terrorist organizations, this vague response leaves an opening for BLM to be seen as an act of terrorism rather than a movement for equality. The label of "terrorist" in a post-9/11 world is a sentence of death. Former President George W. Bush's emphatic statement "We do not negotiate with terrorists" suggests that the only alternative is annihilation. Therefore, once again, Black life is not only dispensable but a problem that must be eradicated. The creation of the "other" is needed to diminish humanity to the point that disregard and removal of life is not only acceptable but celebrated. In the case of "terrorism," the deaths of Sadaam Hussein, Muammar Gaddafi, and Osama bin Laden are public displays of jubilation and patriotism.

Historical Context

January 20, 2009, was a pivotal and benchmark date in American history. Barack Hussein Obama was officially sworn in as the 44th (and first Black) president of the United States. Obama's inauguration, as his campaign slogan suggested, gave "hope" to millions of Americans that maybe this thing called race was no longer a hindrance and that the country had turned a page, moving a step closer to acceptance and tolerance. Many Black and some White Americans could be heard making statements about never thinking of themselves being alive to see the first Black president. Many of these types of statements were full of emotions. Despite this feeling of achievement, there was an air of unease about our newly elected first Black president being harmed, which became the elephant in the room. Rapper Nas made a song entitled, "Black President" that highlighted this anxiety. He says, "What's the black pres' thinking on election night? Is it: 'How can I protect my life? Protect my wife? Protect my rights?'"[3] This feeling of discomfort was very real to Black Americans, and a recent Facebook post from a friend after the deaths of Alton Sterling and Philando Castille in July 2016 evoked these lyrics and what Black America was afraid of. Perhaps, they suggest, our focus has been in the wrong direction:

> When Barack Obama became the first African-American President of the United States of America I had this anxiety going through me like man, I hope he doesn't get hurt, or get attacked or even worse. I, like countless others, was so worried that the first Black President in America was in danger . . . expecting that we had a price to pay for this watershed moment. But, instead, it seems like the sacrifice has been the lives and safety of Black People and the intensification of racism in America.[4]

In other words, while the world watched and hoped for the protection of this single Black man, America's racism and violence was enacted on those that could be harmed: vulnerable, working, poor and middle-class Black citizens.

The U.S. Department of Justice's recent reports on Ferguson, Missouri; Cleveland, Ohio; and Baltimore, Maryland, indicate that there is systemic institutional bias and discrimination within policing agencies against Black people, including excessive force. Although this is new news for many, this has been the lived experience of Black Americans for generations. These experiences of discrimination have been expressed profusely, yet have often fallen on deaf ears. America tends to believe injustice only occurs when reported from the dominant group as opposed to the oppressed who live through these violent experiences. *Uncle Tom's Cabin,* by Harriet Beecher Stowe, and *Black Like Me,* by John Howard Griffin, are both telling examples of injustice not being taken seriously until expressed by those with power.

This oppression and lack of voice and agency must be read not as a singular or isolated point in time but as part of the larger linear narrative of the Black experience in America. Loïc Wacquant argues that the Black experience in America is largely defined by several "peculiar institutions": slavery, Jim Crow, the ghetto, and prisons.[5] The common denominator in all these stages of Black life is the consistent theme of exclusion, which occurs socially, economically, and politically. Thus, the Black body has differing meanings and relationships to Whiteness, based on the fundamental need at a specific point in time. For example, during the slave era the Black body was needed to produce and cultivate goods. Therefore, as an enslaved person (i.e., property), the Black body was a valued commodity that was in a perverse way "protected." Firsthand accounts describe the brutality and violence inflicted on slaves for the purposes of labor needs.

Frederick Douglass writes, "Mr. Covey had acquired a very high reputation for breaking young slaves, and this reputation was of immense value to him. It enabled him to get his farm tilled with much less expense to himself than he could have had it done without such a reputation."[6] The purpose of pain was of value to slaveholders to force labor at cheap costs. Angela Davis writes of Moses Grandy's observation of pregnant female slave violence being gendered, stating, "[A]n especially brutal form of whipping is described in which the woman was required to lie on the ground with her stomach positioned in a hole whose purpose was to safeguard the fetus."[7] The recognition of future labor as a commodity influenced the form of brutality inflicted on the Black body. In sum, violence was exacted not to kill, but to punish and control the Black body.

The rise of Jim Crow when formal slavery came to an end, which was emblazoned in the *Plessy v. Ferguson* ruling of 1896, arguing separate but equal as constitutional, gave way to new forms of violence on the Black body. Unlike under the regime of slavery, where Blackness as property was a valued commodity, the opportunity of freedom gave rise to ritualized death at the hands of White vigilantes. Lynching—a communal spectacle of extrajudicial vigilantism that foresaw public death as normalized violence on the Black body—became a routine in many places around the United States during the late 19th and early 20th centuries. Often, after a Black male was accused of some sort of crime (e.g., rape), mobs would exact revenge, making the defendant a victim to their brand of justice. Some accounts report that these ritualized forms of violence brought thousands of spectators and were uniquely different from previous forms.[8] This difference was due to intent, because it was not to break or punish, but to destroy, as Black life now held no intrinsic value, and Blacks were seen as in many ways competitors for jobs (economic), housing (social), and voting (political) power.

As early as the late 19th century, Blacks began moving north, and the violence associated with Jim Crow followed even as it was legally abolished with the dismantling of federal legislation in the early 1950s (*Brown v. Board of Education*) and followed by the modern Civil Rights Movement. W.E.B. Du Bois recounts many of the experiences of moving north in his seminal sociological work entitled *The Philadelphia Negro*, which explored Black life in the North and found prevalent institutional discrimination and other racist acts.[9] These included legal and illegal segregation and disinvestment through racial covenants, block busting, and redlining, resulting in the early Black urban ghettos. Relegated to segregated communities in Northern cities, Blacks lived in some of the most deplorable conditions, where many of their communities were forgotten and disinvested by local, state, and federal governments, allowing urban decay and poverty to flourish.[10] These ghetto spaces became vacuums of inequality with the rise of White flight, deindustrialization, and the absence of other social institutions. Mindy Fullilove describes these disruptions as the reasons leading to loss of the social networks of previously functional communities and subsequent development of alternative economies: hustling.[11] Criminal behavior spread, and terms such as *Black on Black* crime began to flourish as justifications for Black inequality. In other words, if Black people could just "get it together," all their problems would be solved. This excuse negates systematic inequality and violence exacted on the Black body and community, whether directly through whippings and lynchings, or often by neglect and disinvestment of communities' needs by White supremacy.

The idea of Black criminality was exploited through propaganda to promote the "War on Drugs" and other strict policies that have impacted the U.S. criminal justice system. The synonymous nature of Blackness as criminal permeates American culture of what is perceived as inherently evil, violent, and—most importantly—felonious. This characterization takes the human form of the Black body. Hence, when law enforcement exacts extrajudicial violence on the Black body and kills an individual, victims' behavior, appearance, location, and lifestyle can all be used against them to justify their death and simultaneously make victims appear as perpetrators.[12]

The historical patterns that tether Black victimization to the hands of both individuals and individuals acting on behalf of the state outline and articulate the current climate that #BlackLivesMatter is highlighting: these deaths are not isolated or accidental, but stem from the larger and prominent idea of what Black life is meant to be, which is dead. Anti-Blackness looks at the ways in which Black life is diluted and repackaged by White supremacy and given as "multiculturalism."[13] Jared Sexton writes, "This division is established through the demarcation of the black body and, as such, is both irritated by and dependent upon the volatility of negrophobia."[14] In other words, this fear of Blackness supports anti-Blackness from both racists who want to see Blackness annihilated and liberals who believe in color blindness. The results devalue Blackness by fusing it with others. Beyond this, anti-Blackness ties Blackness and death together as synonymous with each other.[15] The only right a Black person has is to death, regardless of his or her own determination of when that may be. The idea of death is a looming and omnipresent feeling within the Black body not because death is inevitable, but because the human form is a Black body. Considering recent deaths, that feeling of angst and anxiety is present for Black people when they interact with law enforcement because, as evidenced by the increased eyewitness recordings, Black life is taken without regard or repercussion.

How President Obama Responded Personally

It is known that President Obama is a man who is not afraid to speak when the opportunity presents itself, even on a topic as serious and uncomfortable as the unwarranted killings of Black people in the United States. What is unveiled is a typology of his responses that is clear in some ways and ambiguous in others.

Historical Context

President Obama expresses the frustration of communities of color as it pertains to the reasons behind the inequitable use of violence in the United States, namely, the country's own history of systemic violence and marginalization against Black people:

> Now, this isn't to say that the African American community is naïve about the fact that African American young men are disproportionately involved in the criminal justice system; that they're disproportionately both victims and perpetrators of violence. It's not to make excuses for that fact—although black folks do interpret the reasons for that in a historical context. They understand that some of the violence that takes place in poor black neighborhoods around the country is born out of a very violent past in this country, and that the poverty and dysfunction that we see in those communities can be traced to a very difficult history. And so, the fact that sometimes that's unacknowledged adds to the frustration. And the fact that a lot of African American boys are painted with a broad brush and the excuse is given, well, there are these statistics out there that show that African American boys are more violent—using that as an excuse to then see sons treated differently causes pain.[16]

Gender

Research into President Obama's personal responses to unwarranted killings of Black people found no results for notable female victims, including Rekia Boyd in 2012; Sandra Bland in 2015; and, most recently, Korryn Gaines in 2016. The most that could be found about President Obama's response to a Black woman's unwarranted death was a July 23, 2015, press briefing in which members of the media asked the White House press secretary about President Obama's knowledge regarding the death of Sandra Bland:

Q: Has the President been following the situation with Sandra Bland in Texas, and the incident there? And does he have any thoughts or reaction to what's taking place there?

MR. EARNEST: Josh, I know that he is aware of this incident that has received significant media attention over the last week or so. This is a situation that is currently under investigation by local law enforcement and the local prosecutor down in Texas. And so I'm reluctant to wade in with the President's specific thoughts here until the local prosecutors have had an opportunity to conclude the inquiry that they said that they have opened into this matter.[17]

Age

It could be argued that President Obama's most personal response came after the July 2013 acquittal of George Zimmerman—a neighborhood watchman—who killed 17-year-old Trayvon Martin in February 2012. Although he states his acceptance of the jury's decision and his assurance of the judicial system's efficacy, President Obama does not shy away from the reality of his existence as a Black man, despite being the most powerful individual in the world. Here the unique dynamic of the U.S. president in a Black body is apparent, as even Obama was not immune to the perpetual threat of violence:

> You know, when Trayvon Martin was first shot I said that this could have been my son. Another way of saying that is Trayvon Martin could have been me 35 years ago. . . . There are very few African American men in this country who haven't had the experience of being followed when they were shopping in a department store. That includes me. There are very few African American men who haven't had the experience of walking across the street and hearing the locks click on the doors of cars. That happens to me—at least before I was a senator.[18]

Among President Obama's many challenges to the killing, including the legal application of Florida's controversial "stand your ground" law, is the nature of the preceding incident itself. He continues:

> And that all contributes I think to a sense that if a white male teen was involved in the same kind of scenario, that, from top to bottom, both the

outcome and the aftermath might have been different. . . . And for those who resist that idea that we should think about something like these "stand your ground" laws, I'd just ask people to consider, if Trayvon Martin was of age and armed, could he have stood his ground on that sidewalk? And do we actually think that he would have been justified in shooting Mr. Zimmerman who had followed him in a car because he felt threatened? And if the answer to that question is at least ambiguous, then it seems to me that we might want to examine those kinds of laws.[19]

Finally, President Obama concludes with an acknowledgement of U.S. society's evolution on race relations but reminds us that equity and equality are still distant goals:

Each successive generation seems to be making progress in changing attitudes when it comes to race. It doesn't mean we're in a post-racial society. It doesn't mean that racism is eliminated.[20]

Similar personal sentiments are expressed in his remarks on the deaths of two other young Black men—18-year-old Michael Brown and 12-year-old Tamir Rice—in an interview conducted by Jeff Johnson on BET:

When they described their own personal experiences of having been stopped for no reason, or having generated suspicion because they were in a community that supposedly they didn't belong, my mind went back to what it was like for me when I was 17, 18, 20. And as I told them, not only do I hear the pain and frustration of being subjected to that kind of constant suspicion, but part of the reason I got into politics was to figure out how can I bridge some of those gaps in understanding so that the larger country understands this is not just a black problem or a brown problem. This is an American problem.[21]

Class

Perhaps President Obama's strongest statement about the systemic factors that affect unwarranted killings was in response to the April 2015 death of 25-year-old Freddie Gray after an altercation with six Baltimore law enforcement officers. Prominently noted after his death was the fact that Gray frequented Gilmor Homes of the Sandtown-Winchester neighborhood, notorious for its overwhelming poverty and abundance of criminal activity. Following the death of Freddie Gray while in police custody, Black youth in Baltimore led uprisings calling for "justice for Freddie Gray." In his response after the uprising, President Obama leaves no room for anyone to misinterpret the core issues that leave people of color, particularly Black men, in situations that involve unwarranted violence and death. In addition, he confronts the notion as to who is responsible for addressing said systemic barriers:

> And without making any excuses for criminal activities that take place in those communities, what we also know is if you have impoverished communities, that have been stripped away of opportunity; where children are born into abject poverty; they've got parents, often because of substance abuse problems or incarceration or lack of education themselves, can't do right by their kids; if it's more likely that those kids end up in jail or dead than that they go to college; in communities where there are no fathers who can provide guidance to young men; communities that where there's no investment, and manufacturing's been stripped away, and drugs have flooded the community and the drug industry ends up being the primary employer for a whole lot of folks. In those environments, if we think that we're just going to send the police to do the dirty work of containing the problems that arise there, without, as a nation and as a society saying what can we do to change those communities, to help lift up those communities and give those kids opportunity, then we're not going to solve this problem, and we'll go through the same cycles of periodic conflicts between the police and communities, and the occasional riots in the streets, and everybody will feign concern until it goes away and then we go about our business as usual.[22]

What is also notable about this response, undoubtedly influenced by the number of statements made previously about other unwarranted killings primarily by police officers, is President Obama's charge to law enforcement agencies, and especially individual officers and organizations, to become more proactive in addressing the divide between law enforcement and the people whom they have sworn to serve:

> I think it's going to be important for organizations like the Fraternal Order of Police and other police unions and organizations to acknowledge that this is not good for police. We have to own up to the fact that occasionally there are going to be problems here. Just as there are in every other occupation. There are some bad politicians who are corrupt. There are folks in the business community who are on Wall Street who don't do the right thing. Well, there are some police who aren't doing the right thing.[23]

Social Justice

The rising media evidence of unwarranted killings of people of color has inspired a considerable rise in social justice movements and organizations over the past few years, most notably #BlackLivesMatter. Their growing presence in the consciousness and lexicon of the United States is apparent, and so has been the opposition to their causes. When declaring the humanity of Black lives, particularly in response to killings by law enforcement officers, these social justice movements and organizations have been met with responses solely meant to diminish the message. These include responses such as "All Lives Matter" and in the case of law enforcement officers, "Blue Lives Matter." In his uncharacteristically immediate response to the back-to-back killings of Alton Sterling and Philando Castile in Baton Rouge, Louisiana, and Falcon Heights, Minnesota, respectively, in July 2016—both Black men, both at the hands of law enforcement, both incidences recorded and made available to the entire world, and both meeting with an intense backlash within hours— President Obama goes out of his way to emphasize the true purpose of social justice movements to those unaware and convinced otherwise:

> When people say "Black Lives Matter" that doesn't mean blue lives don't matter, it just means all lives matter but right [now] the big concern is that the data shows Black folks are more vulnerable to these kinds of incidents. This isn't a matter of us comparing the value of lives, this is recognizing that there is a particular burden that is being placed on a group of our fellow citizens, and we should care about that. And we can't dismiss it. We can't dismiss it . . . to be concerned about these issues is not political correctness, it's just being American and wanting to live up to our best and highest ideals. And it's to recognize the reality that we've got some tough history and we haven't gotten through all of that history yet.[24]

Points of Reference: Shootings of Law Enforcement Officers

The July 2016 killings of law enforcement officers in Dallas, Texas, and in Baton Rouge, Louisiana, both proven to be attacks in retaliation to the killings of Alton Sterling and Philando Castile earlier that month, provided an unprecedented opportunity to observe President Obama's approach to addressing a situation in which the circumstances were literally reversed. His response suggests that Obama can take a more hard-line stance against the killings of law enforcement officers, as opposed to relatively milder commentaries about killings by law enforcement officers:

> Regardless of motive, the death of these three brave officers underscores the danger that police across the country confront every single day. And we as a nation have to be loud and clear that nothing justifies violence against

law enforcement. Attacks on police are an attack on all of us and the rule of law that makes society possible.[25]

It is interesting to note President Obama's last sentence of the afore-mentioned statement, as it should seem obvious to him, given his past responses, that there are communities of color—not to mention the fami-lies of police brutality victims—who would vehemently make a counter-argument: although attacks on law enforcement officers should be a concern for all Americans, attacks on the Black body, and Black death, only affect those individuals and their families. President Obama has alluded to the neglect of the Black body being a national issue about which all Ameri-cans should be concerned; nevertheless, he makes as extreme and abso-lute a statement as one could, especially in comparison to prior statements about victimization of communities of color, where he introduces—knowingly or unknowingly—some sense of speculation on the part of said communities:

> When incidents like this occur [unwarranted police harassment and shoot-ing of black people], there's a big chunk of our fellow citizenry that feels as if because of the color of their skin they are not being treated the same . . . and that hurts.[26]

Commonalities

Regardless of the victims about whom President Obama is speaking—whether they were persons of color killed unjustifiably by vigilantes or law enforcement officers, or law enforcement officers killed by retaliating rogues, or riots by Black "thugs" after the death of Freddie Gray—the over-arching message that Obama consistently delivers is a call to all Americans to be proactive in addressing the issues that lead to such incidents, as well as his dedication to the cause through his capacity as president:

> But if we really want to solve the problem, if our society really wanted to solve the problem? We could, it's just that it would require everybody say-ing this is important, this is significant, and that we don't just pay atten-tion to these communities when a CVS burns, and we don't just pay attention when a young man gets shot or has his spine snapped.[27]

A similar proclamation and call to action was made a few months prior in response to the grand jury's decision not to bring charges against NYPD officers in the death of Eric Garner:

And as I said when I met with folks both from Ferguson and law enforcement and clergy and civil rights activists, I said this is an issue that we've been dealing with for too long and it's time for us to make more progress than we've made. And I'm not interested in talk; I'm interested in action. And I am absolutely committed as President of the United States to making sure that we have a country in which everybody believes in the core principle that we are equal under the law.[28]

Obama continues with linking the violence of police brutality against the Black body and subsequent reactions from citizens with a call for all of America to remember to unite together in hope, a theme he set in place when running for presidency:

My fellow Americans, only we can prove, through words and through deeds, that we will not be divided. And we're going to have to keep on doing it "again and again and again." That's how this country gets united. That's how we bring people of good will together. Only we can prove that we have the grace and the character and the common humanity to end this kind of senseless violence, to reduce fear and mistrust within the American family, to set an example for our children.[29]

Obama's Administrative Response

In many ways, the persistence of traditional media coverage of police and vigilante killing of Black bodies has been coerced by increasing onsite recording of these murders and subsequent social media presence. In response, the government has also been forced to address this stark evidence of racism and control, and fear of the Black body. Civil rights and social justice movements and organizations, such as #BlackLivesMatter and Standing up for Racial Justice, have elaborated their call for justice for Black lives in response to this increasing evidence of brutality. In the first eight months of 2016 alone, Black bodies have been shot dead by police at 2.5 times the rate of White bodies.[30] Meanwhile, Obama has consistently addressed the fact that killing Black bodies occurs within the context of a history of disinvestment and its outcomes in low-income and Black communities. He insists that the history of segregation has created poor Black communities with little opportunity for upward mobility that requires a broad system of support to redress these wrongs, and that policing is not the remedy.

My Brother's Keeper

One such program addressing this history and attempting to provide a remedy is My Brother's Keeper (MBK). This program was cited as addressing the White House Council on Economic Advisers' 2016 report detailing the significant disparities in education, exposure to the criminal justice system, and unemployment/underemployment that persist between young Black men and other Americans. Introduced in 2014, Task Force Chair Broderick Johnson reflected on the program after two years:

> MBK is about obliterating the barriers our kids face. It's about building strong, lasting bridges to opportunity for boys and girls, young men and young women, no matter what their background or the circumstances into which they were born. It's about investing in what works, acting with a sense of urgency, basing strategies on data and evidence, and having the courage to call out and tear down discrimination in every system and policy where it shows up. And, in two years we could not be more excited about the momentum, energy, and enthusiasm that has been sparked all across the country.[31]

Early Paroling for Nonfatal Felonies

For those already incarcerated, the Obama administration launched a program to commute sentences for nonviolent drug offenders. Initiated in 2015, this program makes eligible approximately 50,000 prisoners for sentence reductions; to date 6000 have been released. Then-Attorney General Eric Holder noted, "This is a milestone in the effort to make more efficient use of our law enforcement resources and to ease the burden on our overcrowded prison system." Because Blacks are incarcerated at 5.1 times the rate of Whites, this program will begin to address the stark imbalance in arrest and sentencing of Black bodies.[32]

Guidance for Gender Bias in Policing

The question of the intersection of gender bias with racial bias has been taken up by Obama's administration in several ways. This administration is the first to have an advisor on gender inclusion on its advisory council. The former vice-president Joe Biden, while a senator in 1994, introduced the Violence Against Women Act, resulting in the formation of the Office on Violence Against Women (OVAW). In 2015, the OVAW, along with the Federal Civil Rights Division and the Office of Community Oriented Policing Services (COPS Office), collaborated to produce guidelines to help law enforcement agencies prevent gender bias. The guidelines offer training on how to prevent bias in responding to sexual and domestic assault victims and transgendered victims. It responds to the Department of Justice's investigation and report on gender bias in policing and helps to address the intersection of gender, race, class, and sexual orientation bias in law enforcement in cities like Baltimore, Ferguson, New Orleans, and others with a significant number of Black communities living in poverty. By mid-2016, OVAW had granted $500 million to support communities addressing sexual and domestic violence by including resources for a culturally specific services program: to include staff representatives of the people, they are providing services and research, and development involving impacted communities as partners. The administration used the 2013 reauthorization of the Violence Against Women Act to deny funding to the state of North Carolina, which passed a discriminatory law against transgendered individuals. This pattern of addressing the intersectionality of human and civil rights violation by the Obama's administration is not evident in previous administrations.

Department of Justice Investigation of Police Misconduct Patterns

Seattle

According to the Department of Justice (DOJ), during the Obama administration there were more federal investigations into allegations of police misconduct that may have violated civil rights than occurred in the previous five years: over 22.[33] In 2011, the DOJ released its report on allegation of the Seattle's police department use of excessive force: "Our investigation finds a pattern or practice of constitutional violations regarding the use of force that result from structural problems, as well as serious concerns about biased policing."[34] The report gathered enough evidence to suggest the practice of biased policing but concluded:

> Finally, while SPD [Seattle Police Department] does not collect or maintain adequate data relating to issues of biased policing, it does collect some data relating both to its street stops and through its Computer Aided Dispatch ("CAD") system. This data too is incomplete and not sufficient to support any conclusion one way or the other regarding biased policing. However, as discussed below, the data does raise red flags regarding whether minorities are subjected to a disproportionate amount of policing.[35]

In 2016, a seated federal judge, appointed by President George W. Bush, commented on the lack of support by SPD in general and the Seattle Police Officer Guild specifically in resisting reforms to increase biased-free policing delineated in the DOJ's consent decree. He ended his comments as officiate of the consent decree with the declaration: "Black lives matter."[36]

New Orleans

Nine months after the Seattle report was released, the DOJ released results of its investigation of police misconduct in the New Orleans Police Department. It found that patterns and practices of unconstitutional conduct and/or violations of federal law occurred in several areas, including use of excessive force; unconstitutional stops, searches and arrests; biased policing, including racial and ethnic profiling; and lesbian, gay, bisexual, and transgender (LGBT) discrimination; a systemic failure to provide effective policing services to persons with limited English proficiency; and a systemic failure to investigate sexual assaults and domestic violence.

Cleveland

In 2014, the DOJ released its report of allegations of police misconduct by Cleveland's division of police: "We have reasonable cause to believe that CDP engages in a pattern or practice of the use of excessive force in violation of the Fourth Amendment of the United States Constitution."[37] Though racial bias or biased/discriminatory policing was never mentioned in the report, the investigation was spurred by several allegations of a pattern of undue use of force against Black bodies.

Ferguson

In 2015, the DOJ released its report of allegations of systematic misconduct by the Ferguson Police Department after the police killing of Black teenager Michael Brown: "This investigation has revealed a pattern or practice of unlawful conduct within the Ferguson Police Department that violates the First, Fourth, and Fourteenth Amendments to the United States Constitution, and federal statutory law. . . . Further, Ferguson's police and municipal court practices both reflect and exacerbate existing racial bias, including racial stereotypes."[38] The first DOJ investigation to specifically conclude and name the population discriminated against in biased policing, the report continues: "Ferguson's own data establish clear racial disparities that adversely impact African Americans. The evidence shows that discriminatory intent is part of the reason for these disparities. Over time, Ferguson's police and municipal court practices have sown deep mistrust between parts of the community and the police department, undermining law enforcement legitimacy among African Americans in particular."[39] Although the DOJ also investigated the fatal police shooting of

Michael Brown, it concluded that its examination did not support federal civil rights charges against the police officer in question, Police Officer Darren Wilson.

Baltimore

Seventeen months later, in August 2016, prompted by the death of a Black man while in police custody, the DOJ released its report of investigation into allegations of a pattern of undue use of force by Baltimore Police Department:

> The Department of Justice concludes that there is reasonable cause to believe that BPD engages in a pattern or practice of conduct that violates the Constitution or federal law. BPD engages in a pattern or practice of: (1) making unconstitutional stops, searches, and arrests; (2) using enforcement strategies that produce severe and unjustified disparities in the rates of stops, searches and arrests of African Americans; (3) using excessive force; and (4) retaliating against people engaging in constitutionally-protected expression.[40]

Confirming some of the systematic use of force in encounter and arrest of people of color generally and Black bodies specifically, none of the previous DOJ reports made it so explicitly clear how structural racism in the American society had created communities of disinvestment and poverty and at greater risk for police violence because of the resultant segregation. It stated:

> [C]onversely, frayed community relationships inhibit effective policing by denying officers important sources of information and placing them more frequently in dangerous, adversarial encounters. We found these principles in stark relief in Baltimore, where law enforcement officers confront a long history of social and economic challenges that impact much of the City, including the perception that there are "two Baltimores": one wealthy and largely White, the second impoverished and predominantly Black.[41]

The DOJ report elaborated the voices of Baltimore citizens in regard to these two Baltimores and how biased policing occurred:

> Community members living in the City's wealthier and largely White neighborhoods told us that officers tend to be respectful and responsive to their

needs, while many individuals living in the City's largely African-American communities informed us that officers tend to be disrespectful and do not respond promptly to their calls for service. Members of these largely African-American communities often felt they were subjected to unjustified stops, searches, and arrests, as well as excessive force.[42]

Like the Ferguson report, Baltimore's DOJ report emphasized the importance of community partnerships to build trust and ensure fair and effective enforcement, better supervision, data collection and analysis, and accountability for misconduct. Like the New Orleans report, Baltimore's report detailed evidence of biased policing against cis-gendered females and transgendered persons, confirming the intersection of race, class, and gender in biased policing. In response to investigations by the DOJ, police departments may enter a consent decree to address the findings. Consent decrees provide some federal funding for police departments to address and remedy the findings of the report. This carrot-and-stick process therefore shows willingness by the Obama administration not only to investigate civil rights abuses by police departments but also invest resources to remediate civil rights abuses by police departments.

The Broad Response of the Federal Government

Training on an Implicit Bias

In 2016, following evidence of chronic harassment and shooting of Black bodies by police officers, the DOJ announced plans to train more than 33,000 federal agents and prosecutors to identify and address unconscious or implicit bias in their work.[43] The agencies impacted include the Federal Bureau of Investigation (FBI); the Drug Enforcement Administration (DEA); the Bureau of Alcohol, Tobacco, and Firearms; and the U.S. Marshals Service.

Gun Control and Congress

During the Obama administration, the increased coverage of police shootings and violence against people of color mobilized proponents of gun control. In June 2016, Democratic Congressman John Lewis (Georgia) initiated a sit-in on the Congress floor in support of legislation for tougher standards for gun control. He was joined by 174 other lawmakers in this unprecedented act.[44]

Collecting Data on Police Violence

In July 2016, the Department of Justice Bureau of Justice Statistics (BJS) released a policy proposal for counting arrest-related deaths, adding to the administration's response to the increased media coverage of police killings and public protests calling for action. Directly and indirectly, Obama's administration has made great strides to research and provide evidence of civil rights abuses in general and systematic racial injustice. Collectively it has put forward policy and funding to address evidenced civil rights injustice, sending a message to the American citizen that the structures that have built and provided the tools necessary to maintain violence against Black bodies, female-gendered and transgendered bodies, and the impoverished must change. This is a powerful message because it moves away from the personal and into the structural and systematic ways civil rights violence against marginalized populations and specifically people of color and the Black body continue.

It would be tempting to speculate, evidenced by the administration's response since Obama's presidency, that the media lifted a history of civil rights abuses previously gone unaddressed, which triggered a renewed movement for civil rights from above. The increased media attention may have been the force necessary for existing structures, now populated with personnel motivated by an Obama presidency of change and measured response to crisis, to address this history and legacy of civil rights abuses—a movement from above. The media also motivated greater public discourse and action, which in turn likely fueled and supported this new direction of the administration. The consistent findings of biased policing across multiple municipalities by DOJ investigations may have then encouraged increased media coverage and public protest and social justice movements. These interactive movements, from below and above, may account for the current level of attention to civil rights abuses in general and racial injustice against the Black body.

Conclusion

Black self-determination is a threat to White supremacy. The most visible image of this determination is the Black body. Therefore, White supremacy is incessantly trying to control it. Since the inception of BLM, reactionary voices have challenged the methods, ideologies, and goals of this organization. Mass demonstration, protest, and acts of civil disobedience were met with critique and disappointment. Many anti-BLM supporters ironically quoted the late Dr. Martin Luther King Jr.'s stance of nonviolence to condemn the current protests against police brutality. This was done not to analyze the teachings of Dr. King, but to deceptively make connections between BLM and violence. In other words, White supremacy has used an altered form of Blackness to negate Blackness, to control Blackness.

Most recently, National Football League quarterback Colin Kaepernick of the San Francisco 49ers protested the American National Anthem by remaining seated during a preseason game. Kaepernick has received hateful backlash from many questioning his motives, patriotism, and reasoning for "insulting" the country that allows him to play a professional sport for a living. This form of resistance by sitting (and now kneeling) could be argued to be the mildest form of rebelliousness. Yet taken not as an isolated incident, but viewed through a holistic lens, Kaepernick's guilt is not for kneeling during the national anthem but his defiance against his Black body being forced to submit to a command given by White supremacy.

Therefore, any form of resistance, regardless of its minor or strong stance, is opposition that must be stopped. The burning of Kaepernick football jerseys are examples of a provisional lynching. In this case, the body cannot be harmed, but the representation—his name and number—can be set ablaze. This is seen not as violence on the Black body, but as safeguarding White supremacy via the mask of patriotism. Until the Black form in its entirety is taken seriously, the continued violence on the Black community, both through direct police and vigilante violence as well as indirect violence, which takes form in the lack of investment, education, and other structural barriers, will endure.

Recommendations to Reduce Unwarranted Killings

The Obama administration has instituted several initiatives to specifically address unwarranted killings by law enforcement—notably, the White House Task Force on 21st Century Policing and the Advancing 21st Century Policing Initiative. Depending on with whom one speaks, one would hear differing opinions on the program as to its actualized and potential impact on reducing brutality of the Black body in the United States. Regardless of what current programs do in the long term, more solutions are needed to properly and thoroughly address the multisystemic issues and barriers that precipitate such outcomes, including the following:

1. *Extend the duration of training academies for incoming law enforcement cadets to include comprehensive cultural understanding programs and introductions to jurisdictional cultures.* Before recent reform recommendations, some police department

academies graduated their cadets in as little as six months, and even afterward many would argue that still more time is needed for future officers to become acclimated to the areas they will serve and, just as importantly, the people they will serve. Challenges aside with infrastructure and manpower, future officers would be better served with a transitional period between graduation from the academy and the beginning of their beat service.

2. *Mandate that all law enforcement officers—from those on the beat to administrators—live within jurisdictional limits.* Particularly for urban locales that have been deprived of adequate economic resources for years, like Baltimore, such a mandate would increase the tax base in a significant manner. Most importantly, it would create instant accountability for law enforcement officers, given that their jobs would directly impact their communities and their neighbors.

3. *Implement programs within police departments that allow officers to address their own trauma.* In the end, law enforcement officers are human beings, just like us, who inherently bring their misperceptions, pressures, and complications to the profession. Without opportunity to fully appreciate their thoughts and feelings as a person, let alone those feelings associated with a highly stressful job, tragedies will continue to manifest. The "blue line" culture must change to acknowledge the humanity of its men and women and give them the space to express fear, confusion, anger, joy, peace, and understanding—all that makes us the complex beings that we are.

4. *Provide comprehensive policy reform and multi-sector funding to reverse the perpetuation of systemic racism.* The institution of racism in the United States has existed since before its founding. The effects of the system are so prevalent that it feels normal, and the way racism manifests is numerous. As previously elucidated, education, housing, sanitation, recreation, mental health and substance abuse, chronic physical disability, police brutality, and many other outcomes can be directly traced to past and present institutionally racist policies. Therefore, a well-defined, macro-level, multidimensional approach is what it will take to begin undoing the pervasive damage that systemic racism has caused. If the Black body is treated and respected like every other body—not just to reduce unwarranted killings but also to provide the opportunity to actualize a quality life—tragedies such as those showcased to the world in recent years will be just that: tragedies, and not an obvious continuation of systemic oppression and dehumanization.

President Obama's Legacy

Will Obama's legacy as a president who personally responded to the chronic systematic brutality against the Black body and communities continue with a new president? Will the administration under a new president continue with what has been implemented, in investigation, policy, and funding? What of future presidents beyond the next two terms? In other words, will the federal attention to the violation of Black bodies become part of business as usual, or will the Trump administration redouble efforts to protect the rights of the Black community?

These questions may be advised by the two threads discussed in this chapter: the presence of a Black man as president and the role of the media and their individual and collective influence on the response by the president and his administration to police violation of the civil rights of Black people. History suggests that if the next and future presidents are White, the status quo that existed under previous White presidents will return: vague interest and negligence concerning the value of Black lives and communities, resulting in violence against the Black body. But the role of social media in pushing a federal-level response during Obama's presidency—despite his race and ethnic identity—cannot be ignored. Therefore, the continued coverage of unwarranted police violence against Black women and men, poor people, and gendered violence is a critical condition and variable in determining how much the next president and his or her administration will engage in stopping this type of individual and structural violence. Likewise, the role of social media and media in general in maintaining attention to #BlackLivesMatter's determination in highlighting and demanding equity in policy and practice is important. The constant consumption of media and the speed of global news coverage ensures that the role of the media will remain critical not only in the responsiveness of the federal government, but in state and local governments as well.

The continued growth of movements like #BlackLivesMatter will also help in determining the level of engagement by a new president and administration. BLM has made public its platform, one of its major points being ending the war on Black bodies: "We demand an end to the named and unnamed wars on Black people—including the criminalization, incarceration and killing of our people."[45] Police brutality is clearly articulated as a major thrust of the BLM campaign. Along with its movement to build political power, its role as a major voice of Black people in America may influence the next president's continuation of Obama's legacy of addressing systematic inequity and inequality in Black communities.

Notes

1. "Will Smith: 'Racism Isn't Getting Worse, It's Getting Filmed,'" 2016.
2. Flores, 2016.
3. Nas, 2010.

4. Salim, 2016.

5. Wacquant, 2006.

6. Douglass and Gates, 2002, p. 383.

7. Davis, 2011, p. 68.

8. Holden-Smith, 1996, p. 31.

9. Du Bois, 2010.

10. Duneier, 2016.

11. Fullilove, 2004.

12. Smiley and Fakunle, 2016.

13. Sexton, 2008.

14. Ibid., p. 16.

15. Brady, 2016.

16. "Remarks by the President on Trayvon Martin," 2013,

17. "Press Briefing by Press Secretary Josh Earnest, 7/23/2015," 2015.

18. "Remarks by the President on Trayvon Martin."

19. Ibid.

20. Ibid.

21. "President Obama on Freddie Gray's Death: 'This is Not New, and We Shouldn't Pretend that It's New,' 2015.

22. "Remarks by President Obama and Prime Minister Abe of Japan in Joint Press Conference," 2015.

23. Ibid.

24. "President Obama on the Fatal Shootings of Alton Sterling and Philando Castile."

25. "Statement by the President on the Shootings in Baton Rouge, Louisiana," July 17, 2016.

26. "Statement by the President on the Shootings in Baton Rouge, Louisiana," July 7, 2016.

27. "Remarks by President Obama and Prime Minister Abe of Japan in Joint Press Conference," 2015.

28. "President Obama Delivers a Statement on the Grand Jury Decision in the Death of Eric Garner," 2014.

29. "Statement by the President on the Shootings in Baton Rouge, Louisiana," July 17.

30. "The Counted: People killed by police in the US," 2016.

31. "My Brother's Keeper," 2016.

32. Nellis, 2016.

33. Picket, 2015.

34. U.S. Department of Justice Civil Rights Division, 2011.

35. Ibid.

36. Miletech, 2016.

37. U.S. Department of Justice Civil Rights Division, 2014.

38. U.S. Department of Justice Civil Rights Division, 2015. https://www.courts.mo.gov/file.jsp?id=95274.

39. Ibid.
40. U.S. Department of Justice Civil Rights Division, 2016.
41. Ibid.
42. Ibid.
43. "Department of Justice Announces New Department-Wide Implicit Bias Training for Personnel," 2016.
44. Walsh et al., 2016.
45. "End the War on Black People," n.d.

Bibliography

Brady, Nicholas. "Riding with Death: Defining Anti-Blackness." *The Progress.* February 20, 2014. https://progressivepupil.wordpress.com/2014/02/27/right-to-death-defining-anti-blackness/.

"The Counted: People killed by police in the US. September 17 2016." 2016. http://www.theguardian.com/us-news/ng-interactive/2015/jun/01/the-counted-police-killings-us-database.

Davis, Angela Y. *Are Prisons Obsolete?* New York: Seven Stories Press, 2011.

"Department of Justice Announces New Department-Wide Implicit Bias Training for Personnel." 2016. Department of Justice. June 27. https://www.justice.gov/opa/pr/department-justice-announces-new-department-wide-implicit-bias-training-personnel.

Douglass, Frederick, and Henry Louis Gates (ed.). *The Classic Slave Narratives.* New York: Signet Classics, 2002.

Du Bois, William Edward Burghardt. *The Philadelphia Negro.* New York: Cosimo, 2010.

Duneier, Mitchell. *Ghetto: The Invention of a Place, the History of an Idea.* New York: Farrar, Straus and Giroux, 2016.

"End the War on Black People." The Movement for Black Lives. (n.d.) https://policy.m4bl.org/end-war-on-black-people/ (accessed September 2016).

Flores, Reena. "White House responds to petition to label Black Lives Matter a 'terror' group." CBS News. July 17, 2016. http://www.cbsnews.com/news/white-house-responds-to-petition-to-label-black-lives-matter-a-terror-group/.

Fullilove, Mindy Thompson. *Root Shock: How Tearing Up City Neighborhoods Hurt America and What We Can Do about It.* New York: Ballantine Books, 2004.

Holden-Smith, Barbara. "Lynching, Federalism, and the Intersection of Race and Gender in the Progressive Era." *Yale Journal of Law and Feminism* 8 (1996): 31.

Miletech, Steve. 2016. "Federal Judge Declares 'Black Lives Matter' During Hearing Over Seattle Police Reform." *The Seattle Times.* August 15. http://www.seattletimes.com/seattle-news/crime/in-tongue-lashing-federal-judge-wont-let-guild-hold-police-reform-hostage/.

"My Brother's Keeper." The White House. 2016. https://www.whitehouse.gov/my-brothers-keeper.

Nas. "Black President." *Genius*. 2010. http://genius.com/Nas-black-president-lyrics.

Nellis, Ashley. 2016. "The Color of Justice: Racial and Ethnic Disparity in State Prisons." *The Sentencing Project*.

Picket, Kerry. 2015. "DOJ police probes and consent decrees spike under Obama." *The Daily Caller*. May 28. http://dailycaller.com/2015/05/28/doj-police-probes-and-consent-decrees-spike-under-obama/.

"President Obama Delivers a Statement on the Grand Jury Decision in the Death of Eric Garner." December 4, 2014. https://www.whitehouse.gov/blog/2014/12/03/president-obama-delivers-statement-grand-jury-decision-death-eric-garner.

"President Obama on the Fatal Shootings of Alton Sterling and Philando Castile." The White House, Office of the Press Secretary. July 7, 2016. https://www.whitehouse.gov/blog/2016/07/07/president-obama-fatal-shootings-alton-sterling-and-philando-castile.

"President Obama on Freddie Gray's Death: 'This is Not New, and We Shouldn't Pretend that It's New.'" The White House, Office of the Press Secretary. April 28, 2015. https://www.whitehouse.gov/blog/2015/04/28/president-obama-freddie-gray-s-death-not-new-and-we-shouldn-t-pretend-it-s-new.

"Press Briefing by Press Secretary Josh Earnest, 7/23/2015." The White House, Office of the Press Secretary. July 23, 2015. https://www.whitehouse.gov/the-press-office/2015/07/23/press-briefing-press-secretary-josh-earnest-7232015.

"Remarks by President Obama and Prime Minister Abe of Japan in Joint Press Conference." The White House, Office of the Press Secretary. April 28, 2015, https://obamawhitehouse.archives.gov/the-press-office/2015/04/28/remarks-president-obama-and-prime-minister-abe-japan-joint-press-confere.

"Remarks by the President on Trayvon Martin." The White House, Office of the Press Secretary. July 19, 2013. https://www.whitehouse.gov/the-press-office/2013/07/19/remarks-president-trayvon-martin.

Salim, Jason. 25 July 2016, 4:45 p.m. Facebook post.

Sexton, Jared. *Amalgamation Schemes: Antiblackness and the Critique of Multiracialism*. Minneapolis: University of Minnesota Press, 2008.

Smiley, Calvin John, and David Fakunle. "From 'brute' to 'thug:' The demonization and criminalization of unarmed Black male victims in America." *Journal of Human Behavior in the Social Environment* 26, no. 3–4 (2016): 350–366.

"Statement by the President on the Shootings in Baton Rouge, Louisiana." The White House, Office of the Press Secretary. July 17, 2016, https://www.whitehouse.gov/the-press-office/2016/07/17/statement-president-shootings-baton-rouge-louisiana.

United States Department of Justice Civil Rights Division. Investigation of the Seattle Police Department. December 16, 2011. https://www.seattle.gov/Documents/Departments/Council/Members/Harrell/DOJ/2012-01usdoj_spd_report.pdf.

United States Department of Justice Civil Rights Division. Investigation of the Cleveland Police Department. December 4, 2014. https://www.justice.gov/sites/default/files/opa/press-releases/attachments/2014/12/04/cleveland_division_of_police_findings_letter.pdf?wpisrc=nl-wonkbk&wpmm=1.

United States Department of Justice Civil Rights Division. Investigation of the Ferguson Police Department. March 4, 2015. https://www.justice.gov/sites/default/files/opa/press-releases/attachments/2015/03/04/ferguson_police_department_report_1.pdf.

United States Department of Justice Civil Rights Division. Investigation of the Baltimore City Police Department. August 10, 2016. https://assets.document cloud.org/documents/3009376/BPD-Findings-Report-FINAL.pdf.

Wacquant, Loïc. "From Slavery to Mass Incarceration: Rethinking the 'Race Question' in the United States." *The Globalization of Racism* (2006): 94–110.

Walsh, Deirdre, Manu Raju, Eric Bradner, and Steven Sloan. 2016. "Democrats End House Sit-in Protest Over Gun Control." *CNN Politics.* June 24. http://www.cnn.com/2016/06/22/politics/john-lewis-sit-in-gun-violence/.

"Will Smith: 'Racism Isn't Getting Worse, It's Getting Filmed.'" *TheGrio.* August 01, 2016. http://thegrio.com/2016/08/01/will-smith-racism-isnt-getting-worse-its-getting-filmed/.

CHAPTER FOURTEEN

HBCUs and Activism in the Post-Obama Era

Felecia Commodore and Robert T. Palmer

Barack Hussein Obama being elected the 44th president of the United States of America marked the beginning of a historic era in U.S. History. As the first African American president, there were many expectations laid at the president's feet. Simultaneously, the election of Barack Obama sparked an ongoing conversation regarding race relations, racism, and identity politics to come to the forefront of the American consciousness. This conversation, along with other events, caused a seemingly renewed interest in historically Black colleges and universities (HBCUs). Though some focused on President Obama's relationships with HBCUs, others focused on the role that HBCUs played and continue to play in the activism and calls to action within Black communities specifically, and larger society as a whole. This chapter explores the role of HBCUs in activism both before and during the Obama era; the way in which campus constituencies engage with identity politics; and the future of the HBCU activism and community engagement after the Obama era.

History of HBCUs and Activism

Founding and Pre–Civil Rights Era

HBCUs were primarily founded during the Reconstruction era to educate newly freed American slaves. Though admissions practices at the institutions were never limited to just Blacks, the primary focus of the
institutions was the education and uplift of Black Americans. However,
there existed various philosophies regarding why and what type of education was best for Black Americans. Three major groups were important
in the early founding of HBCUs: White missionary groups, industrial philanthropists, and Black church organizations, although there are exceptions such as the Freedman's Bureau in Washington, D.C., and their
founding of Howard University. White missionary groups were often
inspired to found institutions for Black Americans that not only provided
them with a formal education but also provided them with a moral education that they felt necessary after being enslaved. There was a benevolent
racist perspective that in order to be productive and moral citizens, Black
Americans needed to be indoctrinated with White Christian morality so
as not to enter society as depraved beings. Industrial philanthropists often
felt that Black Americans needed to go to school to learn a trade or how to
work so that they could contribute to the economic well-being of themselves and the country. However, considering the country's economic infrastructure was built on the foundation of slavery, this seemed a way to
keep the economy stable while still capitalizing on the work of Black bodies. Black Christian groups such as the African Methodist Episcopal (AME)
Church and the African Methodist Episcopal Zion (AMEZ) Church saw
an opportunity exhibit collective power by pooling congregants' monies
and manpower to found institutions that were for the education of Black
people and created for Black people. These institutions became symbols
of Black empowerment. There was also a second wave of HBCUs founded
due to the Second Morrill Act. These land-grant HBCUs also aided in the
educating of Black Americans, particularly in the area of agriculture and
mechanics.

The founding of these institutions, particularly those founded by Black
groups, were activist moments within themselves. At the time, the self-
determination and self-empowerment of Black persons pooling enough
capital to provide Blacks with access to higher education was a radical
movement. There are also many great Black philosophers and social leaders who arose from the academic and administrative halls of HBCUs during this time. W.E.B. Du Bois, Cora Calhoun, Mary Church Terrell, Anna

Julia Cooper, and Booker T. Washington all pushed for the empowerment of Black people in the United States. These included participating in marches for the economic advancement of Black persons; uplift through education for Black communities; and for Black women's right to vote and have access to quality jobs and lives. Even in the early years of their foundation, HBCUs were wombs of activism and served as places where Black leaders could gather, plan, and aggregate in order to organize and fight injustices occurring to Black communities.

Civil Rights Era

Activism has always been at the core of the DNA of historically Black colleges and universities. Steeped in racial uplift, HBCUs have produced strong and valiant leaders who fought to advance the civil rights of Black Americans during the Civil Rights Movements. For example, in the 1960s, the Student Nonviolent Coordinating Committee (SNCC) was founded on the campus of Shaw University. Interestingly, SNCC, which was formed by Ella Baker, started as a conference but grew into a larger organization that had an important impact on the Civil Rights Movement. HBCUs have nurtured and produced other charismatic leaders, from Dr. Martin Luther King Jr., to Stokely Carmichael and Thurgood Marshall, all of whom played an integral role in fighting for equity *for Black* Americans.

HBCUs being places from which activist movements were born would not end. During the late 1950s through the early 1970s, HBCUs continued to be places where students could anticipate in activism and social justice. The U.S. Civil Rights Movement kicked off around 1958 and centered on dismantling the Jim Crow laws of the South as well as attaining equal rights and economic opportunities *for Black* Americans and ending segregation. HBCU campuses and their students were central fixtures in the movement.

Some of the most influential moments in the Civil Rights Movement were the Greensboro sit-ins. The Greensboro sit-ins were a series of civil disobedience protests in 1960 in Greensboro, North Carolina. The sit-ins were instrumental in bringing media attention to the movement and issues of segregation in the South. The four students, commonly known as the "Greensboro Four," who initiated the sit-ins were students at North Carolina A&T University. The four students kicked off a steady stream of students participating in the sit-ins, including more students from A&T and young women from Bennett College. This student led movement eventually led to the formation of the Student Nonviolent Coordinating Committee (SNCC).

The SNCC was a very important organization in the Civil Rights Movement. Some would argue that the SNCC was the organization that was able to bring Black persons from different generations and class levels together to work collaboratively toward ending Jim Crow laws and segregation. SNCC grew from a meeting organized by Shaw University student, Ella Baker. SNCC grew exponentially during the Civil Rights Movement, even gaining supporters from the North. SNCC was a major force in various sit-ins as well as the Freedom Rides. SNCC's strength came from its ability to provide a steady stream of volunteers. Many of these volunteers were students from HBCUs. Ella Baker was one example of HBCU student organizers who emerged during the movement. From the late 1950s to the early 1970s, a number of Black activists would emerge from HBCU campuses. Diane Nash, Martin Luther King Jr., Jesse Jackson, Bayard Rustin, John Lewis, Stokely Carmichael, and Marian Wright Edelman were all notable players in the Civil Rights Movement. They were all also alumni of HBCUs. HBCUs, having missions that were central to the empowerment and uplift of Black people, created environments that often encouraged students to take on leadership roles and fight against racial injustice. Though this was the case at many schools, there were a number of HBCUs that were not always as supportive of students engaging in the very public protests. Some HBCUs had conservative campus environments and frowned upon students being involved in protests, and they would even expel students who were involved or arrested due to protest participation. This theme would present itself repeatedly throughout various eras. However, for the most part, HBCUs not only produced great Civil Rights leaders and activists but also became safe spaces for student activists and protesters to gather. In essence, without HBCUs much of the Civil Rights Movement would not only not have existed but, lacking HBCUs to serve as incubators of thought, meeting spaces, and protest training facilities, may have been stagnant in growth. It was not merely HBCU students who were a part of the movement, but also the institutions themselves.

Post—Civil Rights Era to Obama

There is question as to whether, post desegregation, HBCUs continued to be forces and fixtures within the activism sphere. The answer is yes. On HBCU campuses, you could find protests regarding the U.S. involvement in the Vietnam War, the women's liberation movement, battling apartheid in South Africa, and a host of other issues. Though HBCUs had student activists, the activism that occurred on the campuses of HBCUs provided a platform for the voice of Black student activists and their unique intersectional experience to be heard. Though legal desegregation had occurred, Black students at HBCUs, as many Black students across the nation, experienced racism and social injustices that would provoke them to respond in protest. Student protesters at both South Carolina State University and Jackson State University were killed by police. Not covered as widely as the infamous Kent State University shootings, these campuses' students were responding to the U.S. involvement in the Vietnam War, state-sanctioned violence, and violence against Black bodies in particular.

Just as it was during the Civil Rights era, there were some campuses that continued to push a conservative tone and nature to their institution, and protesters and agitators were not encouraged, but at times discouraged and asked to leave the campus. HBCUs also had a new challenge to face after the dawn of desegregation. With institutions opening their doors to Black students being admitted, HBCUs had to put more time and energy into enrollment management and recruitment to compensate for the hemorrhaging of prospective Black students to predominantly White institutions (PWIs). "Numerous colleges and universities initiated measures to promote racial access and diversity."[1] Enrollment patterns for Black students began to change in response to these efforts. Landmark court cases, such as *DeFunis v. Odegaard* and *Bakke v. the Regents of the University of California* also aided in this enrollment trend occurring. Coupled with this, state and federal government funding would begin to pour more resources into PWIs that would actively recruit Black students and continue to exacerbate the funding inequalities between PWIs and HBCUs. For some institutions, the tenuous funding environments made HBCU leadership hypervigilant about avoiding situations that held the possibility of scaring away investors or upsetting influential board members or state legislators. However, in the late 1980s and during the 1990s, there appeared to be a resurgence of the Pan-African movement in many Black communities. With this resurgence came a greater interest in where Black persons invested and to what companies they gave their money. HBCU students even protested the practice of apartheid in South Africa, likening it to the Jim Crow era many of their parents had experienced. Therefore, though some HBCUs were still hotbeds of highly visible student activism, some HBCU campuses became quiet and calm in the area of student activism.

HBCU Activism in the Obama Era

The Obama Administration placed a variety of issues at the forefront of their social and political agendas. The presence of the administration also conjured up various discussions around race and class that had been bubbling under the surface of conversations of a postracial America. Issues such as college affordability, police brutality against Black bodies, and equal rights for lesbian, gay, bisexual, transgender, and queer (LGBTQ) communities found themselves central to much political and social commentary. HBCU campuses followed suit. Mike Brown's murder in Ferguson, Missouri, sparked a renewed fire under the Black Lives Matter movement that had been in existence since 2004. It also sparked a discussion regarding spaces where Black bodies could be honored and sacred. These discussions brought an increased attention to the value of HBCU environments for Black bodies and Black minds.

Since the era that birthed the Civil Rights Movements, many have claimed activism among college students in general, and those attending HBCUs specifically have quelled over the years. These individuals contend that college students have abandoned the spirit of activism in pursuit of focusing on activities that will polish up their résumés and give them a competitive edge in the workforce. However, since Obama became president of the United States, the spirit of activism seems to have rejuvenated. This is particularly palpable across college campuses in general and those at HBCUs specifically. For example, during the academic year of 2015–2016, college campuses, such as University of Missouri, Harvard, Princeton, and Brown—to name a few—have been replete with students protesting issues of racism, microaggressions, and other forms of oppression.

Although students at HBCUs have protest in solidarity with their peers at the aforementioned institutions, at HBCUs activism among students has been linked to the discriminatory and oppressive treatment of Blacks in the United States more generally. For example, the genesis of the Black Lives Matter movement is linked to the fact that the American justice system as well as White police officers have demonstrated little regard for Black lives. On far too many occasions, Black Americans, particularly young Black boys and men, have been killed for no justification by White police officers, and these individuals are not held accountable by the justice system, undergirded by a system of White supremacy. The Black Lives Matter movement is an attempt by Black and Brown Americans frustrated with the system of injustice to give voice to police brutality and the systematic, modern-day lynching of Black Americans. The current Black Lives Matter movement has roots in the campuses of HBCUs. Representatives from the Black Lives Matter movement have pointed out that Phillip Agnew, an alumnus of Florida Agricultural and Mechanical University (FAMU), has been a key leader in this movement. During his years at FAMU, Agnew became quite engaged in community activism after learning that a 14-year-old boy died in Florida while in police custody. This event, and others like it, served as the impetus for Agnew to become engaged in activism in order to use his voice to make a positive difference in his community. Faculty, staff, and students at other HBCUs have been energized by the Black Lives Matter movement. This energy has manifested in these individuals holding sit-ins and demonstrations on their campuses to indicate their unity and support for the Black Lives Matter movement. For example, at the end of the 2015 fall semester, students, faculty, and staff participated in an on campus sit-in at Howard University to signify their support with the Black Lives Matter movement and the social issues that it represents.

Although HBCUs helped to birth the Black Lives Matter movement, students at HBCUs have held protest in recent times to call attention to other issues, such as the treatment of the LGBTQ students at HBCUs as well as sexual assault issues against Black women on campus.

Given that the Black church played a critical role in the establishment of HBCUs, like a number of churches, a number of HBCUs are conservative. While conservatism is manifested in range of ways it HBCUs, it is particularly palpable in the ways in which faculty interact with students and the treatment of LGBTQ students on the campuses of some HBCUs. For example, in 2002, on the campus of Morehouse College, Gregory Love, a gay student, was repeatedly hit over the head with a bat by Aaron Price because Price alleged that Love tried to look at him in the shower. This incident of gay bashing made national news and highlighted a subculture of homophobia that was present on the campus of Morehouse. Interesting, and unfortunately despite the fact that Love was beaten severely by Price, many students at Morehouse felt that Love got what he deserved because he violated Price's "privacy as a man."

Moreover, in 2007, Robert M. Franklin, then president of Morehouse, emphasized the importance of students conducting themselves according to "five wells"—to be well read, well spoken, well traveled, well dressed, and well balanced.[2] The notion of students being well dressed became controversial when more specificity revealed that in order to be considered well dressed, students had to adhere to an appropriate attire policy. According to Jaschik, some gay students were displeased with the attempts by the historically all male college to regulate student dress, particularly the banning of wearing women's attire. Although gay students felt that Morehouse had strived to improve campus life for gay students under Franklin's presidency, many were bothered by the college's dress code because it inhibited their sense of self-expression and robbed them of the ability to feel unique. It is important to note that although we have used Morehouse College as an example to depict the conservative culture of HBCUs, which manifest into oppressive, homophobic, and discriminatory environments for LGBTQ students, Morehouse is not the only HBCU where conservatism has spurred homophobia and stigmatization. This culture exists across many HBCU campuses because of their founding and connection with the Christian churches. The conditions for LGBTQ students at HBCUs have improved somewhat due to students and other stakeholders calling attention to and raising awareness of the unfair treatment LGBTQ students experience at these institutions. For example, in her keynote address at the HBCU Student Success Summit, an event organized by the Association of Public and Land-Grant Universities, Sharon Lettman-Hicks, executive director for the National Black Justice Coalition, encouraged HBCU presidents to be more proactive in eliminating bias against LGBTQ students on their campuses; however, she touted that HBCUs had made some progress on this issue. She, as well as others, has noted that some HBCUs now have safe zones and resources centers for their students. In fact, Bowie State University in Maryland was the first HBCU to open a center—the Gender and Sexual Diversities Resource Center—for LGBTQ students and their allies. Although North Carolina Center University is the second HBCU to implement a LGBTQ Research Center, a range of HBCUs, such as Howard University, Morgan State University, John C. Smith, and Norfolk State University, have established safe spaces for LGBTQ students. For a list of additional HBCUs that provide a safe space for LGBTQ students, please consult https://www.campuspride.org/resources/outreach-to-historically-black-colleges-universities. Aside from using students' voices, in the form of protest, to call attention to the plight of LGBTQ students on campus, students at HBCUs have also used their voices to address issues of sexual assault against Black women at Black colleges. In her seminal book *Blacks in College: A Comparative Study of Students' Success in Black and White Institutions*, Fleming asserted that HBCUs are male-dominated environments. Despite the fact that on many HBCU campuses today, the number of female students outweigh the number of males,[3] and female students are reportedly more engaged on campus than their male counterparts,[4] it may be somewhat questionable if Fleming's assertion still holds true today. However, when perusing the literature on HBCUs, it became clear that her supposition still holds weight. For example, in 2014, Robert R. Jennings, then president of Lincoln University of Pennsylvania, questioned the motives of female students who alleged that they had been raped by a fellow student. Specifically, he said, while speaking to students at a public forum, "We have, we had, on this campus last semester . . . three cases of young women who after having done whatever they did with young men and it then it didn't turn out the way they wanted it to turn out, guess what they did. They then went to Public Safety and said, 'He raped me.'"

Rightfully, his comments sparked outrage not only throughout the higher education community, but throughout society at large. His deplorable comments essentially made it less safe for women at Lincoln University to report issues of sexual assault because their claims may be viewed as frivolous. Jennings' comments galvanized students, faculty, and staff on HBCU campuses into taking action on social media, on campus, and through other outlets to vent their frustrations and voice their concerns. Although the Board of Trustees at Lincoln University initially stood behind him, due to mounting pressure, Jennings resigned from the presidency on November 24, 2014. More recently, another female student at Spelman College reported being raped by four male students at Morehouse College. The student, a freshman at Spelman, indicated that she went to a party and went upstairs to the bathroom to throw up. When she opened the bathroom, she was surrounded by four men, who took her in a different room and raped her. The student shared that she went to Public Safety on campus to file a police report, but that it took officials at Spelman a month to contact her. In fact, the student alleged that when the dean and public safety officer contacted her, they questioned her about her attire on the night she was raped, and the dean suggested that the student should give the male students a pass because Spelman and Morehouse are brother and sister institutions. At this juncture, both the presidents of Spelman and Morehouse have issued statements about this incident of rape and have promised to conduct a thorough investigation. Although it is not clear what changes will manifest from this case of sexual assault, what is clear is that the case has garnered attention because of students, faculty, and staff using their voices on social media and on campus to foster a campus environment at HBCUs that will take issues of sexual assault against women more seriously. Overall, the spirit of activism has resurged at HBCUs, and through the use of social media, that activism has the ability for those off campus or on other HBCU campuses to buy in. In fact in a survey administered by to HBCU students, a large percentage of students receive their news via Internet sources and social media. In the same way that their predecessors of the Civil Rights Movement used the media to get the larger public to buy in to the movement, current HBCU students have used social media to do the same.

HBCUs are finding that their students are banding together to fight against larger injustices such as politic brutality and the political and economic disenfranchisement of Black persons; they are also finding subgroups of students banding over other shared issues as well. The argument that HBCU campuses lack diversity can be quelled by simply looking at the variety of issues that students are addressing, issues with which they often share an identity. The rise of the role of identity politics in various spheres during the Obama administration had an impact on college campuses, HBCUs included. HBCUs saw their share of demonstrations regarding issues salient to certain subgroups of students; these issues include women's rights, sexual assault and rape, equal rights for non-Christian groups, and the treatment of LGBTQ students. Though a majority of HBCU students may share in Black identity, there are a variety of additional intersections at which students identify. One could argue that it is because of the critical mass of Black students that students are able to become more sensitive to the issues unique to their intersectional experience. This also means that, moving forward, HBCU campuses should be prepared to address not only issues that are unique to Black students but also issues at the intersections of their students' identities.

Future of HBCU Activism

The millennial college student is different from the students in prior generations. Whereas previous generations attended college to "find their purpose," millennials are often attending college for a specific purpose.[5] College has become more of a good to purchase as opposed to an experience. HBCU students are not necessarily different. A majority of HBCUs serve student bodies that are primarily low-income, first-generation college students. However, it is the unique HBCU context that aids in the development of a racial and community responsibility through a culturally sensitive curriculum and institutional mission of uplift. The Obama era brought about a brutally honest conversation regarding race in the United States. Specifically, questions were raised regarding where were the spaces for Black men, women, and youth to feel both safe and free. The HBCU rose as the academic alternative space for students who do not find places of acceptance on the campuses of PWIs. In creating an alternative academic and social space for Black college students, HBCUs simultaneously create places where Black students can engage their full selves with their institution. One of the ways in which students can do this is through participating in student activism and community engagement.

Moving into the next lifespan of HBCUs, the question becomes whether the spirit of activism and community engagement will continue on HBCU campuses. And if this activism continues, what will it look like? Because of a mission of uplift, especially for disenfranchised persons, HBCUs are bound to continue to be places where students speak out against oppressive systems. "For many Blacks, and other racial or ethnic minorities, gaining an education, especially at the collegiate level, is a struggle fought on a cultural battlefield of ideological, economic, and social landmines that they feel they have little power to influence."[6] However, if the Black Lives Matter movement and other recent movements at HBCUs are indicators, the next wave of activism at HBCUs will focus heavily on issues central to the intersectional identities of Black students. Students will not only address issues centered on Blackness; as they become more engaged at the intersections of their identities, it is possible that students' activist patterns will follow. An increased visibility of students grappling with public issues around Black LGBTQ communities, Black women's issues, and issues at the intersection of race and class are to be expected. HBCUs that are heavy in conservatism may find this activism turning inward toward the institution. It is reminiscent of the Howard sit-in in 1968, and it will be interesting to see how students will challenge their own institutions' policies and administrative practices regarding students and students' identities. Identity politics became an integral part of common discourse during the Obama era. It will be important to see what the next administration's influence will be on discourse and activism.

Though HBCU activism is still alive, it is important to note that a few programs have taken the initiative to take their activism and social justice movements to the surrounding communities. Through their "We Are Not Trash" campaign; organic farming to aid with the community's food desert issue; and engaging with city protests in Dallas are all ways in which Paul Quinn College used its spirit of social justice spirit to better not only their campus and students but the communities around them. We also see movements such as the Freedom Fighters at Florida A&M University, collectively fighting against police brutality. Moving forward, it will be important for HBCUs not only to remain active but to ensure their activity is benefitting the communities surrounding them and the communities that support them. Post–Obama era HBCU activism will continue the great legacy of HBCU activism. However, how that legacy will be exercised may be much different from activism as it is currently known. Furthermore, the activist spirit must continue past the sparks ignited during the Obama administration. HBCU students appear to be taking those sparks and ignite fires of their own.

Notes

1. Thelin, 2004, p. 348.
2. Jaschik, 2009.
3. Palmer and Gasman, 2008, pp. 52–70.
4. Harper et al., 2004.
5. Sasso, Dayton, and Rosseter, 2015, pp. 315–330.
6. Giles, 2008, p. 118.

Bibliography

Allen, Walter R., Joseph O. Jewell, Kimberly A. Griffin, and De'Sha S. Wolf. 2007. "Historically Black Colleges and Universities: Honoring the Past, Engaging the Present, Touching the Future." *The Journal of Negro Education,* 76(3): 263–280.

Badejo, Anita. 2016. "Our Hands Are Tied Because of this Damn Brother-Sisterhood Thing." Buzzfeed, January 21. Retrieved from https://www.buzzfeed.com/anitabadejo/where-is-that-narrative?utm_term=.ycV4JEz VaB#.bm8ZNOL192.

Bennet, DeShaun, 2016. "5 HBCUs with LGBTQIA Support Initiatives," Center for MSIs Monday Morning MSI Lineup, February 22. https://msilineup.com/2016/02/22/5-hbcus-with-lgbtqia-support-initiatives/.

Davis, Janel, and Shannon McCaffrey. 2016. "Morehouse Joins Spelman Investigating Rape Allegations." *The Atlanta Journal & Constitution,* May 5. http://www.ajc.com/news/news/spelman-investigating-rape-allegation-involving-mo/nrGgr/.

Fleming, Jacqueline. 1984. *Blacks in College: A Comparative Study of Students' Success in Black and White Institutions.* San Francisco: Jossey-Bass.

Gasman, Marybeth, and Felecia Commodore. "HBCUs: A History and Future of Preparing Activist Leaders." *HBCU Lifestyle,* December 16. http://hbculifestyle.com/hbcu-activist-leaders/.

Giles, Mark S. 2008. "Race, Social Justice, and the Jackson State University Shootings." In Marybeth Gasman and Chris Tudico, eds. *Historically Black Colleges and Universities: Triumphs, Troubles, and Taboos* (105–120). New York: Palgrave, 2008.

Harper, Shaun R., Robert M. Carini, Brian K. Bridges, and John C. Hayek. 2004. "Gender Differences in Student Engagement among African American Undergraduates at Historically Black Colleges and Universities." *Journal of College Student Development,* 45(3): 271–284.

Harper, Shaun R., and Marybeth Gasman. 2008. "Consequences of Conservatism: Black Male Undergraduates and the Politics of Historically Black Colleges and Universities." *Journal of Negro Education,* 77(4): 336–351.

Howe, Neil, and William Strauss. 2000. *Millennials Rising: The Next Great Generation.* New York: Vintage Books.

Jaschik, Scott. 2009. "What the Morehouse Man Wears." *Inside Higher Ed,* October 19. https://www.insidehighered.com/news/2009/10/19/morehouse.

Jaschik, Scott. 2014. "A President's Comments on Rape." *Inside Higher Ed,* October 11. https://www.insidehighered.com/news/2014/11/10/debate-over-university-presidents-comments-rape.

Johnston, Angelina Rae, and Robinson Wise. 2013. "Faithful Slaves and Black Confederates, pt. 4." Publishing the Long Civil Rights Movement. https://lcrm.lib.unc.edu/blog/.

Khosrovani, Masoomeh Dokhi, and Howard Beeth. 2008. The Opinions of African American College Students about U.S. Politics and Political Culture in the Early 21st Century: A Survey in One HBCU. Presented at the National Association of African American Studies Conference. February. Baton Rouge, LA.

Kingkade, Tyler. 2014. "College President Claims Women Lied About Rape When It Didn't Turn Out the Way They Wanted." *Huffington Post*, October 11. http://www.huffingtonpost.com/2014/11/10/lincoln-university-rape_n _6133672.html.

Monroe, Irene. "Can a Morehouse Man Be Openly Gay?" 2009. *Religious Dispatches*, July 3. http://religiondispatches.org/can-a-morehouse-college-man-be-openly-gay/.

Palmer, Robert, and Marybeth Gasman. 2008. ""It Takes a Village to Raise a Child": The Role of Social Capital in Promoting Academic Success for African American Men at a Black College." *Journal of College Student Development*, 49(1): 52–70.

Patton, Lori D. 2011. "Perspectives on Identity, Disclosure, and the Campus Environment Among African American Gay and Bisexual Men at One Historically Black College." *Journal of College Student Development*, 52(1): 77–100.

Richen, Yoruba. 2014. "HBCUs responds to a Call for Greater Inclusion of LGBT Students." *The Root*, September. http://www.theroot.com/articles/culture/ 2014/09/hbcus_respond_to_a_call_for_greater_inclusion_of_lgbt_ students/.

Sasso, Pietro A., Blair Dayton, and Stephanie Rosseter. 2015. "A Generation Divided: An In-Depth View of Millennial Students." In Pietro A. Sasso and Joseph L. DeVitis, eds. *Today's College Students* (315–330). New York: Peter Lang.

"The State of LGBTQ Issues at Historically Black Colleges and Universities." 2012. Campus Pride. Last modified October 12. https://www.campuspride.org/ resources/outreach-to-historically-black-colleges-universities/.

Thelin, John R. 2006. *A History of American Higher Education*. Baltimore: Johns Hopkins University.

Watson, Jamal. 2014. "HBCUs Challenged to Address LGBT, Diversity Issues." *Diverse Issues*, June 19. http://diverseeducation.com/article/65075/.

Wong, Alia, and Adrienne Green. 2016. "Campus Politics: A Cheat Sheet." *Atlantic*, April 4. http://www.theatlantic.com/education/archive/2016/04/campus -protest-roundup/417570/.

CHAPTER FIFTEEN

Standardized Testing, Teacher Accountability, and the School Choice Debate

Nicole McZeal-Walters

Those occupying positions of responsibility and leadership in today's schools have never been without critics or challenges to keep up with today's standards for measuring student achievement and developing strong reform efforts. Educational leaders have been encouraged to be more resourceful with data-driven decision-making, demonstrate even more accountability with teacher evaluation, evidence more political savvy, and provide parents with knowledge about their school options as these relate to their children. Most of these expectations are rooted in the predictable wisdom that education is cyclical, no matter who is at the helm in policy leadership, and that many of the reform efforts of yesteryear are just as prevalent today.

President Barack Obama's presidency changed that narrative and flipped the script with this line of thinking as he worked to gain authentic bipartisan support to ensure each child in America received a quality education. President Obama's legacy furthered the belief that the full academic potential of every child could be reached if the American society allotted the right of nonbiased education, eliminating the socioeconomic and racial divide within today's schools.

At this moment in our country, the decisions our policy leaders make about education over the next years will shape our future for generations to come and will undoubtedly prove to be challenging as the instructive landscape has changed, with many innovations and options readily available. President Obama's administration has been committed to meeting such challenges with the leadership and judgment that today's educators on the state and national level need. We would be remiss if we didn't discuss major educational and political constructs that merit serious consideration that have impacted President Obama's educational policy and will continue to engage such future issues.

Standardized testing, the belief in accountability for teachers, and providing parents a choice for their child's education have become a ubiquitous part of life for students, teachers, and administrators of public schools. It is no secret that these three constructs are critically discussed and dissected in today's educational circles—education is indeed a prickly topic. Teachers have come under fire for being ill prepared, not being highly qualified, or "teaching to the test." Schools have been forced to answer to constituent groups and substantiate low student achievement and a decaying educational infrastructure.

President Obama historically changed the face of accountability by deciding not to obliterate the No Child Left Behind Act (NCLB) and building on the existing infrastructure by leveraging financial resources, illuminating teachers' performance in the classroom—excellent, fair, or poor—and providing parents with leverage to make the best decision related to school choice for their child. In order to fully understand how the president changed the political landscape as it relates to education, a deeper discussion must trace the historical landscape of NCLB and Race to the Top, and we must take a closer look at standardized testing, including examining whether Americans understand the national and international implications of implementation of standardization (high-stakes testing), teacher effectiveness, teacher accountability, and school choice.

NCLB and President Obama's Race to the Top

In 2003, President George W. Bush signed NCLB, which in effect mandated rigorous testing and district-directed labeling of students who did not pass certain designated tests. If scores were below the indicated passage rate for adequate yearly progress (AYP) for at least two successive years, a campus was labeled as "failing" or "in need of improvement." In 2006, nearly more than a fourth of all public schools throughout the country had an "in need of improvement" label.[1]

Many in education decried NCLB, stating that the goals were unattainable due to students being ill-prepared and that standardized tests were not the only way students could learn. It is an argument well positioned. Those who created the standardized tests relating to NCLB readily concede these kinds of tests measure only a small percentage of information that a student truly knows, and that a better, more holistic assessment uses a variety of authentic methods. NCLB required classroom teachers to decrease curriculum content to ensure students spent time on practicing for tests, including those in special education classes, English as a second language (ESL) classes, and at-risk students. NCLB made no distinction between students who were in schools labeled higher socioeconomically and those considered to be in poverty.

Had NCLB been successful, educators would have resoundingly thrown their continued support behind it; instead, states began introducing new laws and key policies to discard the law. President Obama called on Congress to work evenly to fix the law and to work with states in their reform efforts. In 2007, Congress was set to reauthorize NCLB, but because there was such strong opposition, there was no agreement on how the law would be ratified. In absence of the new bill, President Obama provided nearly $4.4 billion for the Race to the Top initiative in an attempt to promote creativity and additional reform. In 2009, in an effort to continue supporting the growing wave of charter schools, Secretary of Education Arne Duncan announced that $5 billion would be allocated to these schools—regardless of mounting data that students did not do as well as supporters claimed, and oftentimes did worse.[2]

Although NCLB started a national conversation about student achievement, unintended consequences have reinforced the wrong behaviors in public education in America. Public education has been fraught with difficulties, including education leaders and policy makers not taking into account the high number of teachers fleeing the profession in droves; leaders questioning the idea of site-based decision-making for their campuses; and policy makers promoting nonsubstantiated rhetoric.

As states move forward with education reform, it is important to understand the notion that NCLB and Race to the Top were both reform efforts that purported to have rigorous standards and whose aim was to increase the quality of educators in the field. Whether educators, policy makers, and parents agree or not, taking a closer look at how standardized testing continues to impact student achievement, and its correlation to teacher quality and efficacy, is important.

A Closer Look at Standardized Testing . . . Has the Government Backtracked on Its Initial Beliefs?

Once considered a means to assess learning, some educators argue that standardized testing has now become an avenue to retain students, halt teacher tenure, and close schools.[3] Further, they posit that the work of teachers in public schools has shifted from inspiring creativity, divergent thinking, and helping students to reach their full potential, to ensuring that their students perform well on standardized tests.[4] Performance-based school accountability, a vestige of NCLB, is now at the heart of Every Student Succeeds Act of 2015 (ESSA), with teachers' performance subject to heightened scrutiny and students' yearly progress seen as measurable.[5] Croft, Roberts, and Stenhouse (2016) refer to this focus on standardized testing and the debates over teacher accountability as "the perfect storm of education reform."[6] Policy makers must be careful that the education of America's youth is not left behind in their efforts to measure adequate yearly progress on standardized tests.

Questions of whether testing should be used to inform instruction or drive instruction abound. Haertel's "How Is Testing Supposed to Improve Schooling?" poses the question of what are the intended uses and interpretations of test scores,[7] Testing should be used for educational purposes, not for accountability purposes.[8] The results of tests should be used to guide instruction, inform instructional practices, and help teachers to hone in on areas of improvement for individual students. School leadership must help teachers improve their classroom skills and assure them that their performance will be evaluated on all measures taken that impact student performance, including, but not only standardized tests.[9] Teacher evaluations, to be fair, should be based on student performance; however, focusing on the changes in scores from assessment alone is not sufficient. Educational reformers and policy makers must understand that there are indirect effects associated with test results that impact the learning and overall quality of educational programs.

Passage of such laws and initiatives as NCLB, the Race to the Top Initiative, and ESSA is indicative of politicians' belief that the educational system in the United States is badly in need of reform. Indeed, President Obama agreed that students are spending too much time in the classroom taking tests, many of them unnecessary, and has urged education leaders in today's schools to make examinations more meaningful for students. The Obama administration shoulders part of the blame in the high-stakes test environment and agrees that too many tests take away from valuable time students could spend fostering creativity, innovation, and authentically engaging with curriculum material.

The debate has even crossed party lines. Republicans and Democrats alike believe that teachers and schools should be held accountable for the state of American education and that accountability measures should be in place to remove low-performing teachers and close or turn around low-achieving schools. The challenge is agreeing to some consensus on what those measures look like and whom they will truly impact. President Obama, in his best efforts, has shared in his consistent messaging that learning should be fun, and those efforts to curb excessive testing will considerably shift how both parties view the importance of doing what is in the best interest of all children regardless of income and resources.

The best interests of students should not be lost to a continued focus on testing so that there are quantifiable measures of student and teacher performance without regard to creativity, intellectual curiosity, social development, and the rigor of curriculum. Students should be allowed to make mistakes without fear of grade retention. Insisting on quality tests that nevertheless only serve to continue to test students, whether for 1 percent of the instructional time or 20 percent, perpetuates the problem of continued testing, even with the Testing Action Plan the federal government plans to put in place.[10] The testing culture of the United States will not replicate the educational successes of other countries whose academic plans are prioritized differently.

Does the American Public Fully Understand the Implications of Standardized Testing?

A shared belief[11] substantiates that, increasingly, more Americans are concerned about the magnitude of standardized testing, and there is expressed confusion related to how other efforts to support this reform will truly impact our nation's students. Some positions taken in the testing debate have been well informed and considerate, and other times there have been blatant misunderstandings. The Obama administration has made some headway in communication efforts by sharing consistent messaging.

President Obama has attempted to provide additional communication efforts by using social media, notably Facebook, to reach the masses in order to share his administration's efforts to support limiting testing. When both political parties are questioned, there is unequivocal agreement that some measurement must be taken. The assumption has been that testing students' knowledge will provide a mechanism to offer improvement. The circumspect issue is that if students are tested repeatedly and there is no improvement, will the information be used to track students into certain programs or to label intelligence? This is what has occurred throughout America's history, and educators and parents alike have expressed concern. How do we support teachers in fielding their innovation and their own thoughts of how best to support their students' creative thinking in the classroom?

Authentic teaching, alternative assessments, and teacher creativity are left behind with continued focus on high-stakes testing. Additionally, students miss out on a love for learning while teachers lose their joy for teaching. Moreover, what is lost with the focus on testing in reading and math is an integrated curriculum that includes history, government, civics, and the arts, as well as additional support needed for English Language Learners and students with disabilities.[12] Students should not dread going to school or become disengaged with content because they fear its only relevance is its relationship to a test. Teachers should be given some autonomy to meet the needs of their students beyond trying to ensure they pass a test.[13]

Increased testing may not be considered the only vehicle that will lead to improved international competitiveness. Although there have been gains in the number of high school graduates and more available workers for the labor force as a result of high school graduation tests, the current wave of educational reform that has resulted in more testing has not translated into closing the achievement gap between Whites and Blacks, or Whites and Latinos, by a significant degree.[14] Students need the 21st-century skills of innovativeness, communication, and collaboration that cannot be obtained from a standardized test.[15] The success of our students and the future of our nation has to be viewed in a lens other than testing.

Policy makers and education reformers must understand that the education of America's youth is not singularly measured with standardized testing. The needs and interests of students are left behind as schools feverishly compete for grants based on test scores and student rankings.[16] A robust curriculum is certainly left behind as school leaders place greater emphasis on testing in reading and math, with less instructional time provided for other subjects.[17] To survive the perfect storm created by countless education reform efforts, policy makers and reformers must recognize the impact of high-stakes testing and what is left behind with their increased focus on testing and teacher accountability. How can we continue the practice of measuring a teacher's effectiveness solely by scores on a standardized test? What are other countries doing in order to support authentic learning?

What Are Other Countries Doing . . . Are We Keeping up with Standardized Testing and Accountability as Compared to Our International Friends?

Unlike most high-achieving nations, critics debate whether the United States has yet developed a national system of supports and incentives to ensure that all teachers are well prepared and ready to teach all students effectively when they enter the profession.[18] Other countries, such as Finland, have invested resources into providing quality education to their nation's children. Finland, for its small size and staggering record of education success, has been a phenomenon that has inspired and baffled many American parents and educators since Finnish schooling became a topic following the 2010 documentary *Waiting for "Superman."*[19] As confirmed in the documentary, Finland has been in the highest global ranks in literacy and mathematical skills for years—outperforming many other postindustrial countries, including America. The reason dates to the postwar period when Finland first began creating comprehensive schools that would provide a quality, high-level education for poor and wealthy children alike. Finland has also focused on quality teacher preparation, providing free health and dental care, psychological services, and hot meals to all students. In addition, Finland has a required curriculum that is one of the most rigorous and that enables teacher creativity, innovation, and a focus on student learning outcomes.

The transformation of the Finn's education system began over 30 years ago as a significant propellant of the country's economic recovery plan—one that American's have long sought to understand and debate as it relates to resources and implantation. Other countries have loudly questioned our political and economic landscape, but in America, officials continue to attempt to introduce marketplace competition in our public schools. In the most recent years, reformists and philanthropists, such as Bill Gates, have put significant funding behind private-sector ideas, such as vouchers, data-driven curriculum, and school choice (all of which are discussed later), which have nearly tripled in the past decade. President Obama has also bet on this competition and attempted to answer this global question: "How can American schools get education right?" His Race to the Top initiative attempted to do that but still has been fraught with criticism based on the competitive nature of the reform effort.

The Race to the Top initiative invited states to compete for funding (federal dollars), using standardized tests to measure teacher quality; implement some sort of teacher accountability; and promote a philosophy that the international community, including Finland, disagrees with. With the Finns, there are no mandated standardized testing, rankings, comparison and competition among students, or loosened teacher qualifications. Compared to American public schools, the Finns seemed to have "gotten it right" and constantly experiment with new innovations.[20]

Spending time in one fourth-grade classroom, a visitor might observe a warm, mentoring environment where students are free to slouch, wiggle, and even giggle from time to time if that's what they want to do. The teacher, a 36-year-old Finnish man, has been piloting a new innovation with self-assessments, and students are encouraged to write daily accounts of their learning and progress and receive constructive feedback in a meaningful and positive manner. Students are also supported in developing meaningful academic dialogue that is not standardized and test driven, and they are given numerous breaks to go outside to "stretch" and engage in creative, free play.

This is in stark contrast to some of America's public schools, especially those in areas where there are students and families of lower socioeconomic status. Oftentimes, resources are scarce; the school day is designed to leave little opportunity for creativity; there is a strong mandate for standardized curriculum; and the teachers may or may not be highly qualified. In addition, assessments are relegated to what is taught for testing purposes, and outdoor time (or "free time") has been eliminated due to the highly relegated schedule of a near "boot camp," a highly drilled-and disciplined schedule, and a stress-and-fear culture of rigor. What would happen if American schools adopted the Finnish method of a more student-centered, creativity-driven class schedule, and not a watered-down curriculum— the very tenets President Obama has lobbied for and exhorted through his policy issues? How might school educators adapt accountability measures, including the practice of how standardized testing is mandated within education policy? Would standardized tests be a factor in how American educators need to be assessed for effectiveness in the classroom? The need to discuss teacher accountability is significant as we try to scaffold standardized testing in measuring effectiveness.

Should Standardized Testing Be the Sole Indicator of a Teacher's Effectiveness in the Classroom? How Is Teacher Accountability Impacted?

There is a widespread sentiment that standardized testing should be a strong measure of how effective teachers are in the classroom, and should be the number-one factor in their ability to impact student achievement. Supporters indicate it's like comparing apples to apples. If all teachers are held to the same criterion of certain scores on a standardized test, then that should be the same across the board—leading to criteria for judging effectiveness. The Obama administration wants schools to do a better job identifying teacher effectiveness—and to put strong plans into place to identify and remediate those who are ineffective. With the Race to the Top initiative, this has propelled many states to establish systems for evaluating teacher effectiveness and to hold districts accountable for student growth as a significant factor in supporting teacher accountability.[21]

To be eligible, states cannot have laws that prevent teacher evaluations from being tied to student's test scores. Teachers' unions fought hard for those laws; they have long opposed using test results to evaluate teachers. One of the main arguments is that results can sometimes vary. Teachers one year may be rated "highly effective," whereas the next year they are merely "effective"—or worse—even though there are no observable changes in their teaching skills and strategies. But these questions remain: Are teachers held accountable at all? With these "variables," are they inclined to be reflective of their own practices to impact instruction and measure standardized testing as a form of true pedagogical knowledge and skill?

Although it is true that teachers must reflect on their own practices in order to evaluate whether they are meeting the needs of their students, what is "too far" as relates to holding them accountable? Should the failure of a student on a high-stakes test be in some way the fault of a teacher? Should any of the demographic information, limited experiences, or other relatable constructs that students bring to the classroom impact how teachers are evaluated? Many school leaders will say that they hold teachers to high expectations and encourage professional opportunities to promote creative and critical thinking, and those other variables should not matter. Others will say the government-sanctioned testing limits creativity and does not allow teachers to be flexible with the curriculum, and that although we say that we want teachers to be creative, innovative, and have high expectations for learners, this is just lip service, and teacher's effectiveness and accountability is indeed impacted. What does the Obama administration say to such vocal criticism of the debate on the dialogue related to teachers?

Policy advocates of NCLB agree that President Obama's position on the importance of teachers and ensuring they understand their role in impacting instruction is the very reason he consistently shares the message that "the most important factor for success in a student's life is not the color of their skin or the income of their parents, it's the person standing in front of the classroom. America's future depends on its teachers—and they must be highly qualified."[22] President Obama has been candid about his belief that, fundamentally, teachers should be held accountable for providing creativity and innovation in their classrooms—and not teach to a test. He is equally vocal that there should be provisions to ensure standards are in place to hold teachers accountable for teaching the content as designated by local policy. The underlying belief here is that the president supports teachers and school leadership to make decisions for what is best for our children.

Supporting strong teachers and leadership was one of the critical pillars of President Obama's education reform agenda. A significant reform item is that President Obama made it a national priority to ensure that teachers retained their jobs during many state and local budget changes. The Obama administration is fundamentally aware that more needs to be done, and has allocated monies ($30 billion) to prevent teacher layoffs throughout the country. Because the teaching profession has been impacted both by teachers retiring and by those leaving because of increasing disgruntlement over the emphasis still placed on teacher accountability, efforts will need to be made to "prime the pipeline" and embed an understanding that teacher accountability should be considered a positive way to support both students and teachers.

The Importance of "Priming the Pipeline" . . . but First, Why Are So Many Teachers Leaving?

Teacher layoffs and those leaving for early retirement is one consideration, but at the other end of the spectrum, with the advent of at least 1 million teachers retiring within the next five years, serious consideration will need to be given to how we "prime the pipeline" for new talent and how we plan to measure teachers' ability to translate teaching into achievement. Before diving into this discussion, we must answer the question "Why are there fewer individuals entering teacher programs in the first place?" The growing list of concerns for teachers include lack of mentoring (pre-service and new teachers) opportunities, career boredom, more financial prospects for STEM (science, technology, engineering and mathematics) careers, the impact of recession on teacher budgets, discipline issues, and—most often cited—test-based accountability and high-stakes teacher evaluations.[23]

In addition, there is a perceived lack of respect for teachers, with many feeling that they have been turned into the education "fall guys" by policy makers, politicians, and media. President Obama has worked to reverse this portrayal by encouraging local education agencies to offer incentives; working to increase teacher salaries to be competitive nationwide; and employing heavier recruitment of candidates in the STEM areas. The STEM capacity continues to be a growing problem, with many school districts saying there are not enough candidates to teach STEM to increase this workforce. Throw in the fact that there are also individuals who complete teacher preparation programs and then decide that they do not want to teach, creating a full-fledge cause for panic in some of our nation's school districts.

In order to offset some of these issues, school districts have taken to creative methods for "priming the pipeline," including working closely with alternative teacher preparation programs, developing merit-based scholarship programs, and providing additional monies for higher-need subjects. Although some praise this effort, serious concern remains as to whether the decline in enrollment is a short-term occurrence or an omen of decreasing enrollment numbers in the future. In addition, there is pressure on universities to make college more affordable in order to broaden accessibility, and on legislators to expand the federal loan forgiveness program for educators.

As a nod to President Obama's partisan support, the Senate Democrats' Reducing Educational Debt (RED) Act attempts to do just that. The RED Act allows loan borrowers to refinance their federal and private student loans at a lower interest rate.[24] President Obama has made no secret of his desire to make community colleges free, and Democratic lawmakers have been unwavering in their support to hopefully bring more teacher candidates to the profession. Now that we've discussed the individual's reasons for leaving the teaching profession (or not entering it at all), **how** do these relate to methods of "priming the pipeline"? Critics on both sides of the teacher effectiveness debate agree that much work needs to be done on how we recruit, retain, and cultivate teachers who have strong habits of quality instructional practices—and how we explain the importance of them understanding just exactly what teacher accountability means. Over the next 10 years, four practices will impact why this process should be done with fidelity and care:

- A shrinking teaching force
- A growing student population
- A lack of diversity among teachers to match the diversity of students
- A need for teachers in specific types of schools, geographic locations, and subject areas

Incentives to attract, prepare, and support good teachers were presented by President Obama in the form of a grant initiative that would challenge educators and lawmakers alike to work together to strengthen the teaching profession. The aforementioned practices support the impetus that teacher recruitment should continue to be at the forefront for adding new teachers to the profession. The added pressure on teachers to know their content, deliver instruction in an authentic and engaging manner, assess students, and provide additional ongoing support will dictate which teachers successfully remain in the classroom and who will be one of the growing numbers leaving the profession. With the efforts to "prime the pipeline," this will help achieve the goal of continuous improvement within the profession.

President Obama's commitment of his national priority of the federal government's role in providing the best educational resources for the public doesn't just end with the conversation on teacher accountability and the standardized testing focus but also engages the public with matters related to the best choices of school option for children today. With the re-authorization of the *Elementary* and *Secondary Act (ESEA)* opportunities in the form of viable grant sources to encourage educational entrepreneurship to expand such school choice options. Let's take a closer look at what affords school choice.

School Choice . . . Educational Options for Our Nation's Children

The historical milieu related to the origin of America's public schools harkens remembrance of public schooling designed to develop a citizenry-based education to develop future lawmakers, teachers, doctors, and other professionals. Today's public schools seems to have gotten away with this original intent because the common model has been changed with testing to separate and track students in groupings sometimes based on test scores, and subjective attribute.[25] The inequities that oftentimes plague our poorest schools, oftentimes populated with students of color, is one that troubles President Obama as he has called for fair measures in our schools. The Digital Divide, language barriers, overidentification of students of color in special education, and unfair disciplinary practices constitute many reasons parents seek alternative options within the public school offering, and President Obama supports them in doing so. School Choice, quite simply, offers innovation in the best of educating our nation's children—even if this means challenging sometimes pervasive negative assumptions.

Despite what some may think, school choice encompasses much more than the mindset of "leaving the public school behind" or relegating parents to selecting schools only within their zip code. Moreover, it does not mean having private school as the only option to educate their child. School choice includes education savings accounts, online learning, vouchers, home schooling, tax credit scholarship programs and the most popular, charter schools and other high quality public schools (which we will revisit later). As we have discussed standardized testing and teacher accountability, school choice also plays an integral role in national debate across education partisan lines as lawmakers debate the parity of our public school education. Frustrated with the options available to them, parents indicate that there is a lack of viable school choices for their children and that they should be able to exercise their right to an appropriate education. Moreover, many want to send their children to different schools but can't afford to move to school districts where traditional public schools are better for their children—and cannot afford private or parochial schooling. With the reauthorization of ESEA, high-quality public schools and charter schools have become increasingly attractive to parents.

Charter schools are public schools that offer educators the autonomy to operate outside of the local and state laws mandated within the traditional public school setting. The goal of charter schools is to provide parents, community leaders, and key stakeholders the space to innovate and provide students with additional opportunities. Local, state, and other organizations sponsor charter schools and oversee their quality to hold them accountable for academic results and responsible fiscal practices.

Next, other public schools are also a comprehensive choice for parents. According to No Child Left Behind, if a child attends a Title I school

> that has been identified by the state under *school improvement*, corrective action, or restructuring, parents can choose to send the child to another public school that is not identified as under improvement. Districts must let parents know each year if their child is eligible to transfer to another school, and districts must give parents more than one transfer option if more than one exists. Districts must pay for students' transportation costs, giving priority to low-income, low-achieving students if there are not enough funds available to pay for all students.[26]

School choice is a concept that doesn't mean elevating once choice over another, or demonizing our nation's schools. School choice means that there is recognition that children have an opportunity to have their individual needs met by an educational system that cares about their future. We owe it to parents across the country, and more importantly their children, to accelerate the momentum for discussing the viable choices for our children. The Heritage Foundation says it best:

Some people say choice is no silver bullet for improving the American education system. That may be true. But choice creates the conditions necessary to spur schools to implement reforms and strategies that work—or risk losing students and their money. Reforms like performance pay for teachers and the elimination of "social promotion" have positive impacts on student learning. The best schools will embrace initiatives that work in order to provide the best education possible to their students.[27]

President Obama's legacy is one that will be shaped by the shared belief of many that no president has made better influence of historic reforms as they relate to education. By creating a blueprint for reform, he successfully implemented policies that enabled children and families to receive parity within their educational rights. Standardized testing, a belief in accountability for teachers, and providing parents a choice for their child's education allowed states and local government to have a transformative hand in school performance and responsibility for all citizens. The impact of such policies will no doubt have lasting effects as it also gave local jurisdictions more impact over creating sustainable goals, supporting attainable and realistic school ratings, and mediating solutions for struggling schools and teachers. President Obama has created a lasting backdrop that will make schools a place where children can learn, teachers can educate, and parents can be active and informed citizens about the educational process.

Notes

1. Stan Karp, "Band-Aids or bulldozers: What's next for NCLB?" *Rethinking Schools* (2006): 10–13.

2. Zach Miners, "Charter Schools Might Not Be Better," US News, June 17, 2009, www.usnews.com/education/blogs/on-education/2009/06/17/charter-schools-might-not-be-better.

3. Bellamy Foster, "The Opt Out Revolt: Democracy and Education," *Monthly Review: An Independent Socialist Magazine* 67 (2016): 1–7.

4. Mike Rose, "School Reform Fails the Test," *American Scholar* 1, no. 84 (2015): 18–30.

5. Zan Crowder and Stephanie Konle, "Gumbo ya-ya or what a person can't hear: Opt-out," *High School Journal* 98, no 4. (2015): 285–289.

6. Sheryl J. Croft, Mari Ann Roberts, and Vera L. Stenhouse, "The perfect storm of education reform: High-stakes testing and teaching evaluation," *Social Justice* 42, no. 1 (2016): 70–92.

7. Edward Haertel, "How is testing supposed to improve schooling?" *Measurement* 11, no. 1/2 (2013): 1–18.

8. Christopher deVinck, "A failing grade for the notion of more testing," *Education Digest* 80, no. 9 (2015): 27–30.

9. Les Stein, "The art of saving a failing school," *Kapplan* 93, no. 5 (2012): 51–55.

10. Ibid.

11. Ibid.

12. Haley Sweetland Edwards, "Leaving tests behind," *Time* 185, no. 5 (2015): 28–31.

13. Richard Ingersoll, Lisa Merrill, and Henry May, "Do accountability policies push teachers out? Sanctions exacerbate the teacher turnover problem in low-performing schools—but giving teachers more classroom autonomy can help stem the flood," *Educational Leadership* 73, no. 8 (2016): 44–49.

14. Ibid.

15. Güliz Turgut, "International tests and the U.S. educational reforms: Can success be replicated?," *Clearing House* 86, no. 2 (2013): 64–73.

16. Ibid.

17. Ibid.

18. Linda Darling Hammond, *The Flat World and Education* (New York: Teachers College Press, 2010).

19. Davis Guggenheim, Lesley Chilcott, "Waiting for Superman," TakePart, July 2010, http://www.takepart.com/waiting-for-superman.

20. William Doyle, "How Finland Broke Every Rule," The Hechinger Report, February 18, 2016, http://hechingerreport.org/how-finland-broke-every-rule-and-created-a-top-school-system/.

21. U.S. Department of Education, "Race to the Top," June 6, 2016, 2016. http://www2.ed.gov/programs/racetothetop/index.html.

22. Ibid.

23. Ibid.

24. Education News, "#InTheRed, Reducing Educational Debt Act Proposed by Democratic Senators," February 2, 2016, https://www.goodcall.com/news/inthered-reducing-educational-debt-act-proposed-by-democratic-senators-04345.

25. Sonali Kohl, "Modern-Day Segregation In Schools," *The Atlantic*, November 18, 2014, http://www.theatlantic.com/education/archive/2014/11/modern-day-segregation-in-public-schools/382846/.

26. No Child Left Behind.

27. Heritage Foundation, January 28, 2013, http://www.heritage.org/research/reports/2013/01/choosing-to-succeed-choosing-to-succeed.

Bibliography

Croft, Sheryl J., Mari Ann Roberts, and Vera L. Stenhouse. "The perfect storm of education reform: High-stakes testing and teaching evaluation." *Social Justice* 42, no. 1 (2016): 70–92.

Crowder, Zan, and Stephanie Konle. "Gumbo ya-ya or what a person can't hear: Opt-out, standardized testing, and student surveillance." *High School Journal* 98, no 4. (2015): 285–289.

Darling Hammond, Linda. *The Flat World and Education.* New York: Teachers College Press, 2010.

deVinck, Christopher. "A failing grade for the notion of more testing." *Education Digest* 80, no. 9 (2015): 27–30.

Doyle, William. "How Finland Broke Every Rule." *The Hechinger Report.* February 18, 2016. http://hechingerreport.org/how-finland-broke-every-rule-and-created-a-top-school-system/.

Education News. "#InTheRed, Reducing Educational Debt Act Proposed by Democratic Senators." February 2, 2016. https://www.goodcall.com/news/inthered-reducing-educational-debt-act-proposed-by-democratic-senators-04345.

Foster, Bellamy. "The opt out revolt: Democracy and education." *Monthly Review: An Independent Socialist Magazine* 67 (2016): 1–7.

Guggenheim, Davis, and Lesley Chilcott. "Waiting for Superman." *TakePart,* July 2010. http://www.takepart.com/waiting-for-superman.

Haertel, Edward. "How Is Testing Supposed to Improve Schooling?" *Measurement* 11, no. 1/2 (2013): 1–18.

Heritage Foundation. "Choosing to Succeed." January 28, 2013. http://www.heritage.org/research/reports/2013/01/choosing-to-succeed-choosing-to-succeed.

Ingersoll, Richard, Lisa Merrill, and Henry May. "Do Accountability Policies Push Teachers Out? Sanctions Exacerbate the Teacher Turnover Problem in Low-performing Schools—But Giving Teachers More Classroom Autonomy Can Help Stem the Flood." *Educational Leadership* 73, no. 8 (2016): 44–49.

Karp, Stan. "Band-Aids or bulldozers: What's next for NCLB?" *Rethinking Schools* (2006): 10–13

Kohl, Sonali. "Modern-Day Segregation In Schools." *The Atlantic,* November 18, 2014. http://www.theatlantic.com/education/archive/2014/11/modern-day-segregation-in-public-schools/382846/.

Miners, Zach. "Charter Schools Might Not Be Better." 2009. *www.usnews.com/education/blogs/on-education/2009/06/17/charter-schools-might-not-be-better.*

Rose, Mike. "School Reform Fails the Test." *American Scholar* 1, no.84 (2015): 18–30.

Stein, Les. "The art of saving a failing school." *Kapplan* 93, no. 5 (2012): 51–55.

Sweetland Edwards, Haley. "Leaving Tests Behind." *Time* 185, no. 5 (2015): 28–31.

Turgut, Güliz. "International Tests and the U.S. Educational Reforms: Can Success Be Replicated?" *Clearing House* 86, no. 2 (2013): 64–73.

U.S. Department of Education. "Race to the Top." June 6, 2016. Accessed August 6, 2016. http://www2.ed.gov/programs/racetothetop/index.html.

CHAPTER SIXTEEN

Use of Deadly Force: Policing and Accountability during the Obama Administration

Kimberly J. Rice, Keith Boeckelman, and Casey LaFrance

Introduction

While never explicitly embracing the "postracial presidency" narrative that some observers predicted when he took office in 2009, President Obama generally downplayed racial issues, particularly during his first six years in office.[1] There were some exceptions, such as his statement in the aftermath of the Trayvon Martin shooting that if he had a son, he would "look like Trayvon"; but overall, Obama addressed racial issues gingerly, adopting the stance that he was "president of everyone." For example, he avoided speaking about whites' responsibility for black suffering, instead emphasizing African Americans' responsibility for their own problems. As a result, many African Americans have expressed "profound disappoint-ment over the president's refusal to forcefully pursue racial and economic justice policies for his most loyal constituency."[2] Their frustrations range from stalled black economic progress in the wake of the Great Recession to unequal sentencing practices to the police misconduct that is the pri-mary focus of this chapter.

Historians are likely to observe that President Obama's tenure in office has coincided with an awakening global consciousness about appropriate police conduct and the mechanisms that have been developed to foster responsive and accountable policing. The highly publicized shootings of unarmed African American men in Ferguson, Missouri; Staten Island; Cleveland; Chicago; Baltimore; and elsewhere, and the subsequent rise of the Black Lives Matter movement, led Obama to adopt a different approach. After receiving criticism from African Americans, in particular, for not speaking out more forcefully, he attempted to adopt rhetoric and policies more explicitly focused on racial justice. While exercising caution after earlier events, he spoke more powerfully as incidents of police violence against African Americans multiplied. In April 2015, in the wake of Freddie Gray's killing in Baltimore, he warned of a "slow-rolling crisis" in police interactions with black citizens.[3] In the policy realm, he advocated for sentencing guidelines that are less punitive toward African Americans, pushed for funding for body cameras for local police forces, and created a task force to address issues arising between blacks and law enforcement.

That Michael Brown, Freddie Gray, and others have become household names seems almost grimly ironic as we remember the legacy of our first African American head of state. This chapter considers in more depth the Obama legacy on race and the police while also examining possible solutions for increasing police accountability. It begins by introducing scholarship that has explored the multiple accountability considerations that influence police management and discretion. Here we discuss four perspectives on public management and types of accountability: bureaucratic, professional, legal, and political. The chapter then proceeds to examine five highly publicized incidents in five cities where African American men died at the hands of the police: Michael Brown in Ferguson, Missouri; Eric Garner in Staten Island; Laquan McDonald in Chicago; Tamir Rice in Cleveland; and Freddie Gray in Baltimore. We examine how Obama responded through rhetoric and policy, as well as how local and state officials tried to enact accountability measures. We then consider proposed reforms such as increased emphasis on community policing, the results of the task force on 21st Century Policing from the Obama administration, and examine new body camera policies in Baltimore and other cities, as well as other possible institutional changes. Finally, we offer some suggestions for political and law enforcement actors to take advantage of the opportunities presented by this shift in public attention and opinion, and discuss some avenues for future research.

Accountability

The responses to each of the incidents of alleged police brutality all share one common thread: a call for accountability. Whether from the cries of family members, the chants of protesters, the speeches of local or national politicians, or in the spin of the media, every response to these incidents is in some way calling for what each stakeholder considers appropriate accountability. When a person dies wrongfully at the hands of the police, then the officer; the department; and local, state, and even national governing bodies are expected to react. Assessing whether these responses meet standards of accountability is complex, however. Even determining what the concept means is difficult. Research in public administration suggests that there are multiple perspectives on how to achieve accountability, as noted above, including bureaucratic, professional, legal, and political. The specific elements of each approach are detailed below.

Bureaucratic Accountability

Bureaucratic accountability is the orthodox view of accountability. This includes the classic, top-down, command and control features that are paramount to bureaucratic organizations. The theoretical glue used to hold this line of thought in place was born out of a desire to firmly distinguish politics and administration, allowing for a set of universal management principles (POSDCORB, POCCC, Peel's Principles, etc.) to be applied in public sector settings such as policing.[4] David Rosenbloom characterizes this model of public administration as one where the bureaucratic agency focuses its efforts on resolving "cases."[5] Individuals with whom law enforcement might interact then would simply be considered numerically, or as "cases" themselves. This approach simplifies the landscape in which law enforcement takes place and intentionally ignores the contextual nuances of policing areas with different demographic, social, economic, and especially political features.

As a result, it creates a form of accountability that emphasizes following rules, standard operating procedures (SOPs), and orders from upper-level managers in a traditional Weberian hierarchy. Bureaucratic accountability, then, creates a strong, albeit overwhelmingly rigid, organization for police and helps to solidify the role of police management. Bureaucratic accountability, however, may ignore the expertise of subordinates in favor of a more rigid hierarchal approach. This observation, among other potential weaknesses of the bureaucratic approach, leads to the concept of professional accountability.

Professional Accountability

Whereas bureaucratic accountability focuses on the top-down hierarchy and subordinates following superiors, professional accountability focuses on giving "expert employees" the authority to make decisions while also making these experts accountable for any failures.[6] Unlike bureaucratic accountability, then, professional accountability focuses on "deference to expertise within the agency."[7] This focus on expertise is a result of increased education and training that marks a professional approach to management, including policing.

As educational opportunities and training expectations grew, so did the focus on specialization and the emphasis on policing as a profession. Here, we see a similar logic at play in that trained professionals in law enforcement are distinct from the members of the public they serve. Moreover, the use of profession-based credentialing became a common expectation for agencies. In practice, this resulted in the modern phenomenon of policing within one's own profession. For example, today we might notice that the first stage of evaluating an officer-involved shooting or other use of force incident is conducted by law enforcement officers who use their expert power base to deem others unqualified to investigate (or, in many cases, even be present during the course of an investigation).

Still, a rift can readily become apparent when one stops to remember that the emphasis on an officer's individual professional training and expertise has the potential to breed loyalty to the profession at the expense of the organization wherein the professional is employed. Thus, an unintended consequence of this movement toward professionalism and professional accountability is the rampant use of discretionary decision-making among law enforcement officers. Although this is partially explained by the fact that even the most comprehensive SOP manual cannot predict, and thus advise on, every possible permutation of law enforcement encounters that officers experience, one can easily see the value in being granted autonomous decision authority in the course of one's work. Hence, although professional accountability would allow for police officers to utilize their unique training and expertise to evaluate an shooting in which an officer was involved, this could result in increased turmoil between a public that views an entire police force as corrupt and a police force that feels it is best suited to determine when a shooting was or was not justified. When this is the case, as in many of the incidents we describe below, many turn to the courts to attempt to hold officers and the police accountable.

Legal Accountability

A legal perspective of accountability for policing, and public administration more generally, rests on there being a "controlling party outside the agency and members of the organization" that can impose a "legal sanction" and decree some obligation to the agency.[8] Thus, legal accountability is the expectation that the legal system will impose sanctions, whether criminal or civil, when agents violate the law. This theory, however, is complicated by the fact that the courts have adopted a pattern of administrative deference, where judges are more likely to rule in favor of public agents like police. Simply, there is precedent to suggest that judges defer to agency determinations and actions. In fact, if one considers perhaps the most famous case of administrative deference, *Chevron v. NRDC*, we can see the Court actually utilizing the professional approach to public administration. Here, the Court ruled that when an administrative agency, the Environmental Protection Agency (EPA) in this case, has interpreted an ambiguous congressional statute, the agency's interpretation should be deferred to by the court unless that interpretation is unreasonable. The Court, in this landmark case, argued that agencies, as experts, should receive deference from judges, who are not technical experts in all areas of policy. Thus, legal accountability, as an expression of a legal perspective of public administration, has been limited by the judicial institution's own precedent and use of a professional approach.

In addition to the general principle of deference, the courts have also shown great restraint in limiting police use of force, remaining always cognizant of the difficult choices police officers face while attempting to balance individual liberties. A landmark case regarding the police use of force is pertinent here. In *Graham v. Connor*, the Court ruled that any cases dealing with alleged brutality would be analyzed under the Fourth Amendment's provision against unreasonable seizure, versus a substantive due process standard that generally protects an individual's liberty interests from arbitrary governmental intervention. Thus, cases dealing with alleged misconduct in use of force would be analyzed according to whether the office violated the Fourth Amendment rights of the individual, not whether the officer denied basic rights of "life, liberty, or property without due process of law."

In placing all police use of force cases under the Fourth Amendment, the Court requires only that the "objective reasonableness" standard be used to determine if an officer was justified in using force.[9] This, importantly, means that judges and juries need only ask "whether the officer's actions are objectively reasonable in light of the facts and circumstances confronting the officer, without regard to the officer's underlying intent or motivation."[10] This analysis requires the court to consider the totality of circumstances and judge from "the perspective of a reasonable officer on the scene, rather than with the 20/20 vision of hindsight."[11] The Court goes on to say that even evidence of "malicious and sadistic" motivations would be subjective and thus should have no bearing on the Fourth Amendment determination in these cases.[12] This approach to Fourth Amendment violations also considers officers' legal right to "qualified immunity," which protects officers from being held liable if their actions were reasonable. For those who would argue that the current cases of officers shootings of these African American men were motivated in part or full by race, or that the circumstances surrounding the shooting did not warrant the officer's response, this precedent and the reasonableness standard affords little relief, legal or otherwise.

Access to legal accountability measures can also be delayed by the length of time it takes to process a case, or barred completely by jurisdictional or threshold issues like standing to sue or failing to exhaust administrative remedies. Further, as agents of the government, police officers are afforded some measure of qualified immunity, meaning even serious charges, like murder, may be difficult to successfully indict. Importantly, when one seeks to hold a public agent, like police, accountable via the judicial system, the ultimate decision will rest in the hands of judges and juries. As is evident through our discussion of the incidents below, however, when a legal solution is unavailable or denied in cases of alleged brutality, many will turn to elected officials for some redress.

Political Accountability

Political accountability can be viewed as part of a political approach to public administration, which emphasizes "the values of representativeness, political responsiveness, and accountability through elected officials to the citizenry."[13] A political approach, then, focuses on responsiveness as a means to accountability. Elections are the most obvious example, although they are imperfect due to incumbent advantages, timing, and other flaws. Other specific techniques include those that hold bureaucrats responsible to elected officials or the public directly, such as legislative hearings or freedom of information and sunshine laws. Affirmative action or diversity programs that make police agencies more representative of the communities they serve also reflect political accountability, as do efforts to subject police actions to civilian review.

Political accountability is often the most complex to navigate because of the different preferences and values held by community members. To compound this troubling feature of political accountability, one must also remember that agencies can easily find themselves weighing the demands of community members with those of elected officials who provide funding for their respective agencies. Thus, as we discuss in our evaluation of reform efforts later, political accountability to a community whose preferences are ever changing can compound issues with community-based reform efforts. In addition, police departments are paramilitary organizations that are likely to view efforts to impose outside accountability, whether from elected officials or civilians, as undue interference. As a result, politicians seeking police accountability through political means may use public mobilization strategies to overcome resistance to change.

Use of Deadly Force in Five Cities

This section considers the cases of five of the most widely covered incidents of African American men killed by police officers. We begin with the death of Michael Brown in Ferguson, Missouri, and end with the death of Freddie Gray in Baltimore. Here we use the lens of the four types of accountability discussed above to analyze the reactions to each of these incidents and to determine if there are any patterns among the cases.

Michael Brown

Although it did not occur first chronologically, the incident that initially focused widespread public attention on police violence against African Americans took place in August 2014 in Ferguson, Missouri, a suburb of St. Louis. There, African American Michael Brown was shot by a white policeman. Early accounts suggested he was surrendering, although later testimony called that conclusion into question. Protests that sometimes turned into looting, arson, and destruction of buildings occurred in the aftermath of the shooting as well as after the November 2014 non-indictment of the police officer, Darren Wilson, who shot Brown. Unrest also spread to many other U.S. cities. The incident fostered the Black Lives Matter movement, and popularized the expression "hands up, don't shoot," which evoked the initial eyewitness accounts of the Brown shooting that suggested he had his hands in the air. Subsequent protestors, including St. Louis Rams football players, popularized the phrase and attendant gesture.

The grand jury in the case found that there was not sufficient probable cause to charge the officer, Darren Wilson, and that he had acted within the scope of the law regarding the shooting. Here, we see both legal and political accountability attempts; however, given that the grand jury failed to indict the police officer, a perceived failure in legal accountability created an opening for political accountability on behalf of the Obama administration and the Department of Justice (DOJ). After the non-indictment, the U.S. Justice Department pursued a separate investigation against Wilson for civil rights violations but ultimately did not file charges. A broader DOJ investigation of the Ferguson Police Department identified a number of factors that fostered distrust between the police and the community.[14] This study found, for example, that the city relied unduly on fines to generate operating revenue, at the expense of routine taxation, and that racial biases were pervasive in the police and court systems. Broader Constitutional rights were ignored as well. The DOJ study found that the Ferguson Police Department violated the Fourth Amendment through conducting stops without probable cause and using unreasonable force. In addition, it interfered with First Amendment rights, including the right to record and protest police activity, and with Fourteenth Amendment antidiscrimination provisions in its treatment of African Americans. As an example of the latter, 95 percent of the people arrested for jaywalking in Ferguson were African American, even though they accounted for about 67 percent of the population.[15]

Although the grand jury failed to indict Darren Wilson, there have been other attempts to invoke some legal liability. In April 2016, in response to the DOJ findings, a federal judge approved a consent decree that would require Ferguson police to wear body cameras, ensure probable cause, and downplay the use of fines as a local revenue source.[16] Additionally, Michael Brown's family has sued both the officer and Ferguson for wrongful death. The case was removed to federal court in July of 2015. Because civil cases only require a preponderance of evidence to find in the plaintiffs favor, as opposed to a reasonable doubt standard in criminal cases, this will likely be the singular avenue of legal recourse for the family. However, as was noted above regarding legal accountability, legal remedies take time and place the decisions in the hands of the judge or jury, which can limit the scope of the case. For example, in the case of the Michael Brown civil suit, his family's claims were narrowed in 2015 when a federal judge limited the number of claims from seven to three.[17]

Beyond the federal action noted above, local political accountability in Ferguson appears to be a work in progress. Before the Michael Brown incident, despite a population that was two-thirds African American, five of the six city council members were white, and whites accounted for a majority of votes cast in local elections.[18] In the 2015 municipal elections, two new black city council members were elected, bringing the total to three. The newly elected body, however, initially dragged its feet on approving the Justice Department recommendations discussed above, before finally agreeing.[19] At this stage, then, it appears that legal accountability has been more apparent in Ferguson than political or bureaucratic accountability.

Following a pattern that would recur as incidents multiplied, President Obama's tone shifted as he spoke about the matter. In his initial comments on the Ferguson incident, he avoided issues of structural racism, did not mention that the police officer who killed Michael Brown was white, and called for "calm" and "healing."[20] As protests continued, he addressed the racial context more explicitly. For example, he said, "[I]n too many communities around the country, a gulf of mistrust exists between local residents and law enforcement. In too many communities, too many young men of color are left behind and seen only as objects of fear."[21]

Eric Garner

A second African American death at the hands of the police occurred in July 2014, when Eric Garner of Staten Island died after being put in a chokehold by a white officer. Initially this incident received little national attention. That changed when, only about a week after the Ferguson grand jury decision, a New York grand jury decided not to indict the Staten Island officer. The non-indictment, which contradicted the city medical examiner's opinion that the death was a homicide, sparked widespread protests. The unrest shut down traffic and included a failed attempt to stop the tree-lighting ceremony in Rockefeller Center. In the wake of the grand jury's decision, the U.S. Justice Department started a separate investigation to determine if a civil rights violation had occurred. The federal grand jury proceedings began in February 2016. As in the case of Michael Brown, the family of Eric Garner also filed a wrongful death suit, which was settled for $5.9 million in July 2015.

President Obama's initial comments on Garner's choking stressed restoring confidence in law enforcement and treating everyone equally, but he also promised not to "let up" in addressing conflict between African Americans and law enforcement.[22] Later, he appeared on Black Entertainment Television (BET) to discuss the issue. He encouraged peaceful protests, arguing that change happens incrementally, and said, "This is not just a Black problem or a Brown problem, but an American problem."[23] Coming in the wake of his refusal to visit Ferguson, Obama's reaction was criticized as too tepid and equivocal. Later he spoke of a "simmering distrust" between the police and minority communities, and proposed $263 million to pay for a portion of 50,000 body cameras for police.[24] State matching funds would also be used for the program. Unsurprisingly, the proposal became bogged down in Congress, but in May 2015, Attorney General Loretta Lynch announced a smaller $20 million initiative to fund body cameras for local police. Obama also imposed regulations concerning the transfer of surplus military equipment to local police departments and created a task force to reform local police practices, the recommendations of which are analyzed in more depth below.

The local context for political accountability differed in New York from that in Ferguson. Mayor Bill De Blasio ran on a platform of reining in police excesses and has enjoyed strong approval among black voters. At the same time, his relations with law enforcement have been tense, due to the mayor suggesting his biracial son should be afraid of the police, and especially after the highly publicized killing of two officers by a mentally unstable man claiming to avenge Eric Garner and Michael Brown. De Blasio and Police Commissioner William Bratton created a program to improve training and emphasize community policing, reflecting attempts at both bureaucratic and political accountability. Despite this, De Blasio, in September 2016, ordered the Law Department to appeal a judicial ruling that would make disciplinary records of one of the officers public. New York Governor Andrew Cuomo is in favor of making disciplinary records public and also set up a process for the state attorney general to oversee incidents when unarmed civilians are killed by the police.

Laquan McDonald

In October 2014, a white police officer in Chicago fired 16 shots, killing 17-year-old Laquan McDonald while he was running away down the middle of a street. The incident was not highly publicized until the following year when video was released and the officer was charged with murder. The officer, Jason Van Dyke, pleaded not guilty to the charges, and in January of 2016, two other officers, Van Dyke's partner, Joseph Walsh, and the lead detective on the case, David March, whose account of the events is controversially different from the available dashboard video, were taken off their regular assignments and put on desk duty. Although this suggests some internal bureaucratic accountability response, many have criticized the time that it has taken for police and prosecutors to respond. Most recently, the original prosecutor, Anita Alvarez, withdrew from the case in May of 2016, requesting a special prosecutor be assigned to move the case along more efficiently. The family of Laquan McDonald settled with the city for $5 million in April of 2015.

In the wake of protests, Chicago Mayor Rahm Emanuel fired the police chief, Garry McCarthy, and created a Task Force on Police Accountability to investigate the incident as well as the larger issue of police relations with minorities in the city. The panel concluded that police disregard the sanctity of life of people of color and recommended replacing the authority that investigates police misconduct with a "transparent and accountable Civilian Police Investigative Agency."[25] An authority such as this would clearly be in contrast to the professional management approach, which suggests that experts (i.e., other police) are best suited to make these types of determinations. In addition, the panel recommended other bureaucratic changes such as improving recruiting among minorities, reinvigorating community policing, and improving officer training with respect to handling young people. In August of 2016, nearly two years later, the department announced that it would seek to fire the seven officers accused of lying about the shooting. Shortly after, in September 2016, at the request of the special prosecutor, a special grand jury was initiated to explore the possibility of a cover-up. Currently, the U.S. Justice Department is also conducting its own investigation.

President Obama's response to the incident in his adopted hometown reflected his earlier ambivalence. In a Facebook post, President Obama said he was "deeply disturbed" by the footage of the McDonald shooting.[26] He also argued, however, that most police "protect our communities with honor."[27] He said little in defense of his one-time White House Chief of Staff, Mayor Rahm Emanuel, whose popularity has plummeted after the incident. Emanuel does not face an election until 2019, limiting direct political accountability. Nevertheless, he clearly is concerned about the implications of this incident for his political career. In late 2015, he apologized before the city council in response to calls for his resignation as mayor. In June 2016, the city released over 100 videos involving police use of force and promised ongoing transparency, suggesting attempts at bureaucratic and professional accountability.

Tamir Rice

In November 2014, 12-year-old Tamir Rice was shot by a Cleveland police officer while playing with a toy gun. In the aftermath, the U.S. Justice Department released a report on the Cleveland police that had been initiated prior to the shooting that found a pattern of excessive force, including the misuse of deadly weapons, tasers, and pepper spray. The report recommended a greater emphasis on community policing, a reform we discuss in more detail below. A local Cleveland Community Police

Commission was also created in response to the report. Later, the city also agreed to a consent decree that will include independent oversight of the police, suggesting a move away from a professional approach that would put oversight in the hands of other police and their superiors. A grand jury refused to indict the officers involved in the shooting, but in May 2016 the city agreed to pay a $6 million settlement to Rice's family, an amount similar to that paid to the families of Eric Garner and Laquan McDonald's. Prior to this agreement, the city had tried to bill Rice's family for his post-shooting ambulance ride. Lawyers for the city had also initially tried to blame Rice's actions for his death but quickly backed away from this position.

The state government created a task force to investigate and make recommendations on police–community relations in Ohio. In its final report, it recommended a few bureaucratic reforms, including more community involvement with the police as well as more explicit policies on the use of deadly force. Many of Cleveland's top local officials resisted calls from community protestors for greater political accountability. Mayor Frank Jackson explicitly rejected the idea in favor of the bureaucratic vision, stating, "You have to make decisions and set policies that are not political. . . . You have to hold people accountable from supervisors who are the main level of accountability—all the way down to patrol people."[28] The mayor further argued that there was "trust" between the community and the police and that the Justice Department's report on Cleveland's problems was inaccurate.[29] He later expressed greater regret for Rice's death, however, and adopted a more apologetic tone toward the family. The city council is divided about whether and how to proceed with some negotiating with local activists and others supporting the status quo. President Obama said little about the events in Cleveland.

Freddie Gray

Finally, in April 2015, Freddie Gray died from a spinal cord injury while in custody of the Baltimore police. Protests and rioting ensued, particularly on the day of the funeral, which featured fires, looting, and attacks on the police. Ultimately, Maryland Governor Larry Hogan declared a state of emergency and called out the National Guard. Baltimore Mayor Stephanie Rawlings-Blake imposed a curfew for several days; fired the police commissioner, Anthony Batts; and decided not to run for reelection, reflecting a hybrid of bureaucratic and political accountability. With respect to the latter, however, the mayor's successor, Catherine Pugh, downplayed racial issues in her successful spring 2016 Democratic primary bid, casting doubt on how much responsiveness will actually occur in the long term. Kevin Davis, the new police commissioner, created a Special Investigations Response Team to investigate use of force incidents, replacing the previously existing Force Investigation Team. It is not clear that this model will be an improvement, however, as it still lacks independence and remains under police department control, contrary to other cities that have instituted independent review entities. Attorney General Loretta Lynch launched a separate federal civil rights investigation into the death of Freddie Gray himself as well as the practices of Baltimore's police department more generally.

Six police officers were charged with offenses ranging from second-degree murder to assault and misconduct in office. In May 2016, Officer Edward Nero, the officer who allegedly illegally detained Gray by not buckling his seatbelt in the van, was fully acquitted of all charges. In June 2016, Officer Caesar Goodson, the officer who allegedly took Gray on the "rough ride" in the van, causing his injuries, was also acquitted. After a third officer was acquitted and another charge resulted in a mistrial, the charges against the remaining two officers were dropped, resulting in no convictions. Following the announcement ending prosecution, the State's Attorney, Marilyn Mosby, criticized the police investigation into Gray's death and said, "We stand by the medical examiner's determination that Freddy Gray's death was a homicide."[30] On the civil law side, as occurred in the settlements of the other cases, Gray's family received a settlement of $6.4 million from the city of Baltimore in September of 2015.

In a news conference in the aftermath of Gray's death, Obama distinguished between rioters, whom he called "criminals" and "thugs," and peaceful protesters expressing "legitimate concerns."[31] He further suggested that the causes of tension between the police and African Americans were a "slow rolling crisis" that could not be solved by fixing the police alone, but required deeper societal changes, although he did not specify exactly what this would entail. In a subsequent interview with radio host Steve Harvey, Obama said, "[E]verybody is starting to recognize that this is not just an isolated incident in Ferguson or New York, but we've got some broader issues."[32]

Accountability Patterns

Each of these incidents reveals issues with the different types of accountability. Specifically, most of the responses by the cities and local governments have included at least some attempt at bureaucratic accountability, but these changes are currently rhetorical in most cases. Suggestions like increased officer training and improved community relations are too new to be determined successful at this time, but it is clear that bureaucratic and political actors in all incidents have at least attempted some response. On the other hand, contrary to the professional approach of management, the attempts to foster some professional accountability have actually rested mainly on taking discretion away from the technical experts, the police, and placing it in the hands of civilians.

Legal accountability has also been difficult for victims to obtain when grand juries refuse to indict police officers. Arguably, the reasonableness standard used by the courts to determine whether an officer violated an individual's Fourth Amendment rights stacks the deck in favor of police. Similarly, when officers are brought forth on murder charges, indictments continue to be difficult to obtain as police are granted a certain level of "qualified immunity" from criminal and civil prosecution. If there has been any success in procuring legal remedies, it has been in obtaining civil settlements in the millions for the families of the dead. These settlements, although hopefully bringing some sense of closure to the families and possibly motivating officials to take some preventive measures so as to not incur additional costs, still do not address any institutional problems in policing in these cities.

Levels of local political accountability varied widely, from minimal in Cleveland to at least discernable in Ferguson, Chicago, and Baltimore. In Ferguson, the makeup of the city council changed to become more representative, although it still does not reflect the racial majority. In Chicago, political heat and the mayor's unpopularity led to heightened transparency, and in Baltimore similar pressures convinced the mayor to decline a reelection bid after she criticized protestors. As in Ferguson, however, elections appear to be a blunt tool of accountability, as the new mayor has deemphasized racial issues. The situation in New York City also shows how complicated it is to assess political accountability, as the mayor has faced strong political pressures and demands from the police. Whether longer-term results will occur in the form of more representative police forces in any of these cities is also an open question.

Reforming Police: Community Policing, Body Cameras and Institutional Change

When we consider how the Obama administration and the individual cities responded to each incident, some patterns of reform are also clear. As more incidents of alleged brutality occurred, calls for reform grew. Moreover, as municipal size increases, so do the bureaucratic complexity and profession-oriented approaches of a city's police force.[33] A painful irony of this fact is that citizen demands and the needs of special populations grow with statistically expected parity in a large city. Thus, a powder keg of tension between police and the residents they serve is introduced. As a result, police agencies, like other government agencies, might often be accused of being out of touch with their residents, which can lead to calls for reform, as has been the case in the incidents described above. Here, we consider the broader reform of Community Oriented Policing Services (COPS), which has evolved as solutions to issues arising from the bureaucratic and professional approaches. In fact, community policing reforms have been suggested following the New York, Chicago, and Cleveland incidents. In considering community policing, we also consider the implications of the pillars of reform recommended by the Obama administration's 21st Century Policing task force and the more specific reform of body cameras and how this particular reform may impact community policing and privacy rights. Finally, we consider some institutional and structural reforms that may be beneficial.

Community Policing

One of the most common and contemporary reforms to law enforcement is the introduction of Community Oriented Policing Services. Colloquially called "community policing," this reform movement is often seen as the cutting edge in developments related to policing and is commonly associated with James Q. Wilson's "broken windows" approach to policing, where small infractions of the law and small problems are taken very seriously so as to set the tone that more egregious crimes will not be tolerated.[34]

Still, despite the enthusiasm and sentimentality associated with community policing as the panacea for all of our current ills with police–citizen relations, the roots of community policing go back as far as Sir Robert Peel's Principles, specifically the second principle, where Peel explicitly declares that "[t]he ability of the police to perform their duties is dependent upon public approval of police existence, actions, behavior and the ability of the police to secure and maintain public respect," and the seventh principle, where Peel states, "The police at all times should maintain a relationship with the public that gives reality to the historic tradition that the police are the public and the public are the police; the police are the only members of the public who are paid to give full-time attention to duties which are incumbent on every citizen in the interests of community welfare and existence."[35] Many of these sentiments regarding the value of community policing can be found in the results of the 21st Century Policing Task Force.

An Executive Order released on December 18, 2014, called for the creation of a task force on 21st-century policing to "identify the best means to provide an effective partnership between law enforcement and local communities that reduces crime."[36] The results of the task force, published in May 2016, offered six "pillars" of recommendations for improving policing, including building trust and legitimacy; making changes in policy and oversight; improving technology and social media use; community policing and crime reduction; training and education; and officer safety and wellness. For our purposes, Pillars One, Two, Four, and Five are the most pertinent, and although Pillar Four explicitly recommends community policing, each of these pillars highlights issues of this reform movement.

Pillar One focuses on "building trust and legitimacy" and reminds police agencies of Peel's previously mentioned admonition to remember that police and the communities they serve have a reciprocal relationship built on trust and legitimacy. Furthermore, Pillar One suggests that individual officers consider their role as a guardian of the public rather than a warrior against it. Finally, Pillar One calls for a more representative police force, where it is more likely that police and citizens share common experiences, identities, and demographic traits. This representativeness, according to Oberweis and Musheno, will enable police to more readily understand the "subject positions" (or mindsets) of those with whom they interact, and we discuss its relationship to community policing in the conclusion.[37]

Pillar Two focuses on policy and oversight. Here the Task Force urges police to establish clear-cut policies, especially related to the use of force, and to ensure that these policy updates, "reflect community values." Moreover, the Task Force asserts that police should "collaborate with community members, especially in communities and neighborhoods disproportionately affected by crime, to develop policies and strategies for deploying resources that aim to reduce crime by improving relationships, increasing community engagement, and fostering cooperation."[38] That these ideas were so important to Peel in 1829 but were largely neglected throughout the 19th and 20th centuries might speak to a larger conundrum associated with the community policing movement and attempts at academic inquiry about this movement.

This problem evinces itself in the inability of practitioners and scholars to develop a uniform operational definition of community policing, catalyzing troubles we might have in designing systems and mechanisms by which community policing might be applied. Consider, for instance, in relation to Pillar Two, that the Law Enforcement Management and Administrative Statistics Survey conducted by the Bureau of Justice Statistics consistently finds that a significant number of municipal police agencies make presentations to a variety of citizen groups and often conduct surveys related to public perceptions of the police; however, very little data exist to suggest that these meetings/presentations and surveys are used to alter police functions and behavior. Cynics might query whether these are activities that are done in a perfunctory fashion to meet criteria for awards of state and federal grant monies. Thus, Pillar Two's recommendation about reflecting community values may be difficult to put into practice.

Pillar Four explicitly encourages community policing as a mechanism by which crime might be reduced. Here, the task force operationalizes community policing as the degree to which police give community members a voice in identifying areas of concern and highlights the need for police to develop a collaborative approach to dealing with these concerns. Collaboration, however, is difficult as well. It is unlikely, for instance, that citizens with disdain for the police would participate in public forums or citizen police academies. Some might even be afraid that unflattering survey responses could lead to retribution from police agencies, especially if pains are not taken to ensure anonymity and confidentiality of responses. This cynicism is spurred by the fact that many agencies designed community-oriented policing systems only when federal grant funding was available through the COPS program, which provided funds for departments to hire additional officers in cities like Baltimore, Chicago, Milwaukee, and Los Angeles, where notable frictions between citizens and police had gone largely unabated for decades. More vexingly, agencies with a truly benevolent motivation for engaging in community policing might quickly realize the inherent difficulties associated with trying to please everyone at the same time. LaFrance provides the example of law enforcement agencies' quandary in creating a presence near bars and clubs to discourage drunk driving.[39] Here, some community members (e.g., MADD, church groups, etc.) might be especially pleased, whereas others such as bar owners and patrons are likely to become angry or feel threatened by the police.

Pillar Five highlights the need for continuous training and educational initiatives beyond the basic academy training many officers receive. Here, it is of special import to mention, training is not just needed for new technologies or new techniques. Instead, training might also include developing awareness of the perspectives and needs of particular citizen groups; however, community members' demands can tend to be fluid and frantic, spurred by the limited amount of time they are willing to give attention to a given issue in the political world.[40] Thus, even the best community policing system will only remain relevant for a finite amount of time as political, social, economic, and technological contexts continue to change.

This complicates the recommendation of Pillar Five as it suggests costly, complex, and continuous training may be necessary for successful COPS. Considering issues associated with one type of newer technology, police-worn body cameras, and the training and education it would require, the problem of implementing many of these pillars becomes even clearer.

Body Cameras

When we consider the recommendations of the Task Force in light of the steps taken by the Obama administration, and more specifically the Attorney General Loretta Lynch, it is no surprise that one of the most popular reforms to policing today is the introduction of police-worn body cameras, as required for example in the Ferguson consent decree noted above. There are a number of reasons, however, that body cameras are not necessarily a universal remedy to the recent controversies surrounding police shootings.

First, it is possible that body cameras can compromise community policing efforts. Although some would place the use of body cameras as a direct component of a community policing initiative, others warn that the use of body cameras could actually compromise community–police relationships. For example, use of body cameras could reduce citizen willingness to engage in casual one-on-one conversations, which according to Simmons "are the smallest building blocks of community policing."[41]

The use of body cameras also includes privacy implications. As one goal of using body cameras is to increase transparency, and ultimately accountability, more people will want to view the footage of these cameras. In any given interaction between police and citizens, there will be others in the frame who may argue their privacy rights are violated when footage is shared with the media or used in court. Moreover, privacy rights must be considered in the storage of footage.[42] How long, for example, will footage be held and available? What should the process be to request that footage be destroyed?

Finally, and most important to our discussion of accountability, body cameras do not always yield expected results. Consider the case of Eric Garner in Staten Island, where there was police vehicle footage that many thought clearly implicated the officers, but still none were indicted. Footage may also be superseded by the "reasonableness standard" from *Graham v. Connor*. For example, if an officer thinks he saw a gun and uses deadly force, but camera footage later shows it was a wallet or cell phone, judges or juries may still rule in favor of the officer if they believe it was reasonable to think it was a gun.[43]

These are all issues with which cities and states grapple as they attempt to construct and implement body camera policies. A recent Brennan Center report examined body camera policies, many of which were pilot programs, in 24 cities. The report examines how policies are crafted to deal with some of the concerns listed above. Of particular interest is the amount of discretion afforded to officers about when they can stop recording. Some cities, like Baltimore's program, piloted in 2015, give the officer the discretion to stop recording if the situation becomes too "sensitive," whereas other programs, like that in New Orleans, require supervisor authorization to stop recording when speaking with victims or witnesses. Additionally, programs vary as to the length of time recordings will be kept. Some programs do not specify a length, whereas others keep recordings for anywhere from 45 days to two years. Finally, programs also vary as to how accessible the footage will be, both to officers who want to review footage and to the general public or media. Some cities, like Chicago, allow officers to view footage before making a statement or report; other cities, like Seattle, do not. For the public or media, most of the cities simply require that usual channels of public records release are followed, but some cities, like Seattle, even go so far as to publish blurry versions online and then allow for requests for clearer video. Overall, the report suggests that there is a lot of variance in how cities are establishing body camera policies and because many of these are pilot programs, a lot remains to be determined about the success of this reform. What is clear, however, is, as the *Harvard Law Review* suggests, that body cameras should "not be used as an excuse to stifle continued conversation about the root causes of police violence and fractured community relations, as body cameras alone will never be the hoped for cure-all."[44]

Prospects for Institutional and Structural Change

Making policy recommendations like increasing the use of body cameras or instituting community policing is a natural response to an ongoing crisis, such as this one. Nevertheless, it is important to step back and consider the workability of various policy options. Evidence from abroad suggests some possible directions for achieving police accountability. For example, England and Wales recently created a new position within the respective hierarchy of each of their 41 police force areas. This new office, the Office of Police and Crime Commissioner (PCC), is charged with overseeing the decisions of officers up to and including the chief constables. Because PCCs obtain office via electoral selection, proponents of this structural reform argue that it will introduce more political accountability into police decision-making in the United Kingdom.[45] Ironically, Cruz argues that police malfeasance in Latin America is rooted in the police force's continued attachment to the "partisan politics" of ages past.[46]

Herbert Kaufman, however, points out some of the difficulties in achieving accountability and notes that we sometimes grow tired of its side effects. He therefore provides a useful window through which we may appreciate the eternal insatiability of humankind. Kaufman's essay explains that we want political accountability and representation as long as the politicians we support are in power and the interests that represent us are given audience. Once other voices successfully lobby for attention, one might begin to think that police agencies have been captured by overzealous interest groups and political actors. At this point, we might begin to see a call for neutral competence and the apolitical execution of policy by specialized experts. This, in turn, might eventually lead us to feel as if these experts are too insulated from our voices. We might then demand a return to representation in the political sense, or we might look to strong executive leadership to right the ship. Although we generally look to the law to provide stability, as time marches on, the following three values—(1) representation (political accountability), (2) neutral competence (professional and bureaucratic accountability), and (3) executive leadership (bureaucratic accountability)—cycle in and out of public consciousness, perennially offering themselves as solutions to the excesses of the other two core values in the cycle. A pessimist may look at this phenomenon and wave a flag of surrender. After all, if the goal posts continue to move, what is the point in trying to march down the field? A more optimistic way to interpret this cycle is to view it in the context of introducing meaningful change into police organizations that will prevent them from becoming stale or overly devoted to one perspective.

Fostering Intraorganizational Communication and Considering Career Stages

In recent years, another area of police reform has attracted the attention of researchers. Although much has been written about the ways in which police agencies can better communicate with stakeholders in their respective communities and in other locations outside their agencies, newer research draws attention to the internal communication dynamics. For instance, LaFrance developed a simple diagnostic tool, the Target Model, to quickly compare the accountability priorities used by frontline officers and members of an agency's command staff when making discretionary choices. This model has the potential to catalyze important discussions about how and why differences in these priorities might exist between rank levels. Many scholars conceptualize the public agency as an organism in its own right, replete with the ability to learn in order to adapt to changing environmental demands.[47] In this sense, the organization can also learn from introspective evaluation, perhaps even before scanning the outside environment. It is important to note that rank level is only one variable that could explain variations in accountability priorities. Other scholars suggest that career stage or years of experience can also influence decision-making.[48] As one acquires experience in a career field (and grows older as a person), values are liable to change even if these changes are so incremental to be unnoticeable right away or if they are so slowly formed that they evince themselves subconsciously. Supervisors and scholars should consider more research and more hands-on interventions to mitigate the effects of career stage or years of experience in police agencies.

Conclusion

Although this chapter has examined multiple forms of accountability and their relationship to incidents of police shootings in five cities, an investigation of proposed reforms as interpreted from the task force reports and actions of leaders in the different cities might reveal more problems than solutions. Unfortunately, the focal points of the reforms seem to read as a call to action for winning political approval from aggregate segments of an agency's respective community in pursuit of a larger goal: validation of police authority over members of the community. In seeking legitimacy from these groups, a more pressing need, to foster sincere, one-on-one empathy with each citizen, is muted.

Scholars such as Michael Harmon and others who focus on a perspective commonly called "unconditional positive regard" or UCR would be disappointed that more effort is not encouraged to cultivate dyadic, mutually constructed, and agreed-upon meaning between each officer and citizen.[49] Pursuing this type of relationship would threaten standardized responses but would come with the much heftier price of engendering respect and trust between police and the community. This would also allow a theoretical and practical bridge to be built between Rosenbloom's political and legal approaches to public administration, driving home the fact that each citizen with whom a police officer interacts possesses individual needs as well as individual rights.[50] Moreover, each individual might be able to better articulate the ways in which police officers care about these needs and rights, regardless of the larger, aggregate community politics in which an interaction, or series of them, is taking place. A better articulation of expectations then could result in better accountability of all types.

Following this normative stream of thought, scholars and practitioners might notice that the post-Obama world of policing is one in which simple representative bureaucratic urges will not heal all wounds. Representative bureaucratic theory has its roots in the larger public administration movement for social equity. This movement developed traction in the late 1960s with the Civil Rights Movement in the United States, culminating in epochal moments such as the first Minnowbrook Conference and George Frederickson's call for a "New Public Administration." Subsequent scholars such as Samuel Krislov and Kenneth Meier carried the torch for this movement, marked by its insistence that government agencies be staffed with public servants who mirrored their service recipients in key demographic characteristics such as race, sex, social class, and more recently, disability, sexual orientation, and gender identity and expression. One can easily see the influence of this perspective on hiring practices in government agencies and the advent of Affirmative Action and Equal Employment Opportunity legislation.

Although representative bureaucracy and closer community contact may not be a recipe for perfection in local law enforcement, it is prudent to remember that the perfect is often the enemy of the good in an area of public service fraught with multiple and competing expectations. Policing in a post-Obama America is likely to be a subject of deep, and justified, scrutiny among academics, citizens, and elected officials. Moreover, the tragically similar events showcased in this chapter are capable of provoking difficult discussions within police departments and catalyzing a great deal of introspection and soul-searching by individual officers. Policing will become a more thoughtful and intentional enterprise as long as pressure is applied from within and outside police agencies. In addition, perhaps the issues we have identified will elucidate opportunities to improve other criminal justice institutions beyond the initial arrest (e.g., prisons, probation programs, drug courts, community service programs). Here too it is probable that the wheels of communication have been sufficiently greased by the display of horrors that can occur when communication regarding expectations is more limited. As with other areas of government, President Obama gracefully exits his office with his legacy entrenched in these words he penned prior to holding the most powerful office on earth:

> Hope is not blind optimism. It's not ignoring the enormity of the task ahead or the roadblocks that stand in our path. It's not sitting on the sidelines or shirking from a fight. Hope is that thing inside us that insists, despite all

evidence to the contrary, that something better awaits us if we have the courage to reach for it. Hope is the belief that destiny will not be written for us, but by us, by the men and women who are not content to settle for the world as it is, who have the courage to remake the world as it should be.[51]

As the light continues to radiate from his fading star, President Obama's words will continue to inspire us to pursue that same sort of hope and change that resonated with a majority of voters almost a decade ago.

Notes

1. Davis and Shear, 2014.
2. Joseph, 2016.
3. Joseph, 2015.
4. Gulick, 1937; Fayol, 1949; Lentz and Chaires, 2007.
5. Rosenbloom, 1983.
6. Ibid., p. 229.
7. Ibid., p. 229.
8. Ibid., p. 228.
9. *Graham v. Connor,* 490 U.S. 386 (1989), p. 388.
10. Ibid., p. 397.
11. Ibid., p. 396.
12. Ibid., p. 397.
13. Rosenbloom, 1983, p. 221.
14. Gupta, 2015.
15. Ibid.
16. Deere, Kohler, and Raasch, 2016.
17. Munsch, 2015.
18. Harrop, 2014.
19. Deere and Taketa, 2016.
20. Dyson, 2016, p. 14.
21. Davis, 2014.
22. Fischer, 2014.
23. Arceneaux, 2014.
24. Feeney, 2014.
25. Babwin, 2016.
26. Stafford and Walters, 2015.
27. Crowell, 2015.
28. Johnson. 2015.
29. Lowery, 2014.
30. Linderman, 2016, p. A11.
31. Fritze, 2015, p. 5A.
32. CNN, 2015.

33. Falcone and Welles, 1995; Sims, 1988.
34. Wilson and Kelling, 1982.
35. Sir Robert Peele's Nine Principles, 2014.
36. President's Task Force on 21st Century Policing, 2015.
37. Oberweis and Musheno, 1999.
38. President's Task Force on 21st Century Policing, 2015.
39. LaFrance, 2009.
40. Downs, 1972.
41. Simmons, 2015, p. 889.
42. Harvard Law Review, 2015.
43. Ibid.
44. Ibid., p. 1797.
45. Baldi and LaFrance, 2013.
46. Cruz, 2009, p. 5.
47. Senge, 2014.
48. Super, 1957; Johnson and LaFrance, 2016; LaFrance and Day, 2013.
49. Harmon, 1981.
50. Rosenbloom, 1983.
51. Obama, 2012.

Bibliography

Alexander, Michelle. 2012. *The New Jim Crow: Mass Incarceration in the Age of Col-orblindness*. New York: The New Press.

Arceneaux, Michael. 2014. "President Obama Takes His Message to '106 & Park.'" *Chicago Defender*, December 9.

Babwin, Don. 2016. "Report: Chicago police have 'no regard' for minority lives." *Springfield State Journal Register*, April 13.

Baldi, Gregory, and Casey LaFrance. 2012. "Lessons from the United States sheriff on the electoral selection of police commissioners in England and Wales." *Policing*: pas048.

Brennan Center for Justice. 2016. "Police Body-Worn Camera Policies." https://www.brennancenter.org/body-cam-city-map. Accessed June 20.

Brodsky, Adam. 2015. "The Lost Year: New York City Since Eric Garner's Death." *New York Post*, July 17.

Bult, Laura. 2015. "Rahm: I am sorry, Chicago. 'Owns' Shooting Fiasco amid Noisy Calls to Quit." *New York Daily News*, December 10.

Chevron v. NRDC. 467 U.S. 837 (1984).

CNN. 2015. "Obama: Freddie Gray Death not an Isolated Incident." *CNN Wire*, April 29.

Cohen, Rachel. 2016. "Baltimore's Next Mayor Doesn't Want to Talk about Racism." http://www.slate.com/articles/news_and_politics/metropolis/2016/04/baltimore_s_next_mayor_doesn_t_want_to_talk_about_racism_almost_every_issue.html. Accessed June 27.

Crowell, Maddy. 2015. "Why is Obama not Speaking up about Rahm Emanuel's Crisis?" *Christian Science Monitor*, December 10.

Cruz, José Miguel. 2010. "Police Misconduct and Democracy in Latin America." *Americas Barometer Insights*, 33: 1–5.

Davis, Julie Hirschfeld. 2014. "Calling for Calm in Ferguson, Obama Cites Need for Improved Race Relations." *New York Times*, August 19.

Davis, Julie Hirschfeld, and Michael D. Shear. 2014. "Unrest over Race is Testing Obama's Legacy." *New York Times*, December 8.

Deere, Stephen, Jeremy Kohler, and Chuck Raasch. 2016. "Ferguson Releases Proposed Settlement with the Justice Department." *St. Louis Post-Dispatch*, January 28.

Deere, Stephen, and Kristen Taketa. 2016. "Ferguson Suggests Changes, Potentially Undermining Much of DOJ decree." *St. Louis Post-Dispatch*, February 10.

Downs, Anthony. 1972. "Up and Down with Ecology—the 'Issue-Attention Cycle.'" *Public Interest*, 28: 38–50.

Dubnick, Melvin. 2005. "Accountability and the Promise of Performance: In Search of the Mechanisms." *Public Performance and Management Review*, 28: 376–417.

Dubnick, Melvin, and H. George Frederickson. 2010. "Accountable Agents: Federal Performance Measurement and Third-Party Government." *Journal of Public Administration Research and Theory*, 20: 143–159.

Dyson, Michael Eric. 2016. *The Black President: Barack Obama and the Politics of Race in America*. New York: Houghton Mifflin Harcourt.

Falcone, David N., and L. Edward Wells. 1995. "The County Sheriff as a Distinctive Policing Modality." *American Journal of Police*, 14: 123–149.

Fayol, Henri. 1949. *Industrial and General Management*. London: Pittman.

Feeney, Nolan. 2014. "Obama Requests Funds for Police Body Cameras to Address 'Simmering Distrust' After Ferguson." *Time.com*. http://time.com/3613058/obama-ferguson-police-body-cameras-funding/. Accessed June 26.

Fischer, Sara. 2014. "Obama on Garner Verdict: We are not Going to let up" *CNN Wire*, December 3.

Frederickson, H. George. 1990. "Public Administration and Social Equity." *Public Administration Review*, 50: 228–237.

Fritze, John. 2015. "Obama Urges U.S. 'Soul-Searching.'" *Baltimore Sun*, April 29.

Goodman, J. David. 2015. "Eric Garner Case Is Settled by New York City for 5.9 Million." *The New York Times*, July 13. http://www.nytimes.com/2015/07/14/nyregion/eric-garner-case-is-settled-by-new-york-city-for-5-9-million.html?_r=0.

Graham v. Connor. 490 U.S. 386 (1989).

Gulick, Luther. 1937. "Notes on the Theory of Organization." *Classics of Organization Theory*, 3: 87–95.

Gupta, Vanita. 2015. "Principal Deputy Assistant Attorney General Vanita Gupta Delivers Remarks at the Colorado Lawyers Committee Annual Lunch."

Denver, CO, May 19. https://www.justice.gov/opa/speech/principal-de
puty-assistant-attorney-general-vanita-gupta-delivers-remarks-colorado.

Harmon, Michael M. 1981. "Action Theory for Public Administration." New York:
Longman.

Harrop, Froma. 2014. "Lesson for Ferguson: Voting Matters." *Denver Post*,
November.

Harvard Law Review. 2015. "Developments in the Law—Policing: Chapter Four:
Considering Police Body Cameras." *Harvard Law Review*, 128: 1794–1817.

Johnson, Jeff. 2015. Cleveland Mayor Frank Jackson on Accountability, Police
Reform, and his Vision for the Future of Policing. *Chicago Defender*,
March 6. http://chicagodefender.com/tag/mayor-frank-jackson/.

Johnson, Richard R., and Casey LaFrance. 2016. "The Influence of Career Stage
on Police Officer Work Behavior." *Criminal Justice and Behavior*, 43:
1580–1599.

Joseph, Peniel. 2016. "Some Initially Heralded His Victory as the Arrival of a
'Post-Racial' America. *Washington Post*, April 22. https://www.washington
post.com /graphics/national/obama-legacy/racism-during-presidency.html.

Joseph, Cameron. 2015. "America's Crisis." *New York Daily News*, April 29.

Kaufman, Herbert. 1969. "Administrative Decentralization and Political Power."
Public Administration Review, 29: 3–15.

Krislov, Samuel. 2012. *Representative Bureaucracy*. New Orleans: Quid Pro Books.

LaFrance, T. Casey. 2009. "The Drunk Trap: Bureaucratic vs. Political Accountability in Local Law Enforcement Management." *Law Enforcement Executive Forum*, 9: 73–87.

LaFrance, Casey. 2016. *Targeting Discretion: A Guide for Frontline Officers, Command
Staff, and Students*. Dahlonega: University Press of North Georgia.

LaFrance, C. and Day, J. 2013. "The Role of Experience in Prioritizing Adherence
to SOPs in Police Agencies." *Public Organization Review*, 13: 37–48.

Lentz, Susan A., and Robert H. Chaires. 2007. "The Invention of Peel's Principles: A Study of Policing 'Textbook' History." *Journal of Criminal Justice*,
35: 69–79.

Linderman, Juliet. 2016. "Prosecutors Drop All Remaining Charges in Freddie
Gray Case." *St. Louis Post-Dispatch*, July 28.

Lowery, Wesley. 2014. "In Cleveland, Distrust Deepens Racial Fault Lines." *Washington Post*, December 17.

Lowi, Theodore J. 1979. *The End of Liberalism: The Second Republic of the United
States*. New York: W.W. Norton.

Meier, Kenneth John. 1975. "Representative Bureaucracy: An Empirical Analysis." *American Political Science Review*, 69: 526–542.

Moncada, Eduardo. 2009. "Toward Democratic Policing in Colombia? Institutional
Accountability Through Lateral Reform." *Comparative Politics*, 41: 431–449.

Munsch, Kate. 2015. "Judge Dismisses Counts in Michael Brown Family Lawsuits:
Report." *Reuters* July 14. http://www.reuters.com/article/us-usa-police
-missouri-idUSKCN0PO2GV20150714.

Nazemi, Sandra. 2009. "Sir Robert Peel's Nine Principals of Policing." Los Angeles Community Policing. http://www.lacp.org/2009-Articles-Main/062609 -Peels9Principals-SandyNazemi.htm. Accessed June 26.

Obama, Barack. 2012. "Victory Speech." National Public Radio. http://www.npr .org/2012/11/06/164540079/transcript-president-obamas-victory-speech.

Oberweis, Trish, and Michael Musheno. 1999. "Policing Identities: Cop Decision Making and the Constitution of Citizens." *Law & Social Inquiry*, 24: 897–923.

Ohio Task Force on Community-Police Relations. 2015. *Final Report*. Columbus: State of Ohio.

President's Task Force on 21st Century Policing. 2015. May. http://www.cops .usdoj.gov/pdf/taskforce/taskforce_finalreport.pdf. Accessed June 27.

Ramsey, Charles H., and Laurie O. Robinson. 2015. *Final Report of the President's Task Force on 21st Century Policing*. Washington: U.S. Government Printing Office.

Rector, Kevin. 2015. "Force Review Squad Altered: Probes of Shootings, Deaths, Linked to Police Officers Revamped." *Baltimore Sun*, September 25.

Romzek, Barbara S., and Melvin J. Dubnick. 1987. "Accountability in the Public Sector: Lessons from the Challenger Tragedy." *Public Administration Review*, 47: 227–238.

Rosenbloom, David H. 1983. "Public Administrative Theory and the Separation of Powers." *Public Administration Review*, 43: 219–227.

Schmadeke, Steve. 2016. "Grand Jury to Look into Possible Cover-up by Chicago Police in Laquan McDonald Shooting." *Chicago Tribune*. September 12.

Senge P. M. 2014. *The Fifth Discipline Fieldbook: Strategies and Tools for Building a Learning Organziation*. Chicago: Crown Business.

Simmons, Kami Chavis. 2015. "Body-mounted Police Cameras: A Primer on Police Accountability vs. Privacy." *Howard Law Journal*, 58: 881–890.

Sims, Victor H. 1988. *Small Town and Rural Police*. Springfield, IL: Charles C. Thomas.

Sir Robert Peele's Nine Principles of Policing. 2014. *The New York Times*. https:// www.nytimes.com/2014/04/16/nyregion/sir-robert-peels-nine-principles -of-policing.html?_r=0

Stafford, Zach, and Joanna Walters. 2015. "Obama Backs Protests over 'Deeply Disturbing Laquan McDonald Shooting" *The Guardian*, November 25.

Super, Donald E. 1957. "A Life-span, Life-space Approach to Career Development." *Journal of Vocational Behavior*, 16: 282–298.

Sweeney, Annie, Jeremy Gorner, and Dan Hinkel. 2016. "Top Cop Seeks to Fire 7 Officers for Lying about Laquan McDonald Shooting." *Chicago Tribune*, August 18.

Wilson, James Q., and George L. Kelling. 1982. "Broken Windows: The Police and Neighborhood Safety." *Atlantic Monthly*, 249: 29–38.

Wrobleski, Tom. 2014. "Sharpton, Mayor Get Low Marks from Island." *Staten Island Advance*, August 27.

Index

About the Editors and Contributors

Editors

Larry J. Walker, EdD, is a researcher and political strategist, Baltimore, Maryland. Dr. Walker is a former Congressional Fellow with the Congressional Black Caucus Foundation (CBCF) and served as the legislative director for Congressman Major R. Owens.

F. Erik Brooks, PhD, is a professor and associate director of the Centennial Honors College at Western Illinois University, Macomb, Illinois.

Ramon B. Goings, EdD, is an assistant professor of educational leadership at Loyola University of Maryland, Baltimore, Maryland.

Contributors

Keith Boeckelman, PhD, professor and chair of political science, Western Illinois University.

Melissa Brown, MA, graduate assistant, University of Maryland, Department of Sociology.

Cassandra Chaney, PhD, associate professor in child and family studies, Louisiana State University.

Felecia Commodore, PhD, assistant professor, Educational Foundations and Leadership, Darden College of Education, Old Dominion University.

Arash Daneshzadeh, EdD, Associate Director–Urban Strategies Council, Lecturer, University of San Francisco.

Paola Esmieu, MSEd, Associate Director for Programs, Penn Center for Minority Serving Institutions.

David O. Fakunle, doctor of philosophy candidate, Johns Hopkins Bloomberg School of Public Health; Policy, Community Engagement and Outreach Fellow, Baltimore City Health Department.

Marisela B. Gomez, PhD, MD, MPH, Social Health Concepts and Practice, Inc.

Kyomi Gregory, PhD, CCC-SLP, assistant professor, Salus University.

Belema Idoniboye, MPP, JD.

Casey LaFrance, PhD, associate professor of political science, Western Illinois University.

Marta N. Mack-Washington, PhD, lecturer, University of Kentucky.

Andrew Martinez, MSEd, research associate, Penn Center for Minority Serving Institutions.

Nicole McZeal-Walters, EdD, Associate Dean and Assistant Professor of Graduate Programs, School of Education and Human Services, University of St. Thomas.

Robert T. Palmer, PhD, Interim Chair and Associate Professor, Department of Educational Leadership and Policy Studies, Howard University.

Clarissa Peterson, PhD, a professor of political science at DePauw University in Greencastle, Indiana.

MaCherie M. Placide, DPA, associate professor, Western Illinois University.

Blanche M. Radford-Curry, PhD, professor of philosophy, Fayetteville State University.

Kimberly J. Rice, PhD, assistant professor of political science, Western Illinois University.

Emmitt Y. Riley III, PhD, assistant professor of Africana studies at DePauw University in Greencastle, Indiana.

Calvin J. Smiley, PhD, assistant professor, sociology, Hunter College (CUNY).

Glenn L. Starks, PhD, senior acquisition division chief for the U.S. Department of Defense.

Donna L. Taylor, MSc, researcher, International Public Policy.

Linda D. Tomlinson, PhD associate professor, history, Fayetteville State University.

Ahmad R. Washington, PhD, assistant professor, Department of Counseling and Human Development, College of Education and Human Development, University of Louisville.

Torie Weiston-Serdan, PhD; CEO and founder, The Youth Mentoring Action Network.

Christopher M. Whitt, PhD, associate professor and chair, Department of Political Science, Augustana College.

www.ingramcontent.com/pod-product-compliance
Lightning Source LLC
Chambersburg PA
CBHW060137280326
41932CB00012B/1551